THE PATH OF THE
SPIRITUAL
SUN

CELEBRATING THE
SOLSTICES & EQUINOXES

BELSEBUUB
WITH ANGELA PRITCHARD

MYSTICAL LIFE
PUBLICATIONS

The Path of the Spiritual Sun: Celebrating the Solstices and Equinoxes
By Belsebuub with Angela Pritchard

Published July 2017 by Mystical Life Publications Ltd.

www.mysticallifepublications.org

ISBN 978-0-9924113-1-2

First edition September 2013, The Path of the Spiritual Sun: Celebrating the Solstices and Equinoxes, eBook (EPUB) ISBN 978-0-9923084-2-1, eBook (Kindle) ISBN 978-0-9923084-3-8.

Second edition September 2016, The Path of the Spiritual Sun: Celebrating the Solstices and Equinoxes, paperback ISBN 978-0-9924113-9-8.

Revised and updated second edition July 2017, The Path of the Spiritual Sun: Celebrating the Solstices and Equinoxes, paperback ISBN 978-0-9924113-1-2.

Belsebuub's official website: www.belsebuub.com

The contents of this book were first published in a series of internet articles on the website www.belsebuub.com between June 2011 and June 2013. We are constantly learning and improving what we do, so the contents of this book may be updated in future editions to reflect corrections or new information. Our field of expertise is esoteric knowledge and spiritual experience; we are not historians or scientists. Therefore the emphasis of this book is not on history or science—rather we have used it to illustrate the core spiritual knowledge found throughout it.

All chapters of this book were jointly authored by Mark Pritchard, who contributed the esoteric knowledge from his own experience of the path of the spiritual sun, and Angela Pritchard, who contributed the historical and academic research, except the ceremonies which were written entirely by Mark Pritchard.

··· Contents ···

Winter Solstice
The Birth of the Spiritual Son

Spring Equinox
Resurrection and Re-integration with the Spiritual Mother

CHAPTER FIVE

DECODING THE ANCIENT MEANING OF THE SPHINX AND ITS ORIGIN AS ANUBIS

Summer Solstice
Ascent to the Spiritual Father
and the Return to Source

PART II:

The Ancient Civilization of the Sun

PART III:
Ceremonies and Rituals for Celebrating the Solstices and Equinoxes

Autumn Equinox

Winter Solstice

Spring Equinox

Summer Solstice

CHAPTER SEVENTEEN

CONCLUSION

Preface

THE PATH OF THE SPIRITUAL SUN UNCOVERS a highly significant knowledge, which has the potential to both decode and explain much of the ancient spiritual wisdom of the past.

It is not an encyclopaedic style compendium of research on the celebration of the sun—that would be a much bigger book, would serve little real purpose in terms of practical understanding, and would also be very boring! Instead it aims to synthesize the deeper meaning behind the celebration of the spiritual sun as something that can be practiced today just as the ancients did thousands of years ago. It uncovers the lost threads that connect the very process of spiritual transformation, with the movement of the heavens and the earth, as well as the remaining fragments of ancient spiritual knowledge we have access to today.

It describes why so many ancient sacred sites align to the sun's major annual stages (the solstices and equinoxes), why so many ancient spiritual teachings share similarities with one another and the sun even though separated by great distances, and reveals the common roots behind many of the religions and traditions still practiced today. I will go so far as to say that the knowledge of the spiritual sun acts as a virtual Rosetta Stone of ancient spirituality.

But to the world this knowledge is lost. After thousands of years of persecution, suppression, destruction, and degeneration, the ancient knowledge of spirituality in its diverse forms of expression has arrived to us in the present day in fragments that no longer form a coherent whole. Much of it was also kept from public circulation to protect it from persecution and perversion.

Testament to this comes from one of the only known expeditions of its kind. In 1895, Gurdjieff helped form a group of around 15 members called "Seekers of the Truth" who traveled to remote locations in order to find ancient esoteric knowledge, often risking their lives and going through extreme hardships to do so. They are said to have traveled across three continents to places that include Egypt, Ethiopia and the Sudan, Mesopotamia, Central Asia, the Gobi Desert, Northern Siberia, Northern India, Australia and the Solomon Islands.

> "During their travels the Seekers studied literature, oral tradition, music, dance, sacred art, architecture and esoteric monuments, and they conducted their own experiments and archeological excavations. Their investigations led to many exciting discoveries related to the science of human transformation, including ancient methods of music composition, architecture, and dance choreography which produced exact and predictable alterations in consciousness in the listener, observer or practitioner.

> From their journeys and research the Seekers concluded that knowledge of human spiritual potential once existed as a complete teaching, but that only widely scattered fragments remained." [1]

> ~ GURDJIEFF'S SEARCH FOR ESOTERIC KNOWLEDGE, BY THE LEARNING INSTITUTE FOR GROWTH, HEALING AND TRANSFORMATION

In some cases we have access to more of these fragments today, thanks to the discoveries of suppressed texts like the Nag Hammadi Library. In another sense we also have less, due to the rapid increase of materialism, corporatization, violent strife in the world, the persecution of those who practice this kind of spiritual knowledge today, and the disruption and destruction of many of the cultural traditions and sacred sites that carried spiritual knowledge.

But even having access to more fragments, as in the case of the previously unknown Nag Hammadi Library, many remain obscured due to the fact that they were encoded by their authors in layers of symbology. On top of this, the symbols used by different cultures to express the same message can often be different. So when trying to piece together the fragments of ancient knowledge, not only are they incomplete, but they are often encrypted in an unknown symbolic script, and also use different codes of encryption to one another.

Sometimes the key similarities amongst this array of fragments stand out— enough to conclude that many of these ancient spiritual peoples tapped into a common source of knowledge, and that they did once explain the mysteries of life and its purpose. But mostly questions remain, such as what is this common source, how did they tap into it, what are these mysteries, and most importantly, how can they be experienced again today?

There is one missing key that has the power to answer these questions and to crack the codes. Researchers only have access to physical artifacts and texts, which they sometimes try and piece together. It's like putting together a puzzle when you don't know what the image of the puzzle is—in fact, when you've never even seen what the puzzle image is before, and you only have a few of the pieces that are not clear because each piece is encrypted, and each using a different code of encryption. Not only that, but some of the pieces don't even belong to the puzzle because so much of the spiritual knowledge of the past got distorted and infiltrated over time!

We can theorize what the puzzle image is going to be forever, but we're never going to really know. Unless, that is... we had gone through the same process of spiritual transformation and gained the same spiritual knowledge in the same ways that these ancient peoples did.

Then we would approach the mystery of the puzzle in a completely different way. We could know what the puzzle picture is, even without the pieces, and could see where the few pieces that we had fit together, and could even explain which pieces are missing and which ones are not part of the puzzle at all. And this is exactly what Mark (Belsebuub) has done.

Anyone can compile information, even in the field of spiritual knowledge, but to synthesize, to get to the essence of it and to explain it so that another can transform themselves through it, requires one crucial ingredient found severely lacking in modern corporatized so-called "spirituality"—and that is first-hand esoteric experience. Unfortunately, commercial spiritual writers will read this book only to take bits and pieces of it to use for their own books, articles, and for-profit ventures. At their own loss, and the loss of those they mislead, these people will miss the magnitude of what has been uncovered here.

Although both Mark and I are listed as the authors of the book, we both had very different roles in putting it together. Both Mark and I did the writing and researching, but it was Mark's own experience of the process of spiritual transformation that is really behind it.

In my research, I would present Mark with the few pieces of the puzzle I could find. He then, using his own experience and knowledge of the process of spiritual transformation, would explain the meaning behind them, allowing each piece to "snap" into place. Mark took a confused (and often dizzying!) mass of incoherent fragments uncovered through sometimes arduous research, separated off what had become distorted or degenerated over time, and distilled the remainder into a coherent and logical revelation of the great thread of universal truth behind so many of the world's ancient sites, sacred texts, and spiritual legends.

The ceremonies were entirely created and written by Mark, who used his experience of the spiritual stages in the process of enlightenment that correspond to each equinox and solstice as the basis and framework for each, and then looked at how the solstice and equinox had been celebrated throughout the ancient world, to incorporate what communicated and symbolized these stages. To his surprise, he came across an obscure Greek reference to a winter solstice ceremony celebrated in ancient Egypt which contained virtually the same ritual he had written into the winter solstice ceremony he'd not long before put together.

This book would not have been possible without the breadth and depth of Mark's own spiritual and metaphysical experience, which is the culmination of over 20 years of his personal inner esoteric work. *The Path of the Spiritual Sun* comes from the knowledge of one who has tread upon the path of the spiritual sun, nearly even to its end where the very references to its stages become almost as rare as those who have passed through them. If Mark is able to make further progress on his inner path and therefore gains more knowledge and experience of its later stages, then there are likely to be changes made to future editions of this book to reflect them.

Mark, having a sense of the intrinsic connection between the process of enlightenment and creation, standing on the verandah with a week to go before the summer solstice, turned and said, "We should do something on the summer solstice." And there began one astonishing revelation after another on the spiritual meaning of the solstices and equinoxes, and on the connection between ancient spiritual teachings and the sun, as we researched and wrote web articles on the next solstice or equinox to come around until we had completed the cycle of the year. After first publishing the contents of this book as separate articles on www.belsebuub.com we eventually compiled them together into a free eBook, which has now been printed in paperback.

What we have put together in terms of the sacred sites, texts and traditions is by no means exhaustive. Firstly, there are a huge number of examples we could have included (with sites still being discovered), but we felt it was only necessary to include enough in order to clearly make a point. Secondly, there is a limit to the time we had before the next solstice or equinox came around, and therefore to the breadth of what we could include. And thirdly, there are no doubt many other sites, texts and traditions linked with the solar year that are largely unwritten about in English, and which were therefore much more difficult and time consuming to find. We hope, however, to add some of these to later editions as we have the time so that even more people can understand the path of the spiritual sun through their own cultural heritage.

Finally, to conclude, I'd ask you to please bear with this book on two counts. Firstly, we are not qualified historians, trained researchers, or academics. Secondly, because so much spiritual knowledge is esoteric (meaning it requires grades of spiritual wisdom and experience to understand), some parts of the book may seem obscure. Despite the difficulties these two things present, it's worth persisting as what you can gain at the very least is an understanding of the wider synthesis of the spirituality from our ancient history—how much more beyond this depends entirely upon how much we can personally spiritually experience.

Angela Pritchard

PART I

The Spiritual Messages in the Path of the Sun

CHAPTER ONE

The Significance of the Solstice and Equinox in Spirituality

THE ANCIENT VENERATION OF THE SUN is one of the greatest celebrations in history. It has been encoded in sacred sites and texts by peoples separated by vast distances for thousands of years across the world—all the way from the Great Pyramids of Egypt, to the megaliths of Stonehenge, and the huge stone statues of Easter Island. The sun is one of the oldest and most universal themes connecting the ancient wisdom traditions of the world.

It's estimated ancient cultures built hundreds (if not many thousands) of huge megalithic structures, stone circles, temples, and secret inner rooms that aligned with the sun at its major annual stages—the solstices and equinoxes—across Europe and Britain, in Africa, Russia, North, Central and South America, Easter Island, Australia, Asia, and other parts of the world.

Most today see it as a form of sun or agricultural worship and pagan cele-bration to do with the seasons—and yet some of these sites have endured as the most enigmatic and mystical places in the world, and remain some of the most advanced sites astronomically, mathematically, architecturally, and spiritually even to this day. Down through the ages they have echoed messages from a Golden Age of spirituality, that have largely been misinter-preted as primitive by a modern world that has become so distanced from natural and cosmic principles that it has failed to recognize what is hidden in plain sight.

Tens of thousands gathered at Stonehenge to witness its alignment to the summer solstice sunrise again in modern times.

The sun and stars, source of all light and life in the universe, are central to a cosmic spirituality that is both ancient and timeless—and as ever-present as always. Its principles have formed the basis of many of the world's religions—unbeknownst even to many of their adherents—and are just as relevant to people searching for spirituality today.

This book delves into the profound spiritual significance of the veneration of the sun, pulling together the sites, texts, traditions, and symbols from around the world that were based on the sun's cycle, to reveal the common thread of spirituality running through all of them. This knowledge has then been used to form a practical guide to celebrate the spiritual sun just as it was in ancient times, incorporating sacred symbols and texts from the ancient Egyptians, to the Druids, Maya, Hindus, and more, for people to re-enliven and experience the spirituality of the cosmos again all over the world.

It's important to note though that the ceremonies in this book are not about a worship of the physical sun. Instead they are like plays that enact the process of individual enlightenment, which can be found in the progress of the spiritual sun throughout the year. They were used in the past, and can likewise be used today, to assist in the perception of the principles of the sun and creation, which are found manifest in nature and can be experienced and understood through celebrations that enact these principles in tune with the cycles of the cosmos.

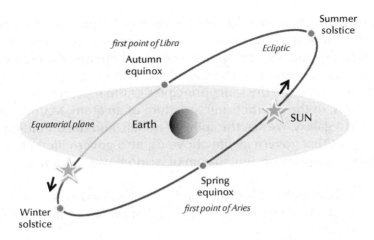

A diagram of the solstices and equinoxes from
the viewer's perspective of the sun from the earth.

The journey of the sun through the sky (or rather our planet's journey around it) goes through four distinct stages every year, which occur at four equidistant points—the autumn equinox, winter solstice, spring equinox, and summer solstice—forming the "wheel of the year." These points mark the main stages in the movement of the earth around the sun and the sun's varying influence over light and darkness, day and night, and the passage of the seasons. But they also hold a greater spiritual significance.

AS ABOVE, SO BELOW

Here the alchemist draws our attention to the relationship between the world contained in the smaller circle in which we find ourselves, and the world contained in the larger circle—that is, between the microcosmic and the macrocosmic, as well as the mathematical principles that apply to both. The alchemist looks above, whilst the figure of the man in the drawing, points below.

It's easy to write off ancient spiritual people as simple-minded nature worshipers. But there is a reason why natural principles are found throughout sacred texts and ancient sites—this is because there are universal principles that govern all of creation, including all life in the largest to the smallest of scales. Thus we can see the same principles of the macrocosmic movement of the planets, in the microcosmic structure of an atom. Mathematically, in the spiral of a galaxy, we see the spiral of a shell, and the unfolding of a fern. The principles that govern all life above us, also govern life here below on earth—which is why an ancient maxim of wisdom was, "as above, so below."

> "Man takes his law from the Earth; the Earth takes its law from Heaven; Heaven takes its law from Tao; but the law of Tao is its own spontaneity." [1]
>
> ~ THE TAO TE CHING, TRANSLATED BY LIONEL GILES

> "The sages of old studied living things to a point of realization that God is most perfectly understood through a knowledge of His supreme handiwork—animate and inanimate Nature. Every existing creature manifests some aspect of the intelligence or power of the Eternal One, who can never be known save through a study and appreciation of His numbered but inconceivable parts. When a creature is chosen, therefore, to symbolize to the concrete human mind some concealed abstract principle it is because its characteristics demonstrate this invisible principle in visible action." [2]
>
> ~ MANLY P. HALL, THE SECRET TEACHINGS OF ALL AGES

Going further, not only do the principles of life and creation govern the outer world, but they also govern the inner, spiritual world. Spirituality exists in the very fabric of the universe. Thus when someone studies creation, they find spirituality and the supernatural. This is why scientists are now theorizing about the existence of other dimensions, parallel universes, and the inexplicable realm of possibilities, energy, and matter, from the study of the behavior and structure of minute particles.

Today, these properties of the universe, in which the same principles apply at the largest to the smallest scales, and both to the inner and outer world, have been described as fractal and holographic. Fractal in that the same fundamental pattern appears at all scales, and holographic in that wholeness is found everywhere and in everything, essentially making the same observations as the ancient maxims of wisdom "as above, so below," and "as within, so without."

The sun in its movement throughout the course of the year then becomes a symbol of something much, much greater than a physical object bringing the change of seasons.

THE SPIRITUAL SUN

The physical sun is a blazing fire—it gives light and life to all things physical. From the physical sun, all creation comes into being. Literally, science theorizes that the universe came from a fiery burst of light called the "Big Bang"—and that the first few elements which emerged from this sudden burst of creation fused to form stars. These stars, through a process of nucleosynthesis, created almost all matter and everything we see, including us, and even now are in a constant process of creation as they produce and eject elements into space.

But life is multidimensional. Mystics have known this throughout time—that there is more to our world than what we perceive with our five senses. With improvements in technology, there are now huge numbers of compelling accounts of life beyond the physical body in other dimensions from near-death experiences, reported by people all over the world, and these numbers are increasing rapidly by the day. Scientists are even theorizing about the existence of multiple dimensions from the behavior of particles existing in multiple places at the same time (in the field of quantum physics).

Because the universe is multidimensional, everything within it, including the sun, has other dimensional aspects.

In the ancient text Pistis Sophia, Jesus speaks of the multidimensional nature of the sun:

> "For the light of the sun in its shape in truth is not in this world, for its light pierceth through many veils and regions." [3]
> ~ JESUS IN PISTIS SOPHIA, TRANSLATED BY G. R. S. MEAD

The sun that exists in the physical world as the fire we see in the sky also exists in the higher dimensions as a spiritual fire and the spiritual source of all creation, which is why there is an overlap in accounts of creation in many ancient cultures between natural and supernatural phenomena. The natural phenomenon is the physical, tangible manifestation of the supernatural phenomenon. That is why many spiritual cultures throughout the world venerated the sun—they knew of its spiritual side.

Manly P. Hall writes in his extensive study of the esoteric teachings of the world:

> "In the majority of cases, the religions of antiquity agree that the material visible sun was a reflector rather than a source of power. The sun was sometimes represented as a shield carried on the arm of the Sun God, as for example, Frey, the Scandinavian Solar Deity. This sun reflected the light of the invisible spiritual sun, which was the true source of life, light, and truth. The physical nature of the universe is receptive; it is a realm of effects. The invisible causes of these effects belong to the spiritual world. Hence, the spiritual world is the sphere of causation; the material world is the sphere of effects; while the intellectual—or soul—world is the sphere of mediation. Thus Christ, the personified higher intellect and soul nature, is called 'the Mediator' who, by virtue of His position and power, says: 'No man cometh to the Father, but by me.'" [4]
> ~ MANLY P. HALL, THE SECRET TEACHINGS OF ALL AGES

Because creation of physical matter comes from the physical aspect of stars, then the higher dimensional parts of matter are likewise created by the stars in higher dimensions. We find references to this in ancient texts. In the Taoist texts of ancient China for instance, creation is described as moving from the subtle and unseen realms (which are higher dimensional), into physical manifestation. The source of these subtle energies is said to be the stars, and the sun is the star with which we share our closest relationship.

> "Trees and animals, humans and insects, flowers and birds: These are active images of the subtle energies that flow from the stars throughout the universe. Meeting and combining with each other and the elements of the earth, they give rise to all living things." [5]
> ~ LAO-TZU IN HUA HU CHING, TRANSLATED BY BRIAN WALKER

In The Vision of Hermes, a text attributed to Hermes Trismegistus and believed to have originated in Egypt prior to Christianity, the spirits of the stars are said to control the universe and have their origin in the "One Fire," which is the spiritual source of creation.

"At the Word of the Dragon the heavens opened and the innumerable Light Powers were revealed, soaring through Cosmos on pinions of streaming fire. Hermes beheld the spirits of the stars, the celestials controlling the universe, and all those Powers which shine with the radiance of the One Fire—the glory of the Sovereign Mind." [6]

~ THE VISION OF HERMES, TRANSLATION FROM THE SECRET TEACHINGS OF ALL AGES BY MANLY P. HALL

Going further, not only does both physical and other dimensional matter have its source in the stars—so too does our own inner spiritual light, called consciousness. The light of the sun and stars is the spiritual source of creation, and gives rise both to matter and the spirit.

"These two things, the spiritual and the material, though we call them by different names, in their origin are one and the same. This sameness is a mystery,—the mystery of mysteries. It is the gate of all spirituality." [7]

~ TAO TE CHING, TRANSLATED BY LIONEL GILES

As many ancient cultures believed, the Milky Way is said to be the place where our souls were born.

"Behold, O Hermes, there is a great mystery in the Eighth Sphere, for the Milky Way is the seed-ground of souls..." [8]

~ POIMANDRES (THE MIND OF THE UNIVERSE) TO HERMES IN THE VISION OF HERMES, TRANSLATION FROM THE SECRET TEACHINGS OF ALL AGES BY MANLY P. HALL

Is it little wonder then, that often when pondering the meaning of life and the question of where we came from, we tend to raise our eyes to the stars or gaze at the sun, and likewise when calling for spiritual guidance or help. This intuitive sense of home has been with humankind throughout the ages. From a scientific perspective, the elements that created our bodies, and all that exists materially, came from the stars. From a spiritual perspective, our consciousness—the spark of divinity within us—also originated in the stars, in higher dimensions, from the greatest source of life and light in creation.

This is why so many ancient cultures, such as the Hindus, Sumerians, Egyptians, Gnostics, Inca, and Maya, all referred to themselves as the "Children of the Sun" or "Children of Light." The Inca literally believed that they were the descendants of the sun, and celebrated their spiritual lineage at the winter solstice.

The sun worship of the past in the more advanced societies was really the worship of the spiritual sun, not the physical sun.

Paracelsus, the great alchemist of the Renaissance, wrote in the 1500s:

"There is an earthly sun, which is the cause of all heat, and all who are able to see may see the sun; and those who are blind and cannot see him may feel his heat. There is an Eternal Sun, which is the source of all wisdom, and those whose spiritual senses have awakened to life will see that sun and be conscious of His existence; but those who have not attained spiritual consciousness may yet feel His power by an inner faculty which is called Intuition." [9]

~ PARACELSUS

There are hundreds of ancient sites aligned to the solstices and equinoxes, some of the most famous sacred texts encode solar events and venerate the sun, and supreme deities in many ancient spiritual teachings are associated with the sun and its attributes. Both the Druids and mystery schools of Greece conducted their initiation rituals and mysteries on the equinoxes and solstices. Throughout the world we see evidence of an ancient religion of the sun.

THE COSMIC SON

Osiris, Jesus, Krishna, and many other great spiritual figures throughout history, have identified themselves with the sun and its fire and light, as the spiritual Son, and as the source of creation—indicating the connection between their incredibly profound spiritual teachings, and the sun, stars, and cosmos.

"Thou shinest in the horizon, thou sendest forth thy light into the darkness, thou makest the darkness light with thy double plume, and thou floodest the world with light like the Disk at break of day. Thy diadem pierceth heaven and becometh a brother unto the stars, O thou form of every god." [10]

~ HYMN TO OSIRIS, TRANSLATED BY E. A. WALLIS BUDGE

"The light which, residing in the sun illumines the whole world, that which is in the moon and in the fire — know that light to be Mine." [11]

~ KRISHNA IN THE BHAGAVAD GITA, TRANSLATED BY SWAMI SWARUPANANDA

"It is I who am the light which is above them all. It is I who am the all. From me did the all come forth, and unto me did the all extend." [12]

~ JESUS IN THE GOSPEL OF THOMAS FROM THE NAG HAMMADI LIBRARY, TRANSLATED BY THOMAS O. LAMBDIN

"After six days Jesus took with him Peter, James and John the brother of James, and led them up a high mountain by themselves. There he was transfigured before them. His face shone like the sun, and his clothes became as white as the light." [13]

~ THE GOSPEL ACCORDING TO MATTHEW 17:1-2

Symbolized by the sun, the Son/Christ is present in many ancient spiritual practices where people were in touch with the divine, given different names, but naturally having key aspects in common. Jesus is known as the Christ, but Christ is more than a name. It's the same cosmic Son—Horus, Quetzalcoatl /Viracocha, Mithras, Krishna, Odin/Wotan, Balder, Hu, Attis—the light and savior of the world. This universal cosmic principle has been celebrated and expressed according to culture, but with many similarities.

"'Jesus' is a hidden name, 'Christ' is a revealed name. For this reason 'Jesus' is not particular to any language; rather he is always called by the name 'Jesus'. While as for 'Christ', in Syriac it is 'Messiah', in Greek it is 'Christ'. Certainly all the others have it according to their own language. 'The Nazarene' is he who reveals what is hidden. Christ has everything in himself, whether man, or angel, or mystery, and the Father." [14]

~ THE GOSPEL OF PHILIP FROM THE NAG HAMMADI LIBRARY, TRANSLATED BY WESLEY W. ISENBERG

As just one example, many of these deities all have the same birthday, which is the date of the winter solstice. This is because the cosmic Son has been allegorized by or has actually been present within different people numerous times, each who have represented the same kinds of events in their lives based on the same spiritual principles. Even today, many people still continue to celebrate the birthday of these deities at the time of the winter solstice. The birth of Mithras is celebrated in Iran as Yalda, in Germany Yule is celebrated in connection with Odin, and the birth of Jesus as Christmas.

In the West there were many traditions which the orthodox called pagan and suppressed as Christianity took hold, but Christianity itself has many similarities with those pagan traditions, which also appear in many other cultures.

People argue that the winter solstice was a pagan tradition which was simply used by the Church as Christ's birthday and that the celebration actually has nothing to do with Christ, and even that Christians adapted pagan myths and symbols to create the story of Jesus' life. Others argue that the pagan people of Europe were simple people whose celebration was little more than a form of nature worship, which they personified into gods. But both ignore the role of the cosmic Son and the many universal principles contained in their religion's forms.

The solstices and equinoxes are a celebration of the spiritual Son, which has been expressed through a number of ancient religions. This is why the Christ, the spiritual Son, or solar hero, was born at the winter solstice, and died and resurrected at the spring equinox in sacred myths throughout the world. What is described by the name "Christ" is not unique to Christianity—Jesus portrayed the path of the Christ in his life, just as Osiris and Mithras did hundreds and thousands of years earlier, and Quetzalcoatl and Hun Hunahpu did vast distances away.

This spiritual Son is both a universal and personal force. At a universal level, the Son is the spiritual force produced from the union of the cosmic Father and Mother in creation. In the Vedas, this spiritual Son is described as the golden child who arises at the dawn of creation.

> "In the beginning there arose the Golden Child (Hiranya-garbha); as soon as born, he alone was the lord of all that is. He established the earth and this heaven... He who gives breath, he who gives strength, whose command all the bright gods revere, whose shadow is immortality, whose shadow is death... He who through his might became the sole king of the breathing and twinkling world, who governs all this, man and beast..." [15]
>
> ~ FROM THE HYMN TO THE UNKNOWN GOD IN THE RIG VEDA, TRANSLATED BY MAX MÜLLER

As the process of creation at a universal level also applies to the creation of the spiritual within us, the Son at a personal level is an aspect of each person's higher Being produced from the union of each person's spiritual Father and Mother in higher dimensions.

Like all things, our Being has its origins in the stars in higher dimensions—the source of all creation. When our consciousness was first created from the stars, it descended through the higher dimensions into matter, and as it did, left higher parts of itself behind in higher dimensions. The spiritual Son, or Christ, is one part of this Being, which is of the same nature as the stars and sun—as a much higher frequency of spiritual energy and light—which is why the spiritual Son is symbolized by the sun. Through their lives and their teachings, those who had their own spiritual Son within or who were representing it, showed how someone can incarnate this higher part of their Being themselves, calling this process enlightenment, self-realization, awakening, liberation, salvation, immortality, etc. The final destination of this journey was always described as the heavens, sky, sun, and stars, as it is ultimately about the return to the divine source of creation and to each person's own higher Being, which has its origin in the stars.

The ancient Christian Gnostics, who followed the esoteric side of Jesus' teachings, describe this in their ancient texts, stating that Christ—this higher part of each person's Being—illuminates the psyche of each person, just as the sun illuminates the earth and a lamp lights up a place.

> "Live with Christ and he will save you. For he is the true light and the sun of life. For just as the sun which is visible and makes light for the eyes of the flesh, so Christ illuminates every mind and the heart. [...]
>
> For everything which is visible is a copy of that which is hidden. For as a fire which burns in a place without being confined to it, so it is with the sun which is in the sky, all of whose rays extend to places on the earth. Similarly, Christ has a single being, and he gives light to every place. This is also the way in which he speaks of our mind, as if it were a lamp which burns and lights up the place. (Being) in a part of the soul, it gives light to all the parts." [16]
>
> ~ THE TEACHINGS OF SILVANUS FROM THE NAG HAMMADI LIBRARY, TRANSLATED BY MALCOLM L. PEEL AND JAN ZANDEE

Both the fire of the sun and earthly fire give light and life, and are what allow us to see in the physical world. Likewise, on a spiritual level, the Son within brings spiritual light and life to our own inner darkness, which is the darkness of the human personality and the subconscious.

THE DIVINITY OF FIRE

The spiritual Son has not only been associated with the sun, but also with fire, as when we look at the sun, we are watching a blazing fire.

Fire is not just the result of combustion as many believe. Instead, matter contains fire; when we witness a fire, we are seeing an object's fiery energy released.

When the fire is burned out, the object once full of color, texture, shape, and substance, has now disappeared and all that remains is grey dust.

Fire destroys things, but few realize that it is also what creates. It is well known in science that literally everything in our universe, all that we see around us, including our own bodies down to the very atoms, originated from within the fiery furnace of the stars. When we look around then, we can begin to see that all we are looking at are modifications of fire. It has been said that all that separates us from the burning stars above is time.

Fire is also what sustains us. Without the light and heat of the sun's fire, and the continual outpouring of its energy, no life could exist—the universe would be nothing but an utterly dark and freezing void. When the sun has set, its light reflected on the moon, the shining fire of the stars, and the fire released from wood that has absorbed and stored the fiery energy of the sun, are what give us light and warmth. Even electricity is a form of fire.

Eventually, Earth and its life will be returned back into the stars billions of years from now, when our planet will be engulfed or burned by the sun as it expands into a "red giant." And so the fiery light of the sun will fulfill its role as the universe's creator, sustainer, and destroyer.

The sun (and stars), so associated with the Son/Christ (as Jesus, Viracocha, Horus, etc.), is a raging fire and that which creates, sustains, and ultimately destroys all of creation. This is why Krishna, who represented the Son in India, is said to be that from whom this universe proceeds, in whom it subsists, and to whom, in the end, it returns.

> "[Krishna said] I will speak to thee now of that great Truth which man ought to know, since by its means he will win immortal bliss — that which is without beginning, the Eternal Spirit which dwells in Me, neither with form, nor yet without it. [...] It is the upholder of all, Creator and Destroyer alike; It is the Light of lights, beyond the reach of darkness; the Wisdom, the only thing that is worth knowing or that wisdom can teach [...]" [17]
>
> ~ KRISHNA IN THE BHAGAVAD GITA, TRANSLATED BY SHRI PUROHIT SWAMI

The Son, born of the union of masculine and feminine forces at the dawn of creation, is the light of the first day, the sun, which is fire.

But life is multidimensional. And so it follows that whilst there is physical fire that appears from within matter, this fire also exists in higher dimensions even when we don't see it, as every physical form has its corresponding multidimensional aspect. Fire's origins trace back into the very highest of dimensions, where it is the force that sustains all life, and even beyond the dimensions into the unknowable, where it becomes impossible to see beyond it to where it came from. This is the realm of Brahman, the incomprehensible, immeasurable creator of all things.

Fire has played an essential part of sacred rituals and ceremonies, and has held a central place on altars and shrines that honor the divine throughout the world since the beginning of history. This knowledge of the spiritual nature of fire has come down, at least in part, from the ancient sacred teachings that originated from a lost global civilization that practiced a religion of the sun, and influenced or gave rise to the religion of ancient Egypt, the Vedic and Hindu religion of India, Zoroastrianism in Persia, the Inca religion of South America, the Druidism of the British Isles, and a number of others in which the sun and fire were seen as manifestations of the divine. Jesus spent time in Egypt and possibly in India and with the Druids, and essentially taught this same religion to his disciples, which is why his teachings share so many similarities with the offshoots of the ancient religion of the sun.

Here are some excerpts on the divinity of fire from the Rig Veda, which is one of the most ancient known sacred texts in the world:

> "I worship the Sacred Fire (Agni), the chosen Priest, God, minister of sacrifice, The invoker [...] Worthy is Agni to be praised by living as by ancient seers... To you, dispeller of the night, O Agni, day by day with prayer Bringing you reverence, we come Ruler of sacrifices, guard of Law eternal, radiant One, Increasing in your own abode." [18]
> ~ THE RIG VEDA, TRANSLATED BY RALPH T. H. GRIFFITH

> "You, oh Fire, shining forth throughout the days, from the waters, from the stones, from the forests and from the herbs, you oh Lord of souls are ever born pure!" [19]
> ~ THE RIG VEDA, TRANSLATION FROM THE AMERICAN INSTITUTE OF VEDIC STUDIES

> "Agni, you beamest forth with light, great Hero, never changed by time. Shining, pure fire (Agni)! with a light that never fades, beam with your fair beams brilliantly [...] He who waters, stones, and trees support, the offspring of eternal Law; He who when rubbed with force is brought to life by men upon the lofty height of earth; He who has filled both worlds with his brilliant shine, who hastens with his smoke to heaven." [20]
> ~ THE RIG VEDA, TRANSLATED BY RALPH T. H. GRIFFITH

The Atharva Veda in its Hymn to the Earth states that divine fire exists within everything—within all the elements, in all life, and in the sun:

> "There is a Divine fire in the Earth and in the plants. The Waters carry the fire and the same fire dwells in the rocks. There is a fire within

human beings, within the cows and the horses are sacred fires. The Divine fire shines from heaven as the Sun. The Divine fire extends the wide atmosphere through the wind. Mortals enkindle the Fire that carries their prayers, which loves clarity." [21]

~ THE ATHARVA VEDA, TRANSLATION FROM THE AMERICAN INSTITUTE OF VEDIC STUDIES

The most ancient scripture of the Zoroastrians, the Zend Avesta, says that the Son of God is fire, and they worshipped fire, just as the writers of the Vedas did:

"Yes, we worship the Creator Ahura Mazda and the Fire, Ahura Mazda's son [...]

We worship the Fire, the son of God, the holy lord of the ritual order." [22]

~ YASNA IN THE ZEND AVESTA, TRANSLATED BY L. H. MILLS

In the text The Vision of Hermes, the divine mind of the universe (who appears as a dragon) reveals to Hermes Trismegistus the mysteries of creation. In the vision, God appears as Fire, and the Son of God as a pillar of flame:

"At the Word of the Dragon the heavens opened and the innumerable Light Powers were revealed, soaring through Cosmos on pinions of streaming fire. Hermes beheld the spirits of the stars, the celestials controlling the universe, and all those Powers which shine with the radiance of the One Fire—the glory of the Sovereign Mind." [23]

~ THE VISION OF HERMES, TRANSLATION FROM THE SECRET TEACHINGS OF ALL AGES BY MANLY P. HALL

"I Thy God am the Light and the Mind which were before substance was divided from spirit and darkness from Light. And the Word which appeared as a pillar of flame out of the darkness is the Son of God, born of the mystery of the Mind." [24]

~ POIMANDRES (THE MIND OF THE UNIVERSE) TO HERMES IN THE VISION OF HERMES, TRANSLATION FROM THE SECRET TEACHINGS OF ALL AGES BY MANLY P. HALL

In an ancient Gnostic text, Jesus equates himself with fire, and says that he is the origin of creation, and can be found everywhere and in everything, just as the Vedic texts describe fire as existing within all the elements:

"He who is near me is near the fire, and he who is far from me is far from the kingdom. [...]

It is I who am the light which is above them all. It is I who am the all. From me did the all come forth, and unto me did the all extend. Split a piece of wood, and I am there. Lift up the stone, and you will find me there." [25]

~ JESUS IN THE GOSPEL OF THOMAS FROM THE NAG HAMMADI LIBRARY, TRANSLATED BY THOMAS O. LAMBDIN

In the ancient Egyptian Book of the Dead, Osiris identifies himself as the son of God and as fire:

"I am the great One, the son of the great One. I am Fire, the son of Fire [...] I have made myself whole and sound. I have become young once more. I am Osiris, the Lord of Eternity." [26]

~ OSIRIS IN THE BOOK OF THE DEAD, TRANSLATED BY E. A. WALLIS BUDGE

In the Bhagavad Gita, Arjuna sees Krishna as a blaze of light and fire, and as pervading the entirety of creation:

"Arjuna said: [...] I see Thee, infinite in form, with, as it were, faces, eyes and limbs everywhere; no beginning, no middle, no end; O Thou Lord of the Universe, Whose Form is universal! I see thee with the crown, the sceptre and the discus; a blaze of splendour. Scarce can I gaze on thee, so radiant thou art, glowing like the blazing fire, brilliant as the sun, immeasurable. Imperishable art Thou, the Sole One worthy to be known, the priceless Treasure-house of the universe, the immortal Guardian of the Life Eternal, the Spirit Everlasting. Without beginning, without middle and without end, infinite in power, Thine arms allembracing, the sun and moon Thine eyes, Thy face beaming with the fire of sacrifice, flooding the whole universe with light." [27]

~ THE BHAGAVAD GITA, TRANSLATED BY SHRI PUROHIT SWAMI

Krishna himself says to Arjuna:

"Remember that the Light which, proceeding from the sun, illumines the whole world, and the Light which is in the moon, and That which is in the fire also, all are born of Me. I enter this world and animate all My creatures with My vitality; and by My cool moonbeams I nourish the plants. Becoming the fire of life, I pass into their bodies and, uniting with the vital streams of Prana and Apana, I digest the various kinds of food. I am enthroned in the hearts of all [...]" [28]

~ THE BHAGAVAD GITA, TRANSLATED BY SHRI PUROHIT SWAMI

In a famous passage of the Yajur Veda, the supreme creator called Narayana (also known as Brahman) is described as a great flame of fire that is said to reside within the heart of every being.

"Whatever all this universe is, seen or heard of—pervading all this, from inside and outside alike, stands supreme the Eternal Divine Being.

He is the Limitless, Imperishable, Omniscient, residing in the ocean of the heart, the Cause of the happiness of the universe, the Supreme End of all striving, manifesting Himself in the ether of the heart which is comparable to an inverted bud of the lotus flower.

There in the heart effulges the Great Abode of the universe, as if adorned with garlands of flames.

Surrounded on all sides by nerve-currents, the lotus-bud of the heart is suspended in an inverted position. In it is a subtle space, and therein is to be found the Substratum of all things.

In that space within the heart resides the great flame of fire, undecaying, all-knowing, with tongues spread out in all directions, with faces turned everywhere, consuming food presented before it, and assimilating it unto itself.

His rays, spreading all round, sideways as well as above and below, warm up the whole body from head to foot. In the centre of That Flame abides the Tongue of Fire as the topmost among all subtle things.

Brilliant like a streak of lightning set in the midst of the blue rain-bearing clouds, slender like the awn of a paddy grain, yellow like gold in colour, in subtlety comparable to the minute atom, this Tongue of Fire glows splendid.

In the middle of that Flame, the Supreme Self dwells. This Self is Brahma (the Creator), Siva (the Destroyer), Hari (the Protector), Indra (the Ruler), the Imperishable, the Absolute, the Autonomous Being." [29]

~ THE NARAYANA SUKTAM FROM THE YAJUR VEDA, TRANSLATED BY SWAMI KRISHNANANDA

The fire of the material sun, the fire of the spiritual sun, the fire within matter, and the flame of our Being within, are all connected. This is why the sun and fire have been seen as living representations of the divine, and so often associated with divinity.

Light is in its nature spiritual and contains everything that is spiritual within it, including love, inner peace, wisdom, joy and happiness, heightened perceptions, etc. Each person's Being is essentially a quality of light that comes from the great light of the creator. This is why the Christ or Son is described as a child of light and identified with the light of the sun, stars, and fire.

As explained further in the following chapters, beings have come into the world of form where there is a duality of light and darkness like individual flames descending from the sun, to unlock the spiritual fire found within the dark sheath of matter and the subconscious, gradually returning to their own spiritual sun, and transforming themselves into beings of light as they do.

"Imperishable is the Lord of Love.
As from a blazing fire thousands of sparks
Leap forth, so millions of beings arise
From the Lord of Love..." [30]

~ MUNDAKA UPANISHAD, TRANSLATED BY EKNATH EASWARAN

This journey of transformation and return to the light I call the path of the spiritual sun—it is the path to liberation, the path to enlightenment.

THE PATH OF THE SPIRITUAL SUN

THE SPIRITUAL SON AS THE EGYPTIAN GOD HORUS.

In sacred texts and traditions around the world, which had as their ultimate aim the attainment of enlightenment, there are references to an ancient spiritual veneration of the sun—it can be found in Egypt, in the beliefs of the Druids, the Maya, Sampsaeans, Hindus, and Incas, in the esoteric texts of Christianity, the Eleusinian mysteries of ancient Greece, the pagans of old Europe, the esoteric schools of Mithraism originating in Persia and found underground in Rome, and in many other places around the world.

This is because the annual journey of the sun is symbolic of the journey of consciousness in its return to source—a journey which is eternal and lies at the heart of existence. Ancient peoples expressed this wisdom according to their time and culture, yet their sacred teachings and symbols share many similarities because many of them were based on the same universal principles.

The correlation between enlightenment and the movements of the cosmos is no coincidence, but part of the greater design of the universe, revealing the process of spiritual awakening to humanity.

In times now lost, different groups of people understood this profound teaching and message that literally comes from above, and knew that the movement of the heavens and earth was intimately linked to the process of a human becoming spiritual, with the sun representing the spiritual Son that merges with a person. For those who partake in the process of enlightenment, the sun is shown in dreams and out-of-body experiences in this spiritual context.

Some believe that the correlation of heavenly movements to the lives of different deities only indicates that different religions borrowed from one another, basing their stories on the pagan traditions of sun worship. But to mystics, this correlation is the result of something hidden and profound that is central to all authentic spirituality—the path to enlightenment.

This path is one that is mirrored in the heavens with the movements of the celestial bodies and is found imbued in the very fabric of life. It has been enacted by "Christified" humans throughout time, and takes place within a spiritually prepared person. It is the basis of the work of awakening, and at the solstices and equinoxes ancient people celebrated its stages in tune with the natural rhythms of the sun and seasons, which are permeated by its principles.

Krishna, in the famous text the Bhagavad Gita, actually refers to the path of the sun—the path of enlightenment, which takes one to the Supreme Primeval Abode beyond birth and death—as being related to the summer solstice, also saying that this path has always existed.

> "Now I will tell thee, O Arjuna, of the times which, if the mystics go
> forth, they do not return, and at which they go forth only to return.
> If knowing the Supreme Spirit the sage goes forth with fire and light,

in the daytime, in the fortnight of the waxing moon and **in the six months before the Northern summer solstice, he will attain the Supreme.** But if he departs in gloom, at night, during the fortnight of the waning moon and **in the six months before the Southern solstice [winter solstice], then he reaches but lunar light and he will be born again. These bright and dark paths out of the world have always existed.** Whoso takes the former, returns not; he who chooses the latter, returns. The sage who knows this passes beyond all merit that comes from the study of the scriptures, from sacrifice, from austerities and charity, and reaches the Supreme Primeval Abode." [31]

~ KRISHNA IN THE BHAGAVAD GITA, TRANSLATED BY SHRI PUROHIT SWAMI

References to this path trace back still even further to more ancient Hindu texts, in the Upanishads:

"The sun gives light and life to all who live,

East and west, north and south, above, below;

It is the prana of the universe.

The wise see the Lord of Love in the sun,

Rising in all its golden radiance

To give its warmth and light and life to all.

The wise see the Lord of Love in the year,

Which has two paths, the northern and the southern.

Those who observe outward forms of worship

And are content with personal pleasures

Travel after death by the southern path,

The path of the ancestors and of rayi,

To the lunar world, and are born again.

But those who seek the Self through meditation,

Self-discipline, wisdom, and faith in God

Travel after death by the northern path,

The path of prana, to the solar world,

Supreme refuge, beyond the reach of fear

And free from the cycle of birth and death." [32]

~ THE PRASHNA UPANISHAD, TRANSLATED BY EKNATH EASWARAN

These same paths in and out of the world, connected to the winter and summer solstice can be found in Mithraism. An author describes the design of the secret caves of Mithras as follows:

> "But this cave was adorned with the signs of the zodiac, Cancer and Capricorn. **The summer and winter solstices were chiefly conspicuous, as the gates of souls descending into this life, or passing out of it in their ascent to the Gods;** Cancer being the gate of descent, and Capricorn of ascent. These are the two avenues of the immortals passing up and down from earth to heaven, and from heaven to earth." [33]
>
> ~ JOHN P. LUNDY, MONUMENTAL CHRISTIANITY

This intrinsic relationship between the principles of life and spirituality is one of the reasons why so many ancient sacred sites, texts, and celebrations combined spiritual and natural phenomena. They can be read in the cosmos and the world around us just as they were by ancient spiritual peoples, as they are timeless and ever-present.

FOLLOWING THE SUMMER SOLSTICE

Around three days following the summer solstice, the sun begins to descend in the sky, and darkness begins to increase as the nights begin to lengthen toward winter. This symbolizes the consciousness, the eternal spark of light within each person, the seed of inner potential, coming out from the spiritual sun and stars, and descending into the darkness of matter and the material world (from heaven to earth), to learn and awaken through the process of life like the seed which is produced from the tree at summer. On a personal spiritual level it also symbolizes the beginning of a new journey on the path of the spiritual sun.

AUTUMN EQUINOX

At the autumn equinox, day and night are equal, but from the autumn equinox onward there is more darkness than light—this is the time of inner death within oneself to ego and evil, and the descent into the underworld to face and overcome one's own inner darkness in preparation for the birth of the spiritual Son/sun within. Many deities descended into the underworld/hades/hell at this time of year, as the seed of inner potential remains dormant indefinitely, and does not germinate, unless it goes into the earth and dies. As the course of the sun throughout the year can also be found in its course through one day, the autumn equinox corresponds to the time of sunset and the cardinal direction of west.

WINTER SOLSTICE

At the winter solstice, darkness is at its maximum, but there is hope in the winter sunrise from which the light gradually increases—this is the time of the birth of the spiritual Son/sun within, and why so many solar deities were born at the winter solstice. The winter solstice finds its parallel with the cardinal direction of south and the time of midnight, which is why Christmas mass is traditionally held at midnight. It is a celebration of the midnight sun, which is a celebration of the birth of light at the time of greatest darkness. The spiritual Son within starts as something small like a child and gradually grows—just as the sun at winter and seed beneath the ground—toward the summer solstice, transforming someone spiritually as it does.

SPRING EQUINOX

At the spring equinox day and night are once again equal, but from this time onward light is greater than darkness. This is the time of the inner Passion and resurrection, the triumph over darkness, and attainment of eternal spiritual life, which is why so many deities die and later come back to life to live eternally at the spring equinox, when the life of spring bursts forth to overcome the forces of darkness and death in the light of the triumphant sun. The spring equinox corresponds to the time of dawn and the direction of east.

SUMMER SOLSTICE

At the summer solstice, the sun has ascended to its highest point in the sky and the light is at its greatest, symbolizing enlightenment and awakening—this is the time of the ascension from earth to heaven, the return to wholeness of Being and the spiritual source from which consciousness originated. Like the flowers and fruits of summer, the life of the spirit is at full bloom and corresponds to midday in the sun's daily journey and the direction north. From the ending of the summer solstice, the sun descends once more to begin the eternal cycle again.

Those who incarnated the Son, and had the role of savior in the world, enacted these events in their lives to show the process of spiritual awakening, and those who do the spiritual work will also go through these same events in their lives as part of this process. It is a process that does not belong to any religion, to any deity, but is so universal that it has taken place within many men and women throughout history, and is continuously repeated in the cycles of the sun.

REMNANTS OF SOLSTICE AND EQUINOX CELEBRATIONS FROM ANCIENT TIMES

Thousands of years ago, using highly advanced knowledge, ancient peoples built huge megalithic structures and temples that aligned with the sun at the equinoxes and solstices. And some—such as the Great Pyramids, Angkor Wat, and Easter Island—even align with each other from across the world. A few traditions of celebrating the solstice and equinox still survive today, although many others passed into history.

THE GREAT SPHINX OF EGYPT GAZES PRECISELY AT THE RISING SUN ON THE EQUINOX.

While traditions often change or lose their meaning through time, these stone monuments have withstood thousands of years. They were purposefully built as giant symbols and thus have kept a knowledge of the path of the spiritual sun, and greater spiritual significance of the solstice and equinox, encoded into their structures for us to still read today.

Here are just some of the ancient markers built by different cultures that align to the solstices and equinoxes:

⚙ The Great Pyramid of Egypt has multiple alignments to the solstices and equinoxes, functioning as an enormous sundial. Its shadow to the north, and its reflected sunlight to the south, accurately mark the annual dates of both the solstices and the equinoxes. Two of its faces are orientated precisely due east and west, which are the exact points of the rising and setting sun on the spring and autumn equinoxes. At certain dates a star aligns with its descending passage on the autumn equinox and on the winter solstice a shadow cast on one of its outer sides is at the same angle as the descending and ascending passages inside.

❁ The Great Sphinx of Egypt gazes precisely at the equinox sun rise and is crowned by the setting summer solstice sun.

❁ The first rays of the rising sun on the summer solstice pass through stone markers to hit the altar stone in the center of Stonehenge in England.

❁ Newgrange in Ireland is a giant one acre mound which receives a shaft of sunlight into a central chamber shaped like a cross at dawn on the winter solstice.

❁ At the ancient city of Angkor Wat in Cambodia, the spire of its central tower aligns with the sun on the equinox.

❁ A giant serpent mound in Ohio in the United States faces the summer solstice sunset.

❁ On Easter Island, seven of the giant stone statues called moai face the equinox sunset, while on another part of the island, fifteen face the summer solstice sunset.

❁ The "sun dagger" in Chaco Canyon in the United States is a stone structure which uses shadow and sunlight to mark the equinoxes and solstices. The ancient city at Chaco Canyon also has various alignments to the solstices and equinoxes.

❁ In Central America, in the ancient Maya city of Tikal, the pyramid shaped temples align with the highest mountain peak in the area at the winter solstice sunrise, and the temples align with each other to mark the equinoxes and solstices.

❁ On the equinox at the pyramid of Chichen Itza in Mexico, the light creates the effect of the feathered serpent slithering down the side of the pyramid.

❁ Two of the thirty caves at Ajanta in India capture the sunlight on the solstices so that the sacred statues of Buddha they contain are illuminated.

✪ The ancient city of Arkaim in the Ural mountains of Russia aligns to the solstices and equinoxes.

✪ A number of temples in Egypt are aligned with the winter solstice sunrise. At the temple of Amun in Karnak, which is the largest temple complex in the world, the sun's rays flood an inner sanctuary of the god Amun with light, and are funneled along a giant temple causeway lined with massive pillars.

An understanding of the symbols used in these ancient sites reveals that many were representing the same spiritual process around the same cosmic events. They indicate the existence of a cosmic spirituality, which could be described as an ancient religion of the sun.

The knowledge encoded into their designs tells us that what happens above is related to our world below, and most importantly, to ourselves. They show the great link between the human and divine, the personal and the cosmic, and the inner and outer world, and were centered around the path of the spiritual sun.

SPIRITUAL SYMBOLS FOUND IN THE COSMOS

Some of the world's most ancient and well known spiritual symbols also encode spiritual principles that are cosmic in their nature.

Symbols operate on many different levels, only being able to be interpreted according to the understanding of the observer. If we understand something, it can become apparently visible in the symbol, but that which is out of our reach will remain hidden and invisible.

While many of us will be familiar with the following symbols, most will be unaware of what these symbols describe. These examples reveal how symbols can actually describe universal principles that operate on many different levels. They encode information about the movement of the earth around the sun, yet at the same time, also reveal how these principles are connected to the journey of consciousness, and operate within the human psyche.

This is why the great maxim of wisdom states, "as above, so below." These symbols reveal how physical, cosmic phenomena are related to inner, spiritual ones, and why the progress of the sun throughout the year was so important to ancient spiritual cultures. As a microcosm of the universe, we are connected to creation in ways we cannot possibly imagine. To someone who understands how to perceive the universe in this way, the outer world becomes a magnificent reflection of our own personal journey through eternity.

YIN AND YANG

The ancient Chinese symbol of the yin and yang can actually be seen when mapping the cycles of light and darkness during the rotation of the earth around the sun. It expresses the principle of duality and polarity, which forms the bounds of all manifest creation. At the same time, the union of these polarities gives rise to everything in creation. It also represents the cycles of light and darkness both the cosmos and our consciousness progresses through.

ANCIENT CHINESE YIN AND YANG SYMBOL.

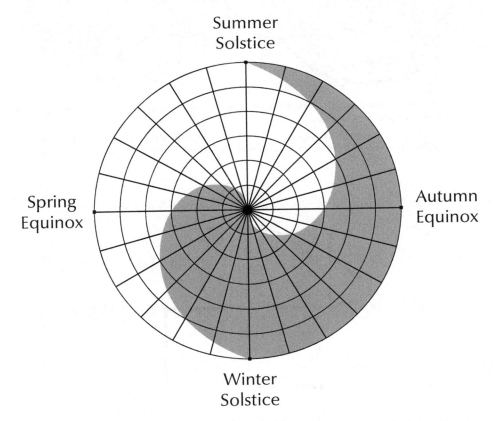

The ancient Chinese symbol of the yin and yang as found in mapping out the cycles of light and darkness throughout the year. (See article by Allen Tsai http://www.chinesefortunecalendar.com/YinYang.htm for more information.)

SWASTIKA

The swastika is one of the most universal symbols, examples of which can be found in numerous cultures of the ancient world that often used it as a symbol of the sun. It illustrates a cosmic principle of movement behind creation, which has its origins in the sun. The four arms can symbolize the four points of the year—the solstices and equinoxes.

IMAGE LEFT: An ancient bowl dated to 4,000 BC discovered in Iraq which shows a swastika and illustrates forces and movements.

IMAGE RIGHT: The same swastika concept found in the art of the pre-Columbian North American peoples who depicted it in connection with their spiritual Son deity, the feathered serpent.

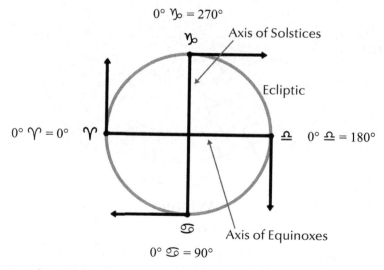

The Precession of the Equinoxes as it is seen on the plane of Ecliptic from the North Pole. This movement can be illustrated by a swastika (See article by Sergey Smelyakov found at http://www.soulsofdistortion.nl/Galactic Alignment.html for a more detailed explanation.)

INFINITY

The symbol of infinity as a figure 8 has been in use at least as early as Roman times. Astronomically, this figure has a reality, as it can be found in the relationship between the sun and the earth in a phenomenon called the analemma, described as follows. If someone were to locate the position of the sun in the sky at the same time every day, whilst standing in exactly the same spot, the location of the sun would change, and the different positions it occupies in the sky plot out a figure 8 every year in a continuous loop—just like the symbol of infinity. The sun's shifting position in the sky occurs because of the slightly altered way we view it from Earth throughout the year, which is due to the elliptical shaped orbit of the earth around the sun, along with the slight wobble of the earth's axis.

The symbol represents the cycling nature of the cosmos and of life, and the axis of ascent and descent that is found within us, and within the wheel of life that consciousness progresses through in its circuit of lives.

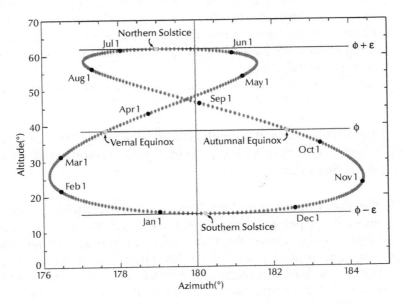

A plot of the position of the sun at 12:00 noon made from the Royal Observatory in Greenwich.

THE DOUBLE SPIRAL

Closely related to the symbol of infinity and the phenomenon of the analemma is the double spiral, one of the most prolific symbols of ancient Ireland, where it's found adorning many of the megalithic sites aligned to the solstices and equinoxes. It has also been found at the site of the ancient solar calendar called the Sun Dagger in  North America, and in the facial tattoos of those who practiced the ancient religion of the sun (described in more detail in chapter seven).

The symbol of the double spiral has cosmological origins, as it can be found in the relationship between the sun and the earth. It is a symbol of the solstices and equinoxes, which is why it was used in the artwork of those who practiced the religion of the sun.

It appears in the pattern the sun's light and shadow traces on the earth over the course of one year.

> "If the shadows of the sun are correlated over the period of one year in chronological order following their curvature they form a double spiral. In winter the spiral is counter-clockwise and the coils are wide. The shadows begin to straighten as equinox approaches, and after equinox they begin to wind into a clockwise spiral and tighten. They contract until the summer solstice, straighten again at equinox and return to a left-handed spiral again in winter to continue the process perpetually." [34]
>
> ~ MARTIN BRENNAN, THE STARS AND THE STONES: ANCIENT ART AND ASTRONOMY IN IRELAND

The artist Charlie Ross also inadvertently discovered this same ancient symbol when in 1971 he created his work for the exhibition titled Sunlight Convergence/Solar Burn.

> "Rather than dispersing sunlight through a prism he decided to focus it into a single point of raw power to create a solar burn. Each day for one year he burned the path of the sun through a large lens into a wooden plank... Each of the 366 planks captured one day of sunlight, a portrait of sunlight drawn by the sun itself. In 1971 Ross discovered that the solar burns traced a double spiral when laid end-to-end." [35]
>
> ~ CHARLES ROSS, BIOGRAPHY

The double spiral is a symbol of the solstices and equinoxes. It has the same meaning and essentially illustrates the same principles as that of the symbol of infinity and the yin and yang.

SPIRALS

The spiral is often found in the spiritual symbology of the ancient Europeans and Britons. At the ancient site of Newgrange in Ireland, the light of the rising sun on the winter solstice enters its innermost chamber. This ancient site is decorated with the symbol of the spiral.

While we often think of our earth's rotational movement around the sun as being in an ellipse on a flat plane, it is really rotating in a spiral around the sun as the sun itself moves at great speed throughout space (at around 450,000 miles per hour) in its own rotation around a greater sun, in an even greater rotation around the center of the galaxy—dragging the planets of the solar system with it in a great whirling spiral. Recent evidence from NASA shows our solar system actually has a tail much like a comet because of its movement through space.

The spin of our earth, rotating around the sun, which is rotating around the galactic center, is a small spiral within larger and larger spirals, almost like the spinning hands of a clock, counting seconds, minutes, and hours of cosmological time.

The entrance stone to the ancient megalithic temple of Newgrange, which aligns to the winter solstice sunrise. It is covered in the symbol of the spiral.

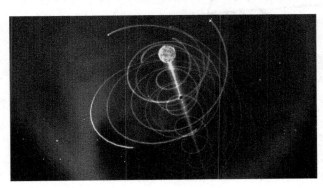

An illustration of the spiraling rotation of the planets of our solar system around the sun as it moves through the galaxy at great speed.

THE PENTAGRAM

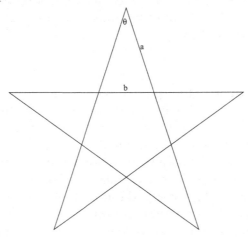

The symbol of the pentagram.
Each of its five arms are a golden triangle.

The symbol of the pentagram is found in pagan spirituality throughout Europe. When pointing upward, it is a symbol of light forces—as its one point over the other four represents consciousness over matter. When pointing downward, it is a symbol of dark forces, as its four points over the one represents consciousness trapped in and dominated by matter.

Incredibly, the pentagram is found in the natural world, and related to cosmic cycles of time. It also contains numbers and angles that were considered sacred by ancient people.

The planet Venus actually traces a pentagram in its orbit around the sun in its relation to Earth every eight years. Both Jesus and Quetzalcoatl were associated with Venus as the morning star.

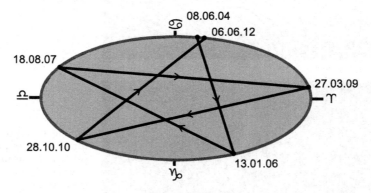

The positions of Venus at its lower conjunctions with Earth between the two transits of 2004 and 2012. Venus' orbit as viewed from Earth assumes an approximate "pentagram" shape, due to the approximate 13:8 ratio between the orbital periods of Earth and Venus.

Each apex of a pentagram is a golden triangle; golden numbers and ratios are found throughout nature and were used prolifically throughout ancient Egyptian art and architecture.

The angle of 108 degrees, as well as 36 and 72, which added together equal 108, occur throughout the pentagram. The number 108 is considered sacred in Buddhism and Hinduism, and is found in the proportions of the sun to the earth, and in the cycle of the earth through its "Great Year," which is a larger cycle of time known as the precession of the equinoxes.

THE CHURNING OF THE MILKY OCEAN

A painting of the famous Hindu teaching called The Churning of the Milky Ocean. Those at the ancient site of Angkor Wat knew how it related to the progress of our earth around the sun in its annual cycle, but also to even greater cosmic cycles.

The Churning of the Milky Ocean is an ancient Hindu teaching that was carved into a mural at the ancient site of Angkor Wat in Cambodia—a site which aligns to the spring equinox.

This mural symbolizes the underlying principle behind the motion of the cycles of the cosmos from the microcosmic scale to the macrocosmic, as well as those related to the journey of consciousness.

It symbolizes the cycles of light and darkness the earth progresses through each year as it rotates around the sun, pivoting upon the equinox, with the winter solstice at the darkest extreme, and the summer solstice the lightest. Numbers of the annual cycle of the sun were also encoded into Angkor Wat, as well as those of The Great Year which our earth cycles through approximately every 26,000 years, and even those of greater cosmic cycles, including huge epochs of time known as Yugas in Hinduism.

It also symbolizes the periods of darkness and light that our consciousness progresses through in its cycles of lives—and that all life, even entire civilizations, transition through.

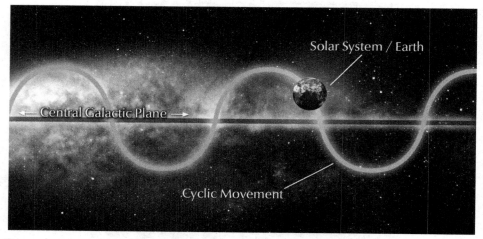

Our solar system, and Earth, cross the galactic plane over very long periods of time in cyclical movements, as if they are pulled back and forth across a central point in a movement much like that depicted in the Churning of the Milky Ocean.

COSMIC CONNECTIONS

The knowledge encoded in ancient sacred sites and texts is not just shared on a planetary level, but also on a cosmic one, as however different the cultural expressions may seem, the knowledge is that of the universal principles governing all of creation and is shared even by inhabitants of other planets and solar systems.

Many spiritual principles and symbols we are familiar with have been found integrated into the unique geometric designs of crop circles, and interactions with extra-terrestrials have revealed they are deeply spiritual beings. The crashed extra-terrestrial vehicle from the famous Roswell incident was described by witnesses as being inscribed with markings reminiscent of Egyptian hieroglyphs, and the temple of Seti I discovered in Egypt has hieroglyphs that look like extra-terrestrial vehicles.

Hieroglyphs carved into the temple of Seti I at Abydos
in Egypt which look like advanced vehicles/craft.

Many of the ancient sites that align to the solstices and equinoxes also align with each other, lying along the same line that runs around the earth within a margin of error of less than one tenth of a degree of latitude (although they are separated by vast distances and are located in some of the most remote places on earth). These sites include the Great Pyramids of Egypt, Easter Island, the Nazca Lines and Machu Picchu in Peru, and the temple of Angkor Wat in Cambodia. Some of these sites are even located at numerologically symbolic degrees from one another. For example, Angkor Wat is situated longitude 72° east of the Great Pyramids and 72 is a number key to the slow astrological cycle our earth progresses through called the "precession of the equinox," which both sites encode in their designs. This begs the question—are these sites all connected, and what can they tell us as a humanity about the cosmic spirituality they all seem to venerate?

The Great Pyramid of Egypt also encodes the speed of light, among many other dimensions related to our planet that seem impossible to measure without the use of advanced technology.

The extraordinary knowledge contained in these sites of the earth's proportions and its astrological cycles reveals that there was a highly advanced input into their designs that combined deep spiritual knowledge with that of the cosmos. This so far remains unexplained by the traditional model of human history, and raises the question of whether there were times in ancient history of cooperation between certain spiritual cultures and interplanetary civilizations.

LOOKING AT THE PAST WITH DISCERNMENT

People often wonder why the ancient builders went to such lengths to create such incredible structures. What many fail to recognize is how they often understood that spirituality and the attainment of enlightenment was the most important aim in life.

However, over time the knowledge of many ancient builders became distorted and lost. What were originally spiritual celebrations either degenerated or were inverted to include human and animal sacrifice and all manner of debauchery, such as found in the mad parties of Sol Invictus in Rome and the blood revelry of the Aztecs. When this happens civilizations are no longer able to hold themselves together, having turned on the very principles that allow them to do so, and thus fall into barbarism and ruin, and can eventually totally collapse and disappear. This degeneration, which happened in some cases over hundreds to thousands of years in different cultures, has unfortunately, in many instances, associated the celebration of the spiritual sun with the worst of human behavior, as when we look back we tend to see civilizations as a whole, rather than being able to distinguish different groups and movements within them, as well as a civilization's periods of spiritual decline.

And so when looking back into the past in search of the traces of spiritual knowledge, it is not possible to do so without confronting the darker aspects of society and human behavior, and the resulting degeneration of spiritual traditions. And whilst this may be uncomfortable to face, it's important to do so now that we are about to delve into the past, to be able to clearly distinguish the different influences that have affected the spiritual knowledge of the world.

DOGMATIC BELIEFS AND RELIGIOUS PERSECUTION

The arrival of the spiritual Son into the world is an incredible event; the Son brings to Earth a profound message of enlightenment that often inspires huge movements of people. Over time these coalesce into religions. However, the mass religions that take root from out of esoteric spiritual knowledge often bear little resemblance to the original wisdom that inspired them (if they were even based on true spiritual knowledge in the first place), as over time, people who co-opt spiritual knowledge, but don't have the spiritual level of the original source, incorporate their own interpretations and cultures into them. And so while these religions can carry spiritual symbols and teachings, they can also incorporate degenerate and barbaric things that were never part of the original message, and are the very opposite of the spirituality of the Son.

Those who had a spiritual level capable of comprehending the mysteries of the spiritual sun were always in the minority, and therefore usually became marginalized and even persecuted by the mass religions that formed, just as the Gnostics (those who followed the esoteric side of Jesus' teachings) were by the early Christians. Their texts were banned as heretical by the early Church, which suppressed and destroyed them en masse, and excluded them from the Bible. This suppression and distortion of the message of Jesus had already started even within the lifetime of Jesus' disciple Peter, who had been given the role of teaching Jesus' message in the West. After Jesus' death, Peter was faced with large numbers of people misappropriating not only Jesus' message, but also his own.

> "But these men, professing, I know not how, to know my mind, undertake to explain my words, which they have heard of me, more intelligently than I who spoke them, telling their catechumens that this is my meaning, which indeed I never thought of. But if, while I am still alive, they dare thus to misrepresent me, how much more will those who shall come after me dare to do so!" [36]
>
> ~ PETER TO JAMES IN THE CLEMENTINE HOMILIES, TRANSLATED BY THOMAS SMITH

Peter then attempts to address the issue by only passing his books on through a process of initiation to ensure they would not fall into the wrong hands. This is an example of how secret schools were formed out of necessity in response to various social pressures.

> "...give the books of my preachings to our brethren, with the like mystery of initiation, that they may indoctrinate those who wish to take part in teaching; for if it be not so done, our word of truth will be rent into many opinions. And this I know, not as being a prophet, but as already seeing the beginning of this very evil. For some from among the Gentiles have rejected my legal preaching, attaching themselves to certain lawless and trifling preaching of the man who is my enemy [Paul]." [37]
>
> ~ PETER TO JAMES IN THE CLEMENTINE HOMILIES, TRANSLATED BY THOMAS SMITH

> "Hear me, brethren and fellow-servants. If we should give the books to all indiscriminately, and they should be corrupted by any daring men, or be perverted by interpretations, as you have heard that some have already done, it will remain even for those who really seek the truth, always to wander in error. Wherefore it is better that they should be with us, and that we should communicate them with all the fore-mentioned care to those who wish to live piously, and to save others." [38]
>
> ~ JAMES IN THE CLEMENTINE HOMILIES, TRANSLATED BY THOMAS SMITH

It was actually Paul's version of Christianity (someone who had never met Jesus and whom the disciples were opposed to) that became widely accepted and popular, while the esoteric interpretation of Jesus' message eventually became persecuted, even though Jesus had given it his own authority in appointing his disciple Peter as its teacher. Paul added many of his own interpretations to the message of Jesus, including statements promoting the suppression of women, which a number of banned texts reveal, was something that Jesus was profoundly against.

A study of the teachings of Jesus, including those that were suppressed and banned from the Bible, reveals a message that shares more in common with the spiritual knowledge of Egypt, the East, and the Druids, than it does with orthodox Christianity, and yet it was often Christianity that suppressed these beliefs as "pagan."

Throughout history, dogmatic believers have ripped people from their cultures in blindly enforcing their doctrines, when the many cultural expressions of spiritual principles form part of the diverse tapestry of nature expressing the same inherent truths and the perpetual creativity of human consciousness. They are cause for mutual celebration and should be preserved and allowed to naturally develop. Whether someone chooses to connect with the spiritual sun through the solar deity of one culture or another generally makes little or no difference, if what is being connected with is the same.

Symbolism, iconography, and parables are simply a means of illustrating principles and imparting knowledge, which is why they can take so many different forms. Through them, mystics have been able to communicate higher spiritual truths. However, an icon is not an absolute truth in itself, and this is where many religious believers get stuck. An icon or symbol is not the spiritual principle; it is a representation of it, just as our reflection in a mirror is not us, but allows us to see and understand ourselves.

Due to their amassed influence and size, religions and not the actual spiritual practitioners tend to become the public carriers of spiritual symbols and sacred texts into the future. However, not having an inner spiritual level, religious believers are unable to comprehend higher truths nor distinguish between what's really spiritual and what's not, and thus exclude the complete body of spiritual knowledge and the deeper meaning of their religious symbols. As has happened so many times in history, whilst an outer shell remains, this complete body of knowledge and the original meaning behind religious traditions then becomes lost, either because it has to be encoded and veiled in symbolism for its protection, or because it is forced underground.

Genuine spiritual practitioners then have to function under the banners of accepted religions in order to survive, whilst teaching real knowledge apart from them and often in secret. So when searching into the past, although many ancient religions carry many spiritual truths, you'll find those who were actually getting knowledge and practicing it were often operating on the edges of society in remote places, and in secret mystery schools. They were not generally large groups of people, but individuals and small groups who emerge in traces here and there, carrying a remarkable wisdom.

THE INFILTRATION OF DARK FORCES

Apart from dogmatism, there is also another influence at work against the expression of the genuinely spiritual. It is impossible to look at spirituality throughout history without finding and having to confront the opposite of the practitioners of the spiritual sun, which are instead those practitioners of darkness. These are people who have sought to awaken in darkness, rather than in light, and part of their goal has always been to suppress human spiritual potential.

These people have likewise operated in secrecy throughout history to avoid detection, which has made looking back into the past a very muddied and murky affair, as wherever you find people attempting to awaken in light, the forces of darkness follow, often attacking them from the shadows. This has caused a real mixing of very different influences and forces within the same scenes on the stage of history—with both those attempting to awaken in light and in darkness operating largely in secrecy at the same time, and both working in opposition to each other.

It is possible however, to separate their influence out, once you become more familiar with spiritual principles. It is difficult for most however, as those seeking to awaken in evil use deception as one of their main methods. Working by stealth and infiltration, they have often taken over, subverted, hijacked, and distorted much of the spiritual knowledge of humanity, even taking over entire spiritual schools and religions. Thus they have often maintained the outward shell of a spiritual teaching, but beneath the surface worked to distort it in order to lead people away from the light, even whilst using the highest sounding of ideals. This makes it even more important and pressing for all sincere people to really understand the spiritual principles of life and creation as much as they possibly can.

There are however, tell-tale signs of the presence of practitioners of dark knowledge, and looking back in history, there are some stark signs of their existence. Some examples of these signs include the tendency to use the number four in their rituals and ceremonies, to strengthen the darkness of materialism; the goal of subjugating and controlling others through force and by stealth; inverting the symbols of light (like the inverted pentagram and cross); mocking and persecuting the spiritual Son; the use of animal and human sacrifice; taking multiple partners and engaging in all manner of sexual deviancies; advocating adultery and fornication; taking pleasure in hurting and persecuting others; and looking to develop occult powers for their own benefit, which they use to impress and mislead people with.

Taken on their own, these things don't necessarily indicate the presence of the dark occult. They can also be indicators of degeneracy, as they are precisely the things that dark practitioners introduce into societies in order to degenerate them. That's why sometimes their mass practice can be found in civilizations throughout history, including at ancient sites, and in many so-called "sacred" texts.

ANIMAL AND HUMAN SACRIFICE

One of the most horrific practices of the dark occult is ritual animal and human sacrifice, evidence for which can be found in many parts of the world.

Perhaps most infamously was its widespread practice by the Maya and the Aztecs of Central and South America. The degree it descended to has shocked the world for centuries since its disappearance after the similarly horrific Spanish conquest. And sadly now many associate the ancient knowledge found at these sites entirely with that practice.

However, there is evidence that their knowledge originated far back in antiquity. Their legends speak of giants, dwarves, and bearded fair skinned peoples who built their sacred sites aligned to the solstices and equinoxes; remnants of this earlier time came down through a veneration of the spiritual sun, the divine son as the feathered serpent Quetzalcoatl, and the sun god Viracocha. Many of these Central and South American sites were built over multiple times, indicating that successive cultures took over and built upon the sacred sites of those they conquered or assimilated—eventually the cultures that took over completely had adopted the savage practice of human and animal sacrifice.

Perhaps nowhere is the evidence clearer for this than in the surviving written legends of the Maya themselves, recorded in their text Popol Vuh.

It recounts how "the nations" were taken over by a small group of people who came under the influence of "gods" who at first asked for animal sacrifice, and then human. The text is written from this group's point of view, and they actually refer to themselves as "bloodletters and sacrificers" as though it were a sacred title. Through sorcery and violence it describes how they subjugated these surrounding nations. Many of the passages are too disturbing to reproduce here, but these excerpts give a glimpse of what has happened similarly in other parts of the world when religious groups have come under the influence of dark forces.

> "But do not reveal yourselves. Do this now and your existence shall become great. You shall conquer all the nations." [39]
>
> ~ THE "GODS" WHO ARE CONSULTED IN POPOL VUH, TRANSLATED BY ALLEN J. CHRISTENSON

> "There they multiplied and became many. They had daughters and they had sons on top of Hacavitz. They rejoiced then, for they had defeated all the nations there on top of the mountain. Thus they had done this. They had surely defeated the nations, indeed all the nations. [...]

> There they put down roots at Chi Izmachi, and there also their bloodletting god increased in greatness. And all the nations, the small and the great, became afraid. They witnessed the arrival of

captive people to be sacrificed and killed by the glory and sovereignty of Lord Co Tuha and Lord Iztayul, in alliance with the Nihaib and Ahau Quichés." [40]

~ POPOL VUH, TRANSLATED BY ALLEN J. CHRISTENSON

Sadly, this text incorporates one of the only records of the spiritual beliefs of the Maya, which includes their description of how creation came to be.

Both Quetzalcoatl and Jesus spoke out against the practice of human and animal sacrifice, but their message was ignored by many in their societies at the time. Jesus could not have been clearer when he said:

"I came to destroy the sacrifices, and if ye cease not from sacrificing, the wrath *of God* will not cease from you." [41]

~ JESUS QUOTED IN PANARION 30.16,4-5 BY EPIPHANIUS (CALLED THE GOSPEL OF THE EBIONITES)

"And to those who supposed that God is pleased with sacrifices, He [Jesus] said, 'God wishes mercy, and not sacrifices' —the knowledge of Himself, and not holocausts." [42]

~ PETER IN THE CLEMENTINE HOMILIES, TRANSLATED BY THOMAS SMITH

"In his study of aboriginal American religions (1882, p. 140), Brinton comments: He [Quezalcoatl] forbade the sacrifice of human beings and animals, teaching that bread, flowers, and incense were all that the gods demanded. And he prohibited wars, fighting, robbery, and other forms of violence to such an extent that he was held in affectionate veneration, not only by his own people but by distant nations as well, who made pilgrimages to his capital. The fact that the Aztecs, who excelled in human sacrifice at their pyramids and temples, still recollected a benevolent, pacifist culture-bringer whose teachings closely paralleled the Biblical Commandments so impressed the Spanish friars that they identified Quetzalcoatl with the Apostle Thomas—an exact analogy to the confusion of Viracocha with St Bartholomew in Peru." [43]

~ THOR HEYERDAHL, THE BEARDED GODS SPEAK

SOME OF THE ORIGINAL KNOWLEDGE SURVIVED

Thankfully, not all spiritual knowledge has been destroyed by dark forces and oppression. Due to the tireless efforts of many brave men and women, there do exist fragments of knowledge that have been kept and preserved. By looking back today with the same shared knowledge as the original esoteric practitioners, someone can recognize the knowledge of the spirituality of light in their ruins and preserved texts, which preceded and survived the degeneration and persecution—allowing someone familiar with esoteric knowledge and experience to understand ancient mysteries where archeologists and academics remain baffled.

But despite the passing of these ancient cultures into history, this knowledge is never truly lost, as it is palpitating throughout the whole of the universe, waiting to be rediscovered by those who choose to search for it.

CONNECT WITH THE HEAVENS AND THE EARTH BY CELEBRATING THE SOLSTICES AND EQUINOXES

Solstices and equinoxes are a time of connection between the heavens and the earth, the personal and the divine, the inner and the outer, the material and the spiritual, and even a time when contact through mystical experiences is made more possible. It is a beautiful time, which unfortunately we as a humanity have lost touch with, as did other cultures who degenerated in the past and lost their spiritual foundation.

By taking part in ceremonies to celebrate the solstices and equinoxes, one is able to use the event for its higher purpose just as the ancients did—to connect with the cosmos, to understand eternal principles through intuitive experience and the cycles of nature, and to take the spiritual nourishment needed to help toward awakening. This is not simply the revival of something past, but the partaking in something eternal that permeates our lives, even if we pay little attention to it.

The whole of creation has been formed to imbue the principles of spirituality, and thus these principles can not only be found all around us, but also within us, allowing us to understand our origins and the true purpose of life whenever we choose to look. This has allowed people throughout the ages to tap into the same universal spiritual knowledge.

"**In everything that is life is the law written. You find it in the grass, in the tree, in the river, in the mountain, in the birds of heaven, in the fishes of the sea; but seek it chiefly in yourselves.** For I tell you truly, all living things are nearer to God than the scripture which is without life. God so made life and all living things that they might by the everlasting word teach the laws of the true God to man. **God wrote not the laws in the pages of books, but in your heart and in your spirit.** They are in your breath, your blood, your bone; in your flesh, your bowels, your eyes, your ears, and in every little part of your body. They are present in the air, in the water, in the earth, in the plants, in the sunbeams, in the depths and in the heights. They all speak to you that you may understand the tongue and the will of the living God. But you shut your eyes that you may not see, and you shut your ears that you may not hear. I tell you truly, that the scripture is the work of man, but life and all its hosts are the work of our God. Wherefore do you not listen to the words of God which are written in His works? And wherefore do you study the dead scriptures which are the work of the hands of men?" [44]

~ JESUS IN THE ESSENE GOSPEL OF PEACE, TRANSLATED BY EDMOND BORDEAUX SZEKELY

The message of the spiritual sun transcends both time and culture and forms a cosmic book for all who can read it.

This crop circle appeared on the summer solstice 2001 in a field in Wiltshire, England, which is significant as Wiltshire is home to Stonehenge—an ancient site aligned to the summer solstice. The symbol in the crop circle correlates with the spiritual meaning of the summer solstice—the sun at the pinnacle of the pyramid represents the attainment of enlightenment, which is represented by the summer solstice as the day of most light in the year. If this crop circle is genuine, it reveals the knowledge of the spiritual sun has been shared not just by some here on earth, but even by those who inhabit other planets, as it is the knowledge of creation.

Autumn Equinox

The Descent into Inner Darkness

CHAPTER TWO

The Spiritual Meaning of the Autumn Equinox

THE PATH OF THE SUN, SYMBOLIZING THE JOURNEY to enlightenment, starts as darkness begins to increase, three days after the summer solstice. This is when the sun begins its annual descent, after having reached its apex at the summer solstice, and the days gradually begin to shorten toward the cold and darkness of winter.

The annual descent of the sun south into darkness is symbolic of the consciousness descending into the darkness of matter, of it coming into a body, into the darkness of the subconscious of the psyche, to join the process of life (referred to as the Wheel of Life in Buddhism). This darkness is necessary for spiritual awakening, as without darkness we would not know light, and it is from darkness (the subconscious) that light (consciousness) is extracted, giving us the knowledge gained from experience.

In the beginning of creation this unique spark of the spirit comes down into matter to learn from life in the universe of duality between darkness and light. Experience, learning, and suffering, propel it in a quest to return to the spiritual source from which it first emanated: from darkness, to the birth of light at the winter solstice, culminating at the summer solstice, when the light is at its maximum, symbolizing enlightenment.

After the sun's descent following the summer solstice, the next stage in the sun's journey is the autumn equinox, when darkness becomes greater than light.

A TIME WHEN DARKNESS IS GREATER THAN LIGHT

The autumn equinox is a mysterious time. It marks an essential passage in the process of enlightenment that is often overlooked, misunderstood, and mistaken as dark and heretical.

Equinoxes occur twice a year—in spring and autumn—when day and night are approximately equal lengths, which is when the sun crosses the equator.

THE SYMBOL OF THE STAR SIGN OF LIBRA.

Interestingly, in the northern hemisphere, the sun enters the astrological sign of Libra at the autumn equinox, which is the sign of the scales and of balance. The glyph for Libra represents the sun setting/rising, expressing the balance between night and day.

The autumn equinox marks a turning point in the earth's annual journey around the sun, as immediately following it the nights become longer than the days, bringing the coming winter—a time of darkness and death.

Remnants of the esoteric meaning of the autumn equinox can barely be found in the few lasting traditions from ancient peoples who celebrated it and knew of its real significance. To discover the esoteric meaning by looking at rituals and traditions is not easy. There are traditions which have been passed down today, but which have strayed from their root meanings. Different civilizations and cultures have added their own veneer, altering and losing much of the original meaning as they themselves lost the understanding of it.

Its meaning has been obscured with time, much more than the other three events in the wheel of the year. As the understanding of spiritual knowledge was lost, its meaning became vague and must have seemed to represent sinister, evil forces. Thus the symbols were given different meanings and turned into other things in the way that Santa Claus now largely symbolizes Christmas day.

Parts of autumn equinox celebrations moved to cross quarter days (cross quarter days are produced when the wheel of the year is divided into eight instead of four; these days are called Samhain, Beltane, etc., in Paganism) and meanings changed into celebrations of the dead, of evil spirits, harvest festivals, bonfires, sacrifices, drunkenness, and debauchery.

So you have to start with a knowledge of the process of enlightenment, to have a basis upon which you can search and piece together the jigsaw. Fortunately the builders of ancient sites, such as the Great Pyramids, left the message of the real meaning in their architecture, which mirrored the meanings found in the cosmos and survived in sketchy details through myths, legends, and religions throughout history.

Traditionally, the autumn equinox is a celebration of the harvest, as it is when summer has finished giving its fruits, which are collected in preparation for winter. But there are other indicators given by the most ancient sacred sites that mark the autumn equinox: a descending passage into a subterranean pit lit by a star of the dragon constellation in the Great Pyramid of Egypt, a seven-scaled feathered serpent of light descending a pyramid in Mexico, a giant Pyramid of the Sun aligned to the equinoxes built on a cave symbolizing the underworld, and seven massive stone statues facing the equinox sunset on Easter Island.

What was known to the ancients is the part darkness plays in the work of spiritual transformation. Those in the orthodox superstitiously fear it, and many in the new age completely ignore it. But at the autumn equinox it can be found in the cycles of the sun—and traces of it can be found here and there in ancient legends and myths that have become distorted over time.

The message contained in the autumn equinox tells us that all things must die before they can be born, all spiritual ascent requires descent first, and all those who long for light must firstly face their own inner darkness and overcome it.

THE RIVAL OF THE SUN

In the ancient myths of Europe the sun god has a rival. He is the god of darkness, whose dominion is the night and the dark half of the year, which begins at the autumn equinox. This opposition between light and darkness has been depicted in the rivalry between the gods Gawain and the Green Knight, Llew and Goronwy, Lugh and Balor, the Oak King and the Holly King, etc.

In ancient Egypt the god Seth was the dark antithesis of the spiritual Son Horus. In Norse mythology, Höder is the god of darkness and blind brother of Balder, the god of the summer sun. In Aztec mythology the spiritual Son Quetzalcoatl has a twin brother called Xolotl, who was the dark aspect of Venus as the evening star, whilst Quetzalcoatl was Venus as the morning star.

An Egyptian statue with the rival god Horus on one side (the god of light), and Seth on the other (the god of darkness).

The god of light is born three days after the winter solstice as the spiritual Son in traditions around the world (including the birth of Jesus as Christmas), because the sun, having reached its lowest and weakest point in the year, then begins its ascent as it gains strength toward summer. The god of darkness, however, is born three days after the summer solstice, as this is when the sun begins to diminish, and the nights and darkness begin to increase toward winter.

Some have confused John the Baptist, whose birthday is celebrated on June 24th (three days after the summer solstice in the northern hemisphere) as the equivalent of the god of darkness found in pagan traditions. John however, has a different role. He can be seen as both symbolic of the avatar, the prophet who announces the coming of the Son in darkness before the light comes, and also the initiate, the one who starts in the darkness of their own subconscious, which is where each person begins the journey toward enlightenment.

It is from the autumn equinox onwards that the nights are longer than the days, and therefore darkness is greater than light. In some pagan traditions, this indicated that the god of darkness reigned supreme at this time of year. This god of darkness can personify and symbolize many different things, as darkness itself has many aspects to understand.

The god of darkness has typically been associated with the Christian idea of "the devil" and "Satan." However, looking into the historical development of these figures, it is clear that "the devil" and "Satan" were at first terms used to refer to different demons, evil forces, and the embodiment of the egos (the darkness we carry within). It appears these terms became confused, becoming used synonymously with each other, and eventually became names for a sole being that was depicted as the evil opposite of God; this being then took on a distinctive character and appearance in the medieval period. However, through out-of-body experiences, I've personally seen that there are no beings called "the devil" or "Satan" that exist in the underworld, although I have seen that demonic entities and evil forces do, which is likely what these terms were originally used to describe.

The god of darkness so associated with the autumn equinox and found in many ancient myths that predate Christianity, can be seen then not as a symbol of Satan or the devil, who came into literary existence much later, but of the darkness that is found in creation, in the cycles of the sun throughout the day and the year, which also exists within us as a microcosm of the universe. The darkness within us is the psychological darkness of our subconscious, which is inhabited by our egos, and is the antithesis of our own inner light, which is our consciousness, and of the aspect of our higher Being represented by the sun, which is the spiritual Son or Christ.

The god of darkness, the devil and Satan, have also all been associated with another figure, called Lucifer. Lucifer became romanticised as the famous fallen angel. However again, going back into ancient texts, the name Lucifer is based on a Latin word, which means "shining one, light bearer" and "bringer of dawn for the morning star;" this same Latin word has also been used to describe Jesus in the Bible, revealing that it was never originally used as the name of a fallen or evil being.

The name Lucifer does however, describe something else that exists in esoteric lore, which is a higher part of each person's Being that acts as a psychological tempter on the path of the spiritual sun. Misunderstood and confused with "Satan" by the orthodoxy, Lucifer in most people's minds is a figure of evil, but in my experience, and in several esoteric traditions, his role is a spiritual one which facilitates someone's awakening. In this regard, Lucifer, the light bringer, is an aspect of our higher Being sent from the spiritual Father who sets the events of the path of the spiritual sun when someone starts that process, and guides them along it. The role of this aspect is to tempt and thus test the walker of the path, and their temptations must be overcome to successfully awaken. Although Lucifer has become synonymous with evil, this association has no real basis in ancient texts; his role as a tempter is to help us to extract the evil from within us in the situations he puts to us in life, providing the opportunities to be able to see (thus Lucifer is a light-bearer), understand, and remove it.

Symbolically, Lucifer is sometimes depicted holding a set of scales, representing balance and justice. The scales also represent the equinox, a time of balance between night and day, which occurs as the sun passes into the astrological sign of Libra, which is also symbolized by a set of scales.

Without darkness there would be no shadow, and it is shadow that allows us to see just as much as light does. Without shadow we could not see form, and there would be no recognition that light even exists.

> "If one does not stand in the darkness, he will not be able to see the light... And to someone who will not know the [root] of all things, they remain hidden. Someone who will not know the root of wickedness is no stranger to it." [1]
>
> ~ JESUS IN THE DIALOGUE OF THE SAVIOR FROM THE NAG HAMMADI LIBRARY, TRANSLATED BY STEPHEN EMMEL

In the work of inner transformation on the path of the spiritual Son, light is extracted from darkness. The subconscious, which is given by nature, is the darkness, and on the path of the spiritual sun, the light of consciousness is extracted from the egos within the subconscious, gradually increasing consciousness within a person until there is total light. This consciousness, once extracted, then contains the knowledge of light, but also the knowledge of the darkness that once trapped it, which has been referred to as "the knowledge of good and evil." This is how knowledge, wisdom, and love are attained on the path of the sun, and why Lucifer is known as the light-bearer.

Each person starts this path in the darkness of the subconscious, and then must go through much learning and suffering in their life to understand and be able to overcome it, and through a spiritual process destroy it to become the light with the knowledge of that light and the darkness that contained it.

THE DEATH OF JOHN AND THE WICKER MAN

A person starts from where they are, which is in the darkness of the subconscious and the world of matter, and why John the Baptist, who represents the initiate, is born when darkness begins to increase in the sun's annual cycle, and light decrease—symbolizing the descent of consciousness into matter.

The Son is the spiritual force which is born within an initiate once they are spiritually prepared enough, symbolically celebrated at the winter solstice when the light begins to increase in the solar cycle, and darkness decrease. As the Son, the light of the spiritual within symbolized as the sun, grows and increases, the darkness of the egos and the subconscious of the initiate, represented by John, must decrease. This reference is found in the Gospels:

"A man can receive nothing unless it has been given him from heaven. You yourselves are my witnesses that I said, 'I am not the Christ,' but, 'I have been sent ahead of Him.' He who has the bride is the bridegroom; but the friend of the bridegroom, who stands and hears him, rejoices greatly because of the bridegroom's voice. So this joy of mine has been made full. He must increase, but I must decrease." [2]

~ THE GOSPEL ACCORDING TO JOHN 3:27-30

The burning of the wicker man, said to have been performed by the ancient Celts at the autumn equinox.

In Celtic traditions, which still survive today, they symbolized this same principle. At the autumn equinox they made a figure from the stems of cut seed, which they burnt by fire representing John Barleycorn, the spirit of the fields, as it is said that he must die in order to become a man. John the Baptist is said to have died six months before Jesus whose death was at the time of the spring equinox, making John the Baptist's death at the time of the autumn equinox—the same time as the symbolic death of John Barleycorn.

The autumn equinox is a time of death, as just as in nature at this time of year the seeds produced at summer fall to the earth and must die before they germinate, and the old must die to make way for the next season of new life, so too must the inferior within us die to make way for the new life of the spirit within.

The one who walks the spiritual path must die inwardly to make way for the spiritual Son whose presence within transforms someone from being an animal, created by the egos which are animalistic in nature, and symbolized by John dressed in animal hair and crying out in the wilderness, into a "true human." This death is an inner one. It is the death of the egos and darkness of the subconscious, which is part of preparing the way for the birth of the spiritual within. John refers to this preparation as "making straight the way for the Lord."

> "John replied in the words of Isaiah the prophet, 'I am the voice of one calling in the wilderness, 'Make straight the way for the Lord.'" [3]
>
> ~ THE GOSPEL ACCORDING TO JOHN 1:23

THE SACRED SEED

The death of the seed at autumn symbolizes another spiritual principle. It's not just plants that contain seeds; we too contain seeds that have the power to create new life. Our seed is contained within our sexual energies, as these energies have the ability to create children, just as the seed of a plant gives rise to the next generation through its seed in the cycles of nature. But our seed not only has the potential to create things physically; it also contains the potential to create spiritual things.

In ancient times, these energies were sometimes symbolized as a sacred seed. In the Eleusinian mysteries of ancient Greece they were symbolized with an ear of wheat. A third century Roman theologian (who is similar to present-day anti-cult figures) writes about an ear of wheat being used in Athenian initiation ceremonies, and how the Athenians believed that this sacred seed was given by God.

> "The Athenians, when they initiate in the Eleusinia, exhibit in silence to the epoptai the mighty and marvelous and most complete epoptic mystery, an ear of cut-wheat. But this ear of wheat is also considered among the Athenians to constitute the perfect enormous illumination that has descended from the ineffable one, just as the hierophant himself declares." [4]
>
> ~ HIPPOLYTUS, REFUTATION OF ALL HERESIES 5.8.39

The seed was considered sacred, as it symbolizes the latent inner seed planted within each person that contains the powers of creation, a power that is given by and belongs to divinity—thus making it something that's ultimately spiritual, and that contains the potential for divinity we each have.

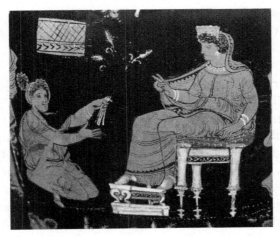

A queen of Eleusis offering a triune of wheat to the
goddess Demeter from a vase dated to 340 BC.

Veiled references to this appear in some of the earliest texts of Hinduism,
called the Upanishads, which talk about the potential found within sexual
energies, which is the seed within us, and its use for spiritual purposes.

"Those who use their days for sexual pleasure
Consume prana, the very stuff of life;
But mastered, sex becomes a spiritual force.
The wise see the Lord of Love in all food;
From food comes seed, and from seed all creatures.
They take the lunar path who live for sex;
But those who are self-controlled and truthful
Will go to the bright regions of the sun." [5]
~ THE PRASHNA UPANISHAD, TRANSLATED BY EKNATH EASWARAN

When used within the practice of spiritual alchemy, the sexual energies
become a spiritual inner fire. Fire, like that found in the sun and stars, reduces
matter back into energy and light, and creates new elements. The feminine
aspect of each person's higher Being, symbolized as a Great Mother goddess,
works within these energies and the inner divine fire to put to death the dark
matter of the egos, and give birth to the spiritual by creating new elements
that crystalize into higher spiritual parts. This practice has been referred to
as Maithuna (as a practice found within some Tantric traditions) in the East,
alchemy in medieval and Renaissance Europe, the practice of HeQi in Taoism,
and the bridal chamber of the Gnostics.

Through an alchemical process of transmutation, light is extracted from
darkness and the initiate creates themselves anew, being "born again"—not
of flesh, but of the spirit.

"Flesh gives birth to flesh, but the Spirit gives birth to spirit. You should not be surprised at my saying, 'You must be born again.'" [6]
~ JESUS IN THE GOSPEL ACCORDING TO JOHN 3:6-7

To be able to create higher spiritual parts with the energies, however, they need to be purified so that they are of a suitable frequency. As the egos are put to death, the initiate's energies become increasingly cleansed, in the purifying inner flames, in preparation for the birth of the Son within. This is the spiritual meaning behind the symbolic transmutation of base metals into gold in alchemy, and the ritual purification, and spiritual cleansing, of John the Baptist.

Like the practitioners of the Eleusinian mysteries, the Maya also considered their staple seed corn (also known as maize) to be sacred; it was associated with their spiritual Son Hun Hunahpu, who was known as the Maize god, and the cakes they made of maize were used to symbolize the sun. It was also said to be the substance that humans were made of, showing how they understood that we ultimately come from the sun, and contain the seeds of the sun, which are the seeds of creative potential that can give birth to the spiritual sun within us.

In the Maya account of creation, humans were created from a mixture of ground corn (seed) and water. The corn was said to be found hidden in a sacred mountain, and was the bones of the buried remains of the Corn Goddess. This hidden potential is symbolic of the same Goddess energy written about in Hindu texts called kundalini. In some Maya accounts the corn is hidden under an immovable rock, just as the Hindus describe this energy as lying latent within the coccyx bone of the human being. The Maya describe how this rock was split open by a strike of lightning, and believe that lightning can take the form of a serpent, just as the Hindus depict the kundalini as a serpent. The serpent is used as a symbol of sexual electricity and fire because it moves like the sine waves of electricity, and both lightning and electricity are a form of fire. The lightning symbolizes how the latent potential within our inner seed is only activated by the electric (serpentine) energy that the Goddess works with in alchemical transformation.

When struck by the lightning, the corn was singed and became three other colors, making four in total: black, white, yellow, and red. These colors represent the change in the sexual energies that occurs in alchemy as they are purified (from black, to white, to yellow and then red), and can be shown to somebody in dreams or out of the body. They have also been depicted in the alchemical texts of medieval and Renaissance Europe. When the energies turn red, the kundalini awakens.

In this Maya account, the human being is the grain, the seed (which is the corn) of hidden potential, whose energies can be transformed in alchemical fire (the lightning).

"When the hero twins were in the underworld battling the Xibalba lords, four wild animals brought news of corn hidden within the great eastern mountain. These corn seeds were the buried remains of Bone Woman, Hun Hunahpu's first wife (Bassie-Sweet 1999, 2001). This goddess and her Classic Period counterpart, the Corn Goddess, represented the ear of corn and its seed. The discovery of corn within a mountain is widespread in the Maya area, and in many of these stories the corn was hidden under an immovable rock that had to be split open by a deity using a lightning bolt (Edmonson 1971:146; Thompson 1970). Another consistent element is that this seed was originally white. When the lightning struck the stone, it singed and burnt some of the white corn, and this resulted in the creation of the other three colors of corn: yellow, red and black. The Maya still categorize corn according to these four colors. Bone Woman thus took on four manifestations representing the four kinds of corn... The Quiché still believe that a lightning bolt splits open the seed at germination (Allen Christenson, personal communication 2001)." [7]
~ KAREN BASSIE, MAYA CREATOR GODS

It is the awakening of the sexual inner fire (symbolized by lightning and the serpent) that germinates our seeds of spiritual potential.

The humans that were created in the Maya account of creation were born into darkness (which is the darkness of the subconscious). It was not until the sun rose in the east from out of a cave that there was light and life. Mithras, Jesus, and Viracocha were all said to have been born into a cave and Krishna into a prison. This is the birth of the spiritual Son/sun within, who brings the light and life of the spirit to our inner darkness.

THE DESCENT INTO THE UNDERWORLD

LOOKING DOWN THE DESCENDING PASSAGE OF THE GREAT PYRAMID.

In the Great Pyramid of Egypt there is a descending passage that leads to a subterranean pit. At midnight on the autumn equinox during certain time periods, a star associated with the god of darkness, who esoterically can be seen as Lucifer, shines down the descending passage into the pit. At the same time, the star Alcyone, the principle star from the Pleiades star cluster around which our own sun and solar system revolves, aligns with the meridian of the Pyramid. Here is a significant ancient clue to the meaning of the autumn equinox. It is before the birth of the god of light at the winter solstice that the initiate must descend into the underworld whilst subjected to the temptations of Lucifer to investigate their subconscious and overcome their egos.

A similar alignment and design can be found at the Pyramid of the Sun at the Maya site of Teotihuacán in Mexico, which shares many of the same dimensions as the Great Pyramid of Egypt. The entire face of the pyramid aligns to the setting equinox sun, and the pyramid is built on top of a cave. The Maya saw caves as gateways to the underworld, and so, like the Great Pyramid of Egypt, we find a similar theme of equinox and descent into the underworld.

Another strange site that shares similar design elements is the mysterious Ratapignata pyramid in France. It aligns to the equinox, and contains a descending stairwell that leads into a subterranean chamber. No one knows who built it, but many believe it was the Knights Templar, an order of warrior monks founded in 1119 AD, that are said to have had people within their ranks that carried the knowledge of many of the secret mystery schools of Europe and the East.

Many sacred sites which encode the symbols of descent at the autumn equinox face the precise cardinal direction of west, which is the direction of the setting sun. These sites include Chichen Itza, the Pyramid of the Sun, and the statues of Easter Island. The fact that these ancient sites align to the sunset, and not the sunrise on the equinox, is an important clue to their meaning. The direction of west, as the place where the sun sets, was associated with death and the descent into the underworld by the Maya, ancient Greeks, and the ancient Egyptians.

> "And they took [and] brought me to a place in which those who were there were like flaming fire, and, when they wished, they appeared as men. And they brought me to the place of darkness, and to a mountain the point of whose summit reached to heaven. And I saw the places of the luminaries [and the treasuries of the stars] and of the thunder [and] in the uttermost depths, where were a fiery bow and arrows and their quiver, and [a fiery sword] and all the lightnings. And they took me to the living waters, and to the fire of the west, which receives every setting of the sun. And I came to a river of fire in which the fire flows like water and discharges itself into the great sea towards the west. I saw the great rivers and came to the great

[river and to the great] darkness, and went to the place where no flesh walks. I saw the mountains of the darkness of winter and the place whence all the waters of the deep flow. I saw the mouths of all the rivers of the earth and the mouth of the deep." [8]
~ THE BOOK OF ENOCH, TRANSLATED BY R. H. CHARLES

The Maya also associated the direction of west with the color black, which they saw as representing death and darkness.

"The black wild bees are in the west. The black laurel flower is their flower. A large black blossom is their cup." [9]
~ THE BOOK OF CHILAM BALAM OF CHUMAYEL, TRANSLATED BY RALPH L. ROYS

The descent at the autumn equinox into the underworld is found not only in sacred sites, but also in ancient myths.

In ancient Babylon, in the autumn, Dumuzi (whose name means "rightful son") became the god who was sacrificed with the cutting of the corn. As the grain was cut and stored, the god was said to go into the underworld to return next year when the sap rose in the trees and vegetation returned to the earth.

His myth was paralleled in Akkadian lore by Tammuz, who died every year at the beginning of autumn, and was reborn in the spring.

At the time of the autumn equinox, an ancient Welsh myth describes how Llew, the god of light, is killed and descends to the underworld.

THE LAW OF THE FALL

The descent into the underworld is related to a universal law—the law of the fall, where someone must first descend before they can ascend, as light is extracted from darkness. This is why ancient myths and monuments symbolize the descent into the underworld (down steps, descending passageways, into caves and subterranean chambers, etc.), and spiritual ascents (up flights of stairs, ascending passageways, leading to the apexes of pyramids, etc.).

The underworld has been described by ancient peoples around the world. Whilst it is a place in the other dimensions which can be seen in out-of-body and near-death experiences—which is why so many ancient peoples had knowledge of it that share so many similarities—it is also connected to the human psyche. The regions of the underworld correspond to the interior regions of the subconscious, which interpenetrate our body and psyche in the present moment.

The autumn equinox expresses the principle of descent, which occurs throughout the path to liberation: before the birth of the spiritual Son within, at the beginning of each of the path's major stages, and before every initiation.

The darkness and underworld is that of the psyche, which someone descends into whilst out of the body in dreams and in out-of-body experiences, and also in the difficult circumstances that arise in their daily life, in order to suffer, learn, and be tested. And in this darkness, Lucifer, each one's own psychological trainer, tempts them to test their will and to reveal what is truly within each person, hidden within the deep, dark caverns of the mind resounding with the voices of the egos that can sometimes be heard in the phase between wakefulness and sleep as we enter the subconscious in dreams, and which exist in the dark crevices of our subconscious.

> "I entered on the steep and savage path...
> Here sighs and lamentations and loud cries
> were echoing across the starless air,
> so that, as soon as I set out, I wept.
> Strange utterances, horrible pronouncements,
> accents of anger, words of suffering,
> and voices shrill and faint, and beating hands—
> all went to make a tumult that will whirl
> forever through that turbid, timeless air...
> A whirlwind burst out of the tear-drenched earth,
> a wind that crackled with a bloodred light,
> a light that overcame all of my senses;
> and like a man whom sleep has seized, I fell.
> The heavy sleep within my head was smashed
> by an enormous thunderclap, so that
> I started up as one whom force awakens;...
> In truth I found myself upon the brink of an abyss, the melancholy
> valley containing thundering, unending wailings,
> That valley, dark and deep and filled with mist,
> is such that, though I gazed into its pit,
> I was unable to discern a thing." [10]
> ~ DANTE, INFERNO, THE DIVINE COMEDY, TRANSLATED BY ALLEN
>   MANDELBAUM

It is never guaranteed that someone will emerge from a descent, as it is only through overcoming one's internal obstacles that they can ascend from out of the darkness back into the light, but this time with more light than they had before.

One of the earliest known representations of the equinox, a symbol of balance, found in an ancient megalithic site in Ireland—showing the eternal winding and unwinding of the sun, from winter solstice, through the equinox, to the summer solstice, and back again.

THE ROLE OF CHAOS

Chaos is a very important aspect of creation, as all of creation emerges from it. The ancient text called the Rig Veda contains one of the oldest and most famous accounts of creation in the world, and says that creation emerged from darkness, void, and water indiscriminate. Likewise, matter is in chaos after the "Big Bang," which many scientists believe was the origin of our universe. Then, as it crystallized, it gradually organized into forms, structure, and order.

This same principle at work on a macrocosmic scale in creation, is also at work when creating the spiritual within—the old and inferior must firstly dissolve into chaos in order to be reduced back into basic elements, which are then refined and purified to create the new and superior.

The descent into the darkness of chaos at the autumn equinox is the descent into psychological chaos. It's in our darkest times that the egos come to the surface, like when under pressure, unwell, abandoned, attacked, unjustly treated, etc. A person has to fight their way out of this psychological chaos by seeing and removing the egos that arise, rather than being overcome by them, and in doing so, gradually establishes order within themselves. As they do, they emerge with greater understanding, and more consciousness, and therefore come out with something superior to what they had before.

This same principle is found in a study of sound called cymatics. It was discovered that as sound moved to higher and higher frequencies, the patterns it formed became more complex, but that the pattern would firstly completely dissolve into chaos before reforming to create the next more complex pattern.

THE SEVEN BODIES OF THE SUN

The energy of the sun and stars is a creative energy; the stars create almost all the elements of the universe in a process called nucleosynthesis. We too contain creative energy, as man and woman united can create a child. The ancients describe a process, often called "alchemy," which directs this creative energy inward, instead of outward, and uses it to create spiritual parts within. These spiritual parts have been called "the children of the bride-chamber" by the ancient Gnostics.

> "But if ye be persuaded and keep your souls chaste before God, there will come unto you living children whom these blemishes touch not, and ye shall be without care, leading a tranquil life without grief or anxiety, looking to receive that incorruptible and true marriage, and ye shall be therein groomsmen entering into that bride-chamber which is full of immortality and light." [11]
> ~ THE ACTS OF THOMAS, TRANSLATED BY M. R. JAMES

They have also been called "solar bodies," as they are created with purified creative/sexual energy/fire, which is of the same nature as the sun and stars.

> "The bones of the king are firm (or, copper), and the limbs of the king are like the stars, the imperishable stars." [12]
>
> ~ THE PYRAMID TEXTS, TRANSLATED BY SAMUEL A. B. MERCER

The Taoist sages called this energy the "golden elixir," and the ancient Egyptians called the bodies it creates the "bodies of gold," like the gold of the resplendent sun; it is the same refined gold many alchemists symbolically sought in their chemical experiments for thousands of years. Jesus referred to them as spiritual garments, as they clothe the different parts of consciousness, acting as the vehicle for the Being in the different dimensions of creation.

> "The common householder, husband and wife, are endowed with *ch'i* blood, *ching* and spirit, and are not different from the great *tao*. Each and every one of them is capable of perfection. The blazing "golden elixir" can be consumed by any man." [13]
>
> ~ TRUE TRANSMISSION OF THE GOLDEN ELIXIR BY SUN JU-CHUNG, TRANSLATED BY DOUGLAS WILE

There are seven solar bodies, as there are seven dimensions, and a vehicle needed for the parts of consciousness and the higher Being in each.

> "There were seven degrees of initiation [in the secret initiatory schools of Mithraism], these degrees allowed the neophyte to proceed through the seven celestial bodies. Allowing the reversing of the human souls descent into the world at birth." [14]
>
> ~ PAYAM NABARAZ, MITHRAS AND MITHRAISM

The ancient Gnostics wrote that there were seven spheres, which are a reference to these seven dimensions, placing above them an eighth, which were the fixed stars as the source of creation and all its dimensions. In the excerpt below, these seven dimensions are referred to as "seven houses"—and the eighth as the place of rest, the sun and stars, and source of creation.

> "Come, compassionate mother.
> Come, communion of the male.
> Come, she that revealeth the hidden mysteries.
> Come, mother of the seven houses, that thy rest may be in the eighth house." [15]
>
> ~ THE ACTS OF THOMAS, TRANSLATED BY M. R. JAMES

An illustration of the celestial spheres, with the seven lower spheres
assigned to planets, and the eighth to the region of the fixed stars.

On Easter Island there are seven statues that face the sunset on the autumn
equinox. These statues represent the seven solar bodies that someone needs
to have prepared before the descent into the darkness and chaos symbolized
by the autumn equinox, which precedes the birth of the spiritual Son within.
Everything needs its vessel, including consciousness, just as it has a physical
vessel to operate within the physical world. Higher parts of consciousness
need vessels to operate within higher dimensions, and to integrate within
the multidimensional structure of a person in the here and now, but these
bodies need to be made of a quality and level of energy that can withstand
and contain the higher frequency energies of the Son.

The kundalini also needs to be raised up the spinal column in each body.
The kundalini is symbolized as a serpent of light because it illustrates light
and energy that moves in waves just like the slithering of a snake. The energy
of kundalini is a higher frequency energy, produced from the purified sexual
energies, which travels up the spinal column as the main conduit of the central nervous system. This creates and transforms the nervous system in each
of the seven bodies so that each body has its electrical system of movement
to move within its dimension, just as the physical body does.

At the pyramid of Kukulcán (the feathered serpent) in Mexico, at the
autumn equinox, a serpent made of seven triangles of light descends the
pyramid—symbolizing the seven bodies and serpentine energy.

IMAGE TOP: The pharaohs of Egypt were laid to rest totally covered in gold with a serpent on their forehead to symbolize the golden bodies and the risen kundalini.

IMAGE LEFT: Buddha depicted with seven serpents, symbolizing the seven risen serpents/kundalinis in the seven bodies.

IMAGE RIGHT: The god Sokar, who later became known as Osiris in Egypt, beneath a mound with the seven solar serpents raised. These seven serpents correspond to the seven solar bodies. The cane he holds is a symbol of the risen kundalini.

In the Acts of Thomas, the disciple Thomas sings about the consciousness as the daughter of light, and that she has seven groomsmen and seven bridesmaids, which symbolize the seven bodies and the seven serpents. The participants of a wedding are used as the symbols because these bodies are created in the symbolic "bridal chamber."

> "The damsel is the daughter of light... And surrounding her her groomsmen keep her, the number of whom is seven, whom she herself hath chosen. And her bridesmaids are seven, and they dance before her." [16]
>
> ~ THE ACTS OF THOMAS, TRANSLATED BY M. R. JAMES

The groomsmen "surround" and "keep her" because the solar bodies are the vessels and vehicles for consciousness, and the bridesmaids "dance before her" because they are the central nervous systems of each body, which give the bodies, and thus the consciousness that inhabits them, movement.

The baptism of John the Baptist is a symbolic reference to the secret practice of alchemy; John's ritual purification of the body through clean water is symbolic of the spiritual purification of the sexual energies in alchemy, and the use of this purified energy to create the seven solar bodies and raise the seven serpents of light.

In the following quote, the number seven appears again symbolically in connection with the purification of a person's inner energies.

> "For only the pure water can mirror forth the light of the sun; and that water which has become dank with filth and murk can reflect nothing.
>
> And when the body and the spirit of the Son of Man have walked with the angels of the Earthly Mother and the Heavenly Father for seven years, then is he like the running river under the noonday sun, mirroring forth dazzling lights of brilliant jewels." [17]
>
> ~ JESUS IN THE ESSENE GOSPEL OF PEACE, TRANSLATED BY EDMOND BORDEAUX SZEKELY

This is how John, the initiate makes "straight the way of the Lord" to prepare for the coming of the Son within, as these bodies will become the vehicles for the spiritual Son in all the dimensions of creation. The wilderness John is in, is a symbol of the aridity of the animalistic state of a person in the absence of the spiritual. All the anger, hatred, lust, pride, etc., of the psyche is of an animal, whereas the Son brings its spiritual nature to us—which is poured out upon us like a refreshing dew.

"Who is it that will rain a refreshing dew on you to extinguish the mass of fire from you along with your burning? Who is it that will cause the sun to shine upon you to disperse the darkness in you and hide the darkness and polluted water?" [18]

~ JESUS IN THE BOOK OF THOMAS THE CONTENDER, TRANSLATED BY JOHN D. TURNER

THE NINE REGIONS OF THE UNDERWORLD

The underworld is a place described by ancient peoples all over the world. In their explanation of creation, the Maya divided the underworld, which they called Xibalba, into nine regions. In Norse mythology they also described hell as having nine regions.

"Below cold and darksome Nifel-heim are the nine divisions of torture in which the souls of the wicked are punished... Then they enter the Na-gates and die the second death. Punishment is given in the nine realms of torture according to the sins that were committed." [19]

~ DONALD A. MACKENZIE, TEUTONIC MYTH AND LEGEND

Dante writes about the structure of heaven
and hell in his work The Divine Comedy.

Dante Alighieri's work The Divine Comedy assigned nine layers to hell (and nine regions to heaven). In Norse mythology creation is said to consist of nine worlds, in the Eleusinian mysteries of ancient Greece there were nine spheres, and the Taoists described a "nine-fold heaven." Hell and heaven are both lower and higher dimensions respectively; each consists of nine regions as described in ancient teachings, and each region of the underworld corresponds to a region of heaven. They are the regions of both lower and higher frequency light and energy that are invisible to the human eye, as they are outside the spectrum of "visible light."

At the autumn equinox at the pyramid of Kukulcán, the Maya symbolized the descent of the initiate with the risen kundalini (serpent energy) through the nine layers of the underworld as a serpent of light that descends the nine terraces of the pyramid.

Each of the nine regions of both the lower and higher dimensions also correspond to the nine regions within the human psyche, as everything, including us, is multidimensional. All matter is energy in vibration, and so these regions exist in the present moment, interpenetrating our psyche, but without us seeing it since their vibrations are outside of the band of frequency the physical eye can perceive. These other dimensional worlds, regions, and realities, have been experienced by many people in lucid dreams, out-of-body experiences, and near-death experiences since ancient times.

The ninth region of the underworld (called the ninth sphere) is the center of the earth, which is the location of the earth's central fire. Likewise, fire exists in the lower anatomy of a human, in the sexual organs. To work in the ninth sphere is an esoteric reference to working with the sacred sexual fire in alchemical, inner transformation.

The ninth sphere, located in the sexual organs, and in the womb of the earth, is also the womb in which the Son/Christ gestates. At autumn, the seeds produced at summer die and then begin to germinate beneath the earth; the descent into the nine layers of the underworld symbolizes the gestation of the Son in the womb of the earth over nine months, before being born at the winter solstice.

The center of the earth is often represented with the symbol of infinity, which is also a symbol of equalization or equinox. This same central axis that exists within the earth also exists within each person, and the forces within a person all revolve from it, both into superior regions (heavens), or into inferior ones (hells); and so it is upon this equinoctial axis that the spiritual work is built. The direction we take all depends on the way the central fire found at the equinoctial axis, our inner creative energy, is used—whether to create the spiritual and imperishable, or material and transitory.

The symbol for infinity
(like the number 8 turned on its side).

To descend requires alchemy. In descending, someone climbs down what is called Lucifer's ladder. After the descent, having completed a work of many trials and tests in the underworld, they then have to climb back up Lucifer's ladder (also known as Jacob's ladder), to ascend. There are nine regions of the underworld and nine heavens. Someone must descend through each of the nine layers of the underworld to reach each of the nine regions of heaven (and each layer of the underworld is suffering), as it is only by overcoming the egos and darkness, found in each region of the subconscious, that we reach to the light of consciousness and its heavenly qualities and feelings.

For each region of both heaven and hell there is a gate to pass through to reach to the next level. Someone can only enter through a heavenly gate if they pass the required internal examination, which tests their spiritual level. Gaining the right to pass through these gates has been called initiation. The ancient Egyptians detailed these gates extensively in their sacred texts.

> "He who is in Sekhem hath inspected me. I stretch out my arms over Osiris. I have advanced for the examination, I have come to speak there. Let me pass on and deliver my message. I am he who goeth in, [I am] judged, [I] come forth magnified at the Gate of Nebertcher. I am purified at the Great Uart. I have done away my wickednesses. I have put away utterly my offences. I have put away utterly all the taints of evil which appertained to me [upon the earth]. I have purified myself, I have made myself to be like a god. Hail, O ye Doorkeepers, I have completed my journey. I am like unto you. I have come forth by day." [20]
>
> ~ THE EGYPTIAN BOOK OF THE DEAD, TRANSLATED BY E. A. WALLIS BUDGE

These gates correspond to the nine chambers of initiation in the mysteries of Odin, the nine days of initiation in the Eleusinian mysteries, and the nine stages of cultivating immortality in Taoism. They have been described by both Jesus and Krishna as existing within the body, as both heaven and hell are not only external places, but also exist within. In the following excerpts, they are referred to as "the city of nine gates," "the house of nine bushes," and "the nine-storied pagoda."

> "I [Peter] replied, asking him, 'What is the name of the place to which you go, your city?' He [Jesus] said to me, 'This is the name of my city, "Nine Gates." Let us praise God as we are mindful that the tenth is the head.'" [21]
>
> ~ THE ACTS OF PETER AND THE TWELVE APOSTLES, FROM THE NAG HAMMADI LIBRARY TRANSLATED BY DOUGLAS M. PARROTT AND R. MCL. WILSON

"Mentally renouncing all actions, the self-controlled soul enjoys bliss in this body, **the city of the nine gates**, neither doing anything himself nor causing anything to be done." [22]

~ KRISHNA IN THE BHAGAVAD GITA TRANSLATED BY SHRI PUROHIT SWAMI

"Ahau spread his feet apart. Then it was that the word of Bolon cacab descended to the tip of his tongue. Then the charge of the katun was sought; nine was its charge when it descended from heaven. Kan was the day when its burden was bound to it. Then the water descended, it came from the heart of the sky for the baptism of **the House of Nine Bushes**." [23]

~ THE BOOK OF CHILAM BALAM OF CHUMAYEL, TRANSLATED BY RALPH L. ROYS

"May Anpu/Anubis make my thighs to become vigorous. May the goddess Sekhmet raise me, and lift me up. Let me ascend into heaven, let that which I command be performed in Het-ka-Ptah. I know how to use my heart. I am master of my heart-case. I am master of my hands and arms. I am master of my legs. I have the power to do that which my KA desireth to do. **My Heart-soul shall not be kept a prisoner in my body at the gates of Amentet** when I would go in in peace and come forth in peace." [24]

~ THE EGYPTIAN BOOK OF THE DEAD, TRANSLATED BY E. A. WALLIS BUDGE

"Mysteriously floating in space hangs a 'precious pearl,' the size of a millet grain, which is variously called the 'great Mahayana prajna (wisdom of the Great Vehicle),' the **'nine-storied pagoda,' the 'Buddha body,'** 'cintamani (talisman-pearl),' 'saddharma (wonderful law),' or the 'marvellous Muni pearl.'" When the adept consumes it, his body sprouts wings and he joins the ranks of the immortals." [25]

~ TRUE TRANSMISSION OF THE GOLDEN ELIXIR BY SUN JU-CHUNG, TRANSLATED BY DOUGLAS WILE

THE WARRIOR ASPECT OF THE MOTHER GODDESS

The Mother goddess in her role as a warrior has been illustrated by different cultures around the world with amazing similarities, showing the universal nature of her existence and one of the parts she plays in creation, which has been associated with the autumn equinox since ancient times.

In ancient Sumer, the goddess Inanna descends into the underworld at the time of the autumn equinox. In Egypt, the mother goddess was associated with the Milky Way during the third millennium BC when it aligned with where the sun rose and set during the equinoxes; illustrations showed her body painted with stars, and depicted her swallowing and giving birth to the sun in a continual cycle of death and rebirth.

The autumn equinox is celebrated in India with the Hindu festival of Durga Puja, also called Navatri, which is dedicated to the Mother of the Universe—the warrior goddess Durga. It is the largest celebration of the spiritual Mother in the world today. Starting at the autumn equinox, the celebration lasts for nine nights and ten days, and Durga is celebrated through nine plants associated with her nine aspects. This symbolizes the nine layers of the underworld and psyche she is intimately related to, as the earth and underworld is her womb.

The Mother goddess, symbolized as a female of great power, is the feminine aspect of each person's own higher Being. Whilst she has loving qualities, she also has powerful, punishing, and destructive ones, represented by the many warrior goddesses around the world. The war that she fights is against the forces of darkness and evil—in Hinduism, the goddess Durga is said to have the power to protect someone from evil and misery through her ability to destroy its cause, which is the ego.

> "[The goddess Durga is] always decked in celestial garlands and attired in celestial robes,—who is armed with sword and shield, and always rescues the worshipper sunk in sin, like a cow in the mire, who in the hours of distress calls upon that eternal giver of blessings for relieving him of their burdens." [26]
> ~ THE MAHABHARATA, TRANSLATED BY KISARI MOHAN GANGULI

Durga is symbolically depicted as fighting huge supernatural battles against legions of asuras (demons). The battleground is said to be our consciousness, and the demons symbolic of our egos.

> "She [Durga] filled the entire sky with her terrible roar, and from the immeasurable din a great echo roared. All the worlds shook and the ocean churned. The earth quaked and the mountains heaved. In joy the gods exclaimed 'Victory!' to the lion-mounted Devi; and with bodies bowed in devotion, the sages praised her.
>
> When the enemies of the gods saw the three worlds in upheaval, they readied their foes for battle and rose up as one, with weapons held high.
>
> 'Aha! What is this?' Mahisasura bellowed in wrath. Surrounded by countless asuras [demons], he rushed toward the sound and then beheld the Devi, who pervaded the three worlds with her radiance, bending the earth under her tread, scraping the sky with her diadem, shaking all the nether regions with the resonance of her bowstring, and standing there, penetrating every direction with her thousand arms.

Thereupon, the battle began between the Devi and the enemies of the gods. Swords and missiles, hurled in every direction, lit up the quarters of the sky...

Amid chariots, elephants, and horses, myriads of other great asuras battled with the Devi... Some hurled spears while others threw nooses; intent on killing her, they began an assault with their swords. But she, the Devi Candika, showered down all manner of weapons and cut through their armaments as if in play.

Praised by gods and seers, she remained serene, even while unleashing her weapons at the asuras' bodies.

Her lion-mount, shaking its mane in fury, stalked among the demon throngs as fire rages through a forest...

Then the Devi, with her trident, club, and volleys of spears, with her swords and other weapons, slew great asuras by the hundreds and brought down still more with the confounding din of her bell." [27]
~ THE DEVIMAHATMYA, TRANSLATED BY DEVADATTA KALI

The goddess Kali portrayed in her aspect as Daksine Kali, which is when she has her right foot forward as a protector. Daksine can be taken to mean "south," as Kali is traditionally seen as facing south in the same direction as the souls who are heading south toward hell, so that she can rescue them. The word Daksine also has connections to the transit of the sun as it travels south after crossing the equator at the autumn equinox. The southern transit of the sun is also connected to the "night of the gods," so she may also be said to be facing the night.

This war against the ego is most clearly portrayed in depictions of the Hindu goddess Kali which means "she who destroys" (not to be confused with the demon Kali, which is written differently in Sanskrit). Kali brandishes a weapon in her hands which beheads numerous demons. Her hands are bloodied and the heads of her enemies hang around her neck. Her enemies are the egos, and she fights them within the person working to change. Kali is said to inhabit a cremation ground, which is the place where the egos are killed and destroyed in divine alchemical fire.

Note: Hinduism is a very ancient religion, which means that although at its root it is a white esoteric teaching, elements of it have also been distorted and infiltrated over time. There are traditions, some of them at least hundreds of years old, which worship the goddess Kali but practice black Maithuna/Tantrism and should obviously be avoided.

IMAGE LEFT: The Aztec goddess Coatlicue with an astonishingly similar necklace, skirt, and appearance as the Hindu goddess Kali.

IMAGE RIGHT: The lion-headed Egyptian goddess Sekhmet.

Like Kali, the Aztec goddess Coatlicue is a Mother goddess with her destructive side emphasized. She bears an astonishing resemblance to Kali, with her teeth, breasts, and tongue bared, wearing a necklace made of human hearts, hands, and skulls. It is said that in her both the grave and womb exist, as the Mother has power over life and death both in a physical and spiritual sense.

In Egypt, Sekhmet is the Mother goddess in her destructive aspect, and her veneration appears to be thousands of years old. Sekhmet has the head of a lion and dresses in red like the Hindu goddess Durga, the color of blood. She is said to be the fiercest of all goddesses—her name means "powerful one," but she also had titles such as "Mistress of Dread," "Lady of Slaughter," "Lady of Flame," and the "one before whom evil trembles." She is the female warrior goddess, and it was said that death and destruction were balm for her warrior's heart. Both Kali and Sekhmet were said to wreak such fierce destruction that they had to be placated to stop them from destroying humankind.

In Buddhism, the warrior aspect of the goddess also bears a resemblance to the Egyptian Sekhmet, Aztec Coatlicue, and Hindu Kali. She is Senge Dongma (Simhamukha in Sanskrit), who was created to destroy demons, and like Sekhmet, she has the head of a lion and can be the color red. But also, like Kali, has been described as the color of dark clouds like those that bring rain or storms, and can appear as dark blue or black. This deep, dark color is that of death and descent, and of the primordial waters of the Mother, like deep space and the ocean, which creation is said to emerge from and disappear back into. Again, like Kali, Senge Dongma is also associated with cremation grounds, and her eyes are wide open, her tongue, teeth, and breasts are bared, she wears a skirt made of tiger skin, and a long necklace made of human bones and severed heads, which are symbolic of the egos as the various self-centered states, "moods," and "personas," she destroys within a person.

The Sumerian goddess Inanna and her lion. The mace in her left hand and the weapons sprouting from her shoulders indicate her war-like nature (from a cylinder seal found in Iraq from the Akkadian Period, circa 2,254–2,193 BC).

The Sumerian goddess Inanna was known as the Queen of Heaven and was a powerful warrior whose chariot was drawn by lions; she was even sometimes symbolized as a lioness in battle. Likewise in Hinduism, the goddess Durga is depicted as a warrior mounted on a lion or tiger. Sekhmet and Senge Dongma were both portrayed with the head of a lion. These Mother goddesses were each associated with lions or tigers as they are such powerful animals, that all are their prey. They are symbolic of the spirit which has the power to defeat all evil.

These goddesses were not only associated with the war against evil, but also with sex, Tantra, and fire. Inanna was a goddess of sexual love.

Senge Dongma is known as the "Guardian of the Secret Tantric Teachings," and is depicted as circled by flames, with mythological links to a cremation ground. Kali is primarily a tantric goddess who inhabits a cremation ground. Durga is "Keeper of the Flame" and Sekhmet is known as "Lady of Flame."

The fire all these goddesses are associated with is the sacred sexual fire within. The warrior aspect of the goddess is so intimately related to Tantrism, sex and fire, because it is in the fire of sexual alchemy that she destroys the egos, and also why she is linked to cremation grounds—symbolic of the incineration of the egos in the inner sexual fire.

IMAGE LEFT: Goddess Kali destroying the egos in the fire of sacred sexuality.

IMAGE RIGHT: The Greek goddess Hecate with a sword and snake in her hands, her arms like those of a strong warrior.

The same deathly aspect of the mother goddess can be found in Greece as Hecate. Hecate has been portrayed as a strong, giant woman holding a torch (or serpent) and sword—her powers are symbolized by her strength and size, as well as the torch of the awakened sexual fire (and kundalini) in one hand, and the sword that puts the egos to death in the other.

There are even traditions in Christianity which depict the Virgin Mary as a warrior defending her children. This is symbolic of our spiritual Mother destroying our egos. Many depictions of Mary as a warrior look similar to those of the Hindu goddess Kali, as like Kali, Mary is often portrayed as standing upon an evil demon with a club raised in combat against it. The Carmelite Order is a Christian monastery that was founded around 1206 AD on the sacred site of Mt Carmel. Their patron is the Virgin Mary whom they see as their Spiritual Mother and protector. A Catholic priest, inspired by their traditions, wrote of Mary as a warrior, saying:

"How strange it seems to think of Mary as a warrior.

The gentle maid of Nazareth, the Virginal Mother, the Mother of the Prince of Peace, is still called—and properly called—"More terrible than army in battle array."

And so she is....

Mary, conqueror of heresies

Mary, triumphant always in the battle with sin.

When then we put on the scapular, which is Mary's uniform, we join in a special way the regiment of which Mary is the queen and honorary colonel.

We pledge ourselves to do battle against the enemy of the human race.

We will be victorious as Mary is victorious, and conquering as Christ is conquering." [28]

~ EXCERPT FROM A NOVENA TO OUR LADY OF MOUNT CARMEL

The Virgin Mary armed with a club to protect her children against evil, as she was sometimes depicted. The painting is titled *Our Lady of Succor* by Giovanni da Monte Rubiano.

In many ancient teachings, the Mother is symbolized as descending at the autumn equinox because she plays a vital role in the descent into the underworld through the knowledge she provides, and her ability to destroy our egos. On the path of the spiritual sun, it is the higher feminine part of someone's Being that has this role.

In ancient religions, the feminine is also very much associated with the cycles of nature and the cosmos, and of all that is transitory and impermanent in creation, which is why in Hinduism she was described as Maya—as all that is illusory and passing. This indicates that feminine energy is the basis of all manifest nature, found expressed on a microcosmic scale in the dynamic cycling of electrons (feminine) around the stable nucleus of protons (masculine) in atoms, and on a macrocosmic level in the cycling of the earth around the sun, the changing of the seasons, the waxing and waning of the moon, and even greater galactic and stellar cycles. The Mother is the giver of nature, the physical body, matter, and the subconscious, symbolized by the growing darkness following the summer solstice, which the consciousness enters into when joining the process of life. Her womb is the earth, and so even the underworld forms part of the learning she provides in the cycles of life and nature.

Whilst this world of Maya places limitations on our ability to perceive spiritual realities, without it there would be no darkness, no duality, no sense of separation, and therefore no knowledge of light. Thus, the Mother provides the incredible world of learning we go into, whilst also having the power to free us from it.

"She creates all this universe, moving and unmoving, and it is she who graciously bestows liberation on humanity. She is the supreme knowledge and the eternal cause of liberation, even as she is the cause of bondage to this transitory existence...

You are Savitri, the source of all purity and protection; you are the supreme mother of the gods. By you is this universe supported, of you is this world born, by you it is protected, O Devi, and you always consume it at the end.

You are the creative force at the world's birth and its sustenance for as long as it endures. So even at the end of this world, you appear as its dissolution, you who encompass it all.

Armed with sword and spear, and with club and discus, waging war with conch, bow and arrows, sling and iron mace, you inspire dread. Yet, you are pleasing, more pleasing than all else that is pleasing, and exceedingly beautiful. Transcending both highest and lowest, you are indeed the supreme sovereign...

You are this entire, manifold world and you are primordial matter, supreme and untransformed...

O Devi, who are the cause of liberation and great, inconceivable austerities: sages yearning for liberation contemplate you with sense restrained, intent upon truth, with all faults cast off, for you are the blessed, supreme knowledge...

O Devi, who remove the sufferings of those who take refuge in you, be gracious. Be gracious, mother of the entire world. Be gracious, ruler of all. Protect the universe, O Devi, who are the ruler of the moving and unmoving.

You alone are the sustaining power of the world, for you abide in the form of the earth. By you, who exist in the form of water, all this universe prospers, O Devi of unsurpassable strength.

Of boundless might, you are Vishnu's power, the source of all, the supreme maya. Deluded, O Devi, is all this universe. In this world, you alone, when pleased, are the cause of liberation.

May your terrible, flaming trident, exceedingly sharp and destroying all asuras, protect us from dread...

May your bell that destroys the daityas' life-force and fills the world with its ringing protect us from all evils, O Devi, even as a mother protects her children...

O ruler of the universe, you protect the universe. You are the essence of all things, and you support all that is. All kings must praise you, O revered one, and those who bow to you in devotion become the refuge of all." [29]

~ THE SEER IN THE DEVIMAHATMYA, TRANSLATED BY DEVADATTA KALI

In ancient China the feminine was symbolized as a dragon, which was described as a creature capable of infinite transformation. In nature, we see transformation continuously taking place, which has its root in the dynamic fluctuations of electrons and their influence upon the form and structure of matter. Ultimately transformation has its root in the mysterious properties of electrons, electricity, and fire, which in higher dimensions have spiritually transformative properties and are related to the sexual energies, which is why Mother goddesses from around the world are associated with birth, death, sex, and transformation.

THE MYSTERY OF THE MINOTAUR AND THE LABYRINTH

The ancient Minoans aligned their ancient sites on the island of Crete to the autumn equinox. Their palace at Knossos is believed to be the location of the legendary labyrinth of King Minos. This King was said to have built a labyrinth to imprison the savage beast called the Minotaur—a half man, half bull creature.

This myth has a symbolic meaning. The autumn equinox is the time of descent into the underworld to overcome the animalistic egos with the aid of the Mother goddess. The labyrinth represents the underworld, as it was said to be a treacherous place that no one could ever find their way out of, just as hell has been described as a place that once people enter, they cannot escape. The Minotaur is a symbol of the ego—of a person turned into a beast by the animalistic egos within. This Minotaur inhabits the labyrinth as our psychological underworld is the place where our egos reside.

In the legend, the Minotaur was the offspring of the Queen of Knossos, the wife of King Minos, as it is the energies of the Mother that are used to create the egos. However, it was also symbolically a royal woman, the King's daughter Adriane, who then assisted the hero Theseus to kill the Minotaur, as the divine feminine also has the power to defeat the ego. It appears the Minoans understood this, as it was the goddess who was worshiped primarily at this site. A Minoan inscription at the palace reads, "Mistress of the Labyrinth," as the underworld is the realm of the Mother.

IMAGE TOP: The Minotaur pictured at the center of a labyrinth, symbolic of the egos that inhabit our psychological underworld.

IMAGE LEFT: Theseus battling the Minotaur in the dark passageways of the labyrinth, symbolic of the initiate who battles their egos within their own psychological underworld—the subconscious.

There are cave complexes on Crete that were very likely used ceremoniously to enact the descent into the labyrinth of the underworld on the autumn equinox, where someone symbolically had to confront the beast of the ego each person carries within.

THE PRINCIPLES OF INNER DEATH AND DESCENT

The autumn equinox symbolizes the principles of inner death and descent on the path of the spiritual sun. It reveals that in order to change, we must firstly face the darkness of own inner underworld, and descend with the aid of our spiritual Mother to fight the egos and evil within, to emerge with the light and knowledge extracted from darkness. Here it is our own personal Lucifer, the light-bearer and psychological trainer, who is the tempter in the work to incarnate the spiritual Son (and eventually return to our spiritual Father).

It is a time of inner death where the seed of latent potential within a person must die (symbolized by the sacred seed), forming the basis of the divine alchemical sexual fire the Mother uses to disintegrate the dark energetic substance of the egos, and fabricate the seven bodies of solar energy, in preparation for the light and life of the Son to be born within, which is symbolized at the winter solstice.

Winter Solstice

The Birth of the Spiritual Son

CHAPTER THREE

The Spiritual Meaning of the Winter Solstice

THE BIRTH OF A DIVINE CHILD AND SAVIOR at the winter solstice has formed a central part of spiritual beliefs throughout the world since the beginning of history—in ancient Egypt as the birth of Horus, the birth of Mithras in Persia, the birth of Jesus at Christmas, the birth of the spiritual Son at Alban Arthan of the Druids, etc. These celebrations have tapped into a universal spiritual principle that is just as relevant now as it was then.

They speak to us of a mysterious and universal understanding of spiritual transformation. All things which come into being must first be born. Even as creation was borne by the great Mother of the universe, so too must we be born of the spirit to become spirit. The winter solstice is a celebration of being "born again"—not of flesh, but of the spirit. It's a celebration of the birth of the spiritual Son, the Christ, within a person's consciousness on the path of the spiritual sun.

Symbolized as a child just as the winter sun is at its weakest, it will grow until reaching its full strength at the summer solstice—just as the spirit grows within a prepared individual to transform them completely from inner darkness into light.

The ancient neolithic temple of Newgrange in Ireland, which has an inner chamber in the shape of a cruciform that aligns to sunrise on the winter solstice, the birth date of Jesus, although thousands of years before he was born.

THE BIRTH OF THE SUN

The meaning of the winter solstice operates on a number of levels. At its core is the birth of the sun—both universally and personally.

The rising of the sun on the winter solstice, out of the darkest day of the year, echoes the birth of the light from out of the dark void during the creation of the universe.

This act of creation is described in a mysterious collection of ancient texts called the Kolbrin, which are said to have been carried out of ancient Egypt to the British Isles thousands of years ago. The account describes the creation of the first light from within the dark void of uncreated light, and shares similarities with ancient Vedic, Sumerian, Taoist, Druidic, and Egyptian creation stories, possibly indicating a common origin. Following are some excerpts:

> "Before the beginning there was only one consciousness, that of The Eternal One whose nature cannot be expressed in words. [...]
>
> He who preceded all existed alone in His strange abode of uncreated light, which remains ever unextinguishable, and no understandable eye can ever behold it. The pulsating draughts of the eternal life light in His keeping were not yet loosed. He knew Himself alone, He was uncontrasted, unable to manifest in nothingness, for all within His Being was unexpressed potential. [...]
>
> Earth was not yet in existence, there were no winds with the sky above them; high mountains were not raised, nor was the great river in its place. All was formless, without movement, calm, silent, void and dark. [...]
>
> Eternal rest is intolerable, and unmanifested potential is frustration. Into the solitude of timelessness came Divine Loneliness and from this arose the desire to create, that He might know and express Himself, and this generated the Love of God. He took thought and brought into being within Himself the Universal Womb of Creation containing the everlasting essence of slumbering spirit.
>
> The essence was quickened by a ripple from the mind of God and a creative thought was projected. This generated power which produced light, and this formed a substance like unto a mist of invisible dust. [...]
>
> The creating word had been spoken, now there was another command and the power going forth smote the sun so its face was lit, and it shone with a great radiance pouring warmth and light upon its sister Earth. [...] The waters upon the bosom of Earth were gathered together and dry land appeared." [1]
> ~ THE BOOK OF CREATION FROM THE KOLBRIN

The ancient Egyptians understood the connection between creation and the winter solstice, as they aligned their Karnak Temple Complex, the largest in the world, to the winter solstice sunrise and dedicated one of the central temples to creation and their supreme creator god Amun. This temple complex was never completed, as successive pharaohs kept making additions to it as a living example of the process of creation and its continuous unfoldment. These additions were even built according to the Fibonacci sequence—a key mathematical principle found in the growth and expansion of life.

The spiritual sun is a living and divine fire, and the source of creation, as explained in ancient sacred texts from around the world. However, as creation follows universal principles, the birth of the sun as the light of the first day also represents the birth of the light of our own spiritual sun within us. It is born into the time of most darkness—the physical sun gives life to the external world; the spiritual sun gives spiritual life to the individual.

THE SPIRITUAL SON

Every genuine spiritual teaching through-out the world had some word for attaining enlightenment, whether it was awakening, self-realization, salvation, imperishability, or immortality, etc. Most still have rem-nants of a divine savior associated with the sun, and many associated the birth of this savior with the winter solstice. This divine savior always taught humanity how to achieve enlightenment, to become a "Son of God," and return to the spiritual source awakened.

Although Christmas is now largely about shopping for many people, the birth of the savior was intended to bring to earth a profound spiritual message for the whole of humankind. This message has been brought to earth anew many times as previous teachings became old, obscure, and locked within religious dogma.

For those who are working toward enlightenment now and have done throughout history, the teaching of these divine saviors had a dual aspect—they taught the work to enlightenment in what they said, but also in the events of their lives.

An ancient depiction of the Madonna and child in Egypt, with Isis/Hathor as the spiritual mother nursing her son Horus.

A study of the events of the lives of the divine savior in different times and cultures, such as Jesus (esoteric Christian), Mithras (Persian), Hu Gadarn (Druid), Horus (Egyptian), etc., reveal that the events of their lives match the progress of the sun throughout the year, and the zodiac.

Many theorize that this happened because the different religions borrowed from one another. Others point to the fact that each of these deities was closely associated with the sun, and therefore were merely representing the astrological worship of the sun to simple-minded sun worshipers, waiting for their crops to grow, etc.

But there is another explanation for this incredible similarity. Often this explanation was only known by the initiates of esoteric schools who encoded the knowledge of it in the symbols of sacred sites. To the public these often complex symbols look obscure and even nonsensical, therefore protecting the knowledge from those who would deride and destroy it. This mechanism has helped to preserve much of the knowledge found in sacred sites up until this day.

Each of these deities was known as a savior of mankind, and a beloved and sacred divine child. Each of these deities was associated with the sun, and all of them born at the time of the winter solstice in a miraculous virgin birth. The lives and stories of these deities tells us of a great mystery, which in the case of Jesus, he came to earth with a mission to reveal both in the events of his life and his teachings.

THE POTENTIAL OF CONSCIOUSNESS

Every human being is a latent spiritual potential that lies dormant like a seed. We live asleep to the greater realities of existence, but whether we choose to realize it or not, each of us has the potential to become an awakened spiritual being. This is why sacred texts from ancient times and still today, always point toward enlightenment as the ultimate goal of life.

Literally, the work of enlightenment is found written in the cosmos in the movement of the sun and stars, which is why so many ancient spiritual cultures incorporated celestial movements into their spiritual monuments and sacred texts. This is what life is created for, so no wonder we find it reflected to us from the heavens, and intrinsic to everything around us. This is so we can always discover our true purpose for being here and realize our own spiritual potential—whenever we choose to search for it.

The creative process which gives birth to the universe also gives birth to the spiritual within a human. Thus the divine savior is not just born into the world, they can be born within us—into the symbolic stables, prison, or cave, which is the spirit entering into the humble and limited personality and body.

"When you come to know yourselves, then you will become known, and you will realize that it is you who are the sons of the living father. But if you will not know yourselves, you dwell in poverty and it is you who are that poverty." [2]

~ JESUS IN THE GOSPEL OF THOMAS, TRANSLATED BY THOMAS O. LAMBDIN

The scene of the annunciation and birth of the "king of heaven" at the Luxor Temple in Egypt (also given the name the Temple of Man by the Egyptologist Schwaller de Lubicz as its proportions seem to correlate with those of the human body, thus the divine king is born into a person). Firstly the goddess Neith (the primordial waters) is told by Thoth that she will become pregnant with Ra (the King of Heaven who later became known as the god Horus). Kneph and Hathor impregnate Neith via the ankh, the key of life, and thus Neith remains "ever virgin." The birth occurs over a birthing brick, and praise is given by the gods to the divine newborn Son. This Egyptian depiction of the birth of the sun god Ra shares many similarities with the birth of Jesus.

THE BIRTH OF THE SPIRITUAL SUN WITHIN

We are born as physical beings, but in order to become spiritual we must be born as spiritual beings. This particular spiritual birth, is the birth of the Son—the spiritual sun—within. The process of the creation in the universe is the same process that creates everything, including both the physical aspect of our being, but also the inner, spiritual aspect of our higher being. Each person's consciousness is a spark of the great spiritual light found in the sun and stars, which is why the Milky Way has been described in ancient texts as the birth place of souls.

"Behold, O Hermes, there is a great mystery in the Eighth Sphere, for the Milky Way is the seed-ground of souls..." [3]

~ POIMANDRES (THE MIND OF THE UNIVERSE) TO HERMES IN THE VISION OF HERMES, TRANSLATION FROM THE SECRET TEACHINGS OF ALL AGES BY MANLY P. HALL

The Inca celebration of Inti Raymi (which can be translated as "The Solemn Christmas of the Sun") is one of the most famous winter solstice celebrations in the world, and is attended by over 100,000 people each year in Peru.

The Inca saw the sun as their natural father and most revered God, and themselves as its offspring. The sixteenth century chronicler Garcilaso de la Vega wrote:

> "They (the Incas) made this solemn celebration to the Sun God in gratitude for having him and worship him as the highest, only and universal God who with his light and virtue raised and sustained all things on the Earth. And in gratitude for him being the father of the first Inca, his wife, and their children, and all his descendants that were sent to the Earth for the universal benefit of people. For these reasons this celebration was the most solemn of celebrations." [4]

We are, literally, the offspring of the sun—created from the stars both physically and spiritually. This is why so many ancient cultures, such as the Sumerians, Egyptians, Gnostics, Inca, and Maya, all referred to themselves as the "Children of the Sun" or "Children of the Light."

> "Believe in the light while you have the light, so that you may become children of light." [5]
>
> ~ JESUS IN THE GOSPEL ACCORDING TO JOHN 12:36

As our consciousness descends from the source into the darkness of matter, it divides and leaves behind parts of itself in higher dimensions, just like the sun's light and power diminishes after the summer solstice, as it descends toward the darkness of autumn.

The ancient text, sometimes referred to as The Hymn of the Pearl, allegorically describes this descent of consciousness (the child) from the spiritual source into the world of matter (referred to symbolically as Egypt), parting from its Father, Mother, and Son (higher parts of our Being), in order to rescue a symbolic pearl in the depths of the ocean (light and wisdom extracted from the depths of darkness and the subconscious), and return to the source with it.

> "When, a quite little child, I was dwelling
> In the House of my Father's Kingdom,
> And in the wealth and the glories
> Of my Up-bringers I was delighting,
> From the East [the direction of the sun],
> our Home, my Parents [Father and Mother]
> Forth-sent me with journey-provision.
> Indeed from the wealth of our Treasure,
> They bound up for me a load.
> Large was it, yet was it so light

That all alone I could bear it...
My Glorious Robe they took off me
Which in their love they had wrought me,
And my Purple Mantle (also)
Which was woven to match with my stature.
And with me They (then) made a compact;
In my heart wrote it, not to forget it:
"If thou goest down into Egypt,
And thence thou bring'st the one Pearl —
(The Pearl) that lies in the Sea,
Hard by the loud-breathing Serpent —
(Then) shalt Thou put on thy Robe
And thy Mantle that goeth upon it,
And with thy Brother [the Son], Our Second,
Shalt thou be Heir in our Kingdom." [6]
~ THE ACTS OF THOMAS, TRANSLATED BY G. R. S. MEAD

The trinity of Father, Mother, and Son, found so often in ancient teachings, represents parts of each person's higher Being. It is through the birth of the Son within, the spiritual fire and light represented by the sun, that our spiritual potential can be realized, like a seed that finally germinates. This is what Jesus referred to when he said that we must be "born again."

"Now there was a Pharisee, a man named Nicodemus who was a member of the Jewish ruling council. He came to Jesus at night and said, 'Rabbi, we know that you are a teacher who has come from God. For no one could perform the signs you are doing if God were not with him.' Jesus replied, 'Very truly I tell you, no one can see the kingdom of God unless they are born again.' 'How can someone be born when they are old?' Nicodemus asked. 'Surely they cannot enter a second time into their mother's womb to be born!' Jesus answered, 'Very truly I tell you, no one can enter the kingdom of God unless they are born of water and the Spirit. Flesh gives birth to flesh, but the Spirit gives birth to spirit. You should not be surprised at my saying, 'You must be born again.'" [7]
~ THE GOSPEL ACCORDING TO JOHN 3:1-7

This need to be "born again" was also taught in the Eleusinian mystery schools of ancient Greece in which the human condition was seen as a tomb, and why the Christ in many different cultures (as Viracocha, Jesus, Mithras, Hu Gadarn, etc.) was symbolized as being born into a cave:

"The soul of man—often called Psyche, and in the Eleusinian Mysteries symbolized by Persephone—is essentially a spiritual thing. Its true home is in the higher worlds, where, free from the bondage of material form and material concepts, it is said to be truly alive and self-expressive. The human, or physical, nature of man, according to this doctrine, is a tomb, a quagmire, a false and impermanent thing, the source of all sorrow and suffering. Plato describes the body as the sepulcher of the soul; and by this he means not only the human form but also the human nature.

The gloom and depression of the Lesser Mysteries represented the agony of the spiritual soul unable to express itself because it has accepted the limitations and illusions of the human environment. The crux of the Eleusinian argument was that man is neither better nor wiser after death than during life. If he does not rise above ignorance during his sojourn here, man goes at death into eternity to wander about forever, making the same mistakes which he made here. If he does not outgrow the desire for material possessions here, he will carry it with him into the invisible world, where, because he can never gratify the desire, he will continue in endless agony. Dante's Inferno is symbolically descriptive of the sufferings of those who never freed their spiritual natures from the cravings, habits, viewpoints, and limitations of their Plutonic personalities. Those who made no endeavor to improve themselves (whose souls have slept) during their physical lives, passed at death into Hades, where, lying in rows, they slept through all eternity as they had slept through life.

To the Eleusinian philosophers, birth into the physical world was death in the fullest sense of the word, and **the only true birth was that of the spiritual soul of man rising out of the womb of his own fleshly nature.** 'The soul is dead that slumbers,' says Longfellow, and in this he strikes the keynote of the Eleusinian Mysteries. Just as Narcissus, gazing at himself in the water (the ancients used this mobile element to symbolize the transitory, illusionary, material universe) lost his life trying to embrace a reflection, so man, gazing into the mirror of Nature and accepting as his real self the senseless clay that he sees reflected, loses the opportunity afforded by physical life to unfold his immortal, invisible Self." [8]

~ MANLY P. HALL, THE SECRET TEACHINGS OF ALL AGES

To be born of the spirit is not a matter of adopting or changing beliefs—for anything to be born, it must follow the same process of creation which we see from the largest of scales, right to the very smallest, throughout the whole of creation.

In the previous quote from the Gospel of John, Jesus refers to the waters and the spirit that moves upon it, which gave rise to the birth of light on the first day. The waters are the feminine aspect of creation, found symbolized in Mother goddesses throughout the world, and the spirit moving upon the waters is the masculine aspect, symbolized by Father gods.

These dual creative forces can be found within every atom as negatively polarized particles called electrons and positively polarized particles called protons, and have been symbolized in ancient creation myths throughout the world as a great Mother and Father who come together to make creation.

They are the dual masculine and feminine aspects of the creator that underlie and give rise to everything in the universe.

In ancient Chinese texts they were called yin (feminine) and yang (masculine).

> "One yin and one yang is called the tao... male and female mingle their ching and all creatures are born." [9]
>
> ~ I CHING (THE OLDEST KNOWN BOOK OF CHINA)

> "All things are brought forth from the subtle realm into the manifest world by the mystical intercourse of yin and yang. The dynamic river yang pushes forward, the still valley yin is receptive, and through their integration things come into existence." [10]
>
> ~ LAO-TZU IN HUA HU CHING, TRANSLATED BY BRIAN WALKER

In ancient India, the supreme creator god Brahman assumed a dual nature in order to create, called Prakriti or Rayi, which is feminine, and Purusha or Prana, which is masculine.

> "The Lord of Beings [...] meditated and produced Prana, the primal energy, and Rayi, the giver of form, desiring that they, male and female, should in manifold ways produce creatures for him." [11]
>
> ~ PRASHNA UPANISHAD, TRANSLATED BY SWAMI PRABHAVANANDA AND FREDERICK MANCHESTER

Similarly, the first being in Egypt that emerged from the unknowable source was called Atum, and the first gods this being created were the male god Shu and female goddess Tefnut.

The Druids also symbolized creation being brought forth by the union of male and female forces. In the beginning, the Druids believed that the sap of the cauldron of the Great Mother goddess Cariadwen was fertilized by three drops of dew from the Word of the Father god Celu and gave birth to a son called Hu Gadarn/Taliesun.

In a Chinese story of creation there existed a cosmic egg that floated in the void. The egg was the opposites of yin and yang totally mingled; as they were mingled, creation was not yet able to come into being. Then within this egg grew the primordial man, P'an Ku, who broke out of the egg and split yin and yang into opposites, creating the sky and the earth, etc. Later, P'an Ku entered a holy virgin as a ray of light, and was born into the world as T'ien-Tsun, the first principle of the universe created from yin and yang (in this story T'ien-Tsun represents the spiritual Son/Christ).

In a Maya account, creation also comes into being from the union of Mother and Father, who give birth to a son of light:

> "Great is its performance and its account of the completion and germination of all the sky and earth—its four corners and its four sides. All then was measured and staked out into four divisions, doubling over and stretching the measuring cords of the womb of sky and the womb of earth. Thus were established the four corners, the four sides, as it is said, by the Framer and the Shaper, the Mother and the Father of life and all creation, the giver of breath and the giver of heart, they who give birth and give heart to the light everlasting, the child of light born of woman and the son of light born of man, they who are compassionate and wise in all things—all that exists in the sky and on the earth, in the lakes and in the sea." [12]
>
> ~ POPOL VUH, TRANSLATED BY ALLEN J. CHRISTENSON

In ancient Gnostic Christian texts that were excluded from the Bible, there are numerous accounts of a spiritual Mother and Father giving birth to a divine Son. Many of these accounts are said to be from Jesus himself.

> "[...] in joy did the Earthly Mother and the Heavenly Father give birth to the Son of Man [...] the spirit of the Son of Man was created from the spirit of the Heavenly Father, and his body from the body of the Earthly Mother." [13]
>
> ~ JESUS IN THE ESSENE GOSPEL OF PEACE, TRANSLATED BY EDMOND BORDEAUX SZEKELY

Male and female energies united give birth to all life. At the dawn of creation, their union gave birth to the sun—the light of the first day—and the entirety of creation. This birth of the sun, at a spiritual level, is the birth of the spiritual sun—the birth of the love, wisdom, and power of the Son within.

THE CREATIVE POWER OF SEX

Sex is the foundation of life. Human life is created from the union of male and female in the birth of a child. In the ancient Hindu text, the Brihadaranyaka

Upanishad, the primordial being, after realizing it was alone, created a woman from its body. From their union humans were born. After this, the woman hid from the man by taking the form of a cow. But he came as a bull and from their union, cattle were born. She then hid as a mare, but he came as a stallion, and from their union all hoofed animals were born. This went on for each of the various animals for which there is a male and female, right down to the ants. This teaching illustrates the creative power of sex found throughout life and the universe, and that the union of male and female forces (called yang and yin in Taoism) gives birth to and creates all life at the largest of scales, right down to the smallest.

A Buddhist depiction of the practice called Maithuna in Hinduism (more commonly referred to as Tantrism in the West).

"In the beginning this was Self alone, in the shape of a person. He looking round saw nothing but his Self [...] But he felt no delight [...] He wished for a second [...] He then made this his Self to fall in two, and thence arose husband and wife. Therefore Yagnavalkya said: 'We two are thus (each of us) like half a shell.' Therefore the void which was there, is filled by the wife. He embraced her, and men were born [...] She then became a cow, the other became a bull and embraced her, and hence cows were born. The one became a mare, the other a stallion; the one a male ass, the other a female ass. He embraced her, and hence one-hoofed animals were born [...] And thus he created everything that exists in pairs, down to the ants. He knew, 'I indeed am this creation, for I created all this.' Hence he became the creation, and he who knows this lives in this his creation." [14]

~ THE BRIHADARANYAKA UPANISHAD, TRANSLATED BY MAX MÜLLER

Some people treat sex as ungodly and taboo, as if it was something separate from spirituality. But spirituality is not separate from life, and thus sex is not separate from spirituality either. Sex is part of the great mystery of creation. In spiritually advanced creation myths, we find the union of male and female forces which give birth to life. Deified in many ancient texts, man and woman are seen as god and goddess with the powers of creation. This is also why in these texts the sexual relationship between a man and woman is viewed as sacred, as in essence it belongs to the processes of divinity unlike any other human relationship. Within this relationship is the potential and power of the divine if used properly.

"The Master said:--'(The trigrams) *Khien* and Khwăn may be regarded as the gate of the Yî.' *Khien* represents what is of the yang nature (bright and active); Khwăn what is of the yin nature (shaded and inactive). These two unite according to their qualities [...] In this way we have the phenomena of heaven and earth visibly exhibited, and can comprehend the operation of the spiritual intelligence. [...] The yang originates a shadowy outline which the yin fills up with a definite substance. So actually in nature Heaven (*Khien*) and Earth (Khwăn) operate together in the production of all material things and beings. [...] Heaven and earth existing, all (material) things then got their existence. All (material) things having existence, afterwards there came male and female. From the existence of male and female there came afterwards husband and wife [...]" [15]

~ I CHING, TRANSLATED BY JAMES LEGGE

Spiritually advanced ancient peoples knew that creation is a process which is universal and which is found from the very largest scale, to the most microscopic. Therefore, they knew that the forces of male and female united give birth on earth, give birth to the universe, and give birth to the spiritual within.

"Join the male to the female in their own proper humidity, because there is no birth without union of male and female." [16]

~ HERMES (QUOTED IN THE TEXT THE STONE OF THE PHILOSOPHERS)

SPIRITUAL BIRTH FROM ALCHEMICAL UNION

Physically, we know that sex between a man and a woman creates a child. Out of a tiny egg, an unmanifested potential springs forth almost miraculously becoming an entirely new human being that grows just as a plant from out of a tiny little seed. Thus we see within man and woman, the primordial forces of the Egyptian father god Amun and his wife, the mother goddess Mut, which give rise to all creation. These three forces have been symbolized time and again, as the creative trinities of Osiris, Isis, and their son Horus (Egyptian); Father, Mary, and Jesus (Christian); Zarathustra, Anahita, and Mithras (Persian); Celu, Cariadwen, and Hu Gadarn (of the Druids); Odin, Frigg, and Balder (Norse/Germanic), and many, many others.

> "In this trinity is hidden the wisdom of the whole world." [17]
> ~ HERMES TRISMEGISTUS IN THE EMERALD TABLET, TRANSLATED BY
> SIGISMUND BACSTROM

This creative potential we each have is mentioned in a number of texts, which say that we are a microcosm of the universe and made in the image of the creator:

> "As large as the universe outside, even so large is the universe within the lotus of the heart. Within it are heaven and earth, the sun, the moon, the lightning, and all the stars. What is in the macrocosm is in this microcosm." [18]
> ~ CHANDOGYA UPANISHAD, TRANSLATED BY SWAMI PRABHAVANANDA AND
> FREDERICK MANCHESTER

> "[...] the sun and moon and all planets, as well as all the stars and whole chaos, are in man [...] For man was created from heaven and earth, and is therefore like them! Consider how great and noble man was created, and what greatness must be attributed to his structure! No brain can fully encompass the structure of man's body and the extent of his virtues; he can be understood only as an image of the macrocosm, of the Great Creature. Only then does it become manifest what is in him. For what is outside is also inside; and what is not outside man is not inside. The outer and the inner are *one* thing, *one* constellation, *one* influence, *one* concordance, *one* duration. . . *one* fruit." [19]
> ~ PARACELSUS, SELECTED WRITINGS, EDITED BY JOLANDE JACOBI, TRANSLATED
> BY NORBERT GUTERMAN

But this power to create is not limited to the creation of a physical child. Within the human being we also find the materials of spiritual creation. From this union of male and female, not only can children be born, but also the Son within, just as the spiritual sun/Son is born from the union of these forces at the dawning of creation.

> "The seed of your body need not enter the body of woman to create life; for the power of the angel of Earth can create the life of the spiritual within, as well as the life of the body without." [20]
>
> ~ JESUS IN THE ESSENE GOSPEL OF PEACE, TRANSLATED BY EDMOND BORDEAUX SZEKELY

> "Within the great cosmic process, the two ch'i—Ch'ien the father and K'un the mother—blend harmoniously and give birth to all creation. Therefore, it is said that in all creation only man is also thus. Man possesses a prenatal and postnatal nature. The prenatal is the spiritual father and divine mother; the postnatal is the mundane father and mundane mother. When the mundane father and mother have intercourse, the mercury arrives and is projected into the lead. When yang bestows and yin receives, this is called "the natural course." When the natural course is followed, then the human foetus is formed and sons and daughters are born. When the spiritual father and mother have intercourse, the lead arrives and is projected into the mercury. When yin bestows and yang receives, this is called "contrary to the natural course." If carried out contrary to the natural course, the holy foetus forms and birth is given to Buddhas and immortals. The principle of forming the holy and the human foetus is one and without distinction. The difference is simply one of following the natural course or going against it." [21]
>
> ~ TRUE TRANSMISSION OF THE GOLDEN ELIXIR BY SUN JU-CHUNG, TRANSLATED BY DOUGLAS WILE

Many ancient teachings refer to harnessing the forces of creation that are present when man and woman unite. The joining of husband and wife together in sexual union within a fully committed and loving marriage was given as a key spiritual practice (though usually in a veiled and coded way), and has been called Maithuna (a practice found within some Tantric traditions) in the East, the bridal chamber of the Gnostic/esoteric Christians, HeQi in Taoism, and alchemy in the Middle Ages, in which man and woman in sexual union are depicted as spiritual co-creators. Within the practice, each partner can use the forces of creation to gradually transform themselves inwardly, until reaching the spiritual level required for the Son to be born within.

Crowned as king and queen in nature, man and woman are co-creators in this seventeenth century illustration, giving birth to the divine child from out of the sexual waters/energies.

"Great is the mystery of marriage! For without it, the world would not exist. [...] No one can know when the husband and the wife have intercourse with one another, except the two of them. Indeed, marriage in the world is a mystery. [...] If there is a hidden quality to the marriage of defilement, how much more is the undefiled marriage a true mystery! It is not fleshly, but pure. It belongs not to desire, but to the will. It belongs not to the darkness or the night, but to the day and the light [...] It is from water and fire that the soul and the spirit came into being. It is from water and fire and light that the son of the bridal chamber (came into being). The fire is the chrism, the light is the fire. [...] 'The Holy of the Holies' is the bridal chamber." [22]

~ THE GOSPEL OF PHILIP FROM THE NAG HAMMADI LIBRARY, TRANSLATED BY WESLEY W. ISENBERG

This sacred sexual practice (which only works within a fully committed and loving marriage), involves the purification of the waters, which are the sexual energies, in preparation for creation; the awakening of the sacred fiery energy called kundalini symbolized as the serpent rising up the spine in ancient India, and crowning the forehead in Egypt; the creation of spiritual bodies in higher dimensions, referred to as the wedding garments by Jesus, and as the imperishable bodies of gold by the ancient Egyptians and Hindus; and many other spiritual processes which must be gone through, until someone has reached a level of spiritual preparedness and purity for the Son to be born within—referred to as "the son of the bridal chamber" in the excerpt above.

"The first integration of yin and yang is the union of seed and egg within the womb. The second integration of yin and yang is the sexual union of the mature male and female. Both of these are concerned with flesh and blood, and all that is conceived in this realm must one day disintegrate and pass away. It is only the third integration which gives birth to something immortal. In this integration, a highly evolved individual joins the subtle inner energies of yin and yang under the light of spiritual understanding. Through the practices of the Integral Way he refines his gross, heavy energy into something ethereal and light. This divine light has the capability of penetrating into the mighty ocean of spiritual energy and complete wisdom that is the Tao." [23]

~ LAO TZU IN HUA HU CHING, TRANSLATED BY BRIAN WALKER

"When one begins to apply this magic it is as if, in the middle of being, there were non-being. When in the course of time the work is completed, and beyond the body there is a body, it is as if, in the middle of non-being, there were being. Only after concentrated work of a hundred days will the light be genuine, then only will it become spirit-fire. After a hundred days there develops by itself in the midst of the light a point of the true light-pole (yang). Then suddenly there develops the seed pearl. It is as if man and woman embraced and a conception took place. Then one must be quite still and wait. The circulation of the light is the epoch of fire.

In the midst of primal transformation, the radiance of the light (yang-kuang), is the determining thing. In the physical world it is the sun; in man, the eye. The radiation and dissipation of spiritual consciousness is chiefly brought about by this energy when it is directed outward (flows downward). Therefore the Way of the Golden Flower depends wholly on the backward-flowing method." [24]

~ THE SECRET OF THE GOLDEN FLOWER, TRANSLATED BY RICHARD WILHELM

We run on electric energy, which travels throughout the nervous system of our body. This means we are each electrically charged, and electrically charged matter creates an electromagnetic field, which is why we have a measurable electromagnetic field around our body. Feminine energies are polarized negatively, and have a negative charge, while masculine energies are polarized positively and have a positive charge. This is the basis of sexual attraction, as positively and negatively charged particles are attracted to one another. When a couple unite sexually, their union creates measurable "sexual electricity" and initiates an electrochemical reaction, which turns their energies into a form of inner fire.

Just as physical fire has the ability to destroy and create things, as does the spiritual fire that creates and ultimately destroys the universe, so does this inner sexual fire have the same ability to create spiritual things within us and destroy the negative aspects of ourselves—allowing us to be "born again" spiritually, and return to the source of creation, the Absolute (the Brahman of ancient India), as an enlightened and awakened Deva, a "Son of God."

> "But as many as received him [Christ], to them gave he power to become the sons of God, even to them that believe on his name: Which were born, not of blood, nor of the will of the flesh, nor of the will of man, but of God." [25]
>
> ~ THE GOSPEL ACCORDING TO JOHN 1:12-13

This is not a matter of adopting or changing beliefs—for anything to be born, it must follow the same process of creation which operates on the largest of scales, right to the very smallest. Above, Jesus refers to the waters and the spirit that moves upon it, which gave rise to the birth of the sun on the first day. The waters is the female force, found symbolized in Mary, Isis, etc., and the spirit moving upon it is the male force, symbolized by the Father, Osiris, etc.

The male and female forces are what give birth to all life. At the dawn of creation, their union gave birth to the sun and the entirety of creation. This birth of the sun, on a spiritual level, is the birth of the spiritual sun—the birth of the force of the Son within.

Without understanding this process of creation and harnessing it, ancient teachings state that any spiritual practice, no matter how rigorous, is ultimately futile in creating the spiritual within.

> "This is the reason that all the sages began their work at the germinal vesicle in which outflowing [of sexual energy/orgasm] had ceased. If one does not establish this path, but sets up other things, it is of no avail. Therefore all the schools and sects which do not know that the ruling principle of consciousness and life is in this germinal vesicle, and which therefore seek it in the outer world, can accomplish nothing despite all their efforts to find it outside." [26]
>
> ~ THE SECRET OF THE GOLDEN FLOWER, TRANSLATED BY RICHARD WILHELM

THE SEEDS OF THE SUN

Within us are planted the seeds of the sun. The spiritual sun that arose at the dawning of creation has deposited its seeds within our own primordial waters, our creative sexual energies, which is the void and deep at the beginning of creation, sparkling with the electricity of unrealized possibilities. These seeds contain the blueprint of the bodies of the sun and a totally new spiritual being within us, just as a tiny seed contains the genetic blueprint for the form of every plant, animal, and human being. This is why the ancient Incas associated corn (their staple seed) with the sun, and revered it as something sacred.

"We invoke the bright and glorious Stars
To which the Heavenly Father
Hath given a thousand senses,
The glorious Stars that have within themselves
The Seed of Life and of Water." [27]

~ THE ESSENE GOSPEL OF PEACE, TRANSLATED BY
EDMOND BORDEAUX SZEKELY

"Know, O Arjuna, that I am the eternal Seed of being." [28]

~ KRISHNA IN THE BHAGAVAD GITA, TRANSLATED BY SHRI PUROHIT SWAMI

The process of birth in the universe is the same at both the macrocosmic and microcosmic level, and both at an inner and outer one. When we were born, our physical body was created by the sexual union of our father and mother. As eternal beings, our consciousness then came to inhabit that body, allowing us to exist in this physical plane. When our physical body dies, our consciousness loses its contact with the physical world and returns to non-physical dimensions as so many people who've had near-death experiences testify. After a period of time the consciousness then reincarnates again in a new baby's body.

Likewise, the spiritual Son comes into the spiritual bodies of the person created from the union of husband and wife in the sacred practice of alchemy. Unlike physical bodies, these spiritual bodies stay with someone unless they fall (and go through the second death in the abyss), which is why this spiritual process is part of the path that leads us to immortality.

The spiritual Son is a part of each person's higher Being, which remains in higher dimensions until it has a body to manifest through, just as our own consciousness remains in other dimensions until it has a physical body to be born into. The bodies the spiritual Son needs, however, have to be able to handle a higher frequency energy—like that found in the blinding light of the sun. Any electrician will tell you, that without the proper cable to carry an electrical charge, the cable will be overloaded and burn out. This same principle is behind the necessity of creating higher frequency spiritual parts within us to act as the vessel for higher parts of consciousness.

"For I maintain that the eyes of mortals cannot see the incorporeal form of the Father or Son, because it is illumined by exceeding great light. Wherefore it is not because God envies, but because He pities, that He cannot be seen by man who has been turned into flesh. For he who sees God cannot live. For the excess of light dissolves the flesh of him who sees; unless by the secret power of God the flesh be changed into the nature of light, so that it can see light, or the substance of light be changed into flesh, so that it can be seen by flesh. For the power to see the Father, without undergoing any change, belongs to the Son alone. But the just shall also in like manner behold God; for in the resurrection of the dead, when they have been changed, as far as their bodies are concerned, into light, and become like the angels, they shall be able to see Him." [29]

~ PETER IN THE CLEMENTINE HOMILIES, TRANSLATED BY JAMES DONALDSON

THE BIRTH OF THE WORLD TEACHER AND SAVIOR

The pre-Inca and Inca creator god Viracocha, who is said to come disguised as a beggar to teach people and perform miracles.

Christmas is not only the celebration of the birth of the divine savior into a human being—it is also a celebration of the birth of the Son into the world as the world teacher. Jesus, Horus, and Mithras were all referred to as a "divine savior." The divine savior has a dual meaning—the Son/Christ both saves the individual by entering into them and transforming them spiritually, and also works to save humanity by teaching the way to enlightenment through the individual that is entered into. The mission of the Son within a person, and thus in the world, is to save all those who wish to transcend the darkness and suffering of their lower nature.

The aspect of each person's Being, the Son, descends into a spiritually prepared person, and is born into the symbolic cave, which is the darkness of the psyche and physical body, to join with the consciousness and raise it back up to the divine source. This is what it means to be saved and why the consciousness has been portrayed as a beautiful damsel in need of rescuing in ancient teachings.

The ancient Thracians, who were Indo-European tribes inhabiting a large area in south-eastern Europe, also practiced an ancient form of sun worship. They built sites aligned to the solstice, believed a Great Mother goddess gave birth to the sun, and revered a rider god on horse-back who was depicted slaying a dragon in order to rescue a damsel. The story of a hero slaying a dragon or serpent is one of the oldest Indo-European myths that spread with the religion of the sun. This same symbolism was later used in Christianity in the famous scenes of St George slaying the dragon, which later again became romanticized in many myths and legends.

St George and the Dragon by Paolo Uccello. St George represents the Son who rescues the consciousness (the damsel) from the cave, which is the darkness of matter and the subconscious. The cave is also the dwelling place of the dragon, which is the embodiment of the egos.

In the ancient Gnostic text Pistis Sophia, which records the teachings Jesus gives his disciples after his ascension, the consciousness is called Pistis Sophia. In this part of the story, Jesus explains how the Son saves the consciousness from the "depth of the chaos" as it doesn't have the power to do this itself:

"It came to pass then after all this, that I [Jesus] took Pistis Sophia and led her into the thirteenth aeon, shining most exceedingly, there being no measure for the light which was about me... It came to pass then, when Pistis Sophia saw her fellows, the invisibles, that she rejoiced in great joy and exulted exceedingly and desired to proclaim the wonders which I had wrought on her below in the earth of mankind, until I saved her. She came into the midst of the invisibles, and in their midst sang praises unto me, saying: 'I will give thanks unto thee, O Light, for thou art a saviour; thou art a deliverer for all time. I will utter this song to the Light, for it hath saved me and saved me out of the hand of the rulers, my foes... And when I was come out of the Height, I wandered round in regions in which is no light, and I could not return to the thirteenth aeon, my dwelling-place. For there was no light in me nor power. My power was utterly weakened. And the Light saved me in all my afflictions. I sang praises unto the Light, and it hearkened unto me, when I was constrained. It guided me in the creation of the aeons to lead me up into the thirteenth aeon, my dwelling-place. I will give thanks unto thee, O Light, that thou hast saved me, and for thy wondrous works unto the race of men. When I failed of my power, thou hast given me power; and when I failed of my light, thou didst fill me with purified light. I was in the darkness and in the shadow of the chaos, bound with the mighty fetters of the chaos, and no light was in me. For I have provoked the commandment of the Light and have transgressed, and I have made wroth the commandment of the Light, because I had gone out of my region. And when I had gone down, I failed of my light and became without light, and no one had helped me. And in my affliction I sang praises unto the Light, and it saved me out of my afflictions.'" [30]

~ PISTIS SOPHIA, TRANSLATED BY G. R. S. MEAD

The influence of the spiritual Son within a person's psyche gradually develops as the person progresses along the path of the spiritual sun. Beginning as a helpless baby, the Son then grows and matures, until eventually fully merging with the consciousness of an individual. Then he is the world teacher, a light unto the world, and the teacher of teachers.

In Persia, Mithras was known as "the Mediator." This is because the Son acts within a person to reconcile, return, and reconnect us with divinity; and as the world teacher, acts as the intermediary between humanity and divinity, becoming the vital link between heaven and earth that guides humanity toward realizing their own inner potential through an understanding of the process of enlightenment.

"Now the Prophet of the truth is He who always knows all things— things past as they were, things present as they are, things future as they shall be; sinless, merciful, alone entrusted with the declaration of the truth. Read, and you shall find that those were deceived who thought that they had found the truth of themselves. For this is peculiar to the Prophet, to declare the truth, even as it is peculiar to the sun to bring the day." [31]

~ PETER IN THE CLEMENTINE HOMILIES, TRANSLATED BY THOMAS SMITH

"This awakening you have known comes not through logic and scholarship, but from close association with a realized teacher." [32]

~ THE KATHA UPANISHAD, TRANSLATED BY EKNATH EASWARAN

Many people become attached to a particular religion, denouncing others as untrue. But much of the world's spiritual knowledge sprouted from universal spiritual truths given to humanity by those who had the Son within throughout time, which is why they have such seemingly inexplicable similarities. Once a person who has the Son within is rejected by that religion and leaves it, the religion loses much of its vital connection with the heavens, becoming something barren and static, like an empty vessel that retains its shell but is no longer filled and renewed with the living knowledge and guidance from above.

And so the Son must come again to give spiritual truth anew through another spiritually prepared person. The aim of a true seeker is to always find the living Son to receive the direct living wisdom of the divine—cosmic, omnipresent, and beyond all religious ideas.

This divine savior is always said to one day return. It was thought that Viracocha would re-appear in times of trouble (just as other Christic saviors such as Jesus, Mithras, and the avatars of Vishnu, etc., are believed to). The ancient Indian creator god Vishnu is said to incarnate in different avatars (the most famous of which are Rama and Krishna) throughout the various ages, and that these incarnations take place in all Yugas and cosmic cycles.

"Whenever spirituality decays and materialism is rampant, then O Arjuna, I reincarnate Myself! To protect the righteous, to destroy the wicked and to establish the kingdom of God, I am reborn from age to age." [33]

~ KRISHNA IN THE BHAGAVAD GITA, TRANSLATED BY SHRI PUROHIT SWAMI

This is the return of the Christ within the individual to teach humanity the way toward enlightenment. Unfortunately however, each time Christ comes the teaching eventually becomes a religion where people await the literal return of Jesus, Viracocha, etc., while the real Christ returns within a person because of their spiritual work (not their religious beliefs) and is rejected by the world and society, teaching the real esoteric wisdom unbeknownst to and even hated by religious believers who lack the understanding of the real esoteric meaning of the teachings, which formed the basis of their religion.

There are many, many men and women who have incarnated the Son and taught humanity throughout time—many of whom are completely unknown to history. However, there are others like Jesus who come with a mission from the divine source to show the way to enlightenment in the events of their lives.

In the legends of the pre-Inca and Inca people, the creator god Viracocha, who is depicted with a crown of the sun and whose image appears in a cliff in the Urubamba Sacred Valley that reflects and refracts the rays of the sun on the winter solstice, rose from Lake Titicaca (or in some sources the cave of Pacaritambo) during the time of darkness to bring forth light. Viracocha made the earth, the stars, the sky, and mankind (the light emerges from the primordial waters, or the cave which is a symbol of the womb, and proceeds to make creation). It was said that he wandered the earth disguised as a beggar, teaching his new creations the basics of civilization, as well as working numerous miracles (just as Jesus did, who had the Son within). He wept when he saw the plight of the creatures he had created.

Expressing himself through the ordinary personality of an individual, the Son brings his wisdom to share, as he has done so many times in the past amongst those who have incarnated him and fully realized him within their psychic/physical/spiritual nature. Viracocha was said to return as a beggar, as the Christ is born into a humble person, disguised and unable to be seen by the ordinary observer because of the rags the Christ is clothed in, which is the personality of the individual.

> "Foolish men, without an understanding of My higher nature as the Supreme Lord of all that exists, disregard Me manifested in the human body." [34]
>
> ~ KRISHNA IN THE BHAGAVAD GITA, TRANSLATED BY SWAMI TAPASYANANDA

In the esoteric Christian text the Acts of Peter and the Twelve Apostles from the Nag Hammadi Library, Jesus disguises himself and gives pearls away to the poor of the city (the poor are those who recognize their inner poverty; the pearls are the "pearls of wisdom," the sacred teaching and the spiritual treasures of the path), while the rich of the city reject him (those who are proud and vain). The apostles meet him as fellow "strangers" as they are all strangers to the world.

> "A man came out wearing a cloth bound around his waist, and a gold belt girded it. Also a napkin was tied over his chest, extending over his shoulders and covering his head and his hands.

I was staring at the man, because he was beautiful in his form and stature. There were four parts of his body that I saw: the soles of his feet and a part of his chest and the palms of his hands and his visage. These things I was able to see. A book cover like (those of) my books was in his left hand. A staff of styrax wood was in his right hand. His voice was resounding as he slowly spoke, crying out in the city, 'Pearls! Pearls!'

I, indeed, thought he was a man of that city. I said to him, 'My brother and my friend!' He answered me, then, saying, 'Rightly did you say, 'My brother and my friend.' What is it you seek from me?' I said to him, 'I ask you about lodging for me and the brothers also, because we are strangers here.' He said to me, 'For this reason have I myself just said, 'My brother and my friend,' because I also am a fellow stranger like you.'

And having said these things, he cried out, 'Pearls! Pearls!' The rich men of that city heard his voice. They came out of their hidden storerooms. And some were looking out from the storerooms of their houses. Others looked out from their upper windows. And they did not see (that they could gain) anything from him, because there was no pouch on his back nor bundle inside his cloth and napkin. And because of their disdain they did not even acknowledge him. He, for his part, did not reveal himself to them. They returned to their storerooms, saying, 'This man is mocking us.'

And the poor of that city heard his voice, and they came to the man who sells this pearl. They said, 'Please take the trouble to show us the pearl so that we may, then, see it with our (own) eyes. For we are the poor. And we do not have this [...] price to pay for it. But show us that we might say to our friends that we saw a pearl with our (own) eyes.' He answered, saying to them, 'If it is possible, come to my city, so that I may not only show it before your (very) eyes, but give it to you for nothing.'" [35]

~ PETER IN THE ACTS OF PETER AND THE TWELVE APOSTLES, TRANSLATED BY DOUGLAS M. PARROTT AND R. MCL. WILSON

THE MEANING OF THE CAVE AND STABLES WHERE THE SON IS BORN

The winter solstice sun is "born" at the darkest point of the year. This is because all creation takes place from out of darkness and chaos, as it did in Egyptian mythology, and in the verses of the ancient Vedic text the Rig Veda.

The cave symbolizes the womb from which all of creation is born and emerges, the primordial chaos. This is why Mithras was born in a cave, and why Jesus was also said to be born in a cave in the Gospel of James. In Armenian tradition, Mithras was believed to shut himself up in a cave from which he emerged once a year, born anew. The god Viracocha was also said to be born in a cave to bring light into the darkness.

A depiction of the birth of Jesus as a baby into a cave. Although it is highly unlikely the creator of this image knew of the esoteric symbolism it represents, the symbols given in the teachings of Jesus have been passed on and retain their meaning.

At the Dinas Mountain in Wales there is a nearby cave that goes by a Welsh name meaning "Voice of God" where the Druids enacted the birth of their solar god Hu Gadarn (the Mabyn Taliesun) from within the cave. The Druid priest acting as Hu Gadarn gave a loud musical shout to which the gathered crowds would reply "Ein Hoes," meaning "Our Life!" [36]

Incredibly, at the ancient neolithic site of Newgrange in Ireland, the winter solstice sunlight enters an otherwise giant dark mound precisely at sunrise. The ray of light illuminates the chamber, which is in the shape of a cross. Here the cross is associated with the spiritual Son on the winter solstice, thousands of years before Jesus. The cross is an alchemical symbol showing the union of phallus and uterus, of masculine and feminine principles, which give birth to all creation and the Son. The Son is born as the sun into the mound, which acts as the womb. Also inside the chamber are found spiral designs, showing the spiraling nature of creation, along with a tri-spiral design, which possibly represented the Mother, Father, and Son trinity of creation and the nativity.

In the nativity scene of the Gospels, Jesus is also said to be born in stables amongst animals. The stables symbolize the physical body, and the animals represent the egos within, which are animalistic in nature, such as anger, pride, envy, hatred, etc. This shows that, although someone must have reached a certain spiritual level for the Son to be born within, they are still in darkness and still have many egos. The Son then works within to destroy these egos, and spiritually transform someone. This is why the Son was often depicted as a warrior and hero that battled evil, as in the Greek legends of Hercules.

Mithras emerges from the rock
holding a torch of fire and a sword.

Stone murals of Mithras found in once secret chambers beneath Rome show Mithras emerging from a rock holding a flaming torch, again associating the spiritual Son with fire and light. The Son brings light to our inner darkness. Mithras is also depicted holding a sword as he emerges, and this shows how the Son comes to oppose the darkness both in the subconscious and in the world.

Krishna is born at the winter solstice into a prison. This symbolizes the birth of the Son into the physical body, which to the divine is likened to a prison because of its constraints and material nature.

The Son is born as a baby at the winter solstice as all things that are born must start small and grow. The sun at this time is small and weak as a baby, and so Horus and Jesus were depicted at this time as babies in a manger.

At the winter solstice the Druids would gather in Wales to watch the sun rise over the sacred mountain of Mynydd Dinas, and believed the sun represented the birth of a divine baby Son who grew as the year progressed toward the summer solstice.[37] This is a representation of the birth of the spiritual within, because just as a baby is born as something that feels and perceives but is not able to do much, the birth of the Son within someone is as a new feeling and new way of perceiving, but yet to become something much more, which the Son within develops into just as Jesus in the Gospels grows to become an adult, progressing through other symbolic events in his life.

Although the light is born at the winter solstice, giving hope, it is still born into darkness and has yet to grow.

THE SPIRITUAL TREASURE FOUND IN THE DEPTHS OF DARKNESS

At a pyramid in Chichen Itza, Mexico, the rising winter solstice sun appears to ascend the nine terraces of the pyramid before shining momentarily at the temple atop the pyramid's peak. This illustrates the birth of the sun/Son, which appears from the lowest point, the womb of the earth, and rises through the nine terraces, which symbolize the nine layers of the underworld, the nine heavens, and nine initiations, which someone goes through to reach resurrection.

GLASTONBURY TOR WITH ITS MAN-MADE TERRACES AND TOWER.

Similarly, at Glastonbury Tor during the winter solstice, the sun appears at the base of the constructed mound, rises up its terraces, and clips the pinnacle of the tower—again symbolizing the rising toward resurrection. Incredibly, the constellation Orion, which is associated with Osiris, the Father of creation, and the star Sirius, associated with Isis, the Mother, also both align with the Tor at the winter solstice. Along with the rising sun, it's as if these constellations created the nativity scene in the sky.

These sites, separated by vast distances and time, symbolize the same process at the same time of year. At the winter solstice, in the womb of the earth, in the midst of darkness and chaos, the spiritual Son is born.

Although Glastonbury Tor has so far been unexcavated, it is possible, as with all ancient sites, to explore it whilst out of the body. The birth of the sun on the winter solstice from the base of the mound is also mirrored within the mound, as in the dimension we are in when out of the body, it contains a series of chambers, the lowest of which houses a golden treasure, which was symbolized in ancient Greece as the Golden Fleece.

A reference to a mysterious and lost site with the same design exists in some legends:

> "The Patriarch Enoch—whose name means the Initiator—is evidently a personification of the sun, since he lived 365 years. He also constructed an underground temple consisting of nine vaults, one beneath the other, placing in the deepest vault a triangular tablet of gold bearing upon it the absolute and ineffable Name of Deity. According to some accounts, Enoch made two golden deltas. The larger he placed upon the white cubical altar in the lowest vault and the smaller he gave into the keeping of his son, Methuseleh, who did the actual construction work of the brick chambers according to

the pattern revealed to his father by the Most High. In the form and arrangement of these vaults Enoch epitomized the nine spheres of the ancient Mysteries and the nine sacred strata of the earth through which the initiate must pass to reach the flaming Spirit dwelling in its central core." [38]

~ MANLY P. HALL, THE SECRET TEACHINGS OF ALL AGES

Nine chambers also exist beneath the Great Sphinx of Egypt, and scans revealed that they each contain an unknown metal object.

Enoch was said to have had a vision which showed that humanity would be destroyed in a deluge, and built his underground temple in order to preserve spiritual knowledge within it so that it would survive into the future. Could either the Great Sphinx, Glastonbury Tor, or another location altogether, be the place where the knowledge of the spiritual sun was buried to preserve it for a future time, or was the legend of Enoch an allegory based on the knowledge of an already existing secret site?

WHY CHRISTMAS IS CELEBRATED THREE DAYS AFTER THE WINTER SOLSTICE

The word solstice literally means "sun stands still." After the winter solstice, the sun for the first time will begin to increase—by both lengthening the duration of sunlight each day and ascending in its position in the sky. For three days however, the sun does not visibly appear to ascend, thus looking like it "stands still" in its path through the sky. In correlation, we find the winter solstice celebrated as the birth of the sun around the 22nd of December (in the northern hemisphere), and the divine savior three days later, once this "standstill" has passed and the sun begins its visible ascent on the 25th of December. Jesus, Horus, Krishna, Mithras, Dionysus, etc., are all said to have been born on the 25th of December. In the southern hemisphere the Incas celebrated their festival of Inti Raymi three days following the winter solstice on around June 24th; over these three days, when the sun stands still, they fasted and refrained from lighting fires in anticipation.

There is a spiritual significance to this. The birth of the spiritual sun on the winter solstice is the birth of the cosmic Son at the dawning of creation. From the Son comes all of creation, just as in ancient India the golden womb created from the male and female forces at the dawning of creation gives birth to Brahma, the creator god, and the entire universe called Brahm-anda.

In the Vedas of ancient India, the supreme creator god Vishnu was known as the triple-strider (as Tri-vikrama and as Uru-krama). It is said that he created the universe, making the dwelling of humanity possible, by taking three steps—one encompassing the earth, the other the air, and the third the heights of heaven, which is his supreme abode. This illustrates how creation takes place in three steps, and the number three is therefore also found in the process of creating the spiritual within us.

The number three is a number of completion and crystalization—of bringing things into realization. In many rituals, it is common that phrases are said three times in an act of crystalizing them.

There are three primary forces in creation, which is the trinity of Father, Mother, and Son.

THE THREE GREAT PYRAMIDS OF EGYPT.

On the path of the spiritual sun, there are three series of nine initiations, and then three steps to merge oneself with the trinity of creation. These initiations and steps are themselves grouped into three major stages on this path, which have been called three mountains. They were represented in ancient Egypt as the three Great Pyramids that align to the three stars in the constellation Orion, called Orion's belt. The Egyptians associated the constellation Orion with the god Osiris, whose life represented the path of the spiritual sun.

This act of going through things three times, each time at a higher level/octave, crystalizes the spiritual within, and allows us to reach from the lower realms of matter where we are, to the brilliant regions of light, like steps that allow our legs to traverse a great height.

This underlying principle of three correlates with the three days of standstill at each extreme of the year—both at winter and summer solstice, as the cycle of the sun pauses in its symbolic creation from the source at the winter solstice, and return back to it at the summer solstice.

THE THREE STEPS INTO THE SEVEN DIMENSIONS

The three primary forces of Mother, Father, and Son, which are negative, positive, and neutral, give rise to all of creation.

"Tao produced Unity; Unity produced Duality; Duality produced Trinity; and Trinity produced all existing objects." [39]
~ THE TAO TE CHING, TRANSLATED BY LIONEL GILES

"[...] among the things that were created the monad is first, the dyad follows it, and the triad [...] This is the pattern <among the> immortals." [40]
~ EUGNOSTOS THE BLESSED, TRANSLATED BY DOUGLAS M. PARROT

But creation, which is in three forces, needs organization, and so it unfolds through the number seven, which is the number through which all of creation is organized, and is found in the seven colors of the spectrum, the seven notes of the musical scale, and seven dimensions of the universe. On the path of the spiritual sun there are seven serpents of light to raise in the seven solar bodies. These bodies correspond to the seven dimensions, and representations of them can be found in ancient Egypt, India, and Easter Island.

The seven moai facing the equinox sunset at Ahu Akivi on Easter Island representing the seven spiritual bodies in the seven dimensions.

As we are multidimensional, in order to incarnate and be born into a person, the Son (like Vishnu) is said to take three steps through the seven dimensions, entering into the body and psyche of a person as he does. Our consciousness resides in the sixth dimension, which is the dimension where the Son is first born from the Mother and Father who reside in the seventh, and is symbolized by the "birth" of the sun on the winter solstice.

To be born into us from the realm of the sixth dimension, the Son firstly enters the mental plane of the fifth dimension (the plane of thoughts and the mind); secondly, he enters the astral plane of the fifth dimension (the plane of emotions); and then finally he enters the physical body. Jesus describes this in the following excerpt, where the regions of our psyche and body are described as a "realm of darkness," "chaos," and "prison." This is because our psyche is our own inner underworld, which the higher parts of consciousness, such as the Son, bring spiritual light to.

"And I went into the realm of darkness and I endured till I entered the middle of the prison. And the foundations of chaos shook. And I hid myself from them because of their wickedness, and they did not recognize me.

Again I returned for the second time, and I went about. I came forth from those who belong to the light, which is I, the remembrance of the Pronoia. I entered into the midst of darkness and the inside of Hades, since I was seeking (to accomplish) my task. And the foundations of chaos shook, that they might fall down upon those who are in chaos and might destroy them. And again I ran up to my root of light, lest they be destroyed before the time.

Still for a third time I went — I am the light which exists in the light, I am the remembrance of the Pronoia — that I might enter into the midst of darkness and the inside of Hades. And I filled my face with the light of the completion of their aeon. And I entered into the midst of their prison, which is the prison of the body. And I said, 'He who hears, let him get up from the deep sleep.' And he wept and shed tears. Bitter tears he wiped from himself and he said, 'Who is it that calls my name, and from where has this hope come to me, while I am in the chains of the prison?' And I said, 'I am the Pronoia of the pure light; I am the thinking of the virginal Spirit, who raised you up to the honored place. Arise and remember that it is you who hearkened, and follow your root, which is I, the merciful one, and guard yourself against the angels of poverty and the demons of chaos and all those who ensnare you, and beware of the deep sleep and the enclosure of the inside of Hades.

And I raised him up, and sealed him in the light of the water with five seals, in order that death might not have power over him from this time on." [41]

~ JESUS IN THE APOCRYPHON OF JOHN FROM THE NAG HAMMADI LIBRARY, TRANSLATED BY FREDERIK WISSE

In each of the three steps, the Son enters into the inferior dimensional regions of the mind and inner structure of the human being, and is born from the sexual waters of the great Mother, which is the chaos and womb of creation inside each person. Upon entering the physical body on the third step, the Son is "born"—bringing his hope and light to us. This is the real Christmas—a personal, sacred, and spiritual event, which is celebrated three days following the winter solstice on Christmas day.

THE BIRTH OF JESUS AS A SYMBOLIC ESOTERIC EVENT

There is a profound symbolic meaning to the birth of Jesus at Christmas, which goes further than the religion of Christianity itself. Many see Christmas as a celebration of the actual birth of Jesus based on the Gospels, while others see it as little more than a time of shopping, pleasure, and leisure. What most people don't realize is that the nativity of Jesus is a profoundly significant spiritual teaching in itself, rich with symbolism and containing a timeless spiritual message that was hidden by design so it could survive and reach far into the future.

Jesus taught on two levels—one, on an exoteric level, which is a public and more basic teaching, and the other was on an esoteric level, which was a highly advanced spiritual teaching for people who were prepared for it.

On an exoteric level, Jesus was understood as a divine savior who taught us to be better people and died for people's sins so they might believe and be saved. On an esoteric level, Jesus taught how to transform oneself spiritually, to remove the cause of sins, become a "Son of God," and attain salvation. Many of the parables, events, and teachings of the Gospels have different levels of meaning that were often symbolic. They can also be found in many of the texts that were kept out of the Bible, such as the Nag Hammadi Library, Pistis Sophia, Gospel of Judas, and Gospel of Mary.

It is obvious that the teaching Jesus gave faced a lot of opposition, both from the government and religious authorities of the time. The esoteric side of the teaching, which was seen as more "heretical," was hidden to protect it from complete destruction. Jesus explained this when he said not to throw pearls before swine, lest they turn and tear you to pieces—he also spoke openly to his disciples, but in a veiled way through parables to the public. This exoteric side of his teaching was taken up by the masses and became a religion that unknowingly passed on the esoteric symbols encoded in the events of his life.

Despite attempts to protect it, much of the original esoteric literature of Christianity has either been destroyed, lost, or locked away, and thus the texts we are left with today contain only fragments of how to do the actual practical work of spiritual awakening. Only select texts that were seen as fit some three hundred years after Jesus' death made it into the Bible, at a time when the Church and the Roman state merged, while everything else was ordered to be destroyed since the Church now had the power to enforce its will. Not only were texts destroyed en masse (only a few copies of which have been discovered over the last hundred years, as they had been hidden in order to save them), but people who had the knowledge of what the texts meant were intensively persecuted as well.

So to be able to understand its symbolic meaning, you have to look at Christmas in esoteric terms, where events have symbolic as well as literal meanings. To deeply understand the symbolic meanings requires access to the source of the symbols, which is not to be found in the physical world, but in the world beyond the physical body in other dimensions. That is their source, as it is the source of all symbolism, spiritual myths, and legends. To access the source requires experience beyond the body, by having out-of-body experiences, astral projecting, and to a degree through objective dreams.

Even if you can do that, you won't be able to get the deeper meanings of most symbols if you are not at the personal level of inner spiritual development that can access them. In other words, to get to the hidden meanings you have to be doing the actual work of self-realization that is described in the sacred teachings of the past.

So when we discuss the symbolic meaning of Christmas, you should be aware that it is discussing it in the terms of its source, in a like manner as the ancient peoples themselves, with a common shared esoteric experience and knowledge. This may make it difficult to understand in places, but it's better to give it a fuller description that takes a little extra study to understand, than it is to give a watered down version that everyone can understand right away. The meanings found in Christmas have been watered down so much throughout history that their deeper meanings have mostly been lost, so I feel that it's better to give a more esoteric version, for the sake of completeness and for a more comprehensive understanding.

There is more to Christmas than the birth of a historical person, or the birth of a tremendous spiritual figure. Esoterically speaking, it is about the birth of the Christ, the cosmic Son that is born within a human—the incredible manifestation of the spiritual within.

Christmas day is a celebration of the birth of Jesus for many people, but it is also the time of birth for many spiritual figures in different cultures, and the time of the process of the winter solstice and solstice celebrations.

Although seen as part of different and diverse traditions, they are related to the same process.

The sun has a physical and spiritual aspect, and in each it is the giver of light and life. This is why the Christ is referred to as the light of the world.

Ancient sun worship at its root is the worship of the spiritual aspect of the sun, rather than purely the physical one, as for the ancient sun worshipers, the physical sun was a symbol of its spiritual counterpart.

In Christianity the spiritual aspect of the sun has been given the name the Christ. It is not simply a name of Jesus. It is the neutral spiritual force that gave rise to creation—a universal divine fire symbolized by the sun, the divine creative light. Christmas celebrates the birth of the Christ within a person.

The symbols of the nativity in an esoteric sense relate specifically to the birth of the Christ within an individual, and its preparation.

He was born in a cave/stables where animals were kept, which represents the Christ's birth in an individual amongst their animal egos. The Christ comes into a person in whom the animal egos live. He works within to destroy those egos. The cave represents the womb of creation. In the multi-dimensional nature of a person, the cave is at the center of the inferior regions inside the earth. He is born as a baby, and helpless, because the Christ when incarnated is small and needs to grow to maturity.

He is wrapped in basic clothes, meaning that the inner bodies which hold him are in a basic state. They will later be developed, from solar to an even higher frequency energy again as golden bodies. He is

The angel of the Lord announcing the birth of Christ to the shepherds.

placed in an animal's feeding trough—where the egos feed, in the sexual waters through the layers of the earth within a person, in the energies of sex.

At the time of his birth there were shepherds watching their flock. They represent the walkers of the path who are also teachers; their flock is the public. An angel of the Lord appeared to them and the glory of the Lord shone around them and announced the birth of Jesus. A heavenly host appeared with the angel saying, "Peace on earth to people He favors." The people whom he favors are the initiates who are prepared inwardly to receive him. They visit him just after his birth, meaning that they reach to the birth of the Christ within themselves.

The star that shone over him represents the Being and its guidance. It is the star of self-realization we aspire to attain one day.

The wise men, who visit Jesus later once he is in a house, represent those who are on the path to enlightenment, worshiping him. They came from the East, which can be translated as from the rising (of the sun). The rising sun symbolizes the birth of the Christ. They worship the baby Jesus, showing that they recognize the Christ. Through the sacrifice of their journey they brought gifts fit for a king, demonstrating their understanding of the Christ as a divine king with the treasures of the world no more than gifts in his spiritual presence.

THE WISE MEN VISIT JESUS.

When you put the nativity and what it symbolizes into an overall context of the meaning of the winter solstice and the following days, you discover an extremely profound teaching.

THE CREATION OF THE FOUR

The number four is related to the process of creation, which is connected to the time of the winter solstice.

The ancient Maya sometimes depicted the sun as "Ah Kin," which is "He of the Sun." He is represented as a human carrying the glyph of the Kin, which is a flower with four petals.

> "Thereupon the heart of the flower came forth to set itself in motion. Four-fold was the plate of the flower, and Ah Kin Xocbiltun was set in the center." [42]
>
> ~ THE BOOK OF CHILAM BALAM OF CHUMAYEL, TRANSLATED BY RALPH L. ROYS

Likewise, ancient Vedic texts describe the sun as a lotus flower with four petals.

> "Now that which dwelling within the lotus of the heart devours food, the same, dwelling as the solar fire in the sky, being called Time, and invisible, devours all beings as its food. [...] the four quarters and the four intermediate points are its petals." [43]
>
> ~ THE MAITRĀYANĪYA UPANISHAD, TRANSLATED BY E. B. COWELL

The ancient Maya believed that the great Father and Mother created the world with four sides.

> "Great is its performance and its account of the completion and germination of all the sky and earth—its four corners and its four sides. All then was measured and staked out into four divisions, doubling over and stretching the measuring cords of the womb of sky and the womb of earth. Thus were established the four corners, the four sides, as it is said, by the Framer and the Shaper, the Mother and the Father of life and all creation, the giver of breath and the giver of heart, they who give birth and give heart to the light everlasting, the child of light born of woman and the son of light born of man, they who are compassionate and wise in all things—all that exists in the sky and on the earth, in the lakes and in the sea." [44]
>
> ~ POPOL VUH, TRANSLATED BY ALLEN J. CHRISTENSON

The ancient Neolithic inhabitants of Ireland divided their sacred landscape into quadrants with a sacred center, which Viracocha was also said to have done in South America. And the Egyptian God Horus was said to have four solar sons who came forth from a lotus blossom and were associated with creation.

Four forms the foundation of life and encompasses the bounds of creation. It is found in the four cardinal directions; the four points of the cross of the year, which are the solstices and equinoxes; the four elements; the dimensions of our physical world which are length, width, height, and time; and the four material bodies within each person—physical, vital, astral, and mental.

The birth of stars, which then produce the rest of matter, can be found in the birth of the Son/sun and child of light, who brings the light of the first day, and proceeds to make the rest of creation. The Son, who in Hindu accounts of creation splits everything into three and stretches it out to make both earth and sky—creating the four corners of the world—is like the expansion of three-dimensional space, as well as the fourth dimension, as described by physicists and the ancient Maya. The fourth dimension is time, which is needed for beings to be able to become conscious of their own existence. Within our three-dimensional world, we find life manifest in form and substance in the flow of time. Thus, in creation, the Son who is one of the three forces of creation establishes the four, creating the space-time continuum in which space and time are joined together to create the four-dimensional object we all live within, which is the foundation of life and found in the movement of the sun, forming a cross of four arms and the rotating swastika.

Whilst providing opportunity for learning and awakening, matter also forms a prison that restricts consciousness, as the number four establishes bounds and limits, just like the four walls of room, tomb, or prison. Whilst the Son is born into the prison, he comes to free us from it—liberating a person eventually into the realms of the spirit where they attain immortality beyond the constraints of time and matter.

THE CHILDREN OF THE SUN

The winter solstice symbolizes the principle of spiritual birth—which, just as it is found in the universe, so is it found within us as a microcosm of creation.

We can realize our enormous spiritual potential that lies deep within our own creative energies like a seed. The Son symbolizes the hope of humanity, bringing light to the darkness of our material existence, and reuniting us with the divinity of our own higher nature.

This knowledge is written in the stars, in the universe. Celebrating the winter solstice offers us the time to reflect on the greatest mysteries of all—of how we came to be, why we are here, and how we can attain the truly spiritual—for those who wish to be "born again" as children of the sun.

Spring Equinox

Resurrection and Re-integration
with the Spiritual Mother

CHAPTER FOUR

The Spiritual Meaning of the Spring Equinox

THE SPRING EQUINOX (ALSO KNOWN AS THE VERNAL EQUINOX) is the time in the earth's annual cycle around the sun in which day and night are equal in length, before the days finally start to get longer after the dominance of darkness during winter, and life springs forth from death. Its deeper spiritual significance reveals the mysteries of spiritual resurrection.

In Christianity, the spring equinox is the time of the Passion, crucifixion, and resurrection of Jesus. Likewise, the ancient Egyptians celebrated it as the time when the god Osiris resurrected, the Thracians celebrated the resurrection of their god Orpheus, the Greeks celebrated the resurrection of their god Dionysus, and the Maya celebrated the resurrection of their Maize God Hun Hunahpu. The Great Sphinx of Giza in Egypt gazes precisely at the rising of the spring equinox sun as a symbol of resurrection. The temple of Angkor Wat in Cambodia aligns to the spring equinox, and depicts the scene of the "churning of the milky ocean"—the struggle between the forces of light and darkness.

Maya Maize God Hun Hunahpu resurrecting from a turtle, on a plate found at a temple at the ancient city of Palenque in Mexico.

Throughout the world, the spring equinox is a time of great confrontation between the forces of darkness and light, in the death and resurrection of the central deities of sacred teachings. It symbolizes what an initiate goes through in a definitive and important stage of self-realization, where the struggle between darkness and light creates the opposition needed to attain immortality. This is symbolized by the dark half of the year on one side of the spring equinox sun, and the light half of the year on the other.

THE CHURNING OF THE MILKY OCEAN

The equinox is the point of balance, upon which everything pivots in its motion, in the universe, in the cycles of the seasons, and within ourselves. On one side of the equinox is the dark half of the year, and on the other the light half, representing the struggle between the forces of darkness (death, descent, and decay) and light (birth, ascent, and life). It is this antithesis that gives motion to all cycles in the universe, and which is likewise found in the spiritual work to awaken. This is why Jesus, Osiris, Quetzalcoatl, etc., faced their greatest confrontation with darkness to attain the light at the spring equinox.

This universal principle is illustrated at the temple of Angkor Wat in Cambodia, which aligns to the spring equinox. It portrays the ancient sacred Hindu teaching from the epic the Mahabharata of the churning of the milky ocean in a giant representation on its walls, and in the design of its temple complex which incorporates the sun and the stars as celestial counterparts of the story.

The story of the churning of the milky ocean, as explained below, shows the fundamental principles that underpin the cycles of the sun throughout the seasons, the cycle of our earth through what is called the precession of the equinoxes, the turn of the Wheel of Life, the cycles of human civilization called Yugas, and the inner spiritual process called resurrection.

Painting of the famous scene of the churning of the milky ocean. All the treasures that have emerged from the ocean surround Vishnu, sitting atop the lotus.

At Angkor Wat, the story of the churning of the milky ocean is illustrated by incorporating both cosmic and spiritual forces that are personified using different symbols.

The central segment of the mural of the churning of the milky ocean at Angkor Wat. Vishnu is the large central figure—above him is Indra, below him the turtle in the ocean, and on either side the demons and devas pulling.

In the huge stone mural it depicts the asuras (demons) and devas (angels) as being in a tug of war. They each hold one end of a giant serpent that is wrapped around Mount Meru (specifically its spur Mount Mandara), representing the axis of the earth as the North Pole. This mountain is balanced on a turtle, which represents the earth, swimming through the great milky ocean of the cosmos—and thus depicts the earth cycling through the year, the constellations, and the Milky Way. As the demons (the dark half of nature's cycles) and devas (the light half) pull back and forth, they rotate the mountain (the North Pole) which churns the milky ocean below (the view of the sun and stars from earth).

In the story, this churning produces Amrita, the nectar of immortality, eventually consumed by the devas, and which allows Indra to return to his abode as the King of Heaven—who in this mural appears above in the sky.

On the spring equinox, the sun rises to crown the pinnacle of the main tower of Angkor Wat, representing Indra as the sun returning to his abode as the King of Heaven. In Hinduism, Mount Meru is the location of heaven as the home of the gods, and is said to be located at the North Pole, which is why Indra as the sun appearing at its peak signals his return to heaven. The Hindus, the ancient Egyptians, the Gnostics, and the Druids, all viewed the northern regions of the sky as the location of heaven and as the place of the fixed and therefore "eternal" region of the stars, as they never set below the horizon.

In 10,500 BC, Angkor Wat and a number of surrounding temples would have aligned to the constellation Draco, which is depicted as a dragon or serpent. The constellation of Draco appears in the region of the circumpolar stars, where it literally wraps around the center of the circle that the North Pole traces through the sky in its processional cycle. The constellation of Draco is therefore the celestial depiction of the great serpent of the story, wrapped around the tower of Angkor Wat as the North Pole, with the stars that make its constellation mirrored in the temples on the ground.

Incredibly, as at other related ancient sites, we find the same mirroring of the cosmos to sacred sites on the ground, the incorporation of advanced astronomical observations, and the knowledge of spiritual forces, symbols, and principles—brought together in an architectural masterpiece.

The story of the churning of the milky ocean encodes a principle that under-lies all cycles in the cosmos, which is why extensive research at Angkor Wat has uncovered that the site encodes numbers related to the annual cycle of the sun, the precession of Earth through the constellations, and the huge epochs of time known as Yugas in Hinduism. The Vedic astrologer, yogi, scholar, and guru of Paramahansa Yogananda, Swami Sri Yukteswar Giri, wrote in his book *The Holy Science* in 1894 that the precession of the equinoxes is due to the sun's orbit around another star, which takes approximately 24,000 years to complete, and that this cycle is related to humanity's level of spiri-tual development through various ages called Yugas. The builders of this site understood this connection, and built their whole temple to illustrate it—even incorporating the sun and stars.

THE CYCLE OF THE SUN

Scholar of South-East Asian studies, Eleanor Mannikka, has researched the numbers encoded into the design of Angkor Wat, including those found in the mural of the churning of the milky ocean, and describes them as follows:

> "In the bas-reliefs at Angkor Wat, the position of the churning pivot would correspond to the position of the spring equinox. The 91 asuras in the south represent the 91 days from equinox to winter solstice, and the 88 northern devas represent the 88 days from equinox to summer solstice. In fact, there are either 88 or 89 devas in the scene; 89 is the Deva atop mount Mandara and is counted with the others. There are 88 or 89 days from the spring equinox,

counted from the first day of the new year, to the summer solstice... In Cambodia, the spring lasted for 3 or 4 days.... Mount Mandara as the churning pivot would symbolize the 3 or 4 days of the equinox period, the northernmost Deva would represent the summer solstice day, and the southernmost asura would correspond with the winter solstice day. In other words, the scene is a calendar. It positions the two solstice days at the extreme north and south, and counts the days between them..." [1]

~ ELEANOR MANNIKKA, ANGKOR WAT: TIME, SPACE, AND KINGSHIP

The design of the mural also depicts greater cosmic cycles which Earth progresses through, as it encodes some of the numbers involved in the precession of the equinoxes along Earth's ecliptic around the sun, which takes approximately 26,000 years to complete. As in the annual cycle of the sun, in this cycle the equinox is also the point of rotation.

The churning of the milky ocean scene also encodes the number 108, as each side occupied by the demons and devas measures 54 cubits. In other parts of the complex there are stone statues of the scene, with 54 demons and 54 devas.

The number 108 is a mysterious number, which is considered sacred in Buddhism and Hinduism. The 108 beads of Buddha's necklace used in meditation practices, where someone slowly passes each bead through their fingers, is sometimes said to represent the cycle of the sun from summer to winter solstice. By pausing at the end of the necklace before changing direction, the practice symbolizes the period where the sun stands still at the solstice, before reversing its direction.

Hindus also divide the ecliptic of the sun, which is the great circle representing the path of the sun through the sky each year, into 27 sections of 4 parts, making a total of 108 steps the sun takes in its journey. And while this may seem arbitrary, the diameter of the sun is approximately 108 times that of the earth, and the average distance from the sun to the earth is 108 times the sun's diameter. There are other occurrences of the number 108 in the cosmos and its cycles, too numerous to detail here.

What is clear is that the site of Angkor Wat was designed to illustrate the principle underlying the cosmic cycles found in the design of the universe.

DARKNESS AND LIGHT IN THE GREATER CYCLES OF LIFE

Human existence also progresses through greater cycles, just as our earth does, which transitions through stages of light, ascent, and evolution (like the waxing of the sun from winter solstice to summer solstice), as well as darkness, descent, and devolution (like the waning of the sun from summer solstice to winter solstice). These cycles have been illustrated in Buddhism as the Wheel of Life (also known as the Wheel of Samsara). Like the dark and light half of the year found in the change of seasons from summer to winter, the Wheel of Samsara also has its periods of light and darkness. As the wheel rotates up it is in light, called evolution, and as it rotates down, it is in darkness, called devolution. Within the Wheel of Samsara is found the progress of the person through their cycle of lives, which Jesus describes as a circuit.

> "Strive thereafter that ye may receive the mysteries of the Light in this time of affliction and enter into the Light-kingdom. Join not one day to another, or one circuit to another, hoping that ye may succeed in receiving the mysteries if ye come into the world in another circuit." [2]
> ~ JESUS IN PISTIS SOPHIA, TRANSLATED BY G. R. S. MEAD

A painting of the Wheel of Samsara in the Sera Monastery of Tibet. Notice the light and dark halves of the middle of the wheel, through which life rotates.

This same rotation is found in the cycles of humanity known as Yugas, which were also encoded in the temple of Angkor Wat—whole civilizations and periods of human existence go through periods of light and progress, as well as darkness and degeneration.

THE STRUGGLE BETWEEN DARKNESS AND LIGHT

This pulling back and forth between light and darkness symbolizes an under-pinning universal principle in creation found in the cycles of cosmic time and human life. It reveals the role of darkness and light in creating movement through its struggle and opposition, and likewise shows the role of darkness and light within ourselves and our lives.

This same struggle between the forces of good and evil takes place within the world, even though most people are completely unaware of it. In life, one is either taking part in this struggle or they are simply the unconscious victims of it. If one is in the struggle, they are either pulling for light, or for darkness. Those who do neither, who do not participate, and do not struggle against darkness, are like the creatures of the ocean of existence that become unconsciously churned around by forces they are completely unaware of.

THE TREASURES

In the churning of the milky ocean, the struggle between darkness and light causes multiple spiritual treasures to emerge from the ocean, a poison that has the power to destroy the universe, and finally Amrita—the nectar of immortality. Without the opposition that darkness brings, there would be no movement and no struggle, and it is from the struggle that the spiritual treasures are produced. The spiritual treasures symbolize the spiritual facul-ties and virtues which someone gains through their struggle against darkness.

THE POISON

The poison that the churning produces is called Kalakuta—it is so terrible that it threatens to destroy creation. Before the nectar can be recovered in the story, this terrible poison must be dealt with first.

The opposition found in life not only brings out the best in people, but also the very worst, and thus opposition also creates poison.

As this is a key principle, it works on many levels. In society for example, poi-son emerges as the negative actions and psychological reactions of people, in the practice of sexual alchemy as lustful desire, and within the individual as the responses of the many egos and the actions that they cause.

136

Shiva at the top of the churning of the milky ocean, swallowing the poison. Beneath him various treasures emerge from the ocean.

The poison within, all the hatred, violence, greed, etc., is brought to the surface from the struggle, both within the individual's psyche and externally in the world. The strength of the egos (emotions such as anger, hatred, etc.) stirred up is so great that it threatens to destroy everything.

As terrible as the poison is, however, its extraction is of great benefit, as the act of churning separates the poison from the nectar. The ocean that is churned is life, the human energies, the psyche, humanity, and all of creation; to have the poison extracted and separated from the nectar in all these things is of great value, as it allows a process of purification to take place. In the work to awaken, one must constantly struggle to purify oneself—to remove what is inferior and cultivate what is superior—and it is the struggle that opposition produces which allows this to happen.

As a universal principle the separation of the poison from the nectar also effectively takes place among groups of people. When the events of life are churned, the nature of people becomes apparent and those who prefer darkness and the ego are revealed—this "churning" can uncover negative people within groups, organizations, and projects of all kinds, who would have otherwise continued influencing things for the worse unnoticed.

For someone doing the spiritual work, the person has to face what is within the depths of their subconscious. When the psyche is churned by the agitation created by opposition, they get to see what is really within them—all the egos that were previously hidden beneath the surface of the ocean (the psyche and subconscious), but which can now be seen, understood, and removed.

THE NECTAR

Finally the nectar, the positive results of the struggle, emerges. Out of opposition comes the nectar of knowledge, understanding, wisdom, information, right action, good events, and what is of value in life to those who are working for greater consciousness.

In alchemy, the elixir of immortality arises—that which the devas set out to achieve in the churning, which grants resurrection.

This struggle to acquire the nectar shows the important role that darkness plays in the awakening of the individual. It is in the opposition to darkness that one is tested, one develops strength, self-knowledge, will, wisdom, and many other qualities, and why before Jesus, Osiris, Quetzalcoatl, etc., resurrect and attain eternal life at the spring equinox, they must firstly face darkness in their betrayal, crucifixion, and death.

THE ROLE OF SPIRITUAL HELP

The demons try to steal the nectar of immortality using cunning and deceit, but instead fall victim to their own inner weakness, which is lust and sexual desire, as they are distracted by an attractive woman sent by Vishnu. Instead, through the help of the god Vishnu, the elixir is then seized and consumed by the devas which gives them the strength to defeat the demons, and allows Indra (the initiate with the Son within) to return to his abode as the King of Heaven. This is symbolic of the resurrection of the Son. In the story, the defeat of the demons was only possible through Vishnu's intervention, and thus without Vishnu's help, Indra would not have been able to return to heaven.

This reveals that if it wasn't for spiritual help, the forces of evil in creation, within ourselves, and in the world would always dominate those of good through the use of cunning and deceit. Jesus, Osiris, Balder, and Hun Hunahpu, who each represented the spiritual Son, are all killed through deceit and betrayal. But as Jesus said, without the will of his Father, he would never have been betrayed and handed over to death in the first place. It is the spirit that allows darkness its place in creation because of the opposition it provides. Vishnu promised the devas that they would have the nectar from the beginning, but that they had to first churn the ocean alongside the demons to acquire it.

> "'Do you refuse to speak to me?' Pilate said. 'Don't you realize I have power either to free you or to crucify you?'
>
> Jesus answered, 'You would have no power over me if it were not given to you from above.'" [3]
>
> ~ THE GOSPEL ACCORDING TO JOHN 19:10-11

THE NECESSITY OF DARKNESS

The Aztec god Xolotl (depicted with the head of a dog and body of a man), the twin brother of Quetzalcoatl, is illustrated as being on a cross. Other images show Quetzalcoatl himself on the cross, vast distances away from where Jesus was crucified.

The forces of darkness, evil, death, and decay are found throughout all of creation, in our lives, and within ourselves, as well as the forces of light, goodness, birth, and growth. All form that we see is made perceptible through the combination of both light and shadow—if there were only darkness, or only light, we could not see. Dark and light both form a necessary part of creation, and also a necessary part of the spiritual work.

The work to awaken consciousness is a fight to overcome the darkness within ourselves, both in our own subconscious and in the events we face in the world, so that the light of the spirit increases within us. This great struggle was depicted in the life of Jesus, Osiris, Hun Hunahpu, and many others at the time of the spring equinox—symbolic of the battle between light and darkness.

Many teachings and philosophies today however, wish to focus only on the positive and the "feel good." Darkness and evil is either ignored, or worse, embraced. When what "feels good" is used as the measure for what is spiritual, then there is a tendency to avoid the truth whenever it doesn't suit our ideas, and instead create superficial beliefs on the whims of feelings and emotions. Thus, things like hell, which have been taught about in all great sacred teachings since ancient times, are virtually a subject of taboo. Many religions on the other hand, have turned what were esoteric teachings intended for individuals to use to attain the divine, into idols of worship, dogma, and belief.

Between the spiritual merchants of today and the world's religions, the understanding of the processes involved in spiritual awakening and human existence is virtually lost. However, the real esoteric knowledge is still here today, and going back into the original esoteric teachings and the understanding of the cosmos and creation, one can see it has also been given throughout history.

The attainment of enlightenment is not done as some today would suggest—simply by realizing it; nor is it done simply through holding a belief at the time of death, as many religions teach. The spirit within, which gives eternal life, is reached by those who are prepared to go through great trials, tests, and suffering—to give up all earthly pleasures, riches, fame, etc., for the treasures of the spirit, which are everlasting. This is demonstrated in the teachings of betrayal, death, and resurrection, found throughout the world.

THE TRAPS

PEOPLE TAKE UP ROCKS TO STONE JESUS.

In order for everything that occurs at the betrayal and death to unfold, and thus the resurrection, a series of traps must be laid to ensnare the initiate. They are set in multiple circumstances in their life, well in advance of the death and resurrection, and come at no fault of their own. These ensure that the necessary circumstances in the life of the initiate will occur—they are set by both the forces of evil, who always oppose those who wish to awaken, and also by the divine beings, who move the circumstances and people in the initiate's life for them to be tested, forming an inescapable snare.

> "Keeping a close watch on him, they [the Pharisees] sent spies, who pretended to be sincere. They hoped to catch Jesus in something he said, so that they might hand him over to the power and authority of the governor." [4]
>
> ~ THE GOSPEL ACCORDING TO LUKE 20:20

> "Then the Pharisees went out and laid plans to trap him [Jesus] in his words." [5]
>
> ~ THE GOSPEL ACCORDING TO MATTHEW 22:15

In the life of Jesus, the Pharisees, the religious authorities, conspire to trap Jesus from early on and he is betrayed through deceit. The Lords of Xibalba (of death and darkness) kill Hun Hunahpu using cunning and deceit. Osiris' jealous brother, Seth, makes a coffin and tricks Osiris into lying in it to see if he will fit, then seals it shut once Osiris is inside with molten metal so Osiris can't get out. The god Loki uses deception to kill the Norse god of the sun Balder. In the churning of the milky ocean, the demons steal the elixir of immortality using deceit.

The force of the Son is love. It comes into the world through a spiritually prepared person, and each time it does, its antithesis, hatred, rises to meet it. Inevitably, the initiate who has the Son within has to face the hatred and evil of the world.

> "[Jesus said] This is the verdict: Light has come into the world, but people loved darkness instead of light because their deeds were evil. Everyone who does evil hates the light, and will not come into the light for fear that their deeds will be exposed. But whoever lives by the truth comes into the light, so that it may be seen plainly that what they have done has been done in the sight of God." [6]
>
> ~ THE GOSPEL ACCORDING TO JOHN 3:19-21

It is not as many people think—the Son doesn't come to affirm people's own ideas and beliefs, but challenges the evil that lies veiled within morality, the law, the human being, and society, and in doing so becomes an obstacle to people fulfilling their desires, egos, pleasures, lust, power, violence, and domination. Osiris was a good king who ruled with love and justice, but Seth was jealous and wanted to rule in his place. Jesus came to give the message of divine truth, but the established religion saw him as a threat to their power.

Those in society who appear to be spiritual, moral, religious, sanctified, and righteous are revealed for what they are—as the light of the Son shines in the darkness of the world, it inevitably exposes their true nature. Those in the world who are full of hate come to attack the Son because their vibration is of hatred and darkness, and they cannot stand the emanations of light and love, nor their deeds being exposed. Evil does its work in the cover of darkness. One by one, as they come out to attack the Son, their own inner evil is revealed. In what is about to unfold, all the people around the Son, even society and the world itself, will be defined.

BETRAYAL

JUDAS LEAVING THE LAST SUPPER TO BETRAY JESUS.

Osiris was betrayed by his brother—someone who was a trusted part of his family. For Jesus, it was his disciple Judas, someone he taught and shared his life with, who handed him over to the Pharisees that falsely accused him and caused his execution.

Joan of Arc had attained a certain stage of the spiritual work, and as part of her mission came here to complete a part of it—that stage was the betrayal. In her life she was betrayed by the King of France, the very person whom she had helped to put on the throne, who left her to be captured by their common enemy the English, leading to her trial and execution based on false allegations.

Another person who was similarly betrayed by the King of France on false charges and burnt at the stake, almost one hundred years earlier, was Jaques de Molay—the last grand master of the Knights Templar, along with a number of others in the order. The records of their trial have been recently discovered in the Vatican Library, and reveal the Pope at the time dropped the accusations against them, but that despite this, the King of France persisted with their execution.

The Templars are believed to have had connections to Freemasonry, with its great wealth of spiritual knowledge; the Templars are said to have fled persecution taking their spiritual knowledge with them to the safe haven of Scotland where it is believed the oldest Lodge of the Masons was founded. The name Freemason has been said to possibly derive from the Egyptian words for sun, "Phre," and child, "Mas," meaning children of the sun, or sons of light—titles also used by the Egyptians and Incas. Tragically, Freemasonry was infiltrated by those with malevolent agendas, as so many other spiritual groups and religions have been throughout human history.

In the Garden of Gethsemane as Jesus prays knowing that people are plotting against him, the disciples sleep, signifying that their consciousness is asleep and thus how they are unaware of what is taking place.

The initiate's faith in the divine is tested, as all the authorities of the world will turn against them and those who they thought were with them, will desert them completely. When Jesus is seized, the disciples flee. All the students of the Son, who like Peter, even declare they will do anything for Jesus, when the time comes to stand by their teacher, hide and deny that they even know them in fear of being attacked themselves. Apart from a few disciples, Jesus' mother, and Mary Magdalene, the crowds who once massed around Jesus crying "Hosanna!" completely abandon him. Weak, vulnerable, and almost completely alone, the initiate must go through the betrayal, an excruciating stage in which they are handed over to people who hate them, who ruthlessly destroy their image and reputation with lies and falsity, and face the condemnation, insults, and scourging of the world.

THE DIVINE ROLE OF JUDAS

Jesus was someone who had already achieved a highly advanced spiritual stage and who was born on earth with a mission—to give the universal teaching of spirituality anew both in what he taught and through the events of his life. Those around him, both consciously and unconsciously, played a role in Jesus' life that would help to demonstrate this teaching. Judas was given the most difficult role by Jesus as one of his most advanced disciples (see the ancient text the Gospel of Judas and book *The Flight of the Feathered Serpent* by Armando Cosani).

Judas symbolizes the traitor which exists within every person, who betrays the force of the Son—all the love, wisdom, happiness, treasures, and riches of the spirit—in return for thirty pieces of silver, which are symbolic of the desires of the egos and the pleasures of the material world, which are spent in passing to leave someone at the end of their life with nothing but remorse and the consequences of their actions.

JUDAS BETRAYS JESUS WITH A KISS, AND HANDS HIM OVER TO THE SOLDIERS.

In one of the Gospels Judas dies by hanging himself. The symbol of Judas hanging signifies the student/disciple who betrays someone with the Son within, as well as on a more personal level, those who having the Son within, exchange him for pleasures of the world (which can happen at different times and in different ways). As they hang, their feet do not touch the ground because they can no longer enjoy the ignorant pleasure of mundane life. Nor does their head reach to heaven, because they rejected and betrayed the spirit. Instead, they are left suspended, without the happiness of a material nor spiritual life.

Judas also represents the force of desire within the psyche, which betrays all that is good within a person. Esoterically, the work of Judas is the work to destroy the egos, and it is at this time that someone must carry out this work in order to achieve the inner death necessary to resurrect.

TRIAL

Defenseless, the initiate is symbolically taken captive and treated as a criminal after all they have done to help others. Joan of Arc, who was the savior of a nation, was kept as a common prisoner, and almost completely abandoned.

JOAN OF ARC IS INTERROGATED IN PRISON.

Jesus is left defenseless, and remains silent at the false accusations made against him to signify how the initiate is made unable to defend themselves during this time. Like Osiris who was sealed in the coffin, the initiate is left completely trapped, and is prevented from defending themselves in the face of their own demise. Many of those whom they knew and helped, instead emerge to give false testimony against them.

> "The chief priests and the whole Sanhedrin were looking for evidence against Jesus so that they could put him to death, but they did not find any. Many testified falsely against him, but their statements did not agree.
>
> Then some stood up and gave this false testimony against him: 'We heard him say, "I will destroy this temple made with human hands and in three days will build another, not made with hands."' Yet even then their testimony did not agree.
>
> Then the high priest stood up before them and asked Jesus, 'Are you not going to answer? What is this testimony that these men are bringing against you?' But Jesus remained silent and gave no answer.

Again the high priest asked him, 'Are you the Messiah, the Son of the Blessed One?'

'I am,' said Jesus. 'And you will see the Son of Man sitting at the right hand of the Mighty One and coming on the clouds of heaven.'

The high priest tore his clothes. 'Why do we need any more witnesses?' he asked. 'You have heard the blasphemy. What do you think?'

They all condemned him as worthy of death. Then some began to spit at him; they blindfolded him, struck him with their fists, and said, 'Prophesy!' And the guards took him and beat him." [7]

~ THE GOSPEL ACCORDING TO MARK 14:55-65

JESUS BEFORE PILATE.

Both Jesus and Joan of Arc are put on trial by the religious establishment. The initiate must be rejected by their own religion, and in rejecting the Son (the real source of spirituality in the world), the religion defines itself as that which opposes the light no matter what they preach.

Despite all the false evidence, the religious pharisees are unable to find any charge against Jesus or Joan as they did no wrong. However, both are finally accused of blasphemy/heresy (today it is cult leader or heretic) as they dared to declare their relationship with divinity, which they had only done for the good of helping others. The Son comes into the initiate as the world teacher, and has done so throughout time to bring the message of awakening to humanity—and for this they are persecuted, attacked, mocked, and hated by many, many people.

Through the trial of the Son, the true nature of society is uncovered. The institutions, dogmas, traditions, and laws, which present themselves as the moral good, are often instead the vehicles of persecution, which are used to suppress the awakening of consciousness—in their persecution of the Son, their true position is revealed. The crowds of humanity call for the release of Barabbas, a real criminal who is symbolic of all the degeneration of the ego, instead of Jesus, thereby choosing hatred over the love of the Son.

The initiate undergoes the flagellation in which they feel every word of the mockery and insults made against them like the lashes of a whip. Then, they receive the crown of thorns, which is Christic will, before being sent again to be condemned by society who shout "crucify him!" That is, humanity at large hates and rejects the Son, and anyone who has the spiritual force of the Son within.

INNER DEATH

The Hindu goddess Kali, symbol of the
great Mother who destroys our egos.

The death of crucifixion is symbolic of inner death—it is the death of the egos in the subconscious, the darkness of non-being, the myself, etc., symbolized in the battles of the Hindu god Indra against Vritra. This death does not arrive inevitably as physical death does, but must be fought for, so that the spirit is freed from the darkness within, just as Indra frees the spiritual treasures contained within Vritra. It is often symbolized as death itself, and this is why death is a central theme in the lives of those who portrayed the work of enlightenment in the events of their lives.

The chambers of the Great Pyramids contain stone sarcophaguses (which are stone coffins), but were found completely empty of burials, as the chambers served as tombs for initiatory rites symbolizing inner death. In order to resurrect, someone has to reach a level of inner death in order to meet the required spiritual purity for attaining eternal life. This is the death of the various egos, such as anger, fear, pride, etc.

However, for these egos to be destroyed, they must be seen and understood. For this, they have to be drawn out from the depths of the subconscious. It is difficulties, unfairness, hardships, etc., that bring out things inside of us that we didn't even know we had within, which is the principle of "the churning of the milky ocean" in motion. On the path of the spiritual sun, someone is put through a form of the Passion and crucifixion in their own lives, and the suffering they go through plunges them into the underworld of their subconscious—in order to churn up the egos they have within so they can be destroyed.

Jesus was crucified at the time of the spring equinox on the "Skull Place," as a symbol of inner death. The site of the Great Pyramids where the Great Sphinx aligns to the spring equinox was also associated with death, as its ancient name was the Necropolis, which means graveyard. At around 10,500 BC the Great Pyramids aligned with the three stars of Orion's belt—symbol of Osiris in the sky, whose death and resurrection was the most central event of his life. Incredibly, the three great pyramids of Teotihuacán in Mexico align just as the Great Pyramids of Giza do—to the three stars of Orion's belt. The largest, called The Pyramid of the Sun, shares almost exactly the same base area as the Great Pyramid in Egypt. These pyramids are built along what is called the Avenue of the Dead, which is another reference to inner death, and the site itself was known as "the place where men become Gods," which is a reference to the spiritual transformation of resurrection.

ALCHEMICAL TRANSFORMATION AND THE GOOD AND BAD THIEF

The death of the Son on a cross, or a tree, is a sacred symbol found throughout the world. Jesus was crucified on a cross, and so was Quetzalcoatl. Attis was said to be crucified on a pine tree at the time of the spring equinox. The Maize God Hun Hunahpu was decapitated and his head hung on a tree. Osiris in a coffin, floated down the river Nile until washing ashore and merging with a tree. Odin strung himself upon a tree as an act of self-sacrifice.

The symbols of both cross and tree are found prolifically in sacred teachings throughout the world and both symbolize the union of feminine/earthly and masculine/heavenly forces—of the human with the divine. The masculine principle is represented by the vertical line of the cross and branches of the tree, and the feminine principle is represented by the horizontal line and roots. This joining of feminine and masculine forces is also symbolic of the sacred sexual practice of alchemy, in which man and woman united harness their creative powers to put to death the egos, and give birth to the imperishability of the spiritual within.

The symbol of the cross also appears in ancient Egypt as the ankh, which was used as the hieroglyphic character for "eternal life," again revealing the connection between the symbol of the cross, the practice of alchemy, and resurrection to eternal spiritual life. Although the exact origin of the symbol is unknown, it's commonly believed to represent the union of masculine and feminine forces, just like the cross and tree of life.

Jesus crucified between the good and the bad thief. With the position of Mary Magdalene at the base of the cross, as well as the symbol of the skull, both the practice of alchemy and inner death are alluded to in this painting. A pyramid even appears on the horizon.

Another symbol related to alchemy that appears in connection with the cross of crucifixion is the good and bad thief that were crucified on either side of Jesus. The good thief represents the one who "steals" or takes the awakened sexual energy in alchemy to use it for spiritual purposes, and the bad thief the one who steals this energy to use it to feed desire. They represent how sexual energy can be used for different purposes.

This symbolism can be found in ancient Egypt. Before they were stripped of their casing, the Great Pyramids were each different colors, and evidence for this remains today. The smallest pyramid was colored black; the second largest was red; and the largest was white, tipped with gold. The pyramids have a number of meanings, but in one the black pyramid represents the bad thief, and the white, the good thief, with the red pyramid representing the crucified Son in between (red being the color of self-sacrifice). This red pyramid was connected to the Sphinx, which aligns to the spring equinox—the time of crucifixion.

Alchemy is the purification and transformation of the energies of the human being, turning them from a dirty, dark state, symbolized by lead and the black pyramid, into a pure, light state, symbolized by the gold that once formed the tip of the Great Pyramid.

The good and bad thief are also symbolized in connection with the constellation of Orion. The three stars in Orion's belt align with the Great Pyramids, and Orion was believed to represent the Egyptian god Osiris who died and resurrected. The constellations of the two dogs Canis Major and Canis Minor are found near Orion's heels in the sky and can also represent the good and bad thief respectively. The constellation Canis Major contains the star Sirius, which was the star of Isis to the Egyptians. Isis is the spiritual Mother who works with the sexual energies (taken by the good thief) to create the spiritual within.

The bad and good thief, and black and white pyramid, on either side of the spiritual Son (the red pyramid), symbolize the struggle between the sexual urge and the will, mirrored in the sky at the time of the spring equinox when the battle between darkness and light are in balance. This symbol is found in the Hindu story of the churning of the milky ocean, as explained previously, in the struggle between the demons (the force of the bad thief, desire) on one side, and the devas (the force of the good thief, the spirit) on the other. In order to resurrect, the bliss of the spirit must triumph over desire, just as the days become longer from the point of the spring equinox onward.

SELF-SACRIFICE

The crucifixion of the spiritual Son at the spring equinox is also a symbol of sacrifice. This kind of sacrifice, which symbolizes a key principle in the universe and the path of the spiritual sun, is not the horrific kind that involves violence and the sacrifice of others, but is the inner kind in which we sacrifice what is inferior within ourselves to gain what is superior (the spiritual within), and make sacrifices in our life out of love for others. This has been called self-sacrifice and is based entirely on selflessness and love.

The cross of crucifixion is not only a symbol of alchemy, but also a symbol of sacrifice and responsibilities. This comes with having greater knowledge, as when we are given spiritual knowledge there is a duty to use it to help others. Jesus symbolized this in carrying the heavy weight of the cross during the Passion, which shows how the initiate can't abandon their responsibilities toward humanity, even as they are being attacked and persecuted.

This principle of self-sacrifice has been symbolized in many ancient teachings. Both Jesus and Joan of Arc allowed themselves to be betrayed and handed over to execution as an act of self-sacrifice in pursuit of a higher cause. In the Hindu story of the churning of the milky ocean, the god Shiva comes forward to swallow the terrible poison that emerges as an act of self-sacrifice to save creation and allow the churning to continue. The Maya god Quetzalcoatl created human beings from an act of self-sacrifice. The Norse god Odin undergoes crucifixion on a tree as an act of self-sacrifice, in order to give the wisdom of his sacred runes to humanity.

ODIN'S SELF-SACRIFICE.

"I know that I hung on a windy tree
    nine long nights,
    wounded with a spear, dedicated to Odin,
    myself to myself,

on that tree of which no man knows
from where its roots run.

No bread did they give me nor a drink from a horn,
downwards I peered;

I took up the runes, screaming I took them,
then I fell back from there..." [8]

~ SAYINGS OF THE HIGH ONE, TRANSLATED BY
CAROLYNE LARRINGTON

The principle of sacrifice exists throughout creation. Energy and materials have to be taken from somewhere in order to create something else. We see this principle at work when creating anything new. Many materials are sacrificed in order to build a house for example. Plants of all kinds, as well as animals, are surrendered to so that other plants and animals can survive. A whole cycle of sacrifice, and of give and take, exists throughout the universe.

"In this world people are fettered by action, unless it is performed as a sacrifice. Therefore, O Arjuna, let thy acts be done without attachment, as sacrifice only.

In the beginning, when God created all beings by the sacrifice of Himself, He said unto them: 'Through sacrifice you can procreate, and it shall satisfy all your desires. Worship the Powers of Nature thereby, and let them nourish you in return; thus supporting each other, you shall attain your highest welfare. For, fed, on sacrifice, nature will give you all the enjoyment you can desire. But he who enjoys what she gives without returning is, indeed, a robber.'

The sages who enjoy the food that remains after the sacrifice is made are freed from all sin; but the selfish who spread their feast only for themselves feed on sin only.

All creatures are the product of food, food is the product of rain, rain comes by sacrifice, and sacrifice is the noblest form of action.

All action originates in the Supreme Spirit, which is Imperishable, and in sacrificial action the all-pervading Spirit is consciously present.

Thus he who does not help the revolving wheel of sacrifice, but instead leads a sinful life, rejoicing in the gratification of his senses, O Arjuna, he breathes in vain." [9]

~ KRISHNA IN THE BHAGAVAD GITA, TRANSLATED BY SHRI PUROHIT SWAMI

This same principle applies when creating the spiritual; in order to have the materials to be able to create spiritual things within, sacrifices must be made within ourselves to be able to provide these materials. These materials are the quintessential energies and elements within a person, and they become the prima materia of the alchemists—the symbolic base substance that is offered up in order to create the golden energies of the sun within. For those working toward enlightenment, the dark energetic substances of the egos, and the energies we use to feed them, are sacrificed so that our energies can be put toward creating things of light within us instead. So for example, selfish pleasures are sacrificed in order to gain love. Low states of all kinds, like aggression and violence, are sacrificed to have inner peace. Negative behaviors and addictions are given up in order to bring about mystical experiences and spiritual states. What is lower then, is sacrificed, or given up, in order to gain what is of a higher nature.

Likewise, this principle applies when creating things for the greater good in the world. For example, we can sacrifice our time and effort voluntarily to create something that will not just benefit ourselves, but many others. In giving charity, we give up things that we could have kept to ourselves, to instead help those in need. Those things which confer a smaller benefit, are given up so that those things which bring a greater benefit can take place.

> "O Ye men, increase the store of goods acquired by honest and fair means to be used in the service of humanity. May your life, be constantly dedicated to this principle. May the spiritually minded people, also, not give up this humanitarian work." [10]
> ~ THE YAJUR VEDA, TRANSLATED BY DEVI CHAND

This same principle of sacrifice applies to spreading spiritual knowledge, so that we give up things in our life in order that fellow beings have the opportunity to find out about spiritual awakening.

> "Those who see themselves in all and all in them, help others through spiritual Osmosis to realize the Self themselves." [11]
> ~ THE KATHA UPANISHAD, TRANSLATED BY EKNATH EASWARAN

At the root of this is the principle "it is in giving that we receive," which is love, and which St. Francis of Assisi wrote about in his famous prayer.

> "Lord, make me an instrument of Your peace...
> O, Divine Master, grant that I may not so much seek to be consoled as to console;
> to be understood as to understand;
> to be loved as to love;
> For it is in giving that we receive;
> it is in pardoning that we are pardoned;
> it is in dying that we are born again to eternal life."
> ~ ST. FRANCIS OF ASSISI

The spring equinox contains the principle of sacrifice. In the churning of the milky ocean, the darkness is on one side of the tug of war, and the light on the other, just like the dark and light halves of the year are on either side of the equinox. It's by giving up the things of darkness within that we gain the light, just as the sun after the spring equinox increases toward the summer solstice.

The self-sacrifice symbolized by the spring equinox is also in giving up everything that someone believes themselves to be—the ideals they hold about themselves, their achievements in life, the place they hold in the opinions of others, etc.—all of which constitute someone's own self-image. This is given up in the process of betrayal and crucifixion, where someone's image is destroyed with lies and falsity. This process exists on the path of the spiritual sun, in part, so that someone sacrifices their attachment to their own self-image and their status in society, as they cannot pass this stage if they don't let go of it. Our image is crucial to our acceptance in society and yet it belongs to the lower nature of the personality and the things of the world, and as such, has to be given up to gain that which belongs to one's eternal Being.

> "But you will exceed all of them. For you will sacrifice the man that clothes me." [12]
>
> ~ JESUS TO JUDAS IN THE GOSPEL OF JUDAS, TRANSLATED BY RODOLPHE KASSER, MARVIN MEYER, AND GREGOR WURST, IN COLLABORATION WITH FRANÇOIS GAUDARD

It is through the death of one's sense of "self" that someone reaches the self-less and yet unique nature of their higher Being—that which is not of this world and which brings a new life. It is where someone gives up their own self-centric will, so that their will becomes as one with the selfless will of the divine Spirit whom they can then truly serve—and that will is love.

> "Father, if you are willing, take this cup from me; yet not my will, but yours be done." [13]
>
> ~ JESUS IN THE GOSPEL ACCORDING TO LUKE 22:42

> "There are two selves, the separate ego
> And the indivisible Atman. When
> One rises above *I* and *me* and *mine*,
> The Atman is revealed as one's real Self." [14]
>
> ~ THE KATHA UPANISHAD, TRANSLATED BY EKNATH EASWARAN

ANUBIS, GUARDIAN OF THE GATEWAY TO IMMORTALITY

At the spring equinox, Anubis plays a central role in spiritual resurrection. In the story of the life of Osiris, the god Anpu (Anubis in Greek) receives the dead body of Osiris and places it in a tomb, and along with the goddesses Isis and Nephthys, resurrects him. This reflects a real role that the higher Being Anubis has in the higher dimensions, which the ancient Egyptians were aware of and depicted.

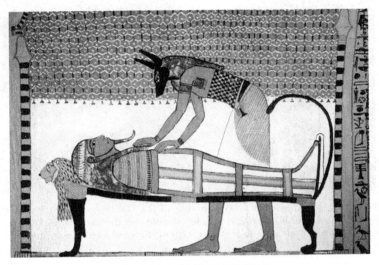

ANUBIS ATTENDING TO THE DEAD.

ANUBIS WEIGHING THE HEART OF A MAN AGAINST A FEATHER ON THE SCALES OF DIVINE LAW.

The ancient Egyptians portrayed Anubis as presiding over the processes of death—a role which he has as head judge of karma in the higher dimensions. He receives those who've just died and judges them according to their deeds in life. He does this along with the forty-two judges of karma. This was depicted in ancient Egypt as the scene of the weighing of the heart, where at death a person has their heart weighed by Anubis on the scales of divine cosmic law.

The god Hermanubis, who was a merger of the Greek god Hermes with the Egyptian god Anubis. Resting on his left shoulder is the caduceus of Mercury, which is an alchemical symbol of two serpents entwined around a winged staff.

It was common in Greece and Rome for Egyptian deities to merge with Greek and Roman ones. In Greece Anubis became the god Hermes, and even merged to form the god Hermanubis, while in Rome he became the god Mercury. Both Hermes and Mercury were also associated with death like Anubis, were both believed to be guides of the dead, and were each depicted with wings. When the initiate lies symbolically dead in the sarcophagus in the higher dimensions before resurrection, Anubis enters the door of the tomb wearing a headdress with the wings of Mercury.

However, few experience firsthand Anubis' role in presiding over inner death as few ever meet the requirements. Anubis not only presides over the process of physical death, but also of spiritual, inner death. It is Anubis who has the role in the spiritual dimensions to administer the initiate upon the stage of inner death preceding resurrection on the path of the spiritual sun.

"The secret ways of Ro-Setawe [the ancient site of Giza], The gate of the gods. Only one whose voice is heard May pass them ... The secret way to which (only) Anubis has access In order to conceal the body of Osiris." [15]

~ THE BOOK OF THE ONE IN THE NETHERWORLD, FROM THE BOOK JACKAL AT THE SHAMAN'S GATE BY TERENCE DUQUESNE

Like Anubis, in the life of Jesus, Joseph of Arimathea wraps the body of the crucified Jesus in linen before he places it in his own tomb. Joseph was a member of the Sanhedrin, which was a council of judges, paralleling Anubis who was seen as a spiritual judge in ancient Egypt.

As lord of karma, and head of the judges of divine cosmic law, Anubis stands as gatekeeper between the realm of earthly mortality and spiritual imperishability, letting only those who meet the requirements pass.

"Anubis, the counter of hearts, deducts Osiris from the gods who belong to the earth, (and assigns him) to the gods who are in heaven." [16]

~ THE PYRAMID TEXTS, UTTERANCE 577, TRANSLATED BY SAMUEL A. B. MERCER

The initiate must pass through Anubis, the guardian between the realm of earthly and spiritual existence, and the head judge of karma, to attain immortal life.

Anubis' role in resurrection was symbolically designed into the ancient site of the Great Sphinx and Pyramids of Egypt. Evidence has come to light that the Great Sphinx of Egypt was originally carved as Anubis in his form as a recumbent African golden wolf, and set down in a sacred lake. Previously the animal Anubis was believed to have been identified with was a jackal, but recent genetic testing has reclassified this species of animal as a wolf. This statue of Anubis was later reshaped by natural and man-made forces over many thousands of years (the Great Sphinx and Pyramids were possibly built around 10,500 BC or earlier), leaving us with the Sphinx as it is today—part man, part lion, that is grossly out of proportion and has obviously been re-carved.

An artist's impression of what the Great Pyramids and Sphinx of Giza may have looked like when they were originally built. Note that the water surrounding the Sphinx actually formed a sacred lake that would have submerged half of its body.

On the spring equinox between approximately 10,970 and 8,810 BC, this giant statue of Anubis would have gazed directly at the constellation we now know of as Leo, but looks just like the recumbent Anubis. This constellation of

Anubis appeared in the sky just before the rising of the sun as Osiris, standing between the path of the sun as it appeared over the horizon and its ascent into the sky, thereby enacting the role Anubis has as gatekeeper between the realm of earthly and immortal existence. It also symbolized Anubis' role in facilitating the resurrection of Osiris, with his constellation appearing just before dawn, and his statue as the Sphinx gazing precisely at the rising sun on the spring equinox, the time of Osiris' resurrection. This incredible alignment and its meaning is explored in detail in chapter five "Decoding the Ancient Meaning of the Sphinx and its Origin as Anubis."

THE RETURN TO THE WOMB

In ancient myths from around the world, creation emerges from the waters of the eternal feminine, which is symbolic of the womb. In Egypt, creation is depicted as emerging from out of the primordial waters, and in Druidic myth, creation emerges from the cauldron of sap of the goddess Cariadwen/Cerridwen. Similarly, creation emerges from the primordial waters in the ancient Vedas of the Hindus and in the legends of the Inca. These primordial waters are those of the eternal feminine womb, the cosmic Mother, which gives birth to the sun, the fire, the Christ/Son, and the light of the first day in the universe from which all of creation unfolds.

The death symbolized at the spring equinox is a return to the primordial waters of the Mother, which is a return to the womb as the place preceding birth. This return to the womb and the resurrection that follows it is found symbolized in sacred teachings and at ancient sites around the world aligned to the spring equinox.

To resurrect and attain eternal life, the Son must be reabsorbed by the Mother, as by returning to the Mother someone returns to the imperishable source of creation—as she was not born of any, but arose from the first Being dividing into male and female. Unlike the Son, because she is not born of any, she is not subject to death, and so by merging with this higher feminine part of someone's Being, a person attains eternal life.

References to the Mother as not being born of any are found in ancient Egypt. The worship of the Egyptian mother goddess Neith can be traced to as far back as seven thousand years ago. Ancient inscriptions referring to her state that she "was the first to give birth to anything, and that she had done so when nothing else had been born, and that she had herself never been born," and also state "I am everything that has been, and that is, and that shall be, and no one has ever lifted my garment," and also "The present and the future and the past, I am. My undergarment no one has uncovered. The fruit I brought forth, the sun came into being." This is perhaps the oldest and clearest reference to the great mother goddess who is not born but is a division of the original creative androgyny, who gave birth to the Son, and the universe, and who remains ever-virgin.

The Son came from the womb of the great Mother, and so to return to the source of creation, the Son must return to his Mother's womb. But a return to the womb is also a time of death, as it is a return to the place which precedes birth. In Maya and Aztec sacred teachings, this is symbolized by Quetzalcoatl being swallowed by the serpent, as the serpent is symbolic of the feminine. Everything that is born must eventually die, and so even the Son must die symbolized by the deaths of Jesus, Osiris, etc.

THE AZTEC CHRIST QUETZALCOATL BEING SWALLOWED BY THE SERPENT.

This return to the womb is symbolized by Jesus' placement in a cave-like tomb, which no one had been placed in before—signifying the return to the womb of the pure and undefiled spiritual Mother. In the Gospel of James, Jesus was also said to be born into a cave, which is a symbol of the womb, and his placement back inside a cave at his death completes the return to the womb. These few symbolic clues are part of the little of what remains of the universal Mother in early Christian writings. A huge part of Jesus' teachings about the spiritual Mother was censored out of history by the orthodoxy, and this has become increasingly apparent as many other early Christian writings have come to light over the last century or so where the Mother is described as part of the Trinity of creation.

In the story of Osiris, he is betrayed by Seth (just as Jesus was by Judas). Seth seals Osiris in a coffin, and then throws the coffin into the Nile River, symbolic of the Milky Way and eternal Mother, which flows out to the sea—this is again symbolic of the return of the initiate to the womb of the spiritual Mother, the primordial waters of creation.

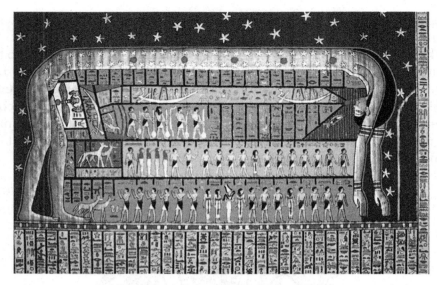

The Egyptian goddess Nut who was symbolized by the Milky Way and who swallowed and gave birth to the sun in a continuous cycle of death and rebirth. This concept of "swallowing" the sun is the same one found in the depictions of the spiritual Son Quetzalcoatl being swallowed by the serpent.

Hathor is one of the most prominent mother goddesses of ancient Egypt. She was depicted as a cow, sometimes with a face shaped like a uterus, to reflect her role of sacred birth. Both she and the goddess Nut were associated with the Milky Way, along with many other mother goddesses around the world. This has an actual basis, as it is now known that the center of the Milky Way is a birthplace of stars—hence the Mother Milky Way giving birth to "suns." The goddess Nut is depicted as stretching across the sky with a body of stars to show her as the Milky Way, giving birth to and then swallowing the sun in an eternal cycle of birth, death, and rebirth. Death for ancient Egyptians was a return to the womb by being swallowed by the goddess (just as the serpent swallows Quetzalcoatl).

Professor I. E. S. Edwards presented evidence that the stone sarcophagus of the Great Pyramid was actually seen as the womb of the goddess Nut (as they were used for initiatory rites and not for burials). As support for this, an ancient Egyptian device for cutting the umbilical cord of a baby at birth was discovered inside the Great Pyramid. However, it was a ceremonial version of the actual instrument, showing that it was not used for actual births, but for initiation rites inside the Pyramid symbolizing death and rebirth.

The Neolithic peoples of Ireland, who built sacred sites like Newgrange around 3,500 BC, also associated the Milky Way with the great Mother. They called the Milky Way "Bealach na Bó Finne," which means the way of the white cow. The Neolithic peoples of Ireland, the ancient Egyptians, and ancient Hindus, all used the cow as a sacred symbol of the great Mother.

In Neolithic Ireland, as in Egypt, they also aligned their temples to the spring equinox using symbols of resurrection and associated the Milky Way with the river around which they built their sacred sites just as the ancient Egyptians did around the river Nile.

At the ancient site of Knowth in Ireland, the symbols of the womb of the Mother, resurrection, and the cross all come together at the spring equinox. Its eastern passage is laid out in a cruciform shape and aligns to the spring equinox. Within it lies the Dagda Cauldron, symbol of the womb. In Irish myth the cauldron was believed to be a vessel of plenty—it is said that no one ever left it hungry, and it never ran out. This symbolizes the nourishing powers of the Mother. It is also said to have had the power to regenerate life so that dead bodies could be placed into the cauldron and drawn out alive and whole again—symbolizing resurrection from the Mother's womb. Knowth was constructed as a mound; the mound itself is another symbol, as it represents the earth as the womb of the Mother. It seems likely that ceremonies symbolizing resurrection were enacted inside the mound of Knowth on the spring equinox, and incorporated the Dagda Cauldron and eastern passage shaped as a cross.

A CEREMONIAL CELTIC CAULDRON FOUND IN GUNDERSTRUP, DENMARK.

The Maize God Hun Hunahpu resurrects from a turtle, known as the tomb of the earth, which is another symbol of the womb. This same enactment is found at the pre-Columbian site of Monks Mound in the United States, where the spring equinox sun appears to rise (or resurrect) from out of a giant mound originally built in the form of a turtle.

The mound, cauldron, tomb, turtle, and waters are all symbols of the womb, which the initiate enters after their death at crucifixion. This is the reabsorption of the Son into the Mother, and it is in the Mother in which both the forces of death and birth are found.

The womb is also the receptacle in which sexual activity takes place. Therefore, the Son's return to the womb also represents the initiate's return to the work of alchemy, to work with the Mother in the processes of inner death and birth—which is the death of the ego, and the creation of the imperishability of the spirit (that which is everlasting). In returning to the womb, the initiate with the Son within works alchemically to transform themselves in order to resurrect. They must destroy their ego states with the help of the Mother and climb up from the center of the earth to its surface to attain resurrection.

SEXUAL SYMBOLS

In the churning of the milky ocean, the ocean represents the Milky Way, but also the sexual waters/energies, which the initiate needs to control so that the spiritual faculties and the elixir of immortality emerge. They must struggle between the pull of sexual desire as the demons on one side, and that of the spirit, symbolized as the devas, on the other. The demons and devas pull back and forth on a giant serpent, which is also a symbol of the sexual energies. Jesus, crucified on a cross, is stretched with his arms across it to a point that is excruciating, signifying the painful struggle between matter and the spirit.

Seth cuts Osiris' body into fourteen pieces, thirteen of which the goddess Isis finds. Thirteen is the symbolic number of death, which represents the inner death of the initiate. The fourteenth piece of Osiris, which is swallowed by a fish, is his phallus, so Isis fashions a phallus of gold. Fourteen is the number of alchemical transmutation, and the gold phallus represents the transformation of the sexual energies into the golden energy of the sun.

A tall stone and round stone at the neolithic temple mound Knowth,
symbolic of the male and female principles and sexual organs.

The Lance of Longinus, which pierced the side of Jesus while he was on the cross, and the Holy Grail used at the last supper and which caught the blood of Jesus from the wound made by the lance, are both sexual symbols. The lance is the male phallus, and the grail the feminine uterus. The wine and blood of Christ are the purified sexual energies. Similar symbols are also found at the Neolithic temple mound Knowth, which incorporated the symbol of the cross at the time of the spring equinox thousands of years before Jesus. Outside the mound is a tall stone beside a short rounded one, representing the masculine and feminine principles.

The Holy Grail became the subject of the esoteric teaching encoded in Arthurian legends, in which the knights of Arthur's round table quested for this sacred relic. In the story, Lancelot is unable to enter the chapel of the grail because he was an adulterer, revealing the sexual purity needed in the spiritual work. It is only Galahad who had the purity required, and upon beholding the grail was made complete and taken up to heaven.

THE ELIXIR OF IMMORTALITY AND THE BODIES OF GOLD

SIR GALAHAD RECEIVING THE HOLY GRAIL.

The Holy Grail, like the symbol of the cauldron of the Neolithic builders of Ireland, is a symbol of the female sexual organs. It is within sex that the wine of the alchemist (our inner energy) is transformed from its impure base state, to the golden solar energies of the spirit.

This transformed sexual energy has been called Amrita and Soma in ancient Hindu texts, and Ambrosia in the Eleusinian mysteries of ancient Greece. It is the "drink of the gods," the elixir of immortality. In the ancient Hindu story of the churning of the milky ocean, this Amrita is produced by the struggle between the demons and devas—which are symbolic of the struggles between the forces of sexual desire on one hand (the bad thief) and the bliss of the spirit (the good thief) on the other. It is in this struggle that the sexual energies are purified.

The demons in the story try to steal the elixir of immortality, symbolizing the bad thief of sexual desire that tries to steal the sexual energies for plea-sure. However, through the help of the god Vishnu, the devas instead gain possession of the elixir. The devas are symbolic of the good thief who takes the sexual energies and uses them to create the imperishable bodies of the spirit. The god Indra who is also present, drinks this elixir, and in doing so, is able to ascend to heaven, just as Galahad did in the presence of the Holy Grail.

The god Indra is symbolic of the initiate with the Son within—he continuously fights Vritra, represented as a dragon that contains the life sustaining treasures of the universe (the waters, light, and cows) which Indra must conquer back, as well as fighting the asuras (demons). This is the fight to rescue consciousness from the darkness of the subconscious (chaos and non-being), which is done in alchemy. Indra symbolically drinks Soma, the purified sexual energies, to give himself the strength he needs in battle—and finally defeats the asuras. This Soma gives him the body of gold he is depicted with.

"In Indra are set fast all forms of golden hue." [17]
  ~ THE RIG VEDA, TRANSLATED BY RALPH T. H. GRIFFITH

In ancient Egypt, the gods are also said to possess the body of gold, which is an imperishable body of the spirit.

"The body of the dead is of gold like that of a god and so it consists
  of imperishable material. 'Rise on your bones of bronze and on your
  limbs of gold, for this body of yours belongs to a god. It does not
  perish. It does not decompose, it does not consume.'" [18]
  ~ THE PYRAMID TEXTS OF QUEEN NEITH, TRANSLATED BY J. ZANDEE

The bodies of gold are formed within by the purified sexual energies and are made of the energy that is the same nature of the sun and stars, which continue as someone's vessels in the higher dimensions, while the physical body dies and decays. These golden bodies are the vehicles used to traverse the higher spiritual realms.

> "Heaven is not the wide blue sky but the place where corporeality is begotten in the house of the Creative. If one keeps this up for a long time there develops quite naturally, in addition to the body, yet another spirit-body." [19]
>
> ~ THE SECRET OF THE GOLDEN FLOWER, TRANSLATED BY RICHARD WILHELM

> "We have drunk Soma and become immortal; we have attained the light, the Gods discovered. Now what may foeman's malice do to harm us? What, O Immortal, mortal man's deception?" [20]
>
> ~ THE RIG VEDA, TRANSLATED BY RALPH T. H. GRIFFITH

Krishna with a golden halo and standing by white cows, symbol of the eternal Mother who works with the initiate to create the golden bodies.

THE DESCENT INTO HELL

The return to the womb is also to enter into the primordial chaos, into darkness, and the underworld. During the three symbolic days he spends dead in a tomb, Jesus descends into hell.

"For as Jonah was three days and three nights in the belly of a huge fish, so the Son of Man will be three days and three nights in the heart of the earth." [21]

~ JESUS IN THE GOSPEL ACCORDING TO MATTHEW 12:40

After Odin's self-sacrifice on the world tree, he then descends into the underworld to drink from the well at its root. Balder also descends to the underworld after his betrayal and death. This is the descent into hellish psychological regions in which someone faces the sufferings like those found in hell itself, and works with their spiritual Mother in the inner death of their egos; it is the force of the spiritual Son within that also works within the initiate to save them by descending into their psychological underworld to fight their egos.

JESUS ENTERS THE UNDERWORLD TO DO BATTLE WITH THE EGOS WITHIN THE SUBCONSCIOUS.

The east-west axis of the temple of Angkor Wat is offset to give a three day anticipation of the spring equinox, which correlates with the three day time preceding the resurrection in which the nights still have dominion over the days.

Numerous sacred teachings throughout the world speak of an underworld. It is the place where those who have not attained immortality undergo the process of the death and decay of their own psychological defects, the egos.

To the ancient Egyptians it was the place of the evil dead called the Place of Annihilation. To the Maya it was Xibalba, meaning Place of Fright. The Hindus and Buddhists call it Naraka. To the Norse it was Hel. In Christianity it is Hell, and in Greek mythology it is Hades, etc. In ancient Egypt the underworld was entered through the jaws of the goddess Ammit, and to the Norse hell was overseen by a queen called Urd. This is symbolic of the Mother who destroys the egos of the dead. Either the Mother works with us in the underworld to destroy our egos during life, or the Mother destroys them in the underworld as we suffer the consequences of our egos after death.

After the Passion and crucifixion, someone descends into the hellish regions of their own psyche, and then needs to work to rise back out in order to resurrect. This descent is into the darkness of the subconscious, as the light of consciousness is trapped within the darkness of the egos and can only be freed through their disintegration.

This is illustrated in the Assyrian story of the death of the solar god Tammuz. After his death, it is the Mother goddess Ishtar who went on a quest to recover the sacred elixir that could restore him back to life. To do so, she had to descend into hell. The guardians of hell stated that she must descend as all lost souls do, which is to give up something at each gate of every descending layer of hell. Ishtar firstly gives up her crown, then her earrings, her necklace, etc., until finally she stands naked before the Queen of Hell who then imprisons her and subjects her to all manner of disease. This symbolizes the descent of the initiate who is increasingly stripped of their faculties, inner strength, possessions, etc., and upon losing each, goes through the particular psychological torment of that region of hell in their own psyche. The work in hell is with the Mother goddess, as the chaos is her womb, and she is the one who has the power to destroy the egos and grant eternal life.

While Ishtar is in hell, the world falls into chaos, as it is she that gives life to the natural world; likewise, while the spiritual Son as the world teacher is tormented and suffers in the womb of the Mother, the sacred spiritual work falls into chaos in the world. Upon seeing this, the gods intervene and pour the waters of life over Ishtar who is healed and then begins her ascent back out of hell—regaining each of her formerly lost powers one by one.

The temple of the grand jaguar in Tikal has nine terraces to its pyramid, which the rising spring equinox sun ascends to crown the pinnacle. As a symbol, the jaguar was considered the night sun—the form the sun takes in its journey through the underworld, so this site may also symbolize the ascent of the Son (as the jaguar and sun) from out of the nine layers of the underworld to resurrect.

The number nine is also symbolic of the ninth sphere, which is the work of sexual alchemy. It is also through the work in alchemy, the work of inner death and birth, that one ascends. The ascent out of the underworld in order to resurrect is a long and difficult climb.

In the mystery schools of Odin, an initiate had to pass through nine chambers in which they were subjected to various trials before being called "resurrected." In Odin's act of self-sacrifice he hangs on a tree for "nine long nights." Jesus was crucified at nine in the morning and darkness covered the land until "the ninth hour." This is symbolic of the trials an initiate goes through psychologically in the nine regions of hell and their corresponding regions in the subconscious, in order to resurrect.

RESURRECTION

Anubis resurrecting the initiate in the presence of the goddesses Isis and Nephthys. Mother goddesses pour the waters of life onto the body to restore it.

Resurrection is the attainment of eternal life, immortality, and imperishability mentioned in many ancient texts and celebrated at the time of the spring equinox.

Life and creation originally sprang from the womb of the great Mother of the universe as described in creation stories throughout the ancient world. That which is eternal is that which never dies—and only that which is never born does not die. In creation myths a divine androgynous being emerges from the great unmanifest and unknowable source. This being divides into male and female in order to create and gives birth to a Son, and the rest of creation.

The Mother goddess is one half of the eternal first being, and therefore is not born of any. When the Son returns to and becomes one with the Mother, the Son becomes immortal, thus resurrecting and attaining eternal life.

> "He called out, saying: 'Whoever has ears to hear about the infinities, let him hear!'; and 'I have addressed those who are awake.' Still he continued and said: 'Everything that came from the perishable will perish, since it came from the perishable. But whatever came from imperishableness does not perish but becomes imperishable.'" [22]
>
> ~ JESUS IN THE WISDOM OF JESUS CHRIST, TRANSLATED BY DOUGLAS M. PARROTT

In the story of Osiris, it is Isis who goes on a quest to bring all the different parts of his dismembered body back together, and bring him back to life. Likewise Ishtar goes on a quest to bring Tammuz back to life by fetching the waters of life. It is the Mother goddess who has power over life and death. If the initiate is able to pass through the death of the egos and fulfill her laws, then the Son is absorbed into the Mother and someone becomes a serpent of light.

> "I tell you truly, the Book of Nature is a Holy Scroll, and if you would have the Sons of Men save themselves and find everlasting life, teach them how once again to read from the living pages of the Earthly Mother. For in everything that is life is the law written. It is written in the grass, in the trees, in rivers, mountains, birds of the sky and fishes of the sea; and most of all within the Son of Man. Only when he returns to the bosom of his Earthly Mother will he find everlasting life and the Stream of Life which leads to his Heavenly Father; only then may the dark vision of the future come not to pass." [23]
>
> ~ JESUS IN THE ESSENE GOSPEL OF PEACE, TRANSLATED BY EDMOND BORDEAUX SZEKELY

To achieve full self-realization someone must return to the source of creation, the Absolute, where all is one. To do that the different parts of the Being that were divided in creation need to unite to form one whole, as it is not possible to enter the Absolute divided. Now the Son has become one with the Mother, the Mother must now return to the Father, so that the consciousness of the individual is completely whole again as one.

> "For truly, no one can reach the Heavenly Father unless through the Earthly Mother." [24]
>
> ~ JESUS IN THE ESSENE GOSPEL OF PEACE, TRANSLATED BY EDMOND BORDEAUX SZEKELY

While the evil of the world celebrated the death of the Son, as Jesus, Osiris, Balder, etc., it is the Son who truly triumphs in the defeat of darkness within a person and in his resurrection, symbolized by the rising of the spring equinox sun. Although the Passion and death of the Son is a tale of human tragedy, the darkness of death and winter has its role in the cycles of life in the universe and on the path of the spiritual sun—and that darkness is overcome by light at the spring equinox and the spiritual resurrection of the individual.

The work from here is to now return to the great Father, known as the ascension and symbolized at the summer solstice.

The resurrected Osiris under the protection
of the great Mother goddess Isis.

"To say: It is beautiful to see, it is peaceful to hear that Osiris stands at the door of the gods.

Thy sanctuary, King, is to thee as a heart of secret places; it opens for thee the double doors of heaven, it opens for thee the double doors of the way; it makes for thee a way, that thou mayest enter there among the gods, that thou mayest live as thy soul.

O King, thou art not like the dead, who art dead, thou art living, thou art alive, together with them, the spirits, the imperishable stars." [25]

~ THE PYRAMID TEXTS, UTTERANCE 667, TRANSLATED BY SAMUEL A. B. MERCER

CHAPTER FIVE

Decoding the Ancient Meaning of the Sphinx and Its Origin as Anubis

THE MEANING OF THE GREAT SPHINX and Pyramids at Giza, Egypt, has eluded the many attempts to understand it using archeology alone. The people who built the Giza site were obviously deeply interested in spirituality. The culture that followed in ancient Egypt, perhaps more than any other, used the intuitive language of symbolism to convey profound spiritual truths—those who had enough inner wisdom could speak this language, while those who did not were rendered incapable of deciphering it. This is why the site at Giza has remained a mystery to most, even though it is one of the most studied sites in the world.

To discover the meaning of the Giza site requires a knowledge of the meaning of the spiritual symbols used in its design. The spiritual knowledge which the builders of the Great Pyramids and Sphinx possessed is timeless, and thus it is possible to unlock this site's meaning through the understanding of this same universal knowledge today, which has found its expression in different forms and cultures in ancient history.

An artist's impression of what the Great Pyramids and Sphinx of Giza may have looked like when they were originally built. Note that the water surrounding the Sphinx actually formed a sacred lake that would have submerged half of its body.

The enigmatic and mysterious Sphinx, great centerpiece to this site's design, holds much of the answer. In this chapter, we will go back as far as possible into the origins of the Sphinx to explore its meaning, using the understanding of the spiritual knowledge of the ancient builders, which we can decipher from their legacy.

THE SPHINX AS ANUBIS

The Great Sphinx being excavated, starting in AD 1817. Its paws are already covered in restoration stones from Roman times and its head is obviously too small in relation to the size of the body, indicating it was re-carved at least once.

To understand the meaning of the Sphinx, we need to firstly uncover its original form, as the form it takes today is the result of multiple restorations dating from at least 1,400 BC.

Anyone who studies photos of the Sphinx can see that it is out of proportion. Its head is much too small for its body, and is far less weathered than the rest of the body and surrounding enclosure. Its head has obviously been re-carved, perhaps numerous times, and its body has been covered with restoration stones dating from thousands of years ago right up until today, giving the Sphinx its leonine shape while masking its original form. So to find the clues as to what it originally was, we have to look further than the Sphinx alone.

A study of the archeology, astronomy, and esoteric messages contained in the structures, objects, and art of the Giza Plateau and Sphinx, point to the Sphinx originally being sculpted as the ancient wolf (previously thought to be a jackal) deity Anubis, facilitator of the process from death to resurrection, agent of cosmic law, and gatekeeper of the passage to immortality.

The Pyramid Texts, carved into the stone walls of the pyramids at Saqqara in Egypt, date from around 2,400 BC and are currently the oldest dated sacred texts in the world. They contain the earliest references to the Great Sphinx and Pyramids of Egypt, and indicate that the Great Sphinx once took the form of the Egyptian god Anubis.

In ancient times the site of the Great Pyramids, where the Sphinx lies, was called Ro-Setawe, the Sacred Land and the Necropolis, and the Pyramid Texts refer to Anubis as "Lord of Ro-Setawe," "Anubis who presides over the Sacred Land" (and also Pure Land, and Secluded Land), and "he at the Head of the Necropolis," which are all ancient references to Anubis standing guard over the site of the Great Pyramids.[1] This may not have been just a metaphysical reference, but a very physical one, as the Sphinx does indeed stand at the entrance to the site of the Great Pyramids.

In ancient times, the Giza site would have been entered by boat as the river Nile reached right up to the Sphinx. Boat quays were discovered protruding from the Valley Temple beside the Sphinx (which was built out of the stones excavated from around the Sphinx when it was first created). Anyone who entered the Giza site had to pass by the Sphinx by arriving via boat and passing by the great statue along a grand causeway leading to the Pyramids.

Modern researchers Robert and Olivia Temple have uncovered the archeological evidence for the Sphinx being Anubis in great detail in their book *The Sphinx Mystery*, but not only does the archeological evidence point to Anubis being the original form of the Great Sphinx, it also ties in with the same kind of spiritual knowledge that is universally represented throughout cultures around the world and in the most ancient sacred texts of Egypt.

Although recognized by millions, the Sphinx has remained an enigma; but by knowing its original form and understanding the principles of esoteric knowledge, its symbolism may be understood and its message decoded.

Aligned to precise cosmic events, lying atop of hidden chambers, surrounded by a sacred lake, and part of an incredible master plan that incorporates the Great Pyramids using advanced geometry, the Sphinx is a monument of magnificent wisdom and scale that symbolizes the attainment of imperishability through resurrection.

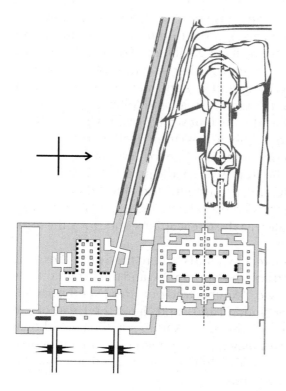

This diagram shows the Sphinx from above. Directly in front of it is the Sphinx Temple, and to its right is the Valley Temple, which has two quays protruding from it (the ones with the spikes protruding left and right) which would have brought people into the Giza site by boat and formed the entrance to the entire Giza plateau. A causeway leads from the Valley Temple (offset at 14° due east) past the Sphinx. The waters of the river Nile would have also reached into the area around the Sphinx, creating a sacred lake. The area around the Sphinx was dug out to create the lake, and the giant blocks excavated used to build the Sphinx and Valley Temples.

In this photo the restoration block-work on the body of the Sphinx can be seen clearly, in multiple layers, revealing beneath it a very weathered original stone. Concrete has been used to fill in the headdress as well as deep rivets in the body. Horizontal signs of weathering can be seen on the wall behind the Sphinx that would have enclosed a lake.

The Great Sphinx aligns to the spring equinox, a time of spiritual resurrection as found in the design of many other ancient sites throughout the world also aligned to this solar event. One of the central spiritual teachings of Egypt is the life of Osiris, which reveals the process of attaining enlightenment—or imperishability as it is called in Egyptian texts. Like Jesus, Osiris is killed and is then resurrected. It is the god Anubis who resurrects Osiris, and who thus formed a central symbolic part of the design of the Giza Plateau and the statue dedicated to this momentous spiritual event.

RESURRECTION

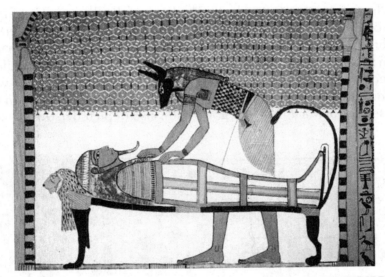

ANUBIS ATTENDING THE INITIATE WHO LIES SYMBOLICALLY DEAD, TO RESURRECT THEM.

In the sacred teachings of ancient Egypt, a person had to undergo a defined spiritual process to pass from mortality to immortality, which led from death to resurrection. Resurrection as a spiritual process can be found in ancient sacred teachings throughout the world and is associated with the time of the spring equinox—the most dominant solar alignment of the Giza Plateau, which the Sphinx gazes precisely toward.

Resurrection was central to the life of the Egyptian god Osiris, just as it was in the lives of Jesus, Tammuz, Dionysus, Attis, Mithras, the Maize God Hun Hunahpu of the Maya, etc., who all resurrected at the time of the spring equinox. The lives of these deities, although appearing in different cultures and times, symbolized the same universal spiritual process also symbolized by the Great Sphinx of Egypt, one of the most ancient and mysterious sacred sites in the world. Each of these deities showed the events and processes involved in reaching enlightenment, which is why they contain so many similarities.

THE GOD ANUBIS

Resurrection is always preceded by death—both Jesus and Osiris were betrayed and killed before they were brought back to life to live eternally. In Egypt, Anubis has a central role in death and resurrection. In the life of Osiris, Anubis resurrects Osiris after he is betrayed and killed by his evil brother Seth.

Anpu (Anubis in Greek) is one of the most ancient gods of Egypt—the record of his veneration pre-dates that even of Osiris. Anubis was depicted as a black recumbent African wolf, or as a man with the head of a wolf, and presiding over the process of death. The wolf head is a sacred headdress Anubis wears in his role in the spiritual realms.

In Egypt, Anubis most famously appears in the scene of the weighing of the heart, illustrating events after death. The heart of the deceased is weighed by Anubis on the scales of divine law (called Maat, which is cosmic order) against a feather to determine how they lived their life, and based on that, what would happen to them next. The following illustration is of Anubis in his role as the head judge of divine law and justice, which he administers along with the other forty-two judges of the divine law, known in ancient Egyptian texts as "The Assessors of Maat," and the god Thoth, also depicted in this scene.

The god Anubis weighs the heart of the dead in the presence of the god Thoth and the forty-two judges of karma, before Osiris who after his resurrection, becomes judge of the dead. This signifies how the initiate (Osiris) achieves becoming a judge through fulfilling all divine laws, and is no longer judged by Anubis, head of the divine law.

ANUBIS AND INNER DEATH

Anubis not only has a role in receiving the dead and judging them, but also in the esoteric process of inner death. Resurrection is always preceded by death, but this death is not a physical one—it is an inner one which takes place as part of a spiritual work. It involves the death of all that is evil, inferior, and dark within oneself, such as hatred, anger, jealousy, lust, etc., in a process of psychological and energetic purification.

In Egypt this turned into a religious belief (as it has happened in other religions) misinterpreted by later generations of people who had lost the ability to understand the esoteric meaning of Egypt's sacred texts. Pharaohs believed instead that their physical death would lead to physical resurrection in the afterlife, and surrounded themselves with jewels and spells that would apparently assure them safe passage in the journey to reach immortality. However, the death of resurrection is an inner one and is achieved in life through a spiritual and alchemical work, and the Great Sphinx and the life of Osiris, along with the life of many other deities, symbolizes how it takes place.

Ro-Setawe and the Necropolis are ancient names for the site of the Great Pyramids and the Sphinx, and Necropolis is a term which means graveyard. In ancient Egyptian texts Anubis was referred to as the Lord of Ro-Setawe, Anubis who presides over the Sacred Land, and Head of the Necropolis. These are all references to Anubis, the god of death, presiding over the Giza Plateau, which was known as the place of the dead.

The reference to the site of Giza being the place of the dead is not a reference to it being an actual graveyard (although the inhabitants of the site later interpreted it this way), but as a place of those who achieve an inner, psychological death. This finds its parallel in the "Place of Skull" where Jesus was crucified, and the "Avenue of the Dead" at the Pyramids of Teotihuacán in Mexico where it is said "men become Gods"—a site which also shares other similarities with the Pyramids of Giza. Little wonder that Anubis, the god with a central role in death and resurrection, stood guard over the site of Giza, dedicated to the spiritual process of attaining imperishability, in which inner death and resurrection were essential.

Anubis in his recumbent form lying atop a coffin. This statue was found among the treasures inside the tomb of Tutankhamun.

Anubis was also known as the "Master of Secrets," and was often depicted as an African wolf recumbent on a coffin, which was said to contain sacred secrets. Indeed, the Great Sphinx does stand guard over incredible secrets, as beneath it lies nine chambers, each containing an unknown metal object.

THE NINE LAYERS OF THE UNDERWORLD

A team of researchers discovered that nine underground chambers lie beneath the Great Sphinx. These symbolize the nine layers of the underworld, which are also found symbolized in other ancient sites around the world, such as the nine terraces of the pyramid of Chichen Itza in Mexico. The Maya and Norse assigned nine levels to hell, just as Dante did in his Divine Comedy.

These chambers beneath the Sphinx represent the layers of the underworld which someone enters at death preceding resurrection, which is why Osiris is cast into the underworld after being killed by Seth, and Jesus descends into hell after his crucifixion. This hell is one experienced internally, where someone suffers hellish psychological states, and must achieve the death of these states in order to surface back from out of the underworld and resurrect, which is why in the quote below Osiris is said to be "weary of the Nine" that he suffered, but now has "no more time there" in the underworld.

> "He comes indeed, Osiris, weary of the Nine, an Imperishable spirit, he that bore more than you, he that suffered more than you, he that is more weary than you, he that became greater than you, he who will be happier than you, he who roars louder than you. You have no more time there!" [2]
>
> ~ THE PYRAMID TEXTS, UTTERANCE 218, BASED ON TRANSLATIONS BY FAULKNER, PIANKOFF, AND SPELEER

Descending into the nine layers also represents the work in what is called "the ninth sphere" which is to work in the practice of sexual alchemy, in the womb of the earth, which is the chaos and crucible of creation, to both destroy psychological states and to create immortal/imperishable spiritual parts within.

THE TOMB

In the life of Jesus, Joseph of Arimathea wraps the body of the crucified Jesus in linen before he places it in a tomb, just as in the life of Osiris, Anubis conceals Osiris' body in a tomb. The two Marys bring spices and perfumes to anoint the body of Jesus, just as Isis and Nephthys do to Osiris.

> "The secret ways of Ro-Setawe [the ancient site of Giza], The gate of the gods. Only one whose voice is heard May pass them... The secret

way to which (only) Anubis has access In order to conceal the body of Osiris." [3]

~ THE BOOK OF THE ONE IN THE NETHERWORLD, FROM THE BOOK JACKAL AT THE SHAMAN'S GATE BY TERENCE DUQUESNE

It is in the stone tomb (symbol of the womb of the great Mother), which in Egypt was built into chambers of the pyramids, where the initiate, lying in the stone sarcophagus, is concealed and attended to by Anubis and resurrects, to emerge from the tomb as an immortal spiritual being.

These tombs were never designed for deceased bodies, but were used for initiatory rites to symbolize the process of inner death. This is why the stone sarcophaguses in the chambers of the Great Pyramids were found empty, and a stone sarcophagus surrounded by water has been discovered in underground tunnels beneath the Giza Plateau.

THE SACRED LAKE OF ANUBIS

Through the research of Robert and Olivia Temple, it has been revealed that the statue of Anubis as the Great Sphinx was once surrounded by a sacred lake—in ancient texts it was referred to as the Jackal Lake, Lake of Fire, Lake of Dawn, Canal of the God, Canal of Anubis, Winding Waterway, Lake of Cool Water, Lake of the Netherworld, and Lake of Life.[4] The recumbent body of Anubis would have been submerged beneath water, which was done for a symbolic reason.

"O King, your shape is hidden like that of Anubis on his belly; receive your jackal-face and raise yourself, stand up." [5]

~ THE PYRAMID TEXTS, UTTERANCE 677 TRANSLATED BY R. O. FAULKNER

Looking at a topographical map of the Giza Plateau, the Sphinx can be seen as set down in an area where the waters of the river Nile would have reached in ancient times during the annual inundation of the Nile to fill the Sphinx enclosure. The vertical signs of weathering (caused by rainfall pouring down) on the Sphinx and its surrounding enclosure, are accompanied by horizontal weathering (caused by water moving side to side). Strange markings around the Sphinx enclosure may have been the location of sluice gates that retained water around the Sphinx to hold the water of the lake.[6]

A channel is also carved along the causeway that leads to the Sphinx. It empties into the Sphinx enclosure, and would have collected rain water runoff from the Giza Plateau to fill the lake.[7] There are also quays protruding from the Valley Temple (which is located next to the Sphinx), so that the Sphinx and Giza area could have been approached by boat.

PURIFICATION OF THE SEXUAL WATERS AND THE FOUR BODIES

The lake around the Great Sphinx was a symbol of the sexual waters/energies, which are purified alchemically in the spiritual work, and used to create the imperishable bodies of gold, which are the vessels of the consciousness in the different dimensions. It is the feminine aspect of someone's higher Being that works within the sexual energies, and is sometimes symbolized as Isis and also as a serpent (the kundalini).

> "O King, your sister the Celestial Serpent has cleansed you upon the causeway in the meadow, you having appeared to them as a jackal... May you govern the spirits, may you control the Imperishable Stars." [8]
>
> ~ THE PYRAMID TEXTS, UTTERANCE 690, FROM THE BOOK JACKAL AT THE SHAMAN'S GATE BY TERENCE DUQUESNE

The extract above refers to the alchemical cleansing of the initiate in the sacred lake of Anubis, which surrounded the Sphinx. The causeway referred to runs from the Sphinx to the second largest of the Great Pyramids, and is described as being in a meadow as in ancient times the Giza Plateau was a green and fertile place.

These are a complete set of four canopic jars, which were used by the Egyptians in the process of mummification and preparation for the afterlife. Each jar held a different organ, and each was guarded by a different god, which also corresponded to the four cardinal directions. Esoterically, these four jars represent the four bodies, which are physical, vital, astral, and mental.

In the Pyramid Texts, the initiate is cleansed in the lake surrounding the Sphinx in which four gods and four jars are involved. This symbolizes the four bodies that are cleansed and purified alchemically: they are the physical, vital, astral, and mental bodies. These bodies need cleansing because they are the bodies through which the egos (inferior psychological states) manifest, and the sexual energies permeate. In the process of cleansing, the egos are destroyed and the sexual energies purified.

> "I travel the Winding Waterway . . . because I am pure, the son of a pure one, and I am purified with these four nemeset-jars of mine which are filled to the brim from the Canal of the God in Iseion [sanctuary of Isis], which possesses the breath of Isis the Great, and Isis the Great dries me as Horus. 'Let him come, for he is pure:' so says the priest of Rē concerning me to the door-keeper of the firmament, and he announces me to those four gods who are upon the Canal of Kenzet [Land Beyond]."9
>
> ~ THE PYRAMID TEXTS, UTTERANCE 510, TRANSLATED BY R. O. FAULKNER

Anubis carries out the process of mummification. Notice the four jars beneath the table, which represent the four bodies that are purified alchemically.

This lake in which the symbolic cleansing takes place is referred to as the Lake of the Netherworld because the lake is a symbol of the sexual energies/ waters within the human being, and these energies permeate through the netherworld region of our subconscious. Our egos exist in this subconscious netherworld and are created from sexual energies (which are the fundamental creative energies within us). The underworld is a real place which we are intimately connected to through our psyche. Being cleansed in the Lake of the Netherworld (also known as Jackal Lake) is to purify the sexual energies/ the waters from the egos through sexual alchemy.

Here the link between Anubis and the god Mercury, with whom he later became associated, becomes clear, since the region of the dead, the netherworld which both Anubis and Mercury guide the initiate through, is the place in which the process of alchemical purification needs to take place preceding resurrection. The caduceus of Mercury, which the god Hermanubis also holds, is an alchemical symbol.

> "My father has remade his heart, the other having been removed for him because it objected to his ascending to the sky when he had waded in the waters of the Winding Waterway. Anubis comes and meets you! And Geb gives you his hand, O my father, (even) he who guards the earth and rules the spirits. I weep deeply, O my father. Oho! Raise yourself, my father, receive these your four pleasant nemeset jars; bathe in the Jackal Lake, be cleansed in the Lake of the Netherworld, be purified. . . . Run your course, row over your waterway like Rē [the sun god] on the banks of the sky. O my father, raise yourself, go in your spirit-state." [10]
>
> ~ THE PYRAMID TEXTS, UTTERANCE 512, TRANSLATED BY R. O. FAULKNER

In Egypt, Horus was the Son in the divine triad of Father, Mother, and Son, just as Jesus was in Christianity, Quetzalcoatl was to the Maya and Aztecs, Viracocha to the Incas, Mithras was in Persia and Rome, etc. As well as Anubis, Horus was also said to resurrect Osiris, as it is the Son within which resurrects in the initiate and purifies them. In the passage below, the Son purifies the internal bodies and energies of the initiate in the lake of Anubis.

> "Horus takes him to his side, he purifies Osiris [the initiate] in the Jackal-lake, he cleans the ka of Osiris in the Lake of Dawn, he rubs down the flesh of the Ka of Osiris as well as his own, with that which is at Re's side in the Akhet-horizon, with what he (Re) receives when the Two Lands (Egypt) are lighted and he opens the face of the gods." [11]
>
> ~ THE PYRAMID TEXTS, UTTERANCE 268, BASED ON TRANSLATIONS BY FAULKNER, PIANKOFF, AND SPELEER

RETURN TO THE WOMB

The sacred lake was also a symbol of the primordial waters, the womb of the eternal Mother, to which the Son (the initiate with the spiritual Son within) must return in order to pass beyond death and rebirth. All that is born dies, and so to achieve immortality the Son must go back to the origin of life and death, and merge with the Mother (who is not born and thus does not die), by returning to the womb of creation. From there the initiate ascends to become one with the eternal Father. This is a going back to the first instance of creation and a return to wholeness in which the Father, Mother, and Son become one; in Egypt, this complete state of being was symbolized by the god Atum.

A Helium Atom

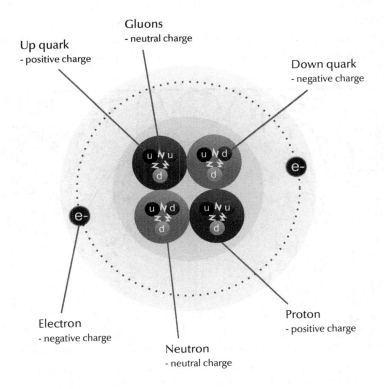

A diagram of an atom which illustrates the three primary forces of creation, as positive (protons), negative (electrons), and neutral (neutrons), which have been symbolized as a spiritual Trinity in sacred teachings as Father, Mother, and Son.

The name Atum is very similar to the word "atom," the basic unit of creation which contains the three primary forces of creation. These manifest as subatomic particles called protons, the positive force of creation (the Father); electrons, the negative force in creation (the Mother); and neutrons, the neutral force in creation (the Son). Subatomic particles themselves are made up of even smaller elementary particles called "up quarks" (which are positively charged), "down quarks" (negatively charged), and "gluons" (the neutral force that binds these quarks together), revealing the same three primary forces that create an atom, but at an even smaller scale. This is an example of the fractal nature of the universe.

Ancient Egyptian texts stated that Atum permeates all of creation. He was the name of the first god that came into existence. He was self-engendered, and from him all other gods came into being. His name is interpreted as meaning "complete one," "lord of totality," "finisher of the world," "the Being of the Being," and "the Great He-She." Atum symbolizes the Monad, the Being that emerged from the source before it divides into different parts and goes into the different dimensions. The spiritual work is to merge the different parts of one's Being together as a complete whole again, which is a return to the state Atum symbolizes—a state of oneness and completion, but with full consciousness and knowledge gained from the experience of life in matter.

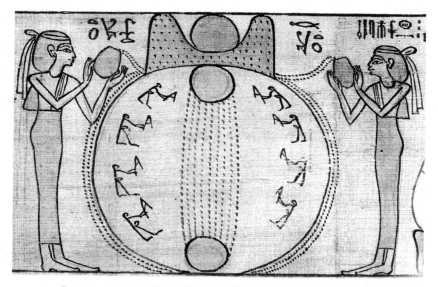

Egyptian painting of the first sunrise at the dawning of creation from the primeval mound that arose from out of the waters.

In Egypt, the process of creation is said to have begun when the god Atum emerged as a mound from out of the primordial waters. Similarly, creation emerges from the primordial waters in the ancient Vedas of the Hindus and in the legends of the Incas. These primordial waters are those of the eternal feminine womb, which gives birth to all of creation. It is following this same process in reverse through which we return to the spirit who conceived us. At death, Osiris is said to return to the heart of Atum, and Atum is said to return all living beings and creation back into the primordial waters from which it came. In this nonexistence, it is said that Atum and Osiris will survive in the form of serpents; when all else passes, only those who resurrect and reach the state of imperishability as Atum will remain. Those who don't awaken are submerged back into the ocean of nonexistence at the end of the great cycle of their lives.

"Osiris: But how long shall I live?

Atum: You will live more than millions of years, an era of millions, but in the end I will destroy everything that I have created, the earth will become again part of the Primeval Ocean, like the Abyss of waters in their original state. Then I will be what will remain, just I and Osiris, when I will have changed myself back into the Old Serpent who knew no man and saw no god. How fair is that which I have done for Osiris, a fate different from that of all the other gods. I have given him the region of the dead while I have put his son Horus as heir upon his throne in the Isle of Fire, I have thus made his place for him in the Boat of Millions of Years, in that Horus remains on his throne to carry on his work." [12]

~ THE BOOK OF THE DEAD, CHAPTER 175, THE CHAPTER OF NOT DYING A SECOND TIME, TRANSLATED BY R. T. RUNDLE CLARK

With its body set down in the lake, the Sphinx would have appeared as a mound, just like the one that emerged from the primordial waters at the beginning of creation, which is why its body is referred to as Atum in the Pyramid Texts.

"Thine arm is like that of Atum; thy shoulders are like those of Atum; thy body is like that of Atum; thy back is like that of Atum; thy seat is like that of Atum; thy legs are like those of Atum; thy face is like that of Anubis." [13]

~ THE PYRAMID TEXTS, UTTERANCE 213, TRANSLATED BY SAMUEL A. B. MERCER

The Sphinx therefore symbolizes the return to a complete and imperishable state of being, in which the Son, Mother, and Father unite to become Atum. Atum is said to be a god of post-existence and pre-existence, being that which is both before and after existence. Those who resurrect (becoming one with the great Mother), and later ascend (becoming one with the great Father), conquer back their state of wholeness as Atum, being beyond birth and death, as one who is eternal.

"You make yourself free of what should be washed away for Atum in [Heliopolis, and you go down] with him. You judge the wants in the Netherworld and stand (as king) over the places of the primeval ocean. You come into being with your father Atum, you are high with your father Atum, you rise with your father Atum. The wants (of the Netherworld) are severed from you, your head (is held) by the nurse of Heliopolis [the city of the sun]."

"You have power over your body, there is no one to oppose you. You are born because of Horus (in you), you are conceived because of

Seth (in you). You have purified yourself in the Hawk nome (Third Nome of Lower Egypt), you have received your purification in the Uninjured-Ruler nome (Thirteenth of Lower Egypt) before your father, before Atum."

"You have come into being, you have become high, you have become a spirit! Cool it is for you in the embrace of your father, in the embrace of Atum."

"Atum! Elevate to you Osiris, enfold him in your embrace! This is your son of your body, eternally." [14]

~ THE PYRAMID TEXTS, UTTERANCE 222, BASED ON TRANSLATIONS BY FAULKNER, PIANKOFF, AND SPELEER

OVERCOMING THE LAW

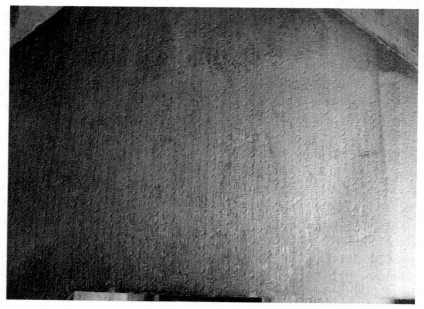

An example of the hauntingly beautiful walls inside the pyramid of Teti I in Saqqara. They are inscribed with a version of the Pyramid Texts—containing esoteric knowledge from a far more ancient time.

As head of the divine law, Anubis stands as gatekeeper between the realm of earthly mortality and spiritual imperishability, letting only those who meet the spiritual requirements pass. On the Giza Plateau as the original form of the Sphinx, Anubis stood at the mystical gateway between the earthly and eternal realm, found in the moment of transition between winter and spring on the dawning of the spring equinox.

"The earth speaks: The doors of the earth-god are opened for you, the doors of Geb are thrown open for you, you come forth at the voice of Anubis, he makes a spirit of you." [15]

~ THE PYRAMID TEXTS, UTTERANCE 437, TRANSLATED BY R. O. FAULKNER

"Anubis, the counter of hearts, deducts Osiris from the gods who belong to the earth, (and assigns him) to the gods who are in heaven." [16]

~ THE PYRAMID TEXTS, UTTERANCE 577, TRANSLATED BY SAMUEL A. B. MERCER

As someone progresses in the work to awakening, they fulfill and thus overcome the different cosmic laws that are upon them and the world, administered by Anubis. The whole of nature and creation is ordered and exists under laws, which govern the way things grow, move, etc., and are studied in physics, biology, genetics, geology, and many other sciences. It is said that in the beginning, Atum first created "life" and "order" and that they were not separate; this order is the laws that are intrinsic to life. However, there are not just laws that govern the physical and natural world, but also those that govern the matters of other dimensions, which include energetic, psychological, and spiritual principles. These laws include those that apply to human interaction, behavior, and spiritual development.

At the stage just preceding resurrection, there are only three laws remaining, which correspond to the three universal principles of creation, which are Father, Mother, and Son. When someone resurrects, the Mother and Son become one. From here is the ascension where someone then becomes one with the Father, and is when the male and female aspects of the being are made whole again. This is a going back to the first instance of creation and the original unified being Atum, which exists under only one law and is therefore no longer under the rule of Anubis. In order to reach this, the initiate must pay all their karma and fulfill all divine laws to pass beyond the laws which Anubis administers.

In the Coffin Texts, the initiate states "I have come . . . to enter the secret gateway By which Anubis is initiated. I have come to Ro-Setawe [name of the Giza Plateau in ancient Egypt] In order to know the Mysteries of the Netherworld into which Anubis is initiated." And also, "I have come in order to enter the gateway that is protected by Anubis." [17]

Anubis is the one who must be satisfied that the initiate has fulfilled everything they need to in terms of the law, before releasing them to become as the Pyramid Texts state, one who is no longer judged, but who fulfills and judges the law themselves.

"Atum, this your son is here, Osiris, whom you have preserved alive.
He lives! He lives! Osiris lives! He is not dead, Osiris is not dead!

He is not gone down, Osiris is not gone down! He has not been judged, Osiris has not been judged! He judges, Osiris judges!" [18]

~ THE PYRAMID TEXTS, UTTERANCE 219, BASED ON TRANSLATIONS BY FAULKNER, PIANKOFF, AND SPELEER

"Horus, hurry! Announce to the gods of the East and their spirits: He comes indeed, Osiris, an Imperishable Spirit! Whom he wills that he live, he lives. Whom he will that he die, he dies." [19]

~ THE PYRAMID TEXTS, UTTERANCE 217, BASED ON TRANSLATIONS BY FAULKNER, PIANKOFF, AND SPELEER

"... Osiris comes indeed, weary of the Nine, an Imperishable Spirit, to reckon hearts, to take kas, to grant kas. His every appointment obliges one (to do his duty), him who he has elevated, and him who applied to him." [20]

~ THE PYRAMID TEXTS, UTTERANCE 218, BASED ON TRANSLATIONS BY FAULKNER, PIANKOFF, AND SPELEER

After his resurrection, Osiris becomes the judge of the dead, just as Anubis had been. The initiate receives their jackal face, which is to achieve the state of existing under the one law of heaven (which is love).

"O King, your shape is hidden like that of Anubis on his belly; receive your jackal-face and raise yourself, stand up." [21]

~ THE PYRAMID TEXTS, UTTERANCE 677, TRANSLATED BY R. O. FAULKNER

THE ASTRONOMICAL ALIGNMENTS OF THE SPHINX

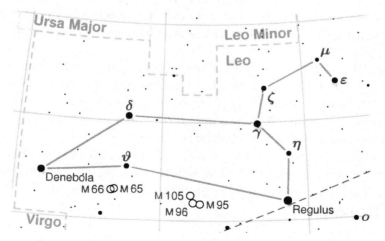

A diagram outlining the constellation of what we now know as Leo.
Regulus, the king star, is the largest in the constellation, and sits at the heart.

THE SPRING EQUINOX

Today, the Sphinx still gazes due east, precisely aligned to the rising sun on the spring equinox—a time intimately connected to resurrection not only in Egypt, but in spiritual teachings throughout the world. Jesus, Tammuz, Dionysus, Attis, Mithras, and many others were resurrected at this time of year. The spring equinox is when the days first begin to grow longer than the nights, and thus life emerges from the death of winter. In its deeper spiritual meaning, the sun, cosmic symbol of the Christ/the Son, rises to overpower darkness.

THE CONSTELLATION OF LEO

Between approximately 10,970 and 8,810 BC (although some have given dates thousands of years earlier) the Sphinx would have also gazed directly at the constellation of what we now call Leo, which rose just before dawn on the spring equinox due to the precession of the equinoxes. The constellation of Leo is depicted as a recumbent lion, which matches the form of the Sphinx.

LEO AS A DOG, NOT A LION

The first record of the constellation of Leo appears in 1,530 BC in Babylonia and was later adopted in Egypt. However, the Sphinx pre-dates this time by many thousands of years—perhaps being built around 10,500 BC or even earlier. Therefore it is possible that the constellation of Leo was seen by the builders of the Sphinx not as a lion, but as the celestial representation of Anubis in his form as a recumbent wolf. The long flat back, curved head, protruding snout, and out stretched paws, match the form of the Sphinx and the hieroglyphic representation of the recumbent Anubis in his wolf form in the most ancient known sacred texts in the world, the Pyramid Texts.

A photograph of an African golden wolf, the animal which Anubis is associated with. Until recently, this animal was believed to be a jackal before genetic testing revealed it is actually a wolf. Translations of ancient Egyptian texts still refer to it as a jackal. Wolves are the ancient ancestors of dogs, which is why the animal of Anubis can also be referred to as a dog.

The ancient site of Abydos in Egypt further connects Anubis to the constellation of Leo. At this ancient site dated to between 6,000–3,100 BC (although possibly much older) lies the mysterious temple known as the Osireion where a deity with the head of a dog that later became associated with Anubis was worshiped. The Osireion temple was unearthed during the construction of the temple of Seti I around 1,280 BC, and later again along with the temple of Seti I in AD 1902, after both had become covered in sand.

The temple of Osireion at Abydos in Egypt. It shares many architectural similarities with the Valley Temple beside the Sphinx, as well as a connection to the deity Anubis as head of the underworld in alignment with the sun and constellation of Leo.

The Valley Temple located beside the Great Sphinx of Egypt. It shares remarkable similarities in building style with the Osireion, another ancient temple. Both are made out of huge unadorned granite blocks.

The Osireion temple closely resembles the unique architecture of the Valley Temple which is located next to the Sphinx—both are made out of huge unadorned granite blocks, which also look very similar to Stonehenge. Like the Sphinx and Valley Temple, the Osireion was covered in sand and forgotten thousands of years ago, periodically being rediscovered even by the pharaohs of Egypt themselves who renovated them. Like the Sphinx and Great Pyramids, the Osireion also encodes the numbers of the Great Year (precession of the equinoxes), the golden mean, and key solar alignments which include the summer solstice, and both sites were centered around the veneration of Anubis. This makes the link between these two sites very strong—it appears that at the very least, the ancient knowledge of the builders of the Great Pyramids and Sphinx was passed on to those who built the Osireion.

On the summer solstice, the light of the setting sun shines through a nearby gap in the Libyan Hills, which intersects the Osireion temple. Due to the precession of the equinoxes, or the progress of the Great Year, the summer solstice occurred in the constellation of Leo in the era of 4,400 BC. During this time at Abydos a deity called Khent-Amenty (also Khentiamentiu or Khentyamentw) was worshiped as a central figure.

Khent-Amenty was depicted with the head of a dog, but was also a variant of a lion deity, and later became associated with Anubis. He was known as "the head of the west" which was a reference to him as the guardian of the underworld, the land of the dead, the entrance to which was seen as in the direction of west as the place of the setting sun. The underworld was believed to be accessed through the gap in the Libyan hills, which lay to the west of Abydos, and which the solstice sun shone through in alignment with the Osireion temple.

> "Equally curious is that Khent-Amenty, a dog-like deity shown recumbent on a black standard, may in fact reflect an earlier understanding of the zodiac. The guardian of the west suggests a match for that guardian of the east, the Sphinx, and both can be related to the same constellation, that of Leo. Primitive cultures have often seen Leo as a dog-like creature, and it has even been suggested that the Sphinx originally depicted a dog. At the time of the earliest pre-dynastic cultures at Abydos, the ancestors of the Thinites around the turn of the fifth millennium BCE, the summer solstice sun was in Leo. So, standing in the sacred grove on top of the Osireion mound, one would have seen the sun set, and there, sparkling in the night sky, would have been Khent-Amenty, the black dog of Leo, guarding the path of eternal life." [22]
>
> ~ VINCENT BRIDGES, ABYDOS, THE OSIREION AND EGYPTIAN SACRED SCIENCE

ALIGNMENT WITH LEO AROUND 10,500 BC

The Sphinx is also mysteriously set low down in the Giza plateau, and beside a giant causeway running from the second largest of the Great Pyramids. The angle of the causeway is slightly offset due east by about 14°. Egyptologists argue that this was because the Sphinx and causeway were incorporated later into the Giza design. Researchers Graham Hancock and Robert Bauval discovered however, that this offset and lowering of the Sphinx mirrored the movement of the constellation of Leo during the era around 10,500 BC at the spring equinox.

When one stands on the causeway, looking toward the Sphinx and the rising sun, one would have witnessed the constellation of what we now know as Leo rising in the sky before dawn so that it would appear head first, as if its body was submerged by the horizon, before fully appearing in its recumbent position. At this moment, one could look across to the Sphinx and see only its head, as if it were submerged in the horizon just like the constellation, with both of them aligned to one another.

The rising of the constellation of Leo preceding the sun mirrors the role Anubis has in the resurrection of the initiate. Anubis, symbolized by the constellation of Leo, appears at the horizon where the sun will rise. The sun must pass through this constellation and the gaze of Anubis (as the Sphinx), to leave the earth and ascend into the sky, the realm of imperishability. At dawn, the sun emerges from the horizon, symbolizing the emergence of the initiate with the Son within from out of the underworld (symbolized by the nine chambers beneath the Sphinx that represent the nine layers of hell/the underworld). As the sun rises, it passes through the symbolic gateway created by the gaze and constellation of Anubis, thus overcoming the divine laws which Anubis administers.

Additionally, at around 10,500 BC the Great Pyramids also aligned with the three stars of Orion's belt. Therefore the monuments of the Giza plateau all had their most dominant alignments around this time, which along with other evidence, reveals that they may have all been built together as part of a master plan.

However, although the date of 10,500 BC is one of the most popularly discussed, due to the precession of the equinoxes, it's possible that these alignments also occurred at an earlier time, which would have been around 37,000 BC. This would coincide closely with the beginning of the king list in Egypt, when the gods manifested as humans.

THE DUAT MIRRORED BY THE GREAT PYRAMIDS AND SPHINX

In ancient Egypt, the realm of the Duat was the dwelling place of the gods, a place that lay beyond the physical world in the area of the constellation of Orion. In the ancient Egyptian text the Book of What Is in the Duat, it states, "whoever shall make the copy of the Duat, and shall know it upon the Earth, it shall act as a magical protector for him, both in Heaven and in Earth, unfailingly, regularly and eternally," alluding to why the ancient builders of the Giza Plateau aligned their structures to this other-worldly realm of the sun and stars.

The three Great Pyramids of Egypt superimposed over the three stars of Orion's belt, showing their correlation.

The Great Pyramids align to the three stars of Orion's belt. To the ancient Egyptians, Orion was the constellation of Osiris, in whose life the process of attaining imperishability was symbolized. In the Pyramid Texts, Unas [the Pharaoh] journeys through the day and night sky to become the star Sabu, or Orion.

"Behold, he has come as Orion, behold, Osiris has come as Orion..." [23]
~ THE PYRAMID TEXTS, UTTERANCE 442, TRANSLATED BY SAMUEL A. B. MERCER

Each year the sun makes a journey through the sky drifting between the constellations of Orion, Leo, and across the Milky Way, symbolically representing the events of the life of Osiris, which are then mirrored at the Giza plateau. Orion corresponds with the Great Pyramids and Osiris, the Milky

Way corresponds to the Nile and the eternal divine feminine known as the goddess Hathor, and Leo most likely with Anubis who resurrects Osiris and is symbolized by the Sphinx.

In the story of Osiris, he is betrayed by Seth (just as Jesus was by Judas). Seth seals Osiris in a coffin and then throws the coffin into the Nile River, symbolic of the Milky Way, which flows out to the sea—this is the return of the initiate to the womb of the great Mother, the primordial waters of creation.

In Maya and Aztec cultures this is symbolized as being swallowed by the serpent. These symbols represent the initiate, the Son, becoming one with the divine feminine principle. But a return to the womb is also a time of death, as it is a return to the place which precedes birth—to the imperishable source of all life.

Incredibly, the Passion (betrayal, death, and resurrection) of Osiris is symbolized by the structures of the Giza Plateau which align to the celestial counterparts that enacted this same drama in the heavens every year.

THE USE OF UNIVERSAL PRINCIPLES IN THE GIZA DESIGN

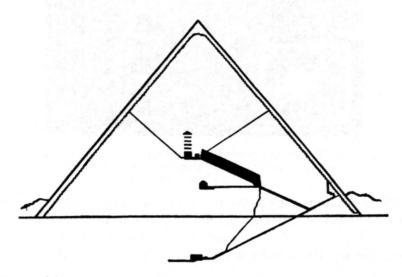

Diagram of the Great Pyramid of Egypt showing its interior passages and chambers. Both the ascending passage (leading to what is called the "King's Chamber") and the descending passage (leading down into the subterranean chamber) are at an angle of 26 degrees, 33 minutes, and 54 seconds.

There is an ancient maxim of wisdom that states "as above, so below." The universal principles of life exist in everything—that is why the same mathematical "logarithmic spiral" is found in the shape of a shell, and the spiral of a galaxy. The same principles that govern the movement of the heavens, the formation and structure of life, and the cycles of growth and decay, etc., also govern the spiritual development of the human being. The whole of life is created for beings to awaken, and is intrinsically imbued with the principles of this process so that we can remember who we truly are and find our way back home.

This is why the builders of the Great Pyramids and Sphinx aligned their sacred structures to the movements of the heavens using sacred geometry, with a precision that is unmatched even today. A study of fifty Egyptian temples revealed that the builders had used highly advanced sacred mathematics in the construction of every single one. A universal principle manifests in numbers, sound, color, natural cycles, the formation of life, astronomy, etc., which are studied in separate and distinct disciplines. However, these are all expressions of the same universal truths. By using the expression of particular principles, whether it be astronomical or mathematical, the builders of the Great Pyramids and Sphinx were able to create places that harnessed these principles energetically and multi-dimensionally, and could be experienced and understood on many different levels beyond the mind.

Researcher Robert Temple discovered that throughout the Giza site, an angle of 26 degrees, 33 minutes, and 54 seconds had been used, stating, "this odd angle of slightly more than 26 degrees is the only acute angle possible for a right triangle to be formed that is known as 'the golden triangle', because it embodies the famous Golden Mean Proportion." [24] It has been used both in two and three dimensions, between all the pyramids, in the slope of the passages inside the pyramids and beside the Sphinx, in the design of the inner chambers, and between the Sphinx and the two largest pyramids. The incredible "invisible" three-dimensional layout of the Giza Plateau, with its stunning multiplicity of sacred geometry from every point and down to minute details with unmatched accuracy (so much that today researchers have barely scratched the surface), reveals that the Sphinx and pyramids may have been built and laid out according to a unified master plan.

This same angle was also used throughout Egyptian artwork, often as the angle the initiate who was being resurrected was tilted on, revealing why the ancient builders wished to harness the energetic power found in this mathematical truth at the site of the Great Sphinx and Pyramids so dedicated to the process of resurrection.

OSIRIS BETWEEN THE PAWS OF THE ANUBIS SPHINX

Critics of the theory that the Sphinx was originally carved as Anubis state that the head of the Sphinx is made of a harder and heavier stone than the body, caused by the strata in the bedrock from which the Sphinx was carved, and that because of this, the body would not have been able to support the weight of Anubis' head without it falling off.

Ram-headed sphinx at the Temple of Karnak
with the figure of a pharaoh between its paws.

However, the ancient Egyptians were master builders. Their statues were built taking into account the fragility of protruding parts like hands and heads, and they incorporated reinforcements into the design to ensure they would last.

You can see an image of an actual Egyptian Anubis sphinx with a pharaoh between its paws at the following URL. It was built as part of the Ramesseum between 1,279–1,212 BC: http://www.mysteriesofancientegypt.com/2010/05/anubis-sphinx.html

There is a large bulge on the chest of the Sphinx. This bulge, now almost completely weathered away, could once have been the image of Osiris or equivalent deity, which would have supported the head of Anubis. Sphinx statues in Egypt often show the figure of a pharaoh between their paws, and this may have been a symbolic design which carried through thousands of years even though the original form of the Great Sphinx did not.

In the constellation of Leo, which the builders of the Sphinx may have mirrored in their design, the brightest star of the constellation is found at the place of the heart. Uncannily, this star called Regulus, is also known as the King Star. This may also indicate why the pharaoh/king came to be situated standing at the heart of sphinxes and again alludes to the possibility that the bulge on the chest of the Great Sphinx could have been the "King" or initiate, represented by Osiris.

In the process of resurrection, Anubis and Osiris are intimately linked, as it is Anubis who facilitates the resurrection of Osiris, and it is on the spring equinox, the sunrise of which the Sphinx gazes at, that the constellation of Anubis (Leo) rises before the sun (symbol of the resurrected Osiris as his son Horus), thus bringing the sun to life. The star Regulus also lies exactly on the ecliptic, which is the sun's perceived path through the sky. The sun passing through Regulus also enacted Osiris as the sun passing through the arms of Anubis to resurrect.

In the Book of the Caverns it refers to "those who are between his [Anubis'] arms," which is an esoteric reference that may have been symbolized by the Sphinx with Osiris between its "arms." In the Book of the Dead, Anubis is depicted laying his hands upon Osiris, saying "I have come to protect Osiris." Sphinxes later had statues of pharaohs between their paws as they were said to protect the pharaoh. This may show that although the knowledge was lost of what the Sphinx originally was, the idea of the pharaoh being protected between its paws continued.

As the spring equinox sun rose, signaling the resurrection of Osiris as his son Horus, the sun would have emerged from the watery horizon, and created a path of light across the river Nile that would have reached the Sphinx and possibly struck the statue of Osiris between its paws, symbolically filling Osiris with the vivifying energy of the sun. The statue of Osiris would have had its lower body beneath the water, as he was often depicted this way to show his symbolic resurrection—rising from out of the underworld and emerging from the primordial waters of the womb and creation to attain eternal life.

HOW THE SPHINX WAS LOST

A partially cleared Sphinx buried in sand up to its shoulders, after having been buried up to its neck. This photo was taken around 1889, but the Sphinx had been buried like this at least once before in the time preceding 1,400 BC.

The knowledge of the original form of the Sphinx was lost thousands of years ago, as it was abandoned, vandalized, re-carved, and restored. Its origins are still unknown as there are no references to who built it, and there are many signs showing that it came from a time before recorded Egyptian history.

A number of researchers and archeologists argue that the Sphinx and its surrounding enclosure show signs of heavy weathering from water. Deep rivets in the stone, which have almost entirely eroded away the original form of the Sphinx, were created by a long period of heavy rainfall. Today, the Giza area is a desert—the last time the Giza plateau had heavy rainfall was at a time called the Nabtian Pluvial that lasted from 10,000 to 3,000 BC. This means that the Sphinx would have existed during this time, but could have been built earlier—possibly being of pre-ice age or pre-flood origin. Archeologist Robert Schoch places the age of the Sphinx to at least as early as 5,000 to 7,000 BC, but researcher John Anthony West believes it could even be as old as 12,500 BC or more.

The original builders of the Sphinx are not known. Instead, using circumstantial evidence, mainstream Egyptology has promoted the idea that the Pharaoh Khafre built the Sphinx and the second largest of the Great Pyramids at around 2,500 BC, even though there are no references to Khafre building either. Restoration block work on the Sphinx is believed to date to as early as this time—which would indicate that the Sphinx was already weathered and in need of restoration by then.

The oldest known sacred texts in the world are called the Pyramid Texts. They have been dated to soon after Khafre's reign (around 2,400 to 2,300 BC), and were discovered on the walls of a number of pyramids at a site called Saqqara. They contain the oldest references to the Sphinx and Great Pyramids, in which they speak of Anpu/Anubis surrounded by a sacred lake at the Giza Plateau. This reveals that at this time, the Sphinx may have still retained its original form. However, they do not contain references to who built the Sphinx or Great Pyramids, leaving the time before around 3,000 BC as a veritable blackout in the history of Egypt.

A few hundred years after Khafre's reign, Egypt was hit with droughts, floods, and plagues for around 150 years. During this time (around 2,150 to 2,040 BC) social order broke down and mobs plundered and vandalized the Giza site. The Sphinx may have been severely damaged during these riots (causing such a disfigurement to the head that the knowledge of what it was may have been lost, also giving cause for later pharaohs to restore the face with their own image), and many artifacts and texts looted and destroyed. The gold pinnacle that topped the Great Pyramid was probably removed at this time. All that survives is what is set in stone and was too large to destroy—the core structures of the Great Pyramids and Sphinx with their encoded and unified mathematical, astronomical, and esoteric wisdom.

Human-headed sphinxes line a causeway at the Luxor Temple in Egypt. These were a later addition to the temple. Human-headed sphinxes such as these did not start appearing in Egypt until around 1,800 BC.

Social order returned to Egypt in around 2,000 BC. After this the head of the Sphinx was re-carved at least once, leaving the final image of Pharaoh Amenemhet II (not Khafre or Khufu, who have been attributed with building it, and look nothing like it) who reigned from 1,876 to 1,842 BC.[25] By this time sphinxes with lions' bodies and the heads of pharaohs or rams were appearing as statues. It is clear that the knowledge of what the Sphinx had been was already lost at large by the Egyptians themselves.

Then, the Sphinx itself was nearly totally lost. Today the area around the Sphinx and pyramids is a parched, sandy desert. In fact, periodically for hundreds and thousands of years at a time, the Sphinx has been covered up to its neck in sand. The famous Dream Stele between the Sphinx's paws records how the Pharaoh Thutmose IV, in around 1,400 BC, had a dream beneath the head of the Sphinx that at the time protruded above the sand. In the dream the Sphinx spoke to Thutmose IV saying that if he restored the Sphinx, in return the Sphinx would make him king.

This reveals that by 1,400 BC the Sphinx had already been long neglected to the sands of time. Rain and the once lush surrounds had long since departed the area, as well as the original civilization of Giza. The focus of Egyptian culture had moved elsewhere.

By the time Thutmose IV had his dream, the Sphinx's head had already been altered and made into the face of a pharaoh. Anyone who views the Sphinx today can see the incredible disproportion between the tiny head of the Sphinx with its large, elongated body. This disproportion was created through one, successively re-carving the head, making it smaller each time; and two, adding block work casing to parts of the Sphinx's body which had the effect of enlarging it.

Images and statues of Anubis/Anpu in his wolf form, associated with death and resurrection continued however, even though his association with the Sphinx had been severed. This knowledge survived through sacred texts that were passed down over thousands of years, with older texts becoming reincorporated into newer ones.

According to a historical account, the Sphinx was vandalized once more by a local Muslim Sheik, who hacked off its nose. Around the same time in AD 1300 after an earthquake shook Cairo, the Great Pyramids were stripped of their outer casing to rebuild the city.

From at least 2,500 BC, successive restorations have been done on the Sphinx, right up until the present day. Ancient Egyptian block work which covers the lower part of the Sphinx's body, including the tail and paws, was later added to by the Greeks and Romans who used the Sphinx as a place of worship during their occupations of Egypt. This has been further added to by modern stones. The addition of all these restoration stones has had the effect of widening the torso, massively enlarging the paws, and adding the curled up tail, to create a leonine form instead. It is now impossible to pull back these stones (no one would give permission) to reveal the original form of the torso, paws, and tail. The Sphinx has also been concreted, lengthening the pharaoh's headdress, smoothing the neck, and filling in huge gaping rivets in the body.

In our times the Sphinx is no longer a site of sacred reverence, but has morphed into a star attraction, replicated in Las Vegas, completely detached from its original esoteric origins. However, through the experience of the same sacred knowledge of the original builders, the Sphinx can once again be understood.

THE GRADUAL LOSS OF THE ESOTERIC KNOWLEDGE OF ANCIENT EGYPT

The pyramids at Saqqara in Egypt which contain the oldest known sacred texts in the world, the Pyramid Texts. These pyramids are clearly poor imitations of the Great Pyramids, and so the texts they contain are also likely to be handed down from a much more ancient and pristine source.

There is no evidence to suggest that the Great Pyramids were ever used as the tombs of pharaohs, although later pyramids were. They served an entirely different and esoteric purpose as temples of initiation and beacons of knowledge. What happened to Egypt, probably a number of times, as has happened to all original esoteric sites and cultures, is that the people there declined in spiritual knowledge. While the ancient sites themselves preserve the original understanding of spirituality, the people who inhabit them invariably lose it as the cycles of nature dictate.

What we see throughout history, repeatedly all over the world, is that the knowledge of spirituality is lost as people themselves lose the capacity to understand and value it. Eventually, the knowledge is turned into a blind religion, the real esoteric practitioners are pushed out, the knowledge becomes distorted, given meanings it never had, and taken over by megalomaniacs and those with entirely selfish and malevolent agendas who then use it as a tool to control and enslave people, at times inverting the practice of the teachings of light into black magic with blood rituals, sacrifice, violence, etc. When the knowledge of spiritual principles is lost, a society declines morally (and spiritually), and thus is no longer able to hold itself together—eventually falling into total destruction and ruin. This sometimes allows other civilizations to rise and give the spiritual knowledge anew in a different form. Life moves in cycles and as Atlantis is said to have fallen, so too will this civilization. This is the cycle of life and death that is visible in all of creation from the most microscopic level, to the most macrocosmic.

Ancient Egypt was undoubtedly once inhabited by a highly spiritually advanced and intelligent people; its greatest achievements are its oldest. There is also no doubt that it eventually descended into a religion ruled by a megalomaniac elite—scenes at temples even came to depict festivals of drunkenness. Originally the Great Pyramids of Egypt were built free of any attribution and were dedicated to the sacred initiatory rites. Later, lavish tombs were created only for pharaohs and nobles to assure them safe passage in the afterlife, laden with riches, and inscribed with various parts of esoteric teachings.

This knowledge, which the elite had reserved for themselves, declined and was eventually interpreted by the public; mass moral decline and degeneration then set in. Excavations have uncovered caches of millions of slaughtered and mummified animals (including newborn puppies) used to appease the gods. One dating from around 747 BC was dedicated to the worship of Anubis in which dogs were bred specifically to be killed and mummified only moments after being born. Obviously this was a totally abhorrent practice and has nothing to do with Anubis in any real sense—revealing just how far society in Egypt had strayed from the original knowledge.

The priests of the once sacred temples, started taking money and gifts for people to buy their way into heaven, rather than upholding the principles of divine cosmic order. This kind of behavior illustrates why the esoteric knowledge was always kept so secret—to maintain its sanctity, and ensure its use for good and rightful purposes. As Jesus would say, "don't throw your pearls before swine lest they trample them underfoot." Not only does the knowledge get trampled upon, but also its practitioners when placed before uncomprehending people.

SPIRITUAL KNOWLEDGE TURNED INTO A RELIGION OF THE AFTERLIFE

The history of Egypt spans many thousands of years during which time the esoteric teachings became a religion merely of the afterlife. Sacred initiatory texts which explain the passage of the initiate in life, through the tests and trials of the path of the spiritual sun, became interpreted as the passage of the soul only after death, as inner death became confused with physical death.

The Egyptians depicted in their texts that unless one attains a spiritual stage, a person does not have immortality, but continues in the deathly dream of the subconscious before entering the jaws of the Egyptian crocodile goddess Ammit known as "the eater of the dead" after the circuit of lives, to be given over to eventual destruction in the underworld, or hell, which the Egyptians called the "Place of Annihilation." This was the fate of the evil dead described by the Egyptians as it is in many other spiritual teachings.

The way to avoid this annihilation changed over time. It was originally through esoteric inner transformation, but it was later supposedly reached through repeating spells, by being buried with charms, and inside lavish tombs.

> "I have passed by the roads of Rosetau [ancient name for Giza plateau] by water and on land; these roads are those of Osiris; they are in the sky. If a man knows the Spell for going down into them, he will be like a god directed by the followers of Thoth. He will indeed go down to every heaven to which he desires to descend. But if he knows not this Spell for passing on these roads, he will fall a prey to the tribunal of the dead, his destiny being that of one who has nothing, and is without (his) justification eternally." [26]
>
> ~ THE BOOK OF THE TWO WAYS, TRANSLATED BY ALEXANDRE PIANKOFF

Instead the focus of the religion became a lavish preparation for the journey in the afterlife, rather than making the journey to attain enlightenment and immortality (or imperishability as it was known in Egypt) within life itself. For enlightenment, material tombs and riches are useless as we only take what we have within ourselves beyond death, and that depends on what we create spiritually within ourselves in life. There is no doubt the Egyptians inherited an incredible knowledge of the realm of the afterlife, but the original builders recognized that this realm did not belong only to death but could be accessed in life, and explored through having out-of-body experiences.

Although the sacred esoteric texts of Egypt became a religion that had steered away from the esoteric toward the mundane, the legacy of ancient Egypt is so great that the knowledge contained in its structures and teachings has remained a source of guidance for initiates throughout the ages.

A SITE FOR SPIRITUAL INITIATION

SUN AT THE PINNACLE OF THE GREAT PYRAMID OF EGYPT.

What is generally known about the Sphinx and the pyramids has been colored by thousands upon thousands of years of culture, multiple restorations, additions, and changes in form and function. But the Sphinx isn't what some have come to believe—a bizarre statue dedicated to a megalomaniac pharaoh. It now re-emerges as a sacred esoteric symbol of one of the most significant stages in spiritual transformation, and an integral part of a message of enlightenment left in the Giza complex by an advanced people long ago.

The Great Pyramids and Sphinx were never built as monuments dedicated to pharaohs, but as purpose-built places for spiritual initiation and esoteric knowledge—with each area of the site having a special form and function related to a stage of the path of the spiritual sun. Whilst out of the body, I have experienced this first hand. The design of the various chambers, passageways, subterranean crypts, and alignments are related to various stages of the spiritual path, with its ascents and descents, times of inner death, resurrection, and ascension to the realms of light, etc., and could be used in initiatory rites that correspond to these stages.

In ancient times, it would have been possible for these initiations to take place within the various areas of the site in the physical world. Using the site physically in this way today is clearly not possible, and hasn't been for thousands of years. However, even though today the site is dilapidated and open to a continuous stream of tourists, the structures of the Pyramids still exist in the higher dimensions, as everything that is physical has its multidimensional aspect. The builders of the Pyramids knew this, and so left a legacy behind not just of physical structures, but of structures that also existed in higher dimensions that would serve as places of initiations out of the body in the higher dimensions for those going through the path of the spiritual sun well into the future.

As the ancient form of the Sphinx, Anubis guards the entrance of the site as the protector of secrets, allowing only those who are initiated to penetrate its mysteries. He guards the gateway that separates those belonging to the physical, earthly realm, and those who are released into the higher, imperishable spiritual realms, making sure that only those who meet the requirements of resurrection pass through. For potentially a few today, the process of spiritual resurrection is as relevant and important as ever to the purpose of life; Anubis and the deities of ancient Egypt still watch over the sacred process in the higher dimensions, while the Giza Plateau still serves as a site for rites of initiation and spiritual resurrection—a part of human experience that is hidden to the uninitiated, and which takes place beyond the body.

Summer Solstice

Ascent to the Spiritual Father
and the Return to Source

CHAPTER SIX

The Spiritual Meaning
of the Summer Solstice

THE SUMMER SOLSTICE IS A TIME to celebrate the light of consciousness within ourselves and within each and every person, and to reflect upon the potential for consciousness to awaken.

The progress of the sun throughout the year symbolizes the process of attaining enlightenment, and the summer solstice is the final climax of this journey as the day of most light in the year. It symbolizes the ascension found in many great spiritual teachings. At the spring equinox, the resurrection and return of the Son/sun to the Mother Goddess is celebrated. Following this, the summer solstice symbolizes the return/ascension to the Great Father Spirit. It is a time to celebrate the triumph of light over darkness in the individual, and the return to wholeness in which the Son, Mother Goddess, and Father God become one great unified consciousness—a complete, whole, and powerful light that enlightens the individual.

The Druids, ancient Egyptians, Maya, Romans, and many others have aligned their sacred sites to the summer solstice and conducted ceremonies on this day. At the Great Pyramids of Egypt the summer solstice sun crowns the head of the Sphinx; the Druids celebrated the marriage of heaven and earth and the defeat of the dark god of the year just as the Egyptians celebrated the defeat of the dark god Seth by Horus as the sun; and in Rome, the festival of Vestalia continued a Druid tradition of guarding the sacred fire.

STONEHENGE, WHICH HAS MULTIPLE ALIGNMENTS TO THE SUMMER SOLSTICE.

Light is spiritual in its nature, and so the sun and stars have a spiritual significance that has its root in higher dimensions—in many ancient teachings they are described as the source of creation. The summer solstice is therefore a highly spiritual time. The summer solstice is described as the gate of ascent out of this world into the realm of spirit by both Krishna, in the famous text the Bhagavad Gita, and in the designs of the secret caves of Mithras.

THE TRINITY AND THE FEATHERED SERPENT

Throughout ancient teachings there are incredible similarities—a divine Son, who is born to a virgin Mother Goddess and great hidden Father, goes through a series of trials before being betrayed, then resurrecting, and later ascending. The events in the life of this spiritual Son and savior nearly always correspond to the solar year and other astrological events.

These famous trinities of Father, Mother, and Son actually symbolize the fundamental energies and forces that exist within creation—found in atoms, the basic building blocks of all matter, as the three forces of positive, negative, and neutral. Paracelsus, the great alchemist of the Renaissance, saw the cosmos as being fashioned from three spiritual substances or principles called a tria prima, which the alchemical substances of salt, sulfur, and mercury signified—salt as substance and solidity, mercury as that which is transformative and fusible, and sulfur as binding these two.

Hindu painting symbolizing the principle of the feathered serpent. The god Vishnu (center) rides his mount Garuda, which is an eagle. His wife, the goddess Lakshmi, is on either side of him in her dual aspect as material energy, and spiritual energy. The eagle holds the serpent; the eagle represents the masculine aspect of the creator (Vishnu), and the serpent, the feminine aspect (Lakshmi).

As what is above relates to what is below, these three primary forces of the universe are also central to the awakening of consciousness and why the stories of Mother Goddess, Great Father, and Divine Son also contained messages about the process of an individual reaching enlightenment. The Trinity of Mother, Father, and Son exist not only as universal forces, but also as higher parts of each individual's consciousness that exist in more spiritual dimensions and which someone reunites with on the path of the spiritual sun.

Full self-realization is a return to the source of creation, the final ring of the Absolute, where all is one. To do that the different parts of someone's Being that were divided as they came into creation reunite to form one whole, as it is not possible to enter the innermost ring of the Absolute divided; we must return as one, just as we did when we left, but with self-consciousness from the experience of duality in the world of matter. When the three forces of creation—Father, Mother, and Son—are one and have returned to the divine source, a person has gone through the process of creation in reverse and re-absorbed the principles of life and divinity.

"It is by love, that the Heavenly Father and the Earthly Mother and the Son of Man become one. For the spirit of the Son of Man was created from the spirit of the Heavenly Father, and his body from the body of the Earthly Mother. Become, therefore, perfect as the spirit of your Heavenly Father and the body of your Earthly Mother are perfect." [1]

~ JESUS IN THE ESSENE GOSPEL OF PEACE, TRANSLATED BY EDMOND BORDEAUX SZEKELY

This fusion of Mother, Father, and Son has been symbolized as the feathered serpent—and can be found as the Maya and Aztec god Quetzalcoatl, the Persian and Roman god Mithras, and prolifically throughout Egypt. The gods Quetzalcoatl, Mithras, and Horus are the Son; the serpent is a symbol of the Mother; and the feathers symbolic of the Father—it is from the union of Father, Mother, and Son that Quetzalcoatl/Mithras/Horus becomes the feathered serpent.

IMAGE LEFT: The feathered serpent in Rome. The Son as Mithras is depicted in the center of the zodiac with the sun atop his head, a serpent wrapped around his body, and wings on his back. Drawing is based on a first century AD Roman white marble relief in the Estense Museum in Modena, Italy.

IMAGE RIGHT: The feathered serpent in Central America. The Son as Quetzalcoatl looks out from the mouth of a serpent that is covered in feathers.

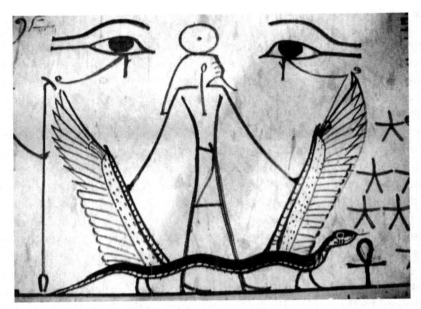

The feathered serpent in Egypt. The sun god in Egypt has the symbol of the sun atop his head and holds out the wings of a feathered serpent. Taken from the illustration of "the 11th hour" from a tomb in the Valley of the Kings.

The serpent is a symbol of the earth (which is substance), and the earthly Mother, as it is an animal that is at all times in contact with the earth. The feathers are those of an eagle, which is a symbol of the heavens (which is spirit) and the heavenly Father, as the eagle is an animal that flies and lives above all others and is thus associated with higher realms. The Son, symbolized by Jesus, Quetzalcoatl, Mithras, etc., is the force that unites the earthly human with its higher, heavenly Being.

In Persia the god Mithras was known as "the Mediator," as the Son is the conciliatory force (who, on the path of the spiritual sun, reunites/reconciles us with divinity). The Son is the miraculous reconciliatory aspect of each person's Being that is both personal and cosmic—the light of the spirit manifest in substance that acts within to unite and integrate the earthly human with heavenly divinity, joining the serpent with the feathers so it can fly. This is why the Son has been referred to as the light and savior of humanity in so many sacred teachings.

> "Dear friends, let us love one another, for love comes from God. Everyone who loves has been born of God and knows God. Whoever does not love does not know God, because God is love. This is how God showed his love among us: He sent his one and only Son into the world that we might live through him." [2]
>
> ~ 1 JOHN 4:7-9

CREATION IN REVERSE

Enlightenment is the process of creation in reverse, as it is the return of the individual to the divine source we were created from. In creation myths, a divine androgynous being firstly emerges from the great unmanifest and unknowable source. This being divides into the duality of masculine and feminine, of Father and Mother, in order to create and give birth to a Son, who then makes the rest of creation. These myths not only describe the creation of the universe, but because the process of creation is the same on a macrocosmic and microcosmic level, and a cosmic and personal level, they also describe the creation of our own unique Being which emerged from the source of creation and divided into its various parts as it came into the dimensions of life.

To follow this process in reverse a person firstly fuses with the Son of their higher Being (symbolized at the winter solstice), then the Son returns to and fuses with the Mother (symbolized at the spring equinox, and as the Son being swallowed by the serpent), then the Son-Mother returns to and fuses with the Father (symbolized at the summer solstice, and as the serpent being swallowed by the eagle). The feathered serpent—the three forces of creation, as Mother, Father, and Son—a unified self-realized androgynous being, which is now whole, then returns on the wings of spirit from the earth to the spiritual realm, the divine source of creation called the Absolute.

> "I am the one who is with you always. I am the Father, I am the Mother, I am the Son. I am the undefiled and incorruptible one." [3]
>
> ~ JESUS IN THE APOCRYPHON OF JOHN FROM THE NAG HAMMADI LIBRARY

> "It is imperative that not a single thought remain and that the tiniest speck of dust be transformed. There must be no perceived distinction of self and other; enmity and kindness must be seen as one; far and near, intimate and distant must be united as one body; birds and beasts, insects and fish are all of the same ch'i. One's lofty tao and weighty te are equal to heaven's. Following this, in the midst of obscurity and utter silence, the blessing is received and the 'mysterious pearl' presented in all its splendour and brilliance, more precious than words can tell. When the 'pearl' is consumed, the body sprouts feathered wings, and 'disappearing from Mount Wu-I' flies to the paradise of the immortals." [4]
>
> ~ TRUE TRANSMISSION OF THE GOLDEN ELIXIR BY SUN JU-CHUNG, TRANSLATED BY DOUGLAS WILE

THE THREE RINGS OF THE ABSOLUTE

The symbol of the divine source of creation called the Absolute, consists of three concentric rings. These rings represent the three primary forces that emerged from the unmanifest source of creation, as the Trinity of Father, Mother, and Son. The outer ring is reached when someone merges with the Son, which they need to do before they can reach the second inner ring where they merge with the Mother. It is only by reaching the second ring that they can then reach to the innermost ring where they merge with the Father. From there a person's consciousness has become whole again, which is represented by the dot of the innermost ring, symbolizing unity. From unity they can return to the unmanifest source of creation.

In Dante's Divine Comedy, he describes his vision of the creator appearing to him as three orbs, which are the three concentric rings of the Absolute.

> "In that abyss of radiance, clear and lofty, seemed, methought, three orbs of triple hue, clipt in one bound: And, from another, one reflected seemed, as rainbow is from rainbow: and the third seemed fire, breathed equally from both." [5]
>
> ~ DANTE, THE DIVINE COMEDY, PARADISO CANTO 33, TRANSLATED BY ALLEN MANDELBAUM

The three rings of the Absolute were depicted in this illustration of Dante's vision of the supreme creator of the universe; it is the same pattern that appears in the cosmic microwave background of the universe, and in the vibration of the mantra Om. How did the authors of the mantra Om and Dante know?

This three ringed pattern appears in some remarkable places.

Scientists have measured the cosmic microwave background, which is the microwave glow, present everywhere all at once, left over from the creation of the universe. Incredibly, it was the symbol of the Absolute, the three concentric rings, which appeared in it.

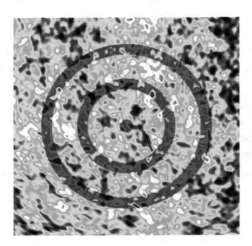

Three concentric rings were discovered in the cosmic microwave background of the universe (study done by Penrose and Gurzadyan; see more here http://arxiv.org/ftp/arxiv/papers/1011/1011.3706.pdf).

The same symbol of the Absolute also appears in connection with the mantra Om from the ancient Vedic texts of India—perhaps the most famous mantra in the world—which is said to represent the Absolute and the sound present at the creation of the universe, which begs the questions—how did the authors of the Vedas know? When a recording of this ancient Sanskrit mantra (which was made inside the chamber of the Great Pyramid of Egypt) was played using a CymaScope (by John Stuart Reid and Erik Larson) it created the three ring symbol of the Absolute (see: http://www.youtube.com/watch?v=Yw13EAX3cZk or do a search for "cymatic imagery of the Om chant"). This field of study is called cymatics, which demonstrates the visual effects of sound upon matter and the geometric shapes and patterns it creates.

The pattern of concentric rings is also found in a number of sacred sites around the world aligned to the solstice, including Arkaim in Russia, Stonehenge in England, and Goseck Circle in Germany (which each lie along the same line of latitude), and the lost island of Atlantis was also described as having its major city laid out in three concentric rings.

At the winter solstice, the spiritual Son is born within a spiritually prepared person. At the spring equinox, this Son dies, becomes one with the great Mother of the universe, and resurrects. At the summer solstice, the Mother and Son ascend to the Father, so that the forces of Son, Mother, and Father become one—returning as they left, through the three rings of the Absolute.

ASCENSION

"Jesus said, 'Do not hold on to me, for I have not yet ascended to the Father. Go instead to my brothers and tell them, 'I am ascending to my Father and your Father, to my God and your God.''" [6]

~ THE GOSPEL ACCORDING TO JOHN 20:17

Ascension is a stage that occurs on the path of the spiritual sun—it is when the Son returns to the Father and is symbolized by the summer solstice. It is found in the life of Jesus: his ascension occurred sometime after the spring equinox, which is when he resurrected. In the quote above, Jesus appears first to Mary Magdalene after he resurrects but tells her he has not yet ascended, as at this stage he has become one with the great Mother but not yet with the Father.

References to Jesus' ascension in the Bible are extremely brief and vague. Some of these references, which are often only one line, were actually added to the Gospels later, so in looking for more extensive and perhaps more authentic references to the ascension, we have to look elsewhere.

There were many highly spiritual works that were excluded from the Bible and which contain secret and advanced teachings Jesus gave directly to the disciples. Many of these texts have only resurfaced in the last century or so after remaining hidden or lost for over a thousand years.

In one of these texts called Pistis Sophia, the ascension of Jesus is witnessed by the disciples in great detail, and explained by Jesus himself who returns to the disciples after his ascension to relate it to them.

> "It came to pass then, when the sun had risen in the east, that a great light-power came down, in which was my Vesture, which I had left behind in the four-and-twentieth mystery, as I have said unto you. And I found a mystery in my Vesture, written in five words of those from the height: *zama zama ōzza rachama ōzai*, —whose solution is this: 'O Mystery, which is without in the world, for whose sake the universe hath arisen, —this is the total outgoing and the total ascent, which hath emanated all emanations and all that is therein and for whose sake all mysteries and all their regions have arisen, — come hither unto us, for we are thy fellow-members. We are all with thyself; we are one and the same. Thou art the First Mystery, which existed from the beginning in the Ineffable before it came forth; and the name thereof are we all. Now, therefore, are we all come to meet thee at the last limit, which also is the last mystery from within; itself is a portion of us. Now, therefore, have we sent thee thy Vesture, which hath belonged to thee from the beginning, which thou hast left behind in the last limit, which also is the last mystery from within, until its time should be completed, according to the commandment of the First Mystery. Lo, its time is completed; put it on [thee].'" [7]
> ~ JESUS IN PISTIS SOPHIA, TRANSLATED BY G. R. S. MEAD

The ascension is described in association with the rising sun in the east—the spiritual sun, which is referred to as the last limit, and the place that all emanations have emanated from, being the source of creation. The Mystery of Jesus' garment, which he had left behind and now returns to, comes to him at his ascent, and is described as the reason why the whole of the universe with all its regions was created, making it the purpose of existence. Incredibly, the word zama on Jesus' vesture is also known as an ancient Mayan word, which means "to dawn" or "sunrise."

The text goes on to describe the Vesture of light that Jesus is clothed in as being three-fold, and producing three different types of light. These three lights correspond to the three rings of the Absolute and the three primary forces of creation (Father, Mother, and Son). After Jesus ascends, these three lights and vestures are one in him, as the Father, Mother, and Son of the Being are now unified.

> "...the heavens opened, and they saw Jesus descend, shining most exceedingly, and there was no measure for his light in which he was.

For he shone more [radiantly] than at the hour when he had ascended to the heavens, so that men in the world cannot describe the light which was on him; and it shot forth light-rays in great abundance, and there was no measure for its rays, and its light was not alike together, but it was of divers kind and of divers type, some [rays] being more excellent than others; and the whole light consisted together. It was of threefold kind, and the one [kind] was more excellent than the other. The second, that in the midst, was more excellent than the first which was below, and the third, which was above them all, was more excellent than the two which were below. And the first glory, which was placed below them all, was like to the light which had come over Jesus before he had ascended into the heavens, and was like only itself in its light. And the three light-modes were of divers light-kinds, and they were of divers type, one being more excellent than the other..."[8]

~ PISTIS SOPHIA, TRANSLATED BY G. R. S. MEAD

In Pistis Sophia, Jesus also narrates the story of the journey of conscious-ness through many perils in the world of matter until its final return to the divine source from which it came. At the end of its journey to awakening, he describes its final ascension where it becomes one with the Ineffable, called "the One and Only." This one and only is the Monad, the Being of each person before it divided into creation, and the ascension of Pistis Sophia in the story is the return to this wholeness of Being.

"And the soul which receiveth the mystery of the Ineffable, will soar into the height, being a great light-stream... and goeth to the region of the inheritance of the mystery which it hath received, that is to the mystery of the One and Only, the Ineffable, and until it becometh one with its Limbs."[9]

~ JESUS IN PISTIS SOPHIA, TRANSLATED BY G. R. S. MEAD

This ascension doesn't happen physically, but in higher dimensions, which is why in the excerpt above Jesus describes the soul and not a physical person as ascending, and describes this soul as ascending into a higher region—a region that is clearly not in the physical plane. Outwardly then, a person who ascends appears the same, but inwardly they are changed.

This is possible because all the dimensions of life are here and now. However, the average person is unable to perceive this and doesn't have the spiritual parts such as the Son, Mother, and Father within their consciousness. These higher aspects of consciousness exist in higher spiritual realms and give this higher perception, while the average person has just base consciousness and is unable to perceive much more than its simpler emanations allow.

Moreover, basic consciousness is sixth dimensional only and contains only the spiritual emanations of its plane, whereas the higher aspects of someone's Being are able to give the spiritual emanations from these higher planes. It is only once the consciousness of someone reunites with the higher spiritual parts of their Being on the path of the spiritual sun that they then contain the spiritual emanations of that higher part and plane permanently—this gives a much greater perception of multidimensional reality in the here and now, and the capacity to feel higher states such as peace and love far more than anyone who has not reunited with these parts is able to.

This is the meaning behind many of the sayings of Jesus.

"His disciples said to him, 'When will the kingdom come?'

[Jesus said] 'It will not come by watching for it. It will not be said, "Look, here!" or "Look, there!" Rather, **the Father's kingdom is spread out upon the earth, and people don't see it."** [10]

~ THE GOSPEL OF THOMAS FROM THE NAG HAMMADI LIBRARY, TRANSLATED BY STEPHEN PATTERSON AND MARVIN MEYER

"He who will receive that light will not be seen, nor can he be detained. And none shall be able to torment a person like this, even while he dwells in the world. And again when he leaves the world, he has already received the truth in the images. **The world has become the Aeon (eternal realm)**, for the Aeon is fullness for him." [11]

~ THE GOSPEL OF PHILIP FROM THE NAG HAMMADI LIBRARY, TRANSLATED BY WESLEY W. ISENBERG

"Jesus said, 'If your leaders say to you, "Look, the (Father's) kingdom is in the sky," then the birds of the sky will precede you. If they say to you, "It is in the sea," then the fish will precede you. **Rather, the (Father's) kingdom is within you and it is outside you.** When you know yourselves, then you will be known, and you will understand that you are children of the living Father. But if you do not know yourselves, then you live in poverty, and you are the poverty.'" [12]

~ THE GOSPEL OF THOMAS FROM THE NAG HAMMADI LIBRARY, TRANSLATED BY STEPHEN PATTERSON AND MARVIN MEYER

Jesus further explains that someone who fuses with the Ineffable is of an unimaginable spiritual stature, and yet is a "man in the world."

"Now, therefore, amēn, I say unto you: Every man who will receive that mystery of the Ineffable and accomplish it in all its types and all its figures, he is a man in the world, but he towereth above all angels and will tower still more above them all...

He is a man in the world, but he will rule with me in my kingdom.
He is a man in the world, but he is king in the Light.
He is a man in the world, but he is not one of the world.
And amēn, I say unto you: That man is I and I am that man." [13]
~ JESUS IN PISTIS SOPHIA, TRANSLATED BY G. R. S. MEAD

This same understanding also appears in Taoist texts:

"Those with determination must find true teachers to instruct them on the 'three stages' and 'three gates'; transmit the 'nine zithers' and 'nine swords'; explain the order of 'obtaining the medicine,' the 'elixir,' and the 'mysterious pearl'; and detail the attainments of the 'earthly and heavenly immortals.' For these, the 'feathered wheels' are not needed to convey them to the Jade Pool 20,000 miles distant, for it is just feet away. One need not mount the celestial winds to the brilliance of the 'ninefold heaven.' Suddenly opening my eyes, the immortals Chang, Ko, Chun, and Lu become my comrades, and the serenity of heaven is my home." [14]
~ TRUE TRANSMISSION OF THE GOLDEN ELIXIR BY SUN JU-CHUNG, TRANSLATED BY DOUGLAS WILE

And in Hindu texts:

"The Self is hidden in the lotus of the heart. Those who see themselves in all creatures go day by day into the world of Brahman hidden in the heart. Established in peace, they rise above body-consciousness to the supreme light of the Self. Immortal, free from fear, this Self is Brahman, called the True. Beyond the mortal and the immortal, he binds both worlds together. Those who know this live day after day in heaven in this very life." [15]
~ THE CHANDOGYA UPANISHAD, TRANSLATED BY EKNATH EASWARAN

THE RETURN TO THE SOURCE OF CREATION

This fusion of the consciousness with the great, ineffable source of creation that Jesus describes can be found symbolized at the Great Pyramids of Egypt at the summer solstice.

On the summer solstice, the sun sets between the second largest of the pyramids and the Great Pyramid. As it does, it creates the Egyptian hieroglyph for the first act of creation—the two pyramids act as the mounds either side of the sun as it rose for the first time. However, in this case the sun is setting not rising, indicating that this is a process of creation, but in reverse. Instead it depicts the sun going back to the source of creation.

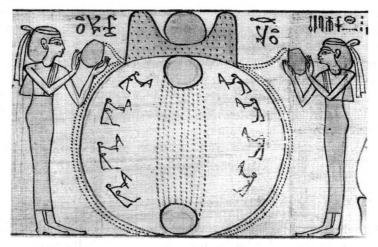

IMAGE TOP: An artist's rendition of the actual alignment of the summer solstice sun setting between the two largest Great Pyramids of Egypt, crowning the Sphinx in the foreground.

IMAGE BOTTOM: Egyptian painting of the first sunrise at the dawning of creation from the primeval mound that arose from out of the waters. At the top is the "horizon" hieroglyph with the sun appearing between two mounds, which looks like the setting summer solstice sun at the Great Pyramids.

In the esoteric Christian text Pistis Sophia, Jesus teaches his disciples that there are twenty-four mysteries, and that the first mystery is also the last mystery—that is, from where everything came, is also where it returns, just as the sun returns to its point of origin each day after twenty-four hours, and also every year.

> "And Jesus said to his disciples: 'I am come forth out of that First Mystery, which is the last mystery, that is the four-and-twentieth mystery.' And his disciples have not known nor understood that anything existeth within that mystery; but they thought of that mystery, that it is the head of the universe and the head of all existence; and they thought it is the completion of all completions..." [16]
>
> ~ PISTIS SOPHIA, TRANSLATED BY G. R. S. MEAD

This completion of all completions applies not just to everything that exists, but also to the process of awakening consciousness.

THE MARRIAGE OF HEAVEN AND EARTH, AND THE TREE OF LIFE

Summer solstice celebrations in Europe today still echo some of the ancient midsummer celebrations of the Druids. At the summer solstice the ancient Druids are said to have celebrated the marriage of heaven and earth, and many actual marriages were conducted at this time.

The pagan maypole still used in dances at midsummer was a symbol of the marriage between heaven and earth. It is symbolic of the Tree of Life, World Tree, and Axis Mundi found in sacred teachings throughout the world with its roots in the earth (feminine) and branches in the heavens (masculine), forming a connection between these two realms.

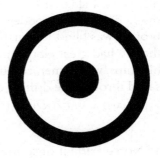

A maypole in Germany with the ring pierced by the pole, symbol of the united masculine and feminine forces, of heaven united with earth.

When the maypole is viewed from below or above, it creates the symbol of the sun, in which the circle represents the feminine and the central dot the masculine.

These also correspond to the inner two rings of the Absolute, which also correspond to the Mother and Father.

Through the unification of these two forces within a person, they become a connection between heaven and earth, and are able to bring heavenly forces, teachings, messages, etc., to the earth, serving as a vital link for humanity by bringing knowledge of otherwise inaccessible divine realms and beings to the world. This is why Odin is able to bring the knowledge of runes to humanity after his self-sacrifice on the World Tree, and after his subsequent journey to its root in the underworld where he sacrifices his eye to be able to drink from the well of "remembrance." After his betrayal and death, Odin's son Balder goes on to discover golden tablets containing the secrets of the runes, which it's said he will use when he returns to initiate a new golden age.

"Balder the beautiful was the most noble and pious of the gods in Asgard. The whitest flower upon earth is called Balder's brow, because the countenance of the god was snow-white and shining. Like fine gold was his hair, and his eyes were radiant and blue. He was well loved by all the gods, save evil Loke, who cunningly devised his death. Balder, the summer sun-god, was Odin's fairest son; his mother was Frigg, goddess of fruitful earth and sister of Njord. His brother was blind Hodur. On Balder's tongue were runes graven, so that he had great eloquence. He rode a brightly shining horse, and his ships, which men called 'billow falcons,' were the sunbeams that sailed through the drifting cloudways." [17]

~ DONALD A. MACKENZIE, TEUTONIC MYTH AND LEGEND

In the Norse Edda it describes how the sacred world tree unites the nine worlds, which are also the nine regions of the psyche—the nine heavens, and city of nine gates. This tree of life is symbolic of the structure of divinity within us (consisting of the imperishable bodies and the different parts of our higher Being), which when it is created, connects what is above with what is below.

"I remember the nine worlds, nine giantesses [who personify each land], the glorious [world tree], Mjötviðr [that unites them]..." [18]

~ THE POETIC EDDA, VÖLUSPÁ 2

The ancient Egyptian symbol of Osiris as the *djed* pillar, with the feathers of the heavenly Father and serpent of the earthly Mother crowning his head, united through the Son/sun, is also a symbol of the Tree of Life. This symbolism was encoded into the events of Osiris' life, as after his death he becomes one with a sacred tree that becomes a great pillar of a king's palace (symbolic of the kingdom of heaven).

The Egyptian symbol of the *djed* pillar which represents the god Osiris as the symbolic pillar of the temple, the world tree, and axis mundi. It shows the four bodies—physical, vital, astral, and mental—as the four notches on the pillar. The spirit sits upon these as the double feather plume, serpents, and sun disk. The serpents represent the Mother, the feathers the Father, and the sun the Son, making up the three forces of the trinity of creation as the symbol of the feathered serpent. The feathered serpent can also be found in Mithraic, Maya, and Aztec spirituality and has the same meaning. The four bodies plus the three forces (of the trinity) correspond to the seven bodies (physical, vital, astral, mental, causal, buddhic, atmic) and seven dimensions.

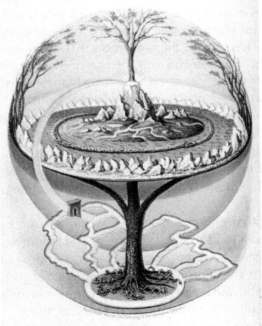

A depiction of the Tree of Life as described in the Norse mythological texts the Prose Edda.

"And just as the roots of the tree
Sink into the earth and are nourished,
And the branches of the tree
Raise their arms to heaven,
So is man like the trunk of the tree,
With his roots deep
In the breast of his Earthly Mother,
And his soul ascending
To the bright stars of his Heavenly Father.
And the roots of the tree
Are the Angels of the Earthly Mother,
And the branches of the tree
Are the Angels of the Heavenly Father.
And this is the sacred Tree of Life
Which stands in the Sea of Eternity." [19]

~ THE ESSENE GOSPEL OF PEACE, TRANSLATED BY EDMOND BORDEAUX SZEKELY

"See, oh Sons of Light, the branches of the Tree of Life reaching toward the kingdom of the Heavenly Father. And see the roots of the Tree of Life descending into the bosom of the Earthly Mother. And the Son of Man is raised to an eternal height and walks in the wonders of the plain; for only the Son of Man carries in his body the roots of the Tree of Life; the same roots that suckle from the bosom of the Earthly Mother; and only the Son of Man carries in his spirit the branches of the Tree of Life; the same branches that reach to the sky, even so to the kingdom of the Heavenly Father." [20]

~ JESUS IN THE ESSENE GOSPEL OF PEACE, TRANSLATED BY EDMOND BORDEAUX SZEKELY

The marriage between heaven and earth is a symbolic and spiritual one that represents the union of the feminine and masculine parts of someone's higher Being.

The first being that emerges from the Absolute source of creation at the dawn of time in creation stories around the world is androgynous, and divides into male and female in order to create—just as the androgynous Adam divides into Adam and Eve, the supreme androgynous creator god Atum in Egypt first creates the male Shu and female Tefnut, and likewise in India Brahman creates through the masculine Purusha and feminine Prakriti, etc.

In order to return to the source of creation, we retrace the steps we took when we left, and undergo this process in reverse. We emerged as an androgynous being, and so we can only return as an androgynous being. This is not a physical or biological change, but an inner spiritual one—references to which can be found in many ancient texts.

> "…it will lead your souls into the Light of lights, into the regions of Truth and Goodness, into the region of the Holy of all holies, into the region **which there is neither female nor male**, nor are there forms in that region, but a perpetual indescribable Light." [21]
>
> ~ JESUS IN PISTIS SOPHIA, TRANSLATED BY G. R. S. MEAD

> "Jesus said to them, 'When you make the two one, and when you make the inside like the outside and the outside like the inside, and the above like the below, and **when you make the male and the female one and the same**, so that the male not be male nor the female female; and when you fashion eyes in the place of an eye, and a hand in place of a hand, and a foot in place of a foot, and a likeness in place of a likeness; then will you enter the kingdom.'" [22]
>
> ~ THE GOSPEL OF THOMAS FROM THE NAG HAMMADI LIBRARY, TRANSLATED BY THOMAS O. LAMBDIN

> "Of the Immortal Man it should be said that He is hermaphrodite, or male and female, and eternally watchful." [23]
>
> ~ HERMES TRISMEGISTUS IN THE VISION OF HERMES, TRANSLATION FROM THE SECRET TEACHINGS OF ALL AGES BY MANLY P. HALL

> "The perfect Savior said: 'I want you to know that he who appeared before the universe in infinity, Self-grown, Self-constructed Father, being full of shining light and ineffable, in the beginning, when he decided to have his likeness become a great power, immediately **the principle (or beginning) of that Light appeared as Immortal Androgynous Man**, that through that Immortal Androgynous Man they might attain their salvation and awake from forgetfulness through the interpreter who was sent, who is with you until the end of the poverty of the robbers." [24]
>
> ~ THE WISDOM OF JESUS CHRIST, TRANSLATED BY DOUGLAS M. PARROTT

This reunion of the masculine and feminine parts of someone's Being is symbolized as a marriage, because when separate, a man and woman are seen as incomplete, but when united together in marriage, they become as one, just as masculine and feminine are the dual aspects of the one supreme creator. Marriage and sex are extremely sacred, as they contain the powers and principles of divinity. In the following excerpt the feminine aspect of the Being (Pistis Sophia) is reunited with the masculine aspect, and their union is described as a kiss.

"Grace and truth met together, and righteousness and peace kissed each other. Truth sprouted forth out of the earth, and righteousness looked down from heaven... 'Truth sprouted out of the earth,' because thou wert in the lower regions of the chaos. 'Righteousness' on the other hand which hath 'looked down from heaven,' it is the power which hath come down from the height through the First Mystery and hath entered into Pistis Sophia." [25]

~ MARY MAGDALENE IN PISTIS SOPHIA, TRANSLATED BY G. R. S. MEAD

This marriage of heaven and earth celebrated at the summer solstice is symbolic of the fusion of the spirit with the human.

THE VIRGINS OF THE SUN

The consciousness as a bride of divinity was celebrated in Rome at the summer solstice, and was based on ancient Druid traditions.

In Rome, the summer solstice was celebrated at the festival of Vestalia. It was the time of year when ordinary women were allowed to enter the sacred temple of the goddess Vesta, who was protector of the sacred flame, and of chastity and marriage. The temple was always kept by Vestal Virgins who tended a sacred fire that continuously burned in a shrine and were always dressed as brides. No men were allowed to ever enter the temple of Vesta, not even the head of the Roman Empire.

Statue of a Vestal Virgin of Rome.

This practice appears to be a continuation of a Druidic one, as at Kildare in Ireland there was a sacred sanctuary of the Celtic goddess Brighid which nineteen virgin Druidesses guarded, and which no man was allowed to enter nor even look upon. The priestesses had the duty of attending the sacred fire of the Goddess Brighid that continuously burned, just as the Vestal Virgins did in Rome. This role was eventually assumed by nuns when the site became Christian, who themselves were called "Brides of Christ." The original Druidic priestesses were called "Inghean au dagha," which means "the daughters of fire," and were believed to symbolize the virgin daughters of the flame. They were said to have sung the following song, in which the virginal consciousness is the bride taken to heaven by the sun:

"Bride, excellent woman, sudden flame, may the fiery, bright sun take us to the lasting kingdom." [26]

Interestingly, there is also evidence of priestesses at the ancient site of Machu Picchu who similarly were called "the Virgins of the Sun." Like the Vestal Virgins of Rome, they tended a sacred fire and were committed to vows of celibacy. The female priestesses of the Guanches, the ancient Indo-European inhabitants of the Canary Islands, also share similarities.

"In addition to male Shamans, the Spanish priests had also documented the existence of a spiritual order of Guanche holy women called "Harmagadas," who were like vestal virgins. Parallels are noted between them and the priestesses on the banks of the Nile in ancient Egypt. They lived together in stone temples called "Tamoganteen Acoran" (house of God)... These holy women were distinguished from other women by their long white garments... The Harmagadas never married, but served as midwives, performed rites of baptism, rain ceremonies and various other sacred functions. Historians and anthropologists agree that these women formed a very important component of the Guanche spiritual order and their theocratic government." [27]

~ GORDON KENNEDY, THE WHITE INDIANS OF NIVARIA

The Romans, Incas, Druids, and Guanches all followed a form of solar religion, and so it is likely that the tradition of the order of the Harmagadas, the Virgins of the Sun, Druidesses, and Vestal Virgins, have some common influence, and that it was a practice that traveled to different parts of the world with the spread of the ancient religion of the sun. Unfortunately however, at least the Romans and Inca distorted and added barbaric practices into this tradition of priesthood, including punishment by death for any violation of the code of virginity.

In Rome, the Vestal Virgins had to commit to thirty years of virginity. These vows of celibacy, however, appear to have been based on a literal interpretation of virginity, which was a distortion of the esoteric meaning of the virginity of consciousness. The priestesses of the temple are symbols of the consciousness, which is feminine in nature; virginity is symbolic of an inward energetic state of purity in which the sexual energies are undefiled by the egos, and in which consciousness, like a holy bride, is faithfully committed to reuniting with the higher aspects of its Being.

> "Wise men of old gave the soul a feminine name. Indeed she is female in her nature as well. She even has her womb. As long as she was alone with the father, she was virgin and in form androgynous. But when she fell down into a body and came to this life, then she fell into the hands of many robbers. And the wanton creatures passed her from one to another and [...] her. Some made use of her by force, while others did so by seducing her with a gift. In short, they defiled her, and she [...] her virginity." [28]
>
> ~ THE EXEGESIS ON THE SOUL FROM THE NAG HAMMADI LIBRARY, TRANSLATED BY WILLIAM C. ROBINSON JR.

The sacred fire the priestesses tend is the flame of the spirit within, and also the sexual fire, which they symbolically protect from defilement—that is from the lower and polluted energies of the egos, and from adultery, lust, and fornication. This is not done through sexual abstinence, but within marriage through a sacred alchemical practice that purifies the internal energies in sex itself—called the bridal chamber in esoteric Christianity, Maithuna/Tantrism in the East, HeQi in Taoism of ancient China, and symbolized as the alchemical transformation of lead into gold.

Ancient Gnostic texts, such as the Exegesis on the Soul quoted previously, tell the incredible story of consciousness—its fall into matter, perilous trials against darkness, and ultimate goal to ascend to heaven. The quote states that we were originally androgynous—a state we lost as we came into creation as our consciousness split into various parts that stayed above in the different dimensions until an aspect of it came down to inhabit a physical body. This aspect of consciousness then became defiled by the various ego states that were created, such as lust, greed, anger, hatred, violence, envy, etc., which are referred to as robbers because they steal the light and powers of consciousness.

The summer solstice signifies the regaining of the powers and pure state of consciousness—an inner state gained through the practice of energetic purification in alchemy and the elimination of the egos—and its ascent to the place it originally descended from, but with the knowledge gained from its experience in matter.

In the life of Jesus, Mary Magdalene played the symbolic role of the aspect of consciousness that descends into matter and falls into spiritual destitution. In his casting out of the seven demons from Mary and redeeming her, Jesus enacted how consciousness is saved by the higher aspect of the Being called the spiritual Son/Christ and how these two parts of someone's Being become joined on the path of the spiritual sun, so that the consciousness becomes as the "bride of Christ," which is why in Gnostic texts Mary Magdalene was often referred to as the consort of Jesus, and bride-like Druid priestesses sang of being taken up to heaven by the sun.

Below, Jesus refers to consciousness as a drop from the Light, who he as the Great Savior saves from "the robbers", awakens and joins with.

"All who come into the world, like a drop from the Light, are sent by him to the world of Almighty, that they might be guarded by him. And the bond of his forgetfulness bound him by the will of Sophia, that the matter might be <revealed> through it to the whole world in poverty, concerning his (Almighty's) arrogance and blindness and the ignorance that he was named. But I came from the places above by the will of the great Light, (I) who escaped from that bond; I have cut off the work of the robbers; I have awakened that drop that was sent from Sophia, that it might bear much fruit through me, and be perfected and not again be defective, but be <joined> through me, the Great Savior, that his glory might be revealed..." [29]

~ JESUS IN THE WISDOM OF JESUS CHRIST, TRANSLATED BY DOUGLAS M. PARROTT

"Now it is fitting that the soul regenerates herself and become again as she formerly was. The soul then moves of her own accord. And she received the divine nature from the father for her rejuvenation, so that she might be restored to the place where originally she had been. This is the resurrection that is from the dead. This is the ransom from captivity. This is the upward journey of ascent to heaven. This is the way of ascent to the father. [...]

From heaven the father sent her her man, who is her brother, the firstborn. Then the bridegroom came down to the bride. She gave up her former prostitution and cleansed herself of the pollutions of the adulterers, and she was renewed so as to be a bride. She cleansed herself in the bridal chamber; she filled it with perfume; she sat in it waiting for the true bridegroom." [30]

~ THE EXEGESIS ON THE SOUL FROM THE NAG HAMMADI LIBRARY, TRANSLATED BY WILLIAM C. ROBINSON JR.

While the spiritual Son/Christ represents the masculine child, of the spiritual Mother and Father, the "Virgin of the Sun," "Daughter of the Flame," and "Bride of Christ," represents their daughter, the feminine child, which is called consciousness. In many texts that record the teachings of Jesus, but which were excluded from the Bible, consciousness is often called Sophia, and the spiritual Son/Christ is referred to as her consort and brother. This consciousness is the spiritual part of a much greater Being that exists within each person, and which gradually reunites with the other parts of its Being—the Son, Mother and Father—on the path of the spiritual sun.

HOLY WELLS AND HOLY WATER

The symbolic Roman and Druid virgins that tended the sacred fire in the temple of the goddess also kept sacred waters—the Vestal Virgins of Rome carried sacred water from a holy spring for summer solstice ceremonial purposes which they did not allow to ever touch the ground lest it be defiled, and the Druid priestesses kept a holy well at their sanctuary which was said to have special healing properties. In pagan traditions, these holy waters are meant to be especially magical and powerful at the summer solstice. Both the Osireion temple in Egypt, and the ancient ruins of the Druid site on Tallaght Hill in Ireland, align to the summer solstice and incorporate water. Summer solstice ceremonies based on ancient traditions in South America are held at sacred springs, lakes, and waterfalls.

The significance of healing water on the summer solstice in Druid traditions can be traced back to ancient celebrations that took place on midsummer.

In the beginning of creation, the Druids believed that the sap of the cauldron of the great Mother goddess Cariadwen/Cerridwen was fertilized by three drops of dew from the Word of the Father god Celu—the dew containing the warmth of the sun. From the action of these masculine and feminine principles united by the warmth of the sun, symbolized by the Son/Christ called Hu Gadarn, they believed everything came into being.

There is record that in Wales the Druids may have celebrated the summer solstice using holy water from a holy well. This ancient Welsh festival is called Gwyl, meaning something like "dew place." In Lithuania where many pagan traditions are still celebrated, midsummer is called Rasos, which means "Dew Holiday." On the morning of the summer solstice, there are some young women in Lithuania who still wash their faces in dew today. As part of summer solstice celebrations in Russia, called Kupala, people also still wash their faces in morning dew.

Dew itself is formed by a natural process of distillation in which water is released from the earth that has been warmed by the sun, cools in the atmosphere, and condenses on surfaces. Distillation is a method of purifying water; it also occurs in the process of inner energetic purification in sexual alchemy. The use of dew symbolizes the purified energies (the sexual waters) separated from the earth (the material world) and united with the sun (the light of the spirit). It also represents the pure emanations of the Father.

"Thou purifiest thyself in the dew of the stars." [31]
~ THE PYRAMID TEXTS, UTTERANCE 214, TRANSLATED BY SAMUEL A. B. MERCER

The Druids are said to have performed baptismal rites on the summer solstice—a day they called Dydd Syl Gwyn, or Holy Sun Day—using holy water, as baptism symbolizes the purification and cleansing of the internal energies in alchemy. Baptism later became incorporated into the celebration of the Christian Pentecost, which also occurs around midsummer.

TWO DRUIDS, ONE WITH AN OAKEN WREATH ON HIS HEAD.

"The form in which you created the sun, <in which> you created the earth! The form of the moisture of heaven, the substance of heaven, the yellow blossom of heaven! How did I create your sun? <How did I> create your moon? How did I create your precious stones? I created you. When you were sprinkled with water, you remembered the force of the sun." [32]

~ THE BOOK OF CHILAM BALAM OF CHUMAYEL, TRANSLATED BY RALPH L. ROYS

The following excerpt from the Odes of Solomon—which is a text that the disciples of Jesus studied—contains a reference to dew upon the face, as practiced by the ancient pagans. The imagery of summer is associated with the eternal realm of light, beauty, and fragrance the soul ascends to.

"And I abandoned the folly cast upon the earth,
And stripped it off and cast it from me.
And the Lord renewed me with His garment,
And possessed me by His light.
And from above He gave me immortal rest;
And I became like the land which blossoms and rejoices in its fruits.
And the Lord is like the sun
Upon the face of the land.
My eyes were enlightened,
And my face received the dew;
And my breath was refreshed
By the pleasant fragrance of the Lord.
And He took me to His Paradise,
Wherein is the wealth of the Lord's pleasure.
I contemplated blooming and fruit-bearing trees,
And self-grown was their wreathed-crown.
Their branches were flourishing
And their fruits were shining;
Their roots were from an immortal land.
And a river of gladness was irrigating them,
And the region around them in the land of eternal life." [33]

~ THE ODES OF SOLOMON, TRANSLATED BY JAMES H. CHARLESWORTH

Greenery and flowers are used in pagan celebrations of the summer solstice that have survived throughout Europe today, and are used in the Christian celebration of the Pentecost, which occurs around the time of midsummer, to decorate churches. This is one of many examples of the Christian tradition incorporating pagan symbolism in its celebrations—the greenery and flowers symbolize the realm of the spirit, as a place of eternal summer and light.

"The Druids saw that flowers and their sweet perfume were not provided to supply nourishment to build up carnal bodies, but were provided by the tender eternal Author of the Universe to gratify the sense of the beautiful in human souls. They, therefore regarded flowers and hues of landscapes, as harbingers of a world of beauty, and eternal summer, beyond this life." [34]

~ MORIEN O. MORGAN, THE ROYAL WINGED SON OF STONEHENGE AND AVEBURY

"Those who sow in winter reap in summer. The winter is the world, the summer the other Aeon (eternal realm). Let us sow in the world that we may reap in the summer." [35]

~ THE GOSPEL OF PHILIP FROM THE NAG HAMMADI LIBRARY, TRANSLATED BY WESLEY W. ISENBERG

THE EARTH CROWNED BY THE SUN

MIDSUMMER CROWN.

Wreaths form a large part of midsummer celebrations in Europe which originated in ancient times. Women wear wreaths of flowers and men wear wreaths of oak leaves. Wreaths of flowers and greenery are floated upon the waters of lakes and streams, and also adorn the maypole, which is danced around on the summer solstice.

Symbolic references to the wreath can be found in the ancient texts of esoteric Christianity, and at the Sphinx which is aligned to the summer solstice in Egypt.

The wreath is the eternal crown of the spirit, which creates the halo famously depicted in artwork throughout the world.

On the summer solstice, the day of most light in the year, the sun sets precisely between the two largest Great Pyramids of Egypt, creating a halo of light around the head of the Sphinx.

In the esoteric Christian text Pistis Sophia, Jesus sends down a light stream which forms a wreath around the head of the ascending Pistis Sophia—the central character of the story, who symbolizes the feminine aspect of someone's higher Being.

> "And moreover by commandment of myself, the First Mystery which looketh without, the light-stream which surrounded Pistis Sophia on all her sides, shone most exceedingly, and Pistis Sophia abode in the midst of the light, a great light being on her left and on her right, and on all her sides, **forming a wreath round her head.**" [36]
> ~ JESUS IN PISTIS SOPHIA, TRANSLATED BY G. R. S. MEAD

In interpreting the above passage in Pistis Sophia, Mary the mother of Jesus refers to another ancient esoteric Christian text that was later brought to light called the Odes of Solomon—quoting the following passage, which explains that the wreath is actually the Father, who is referred to as the Lord.

> **"Like a wreathed-crown on my head is the Lord,**
> And never shall I be without Him.
> The wreathed-crown of truth is plaited for me,
> Causing Your branches to blossom within me,
> For it is not like a parched crown
> That fails to blossom.
> But You have lived upon my head,
> And You have blossomed upon me.
> Your fruits are full, even complete;
> They are full of Your salvation." [37]
> ~ THE ODES OF SOLOMON, TRANSLATED BY JAMES H. CHARLESWORTH

At the summer solstice, the Son who is one with their Mother is crowned by the Father (who is as a King in the spiritual realms).

This same symbolism can be found at the most famous ancient site in the world with a summer solstice alignment. Stonehenge aligns to the summer solstice sun both at sunrise, when its inner sanctuary receives the rays of the sun, and at midday, when the sun overhead aligns with the center of its stone circle. Some believe that its circle of stones is a symbol of the earth, and that its alignment to the summer solstice symbolized the sun crowning the earth—which again is symbolic of the Son-Mother (the serpent and earth) crowned by the Father (the wings and summer sun). The summer solstice sun at midday, aligning directly overhead the center of Stonehenge, would have created the symbol of the sun ⊙ just as the maypole does, which is the symbol of the united feminine and masculine parts of someone's higher Being.

THE END OF DARKNESS

Seth is the god to the left and Horus to the right
in this image, crowning the initiate in the center.

In ancient Britain the god of light was the Oak King, and the god of darkness was the Holly King. The Oak King reigned during the half of the year from the winter to summer solstice, when the sun's light progressively increases/waxes. The summer solstice was the height of his reign as the day of most light.

The Holly King instead reigned from after the summer solstice to the height of winter, which is when the sun's light progressively decreases/wanes until reaching the time of most darkness in the year.

Similarly in ancient Egypt Horus was the god of the sun and light, while the god Seth was the personification of darkness. At the summer solstice Horus finally defeated Seth in battle, and was crowned King.

Horus and the Oak King are symbols of the Son/Christ, whilst Seth and the Holly King can be seen as symbols of Lucifer. Lucifer plays a role in the work of spiritual awakening, as he is the tempter and psychological trainer—stirring our sexual passions and desires from within the subconscious, the dark part of our psyche, so that we can see, understand, and overcome them, and transform subconscious to consciousness, lust into love, and darkness into light. This is why esoterically he has been referred to as "the light bringer."

In the ancient text Pistis Sophia, Jesus is described as ascending on the fifteenth day of the month of Tybi on a full moon. The number fifteen was assigned to Lucifer in ancient traditions of Tarot and numerology. The numbers one and five added equal six, which is the number of sexual desire. This reference is symbolic of the defeat of Lucifer, of all temptation and desire, and the transformation of the moon (which is a symbol of the subconscious) so that it is fully illuminated by the light of consciousness.

> "And it came to pass then, on the fifteenth day of the moon in the month Tybi, which is the day on which the moon is full, on that day then, when the sun had come forth in his going, that there came forth behind him a great light-power shining most exceedingly, and there was no measure to the light conjoined with it... Then Jesus ascended or soared into the height, shining most exceedingly in an immeasurable light. And the disciples gazed after him and none of them spake, until he had reached unto heaven; but they all kept in deep silence. This then came to pass on the fifteenth day of the moon, on the day on which it is full in the month Tybi." [38]
>
> ~ PISTIS SOPHIA, TRANSLATED BY G. R. S. MEAD

To be able to ascend to the Father, Lucifer and all his temptations must firstly be overcome. At the summer solstice, Lucifer is finally defeated, just as Horus defeats Seth and the Oak King defeats the Holly King. Lucifer has fulfilled his role as the "light-bringer," as at the summer solstice the light is made complete. He is absorbed into the light of the spirit, and inner darkness is no more.

> "Let thy messengers go; let thine envoys hasten to thy father, to Atum.
> Atum, let him ascend to thee; enfold him in thine embrace, for there

is no god, who has become a star, who has not his companion. Shall I be thy companion?

Look at me; thou hast regarded the form of the children of their fathers, who know their speech. They are now imperishable stars.

So shalt thou see those who are in the Palace: that is Horus and Seth." [39]

~ THE PYRAMID TEXTS, UTTERANCE 215, TRANSLATED BY SAMUEL A. B. MERCER

The summer solstice is also the stage on the path of the spiritual sun when the egos are finally defeated, which is the defeat of all the evil and darkness within a person. In the following excerpt Jesus takes all the power out of the seven-headed monster, which is symbolic of the self-willed and selfish egos whose seven heads represent the seven sins.

The woman described in the book of Revelation
who treads upon the seven headed beast.

"And I led Pistis Sophia forth from the chaos, she treading under foot the serpent-faced emanation of Self-willed, and moreover treading

237

under foot the seven faced-basilisk emanation, and treading under foot the lion-and dragon-faced power. I made Pistis Sophia continue to stand upon the seven-headed-basilisk emanation of Self-willed; and it was more mighty than them all in its evil doings. And I, the First Mystery, stood by it and took all the powers in it, and made to perish its whole matter, so that no seed should arise from it from now on." [40]

~ JESUS IN PISTIS SOPHIA, TRANSLATED BY G. R. S. MEAD

RETURN TO THE LIGHT

The stages of the path of the spiritual sun that are symbolized at the time of the summer solstice are the ascension to the Father and the return to the divine androgynous state and to source. Although I am going through these specific stages, I have not completed everything and so there are processes and events that I have no knowledge of. This means that the description of the stages of the path symbolized at the summer solstice is incomplete, and in places may need correction. But I can explain with certainty what I have gone through, and this is enough for me to be able to describe most of the overall meaning of ascension and return to source with some clarity. Should I go through more of this path, I will be able to add more to the understanding of this event.

In the path of the spiritual sun, the sun at the summer solstice represents the ascension, enlightenment, and the return to the divine source. It is the culmination of the individual's journey to enlightenment that has been represented in the solstices and equinoxes of the year.

The celebration of the summer solstice is the celebration not only of the life-giving power of the sun, but is the celebration of the complete awakening of the spiritual Son, symbolized by the physical sun. After the end of the summer solstice, the cycle of the year in its symbolic depiction of the work to awakening begins again, as the sun starts to descend in its annual journey.

Around three days after the summer solstice in the northern hemisphere, the birth of John the Baptist is celebrated as St. John's Day. This is no coincidence, as following the summer solstice is the "birth" of darkness in the wheel of the year when the sun's light begins to decrease, which is a return to the beginning of the descent of consciousness into matter.

And so completes the cycle of the sun in its journey each year; and as it completes it begins again, repeatedly teaching its sacred wisdom through creation to the individual sparks of consciousness that each contain creation's wondrous potential—and that like the seed that lies dormant beneath the earth at autumn, if it dies, can have the life of the spirit germinate within at the winter solstice, and grow to magnificent full bloom at summer.

It was said that at the summer solstice the Oak King, the god of light, withdrew to the realm of the northern circumpolar stars, which are the stars that rotate around the North Pole. The ancient Egyptians called them, "the ones not knowing destruction," and believed that this was the place immortals ascended to as these stars are always visible and never set below the horizon. One of the shafts of the King's Chamber in the Great Pyramid was designed to always sight these stars. This symbolizes the ascent into the eternal realms of divine light, which have their source within the stars in the higher dimensions.

"The door of heaven is open, the door of earth is open,
apertures of the (heavenly) windows are open,
the steps of Nun are open,
the steps of light are revealed
by that one who endures always.
I say this to myself when I ascend to heaven,
that I may anoint myself with the best ointment and clothe myself
with the best linen,
and seat myself upon (the throne) of "Truth which makes alive";
while my side is against the side of those gods who are in the north
of the sky,
the imperishable stars, and I will not set..." [41]
~ THE PYRAMID TEXTS, UTTERANCE 503, TRANSLATED BY SAMUEL A. B. MERCER

Without the birth of the Son within, at death we leave by the gate of the winter solstice, but in the darkness preceding the birth of the sun, having not realized our true potential, only to return again. The summer solstice is the gateway for those who have actualized the light of the sun within, and are leaving this world for the realms of imperishability and divine light. For those wishing to return to their Being, the spiritual sun—our own star—is waiting for us.

"'Come, my child,' says Atum, 'come to us,' say they, say the gods to thee, Osiris. 'Our brother is come to us, the eldest, the first begotten of his father, the first born of his mother,' say they, say the gods." [42]
~ THE PYRAMID TEXTS, TRANSLATED BY SAMUEL A. B. MERCER

"May you open your place in heaven amongst the stars of heaven!
You are indeed the unique star..." [43]
~ THE PYRAMID TEXTS, UTTERANCE 245, BASED ON TRANSLATIONS BY FAULKNER,
   PIANKOFF, AND SPELEER

"Jesus said to them, 'Stop struggling with me. Each of you has his own star...'" [44]

~ THE GOSPEL OF JUDAS, TRANSLATED BY RODOLPHE KASSER, MARVIN MEYER, AND GREGOR WURST, IN COLLABORATION WITH FRANÇOIS GAUDARD

"The path to immortality is hard, and only a few find it. The rest await the Great Day when the wheels of the universe shall be stopped and the immortal sparks shall escape from the sheaths of substance. Woe unto those who wait, for they must return again, unconscious and unknowing, to the seed-ground of stars, and await a new beginning. Those who are saved by the light of the mystery which I have revealed unto you, O Hermes, and which I now bid you to establish among men, shall return again to the Father who dwelleth in the White Light, and shall deliver themselves up to the Light and shall be absorbed into the Light, and in the Light they shall become Powers in God. This is the Way of *Good* and is revealed only to them that have wisdom [...] Thus preached Hermes: 'O people of the earth, men born and made of the elements, but with the spirit of the Divine Man within you, rise from your sleep of ignorance! Be sober and thoughtful. Realize that your home is not in the earth but in the Light. Why have you delivered yourselves over unto death, having power to partake of immortality? Repent, and *change your minds*. Depart from the dark light and forsake corruption forever. Prepare yourselves to climb through the Seven Rings and to blend your souls with the eternal Light.'" [45]

~ THE VISION OF HERMES, TRANSLATION FROM THE SECRET TEACHINGS OF ALL AGES BY MANLY P. HALL

PART II

The Ancient Civilization of the Sun

CHAPTER SEVEN

The Lost Civilization
of the Sun

THE PRACTICE OF THE RELIGION OF THE SUN traces its origins far back in time, to a period before written history. It's worth bearing in mind that officially recognized written history only starts around 2,500 BC, and yet we know that this represents a fraction of human existence. This chapter explores some of the evidence for a once widespread civilization carrying the knowledge of the spiritual sun that history does have some knowledge of, and which gave rise to many of the world's spiritual traditions, sacred texts, and ancient megalithic sites, many of which are referenced in this book.

To be able to make sense of our ancient past, it's a topic worth understanding, at least from a broad point of view. It's a huge topic though, and can sometimes feel quite overwhelming, as archeological discoveries continue to be made, and there is already a vast body of witness accounts, ancestral and oral histories, archeological evidence, preserved monuments and texts, etc., on the subject—only a tiny amount of which are provided here as examples. The idea is hopefully to give enough of an overview to put the knowledge in this book into its ancient historical context; anyone who wishes to learn more about it can find an almost endless source of writing on the subject.

We've used the available evidence to piece together what happened in the past, but new pieces of evidence and breakthroughs in dating techniques, etc., can turn long-held assumptions on their head, and in the field of archeology they tend to do so on an almost daily basis. That's why from our personal perspective, our understanding of history is something fluid—and we feel that everyone should always be ready to reevaluate the accepted views of history. We've often had to reevaluate sometimes long-held views on history as we've come across new information, but we feel that's the only way to approach its study, as otherwise our views simply get in the way of truth. Ultimately, the only vested interest anyone should have in looking at history is in finding the truth, and the truth belongs to all of us to study, make sense of, and to use.

The following is as much as we've been able to piece together so far, and we'll continue to add to it as we discover more.

THE SURVIVORS OF THE FLOOD

Many oral histories, including those of the ancient Egyptians, Hindus, as well as those of the North, Central, and South American pre-Columbians, speak of cataclysmic events that destroyed prior civilizations (the last of these is popularly referred to as Atlantis), and recount how survivors took the knowledge from this previous age to found a new civilization in the current human age in which we still live.

Lucy Thompson was one of the first North American pre-Columbian women to write down the oral histories of her people. She describes the civilization of the Wa-gas that once extended across the entire North American continent, and what they told her people.

Photograph of
Lucy Thompson
taken in 1916.

"When the Wa-gas first arrived on this continent they handed down the traditions to us that it was in-habited by a giant race of people when they first came. These giants were represented by the Wa-gas as being very swarthy in complexion, and they used implements so large that no ordinary man could lift them. It was an age when large animals roamed the earth, and it seems the birds and fowls were all very large in size. It appeared to be the first age, and was the age of the giants. The recollections transmitted by the Wa-gas were that these giants were very cruel and wicked. It was said that God became displeased with them and destroyed them and they all perished from the earth. It was also said that God appeared to the High Priest of the Wa-gas and told them that he was going to destroy the giant race and that the Wa-gas themselves would survive upon the earth as a new people." [1]

~ LUCY THOMPSON, TO THE AMERICAN INDIAN; REMINISCENCES OF A YUROK WOMAN 1916

The oral histories of the Hopi people in North America record how the people who survived a flood established a civilization in North America. The Hopi describe a series of world ages, in which humans had to take shelter within the earth (in what they describe as "ant hills") as the ice caps (called "twins") shifted, to afterwards re-emerge once it was safe to repopulate the world. This was said to happen at the end of the First and Second World. Frank Walters in his *Book of the Hopi* states that the description of the emergence from the Third World into our present Fourth World was different. It was not a reemergence like the last two, but was instead a sea voyage undertaken by those deemed worthy to survive the most recent catastrophe.

Similar oral histories exist amongst the peoples of South America.

"The South American legends speak of a time of great trouble, where mankind was at its lowest ebb and state of debauchery. I believe the world had been hit by an asteroid or similar, which had plunged it back into the dark ages of subsistence survival. In this terrible atmosphere of rampant human cannibalism and the dangers of constant predation, the all-powerful enlightened ones turned up to deliver everyone out of their fallen state and establish functioning civilisation anew. The enlightened ones taught the special sciences of civilisation by numbers that could be memorised and encoded into all public buildings, etc." [2]

~ MARTIN DOUTRÉ, ARCHEOASTRONOMER AND AUTHOR OF WWW.CELTICNZ.CO.NZ

"Immediately north of Columbia and Venezuela, the Cuna Indians of Panama, who practiced writing on wooden tablets, had a tradition that after a devastating flood, '...there appeared a great personage who... taught the people how to behave, what to name things, and how to use them. He was followed by a number of disciples who spread his teachings...' (D. B. Stout, Handbook of South American Indians, vol. IV, p. 267.)" [3]

~ THOR HEYERDAHL, THE BEARDED GODS SPEAK

As we will explore further, it is very apparent in the oral histories and archeological evidence that a group of survivors from a flood did indeed travel the world by sea to establish civilizations and many ancient sacred sites aligned to the sun in different continents.

Central to the knowledge carried by these survivors was the religion of the sun, which is why the most ancient cities, mysteries, texts, and sacred sites, incorporate solar symbolism and alignments.

> "Sun worship played an important part in nearly all the early pagan Mysteries. This indicates the probability of their Atlantean origin, for the people of Atlantis were sun worshipers. The Solar Deity was usually personified as a beautiful youth, with long golden hair to symbolize the rays of the sun. This golden Sun God was slain by wicked ruffians, who personified the evil principle of the universe. By means of certain rituals and ceremonies, symbolic of purification and regeneration, this wonderful God of Good was brought back to life and became the Savior of His people. The secret processes whereby He was resurrected symbolized those cultures by means of which man is able to overcome his lower nature, master his appetites, and give expression to the higher side of himself. The Mysteries were organized for the purpose of assisting the struggling human creature to reawaken the spiritual powers which, surrounded by the flaming ring of lust and degeneracy, lay asleep within his soul. In other words, man was offered a way by which he could regain his lost estate." 4
>
> ~ MANLY P. HALL, THE SECRET TEACHINGS OF ALL AGES

Krishna refers to an ancient dynasty of the sun whose knowledge was given to a man called Manu—chosen by the god Vishnu to survive a catastrophic flood in a boat and then reinitiate civilization in a new age. Manu was said to have passed the knowledge of this ancient path to a lineage of divine kings. This is a reference to the knowledge of the spiritual sun passing to the beginnings of our current human age.

> "The imperishable philosophy I taught to Viwaswana, the founder of the Sun dynasty, Viwaswana gave it to Manu the Lawgiver, and Manu to King Ikshwaku! The Divine Kings knew it, for it was their tradition. Then, after a long time, at last it was forgotten. It is the same ancient Path that I have now revealed to thee, since thou art My devotee and My friend. It is the supreme Secret." 5
>
> ~ KRISHNA IN THE BHAGAVAD GITA, TRANSLATED BY SHRI PUROHIT SWAMI

The oldest known sacred texts in the world—the Pyramid Texts of ancient Egypt and the Rig Veda of ancient India, both describe a religion of the sun, which had its origins in more ancient times, and which these texts are fragmentary remnants of.

> "The *Vedas* contain spiritual, occult and cosmic secrets that we are just beginning to become aware of. The great India based religions of Hinduism, Buddhism, Jainism and Sikhism may represent only later aspects of ancient enlightenment traditions that were probably more common during the Vedic era. The *Vedas* represent the remains of these early traditions, of which there were no doubt many more.
>
> Vedic literature portrays an ancient solar religion of Yoga and enlightenment, such as was once common throughout the entire world. The Sun is a symbol of the higher Self, the *Atman* or *Purusha* of yogic thought. This Vedic religion of light is a religion of consciousness, which is the supreme form of light." [6]
> ~ DAVID FRAWLEY, FOUNDER AND DIRECTOR OF THE AMERICAN INSTITUTE FOR VEDIC STUDIES

One of the "Founding Fathers" of the United States, who was also a Freemason, wrote how the religion of the sun is the most ancient of religions and came from a time before recorded history. From these most ancient and unknown origins, he describes how it spread throughout the ancient world and eventually emerged in Christianity and Freemasonry.

> "Masonry (as I shall show from the customs, ceremonies, hieroglyphics, and chronology of Masonry) is derived and is the remains of the religion of the ancient Druids; who, like the Magi of Persia and the Priests of Heliopolis in Egypt, were Priests of the Sun. They paid worship to this great luminary, as the great visible agent of a great invisible first cause whom they styled 'Time without limits.'...
>
> The christian religion and Masonry have one and the same common origin: both are derived from the worship of the Sun...
>
> At what period of antiquity, or in what nation, this religion was first established, is lost in the labyrinth of unrecorded time. It is generally ascribed to the ancient Egyptians, the Babylonians and Chaldeans, and reduced afterwards to a system regulated by the apparent progress of the sun through the twelve signs of Zodiac by Zoroaster the law giver of Persia, from whence Pythagoras brought it into Greece...
>
> The worship of the Sun as the great visible agent of a great invisible first cause, 'Time without limits,' spread itself over a considerable part of Asia and Africa, from thence to Greece and Rome, through all ancient Gaul, and into Britain and Ireland...

As the study and contemplation of the Creator [is] in the works of the creation, the Sun, as the great visible agent of that Being, was the visible object of the adoration of Druids; all their religious rites and ceremonies had reference to the apparent progress of the Sun through the twelve signs of the Zodiac, and his influence upon the earth." [7]

~ THOMAS PAINE, AN ESSAY ON THE ORIGIN OF FREE-MASONRY (1803-1805)

The religion of the sun was, for thousands of years, the dominant religion of the ancient world. If you trace it back far enough, its origin stretches well beyond recorded history (which only goes back a few thousand years BC) into the most ancient sacred texts, and from there, into the most ancient of myths and legends.

Oral histories, written accounts, and the evidence on and under the ground, reveals a time when an advanced civilization of people traveled the globe taking their carefully preserved sciences and spiritual knowledge with them, and used it to establish some of the most famous and enigmatic sacred sites on the planet—many of which we'll explore later in this book.

THE MAKING OF SACRED PLACES ALIGNED TO THE COSMOS

Wherever these ancient people tended to travel, woodhenges, megaliths, pyramids, and mounds, were built that aligned to the solstices and equinoxes, and also particularly to the constellation Orion. This combination of aligning sacred sites to the constellation of Orion and to the sun at the solstices and equinoxes is found at the Great Pyramids of Egypt, the ancient city of Great Zimbabwe, Glastonbury Tor, the cities of the Hopi including Chaco Canyon, the statues of Easter Island, and the Nazca Lines in Peru. Apart from building sites, there is evidence that they also refurbished many pre-existing ancient sites that had survived even earlier cataclysms.

"In remote antiquity, there was a very mobilized group of cousin nations who traveled across the entire globe and wherever they settled long term they built code-bearing complexes to preserve and teach their sciences. To ensure that profound scientific knowledge would not be lost, they erected precisely positioned pyramid and hump mounds, concentric ring mounds, geometric earth embankments, henges complete with internal stone markers, standing stone circles, obelisk complexes, sighting pits, cairn markers, etc. In each case the selfsame measurement standard, as well as length and angle codes on one site will duplicate that found on another, even a continent or two removed." [8]

~ MARTIN DOUTRÉ, THE CHINESE PYRAMIDS AT XI'AN, SHAANXL

Using their great astronomical, navigational, and surveying knowledge, they were even able to align sacred sites to one another across vast distances. In Ireland for example, sites were aligned from its east to west coast, stretching a distance of 135 miles; but if that weren't feat enough, they were also aligned across continents and entire oceans—the Nazca Lines and Machu Picchu in Peru, as well as the statues of Easter Island, all lie on the same line around the earth aligning to each other and to the Great Pyramids of Egypt.

The fact that they aligned the sacred sites they established to the Great Pyramids, and aligned many of them to the same constellations, reveals how these bringers of knowledge understood the important spiritual significance of the Great Pyramids as a great hub of cosmological knowledge and spirituality, as we'll explore further on.

This time of the lost civilization of the sun was a time in which large numbers of people cooperated in the building of giant structures with incredible precision using materials and incorporating alignments from vast distances away, which would have required times of relative peace and prosperity. It was also a time when many remote places of the world were explored and inhabited for this purpose.

The evidence of those who carried the knowledge of the spiritual sun to distant parts of the world is being uncovered in vast quantities in some of the most unexpected places. They have been called the Wa-iti in Africa, the Aryans in Central Asia, the Viracocha-Runa (or people of the sea-foam) surviving in part as the Chachapoyas in Peru, the Turehu people in New Zealand, the Wa-gas and their descendants the Anasazi in North America, and so on—with each culture using different names to describe them.

> "When The Indians first made their appearance on the Klamath river it was already inhabited by a white race of people known among us as the Wa-gas. These white people were found to inhabit the whole continent, and were a highly moral and civilized race. They heartily welcomed the Indians to their country and taught us all of their arts and sciences... For a vast period of time the two races dwelt together in peace and honored homes, wars and quarrels were unknown in this golden age of happiness. No depredations were ever committed upon the property of their people, as the white people ruled with beacon light of kindness, and our people still worship the hallowed places where once they trod. Their morals were far superior to the white people of today, their ideals were high and inspired our people with greatness. After we had lived with these ancient people so long, they suddenly called their hosts together and mysteriously disappeared for a distant land, we know not where... It was a sad farewell when they departed from this land, for our people mourned their loss, as no more have we found such friends as they, so true and loyal.

In their farewell journey across this land they left land-marks of stone monuments, on the tops of high mountains and places commanding a view of the surrounding country. These land-marks we have kept in repair, down through the ages in loving remembrance. I have seen many of these land-marks myself (and often repaired them) that they left as a symbol of the mystic ages and the grandeur of a mighty nation that passed in a single season...

This is said to be the reason why some of our people are very fair. Some of the Indians are still looking for their return to the earth, when they come back it is believed that peace and happiness will reign supreme again over this great land and all evil will be cast out." [9]

~ LUCY THOMPSON, TO THE AMERICAN INDIAN; REMINISCENCES OF A YUROK WOMAN 1916

THE ARRIVAL OF THE WISDOM BRINGERS

In many ancient texts and ancestral histories, there is a wisdom bringer who is divinely appointed to re-establish civilization after a flood. Thoth of Egypt, Manu of the Hindus, and Viracocha of the Incas, have all been described as wisdom bringers who traveled by boat carrying the knowledge to initiate a new civilization based on spiritual principles.

Histories of the Hopi people describe how a wisdom bringer called Maasaw had been appointed to help the survivors of the catastrophe to establish their civilization in North America and gave them divine laws to live by.

"...at the beginning of the Fourth World, they [the Hopi] were greeted by Maasaw, the caretaker of the land. He had also been appointed the head of the Third World... He ordered the survivors to separate into clans, to begin a series of migrations across the continent, whereby the stars would guide them. Eventually, they would meet again and settle. Maasaw gave each clan one or more sacred tablets, which would guide them along their migrations.

To each clan, he also gave a small water jar, which was magical, and came with instructions, which included a description on how to make a new water jar, in case the old one was broken or needed replacing. The Hopi argue that this water jar is the missing ingredient in how to make sense of the locations chosen by the Ancestral Puebloans to live: the water jar meant that they could settle miles away from rivers, as the water jar allowed them to create springs and rivers wherever they settled...

Finally, the Hopi argue that each clan was supposed to complete four migrations, but that only some did, specifically those that kept the "door on top of their heads" open and realised the purpose and

meaning behind the four migrations, which was that these migrations were purification ceremonies. Once completed, they would return to the sacred circle, to establish the Hopi Mesas, their permanent settlement – until the advent of the Fifth World." [10]
~ PHILIP COPPENS, THE WANDERERS OF THE FOURTH WORLD

The reference to being guided by stars and sacred tablets, is actually a reference to the wisdom bringer Maasaw giving people the directions to build their sacred sites and cities in the formation of the constellations Sirius and Orion, as well as in alignment with the solstices and equinoxes, as the sites of the Anasazi/Hopi are built to mirror these constellations on the ground. Incredibly, this practice of aligning sites to these specific constellations and to the sun is found at the site of the Great Pyramids of Egypt, and many other sacred sites around the world, which as we will see, people like Maasaw had a connection to. Sirius and Orion were particularly central in ancient Egypt as the representations of the goddess Isis and god Osiris.

In Central and South America similar peoples were recorded as arriving and bringing knowledge—they were described as fair skinned men with beards and long flowing robes. The peoples of Central and South America called the main wisdom bringer various names. The Inca called him Virachocha, the Maya called him Kukulcan, to the Tzendal he was called Votan, to the Aztecs he was called Quetzalcoatl, to the Chibchas he was Bochica, being called Zume east of the Andes, and so on.

Oral histories of the Inca describe the arrival of Viracocha, who came to South America to help establish civilization, and how he oversaw the building of the ancient megalithic site of Tiwanaku/Tiahuanaco:

"During the first generations after the Conquest, however, the myths and traditions of the legendary pre-Incas were still alive in Peru, and when the famous historian Prescott began to analyse the early Spanish documents and manuscripts in the archives of the Royal Academy of History at Madrid, he came to the following conclusion concerning the early Inca beliefs [1847,Vol.I,p.9]: "The story of the bearded white men finds its place in most of their legends." he also wrote [Ibid]: "Another legend speaks of certain white and bearded men, who, advancing from the shores of Lake Titicaca, established an ascendancy over the natives, and imparted to them the blessings of civilisation. It may remind us of the tradition existing among the Aztecs in respect to Quetzalcoatl, the good deity, who with a similar garb and aspect came up the great plateau from the east on a like benevolent mission to the natives. The analogy is more remarkable, as there is no trace of any communication with, or even knowledge of, each other to be found in the two nations."

...Early chroniclers... have shown that there were memories in aboriginal Peru of important cultural, religious, and political events of pre-Inca times all centering about Lake Titicaca, and more specifically Titicaca Island and the megalithic site of Tiahuanaco. Both places are near the southern end of the same lake, and both have ecclesiastical ruins of superior workmanship of admittedly pre-Inca origin. Here Viracocha is remembered as having made his first appearance among the Indians, and here he built his first abode, from which he spread his culture and benefits all over Peru. Here too, the white and bearded men, the virachocha-runa or Sea-foam people were active during Viracocha's reign, until they were sent by their chief, on their final mission northwards, or killed in the local fighting." [11]

~ THOR HEYERDAHL, AMERICAN INDIANS IN THE PACIFIC

Oral histories of the Maya describe how the wisdom bringer Kukulcan caused the building of structures at Chichen Itza in Mexico. Note the similarities between the name Kukulcan and Cúchulainn—a legendary ancient Irish hero who was the son of Lugh, the god of light (who himself was called "the Son of the sun," and therefore a descendent of the sun). Both Lugh and his son Cúchulainn belonged to the people called the Tuatha Dé Danaan who were responsible for bringing the ancient religion of the sun to Ireland, and building many sacred sites aligned to the sun at the solstice and equinox there. Could the Cúchulainn who brought the religion of the sun to Ireland, be the same Kukulcan who brought it to Central America? The following mention of Kukulcan's four brothers coming from four tribes would match the ancient records of Ireland being divided into four kingdoms:

"The natives affirmed, says Las Casas, that in ancient times there came to that land twenty men, the chief of whom was called 'Cocolcan,'... They wore flowing robes and sandals on their feet, they had long beards, and their heads were bare... Kukulcan seems, therefore, to have stood in the same rela-tion in Yucatan to the other divinities of the days as did Votan in Chiapa and Quetzalcoatl Ce Acatl in Cholula. We learn from Brinton [Ibid., p.162] that Kukulcan was one of four 'brothers' each ruling his own tribe. One of the others having died or departed, and two been put to death, only Kukulcan re-mained. He instructed the people in the arts of peace, and caused various important edifices to be built at Chichen Itza. He also founded and named the city of Mayapan. It is at least interesting to note that Kukulcan is simply a translation of Quetzalcoatl. *Kukul* is the Maya term for the *Quetzal*-bird, and *kan* is a serpent. [Verrill 1929, p.101.]" [12]

~ THOR HEYERDAHL, AMERICAN INDIANS IN THE PACIFIC

Tzendal traditions record the arrival of a wisdom bringer called Votan. Note the similarity of the name with Wotan (pronounced Votan as the letter 'w' is pronounced 'v' in German), which is a Germanic derivative of the Norse wisdom bringer Odin. In some South American legends this wisdom bringer was known as "the wanderer;" incredibly Odin was also known as the wanderer and wisdom bringer in Scandinavia, and was likewise depicted with a long beard. Other strange evidence furthers this connection. Odin was said to have discovered and imparted the magical writing called runes to the peoples of Scandinavia, and stones carved with runes have been found in South America. Likewise Votan in South America is credited with bringing them the language of hieroglyphic signs, and we find different hieroglyphic writing types emerging at many ancient sites, including ancient Egypt and Easter Island.

The wisdom bringer Wotan is believed to have been adopted by Germanic and Norse cultures as a god, just as Votan was by the Central and South Americans. Wotan/Odin's origins are unknown, but theories have speculated that both he and Cúchulainn are of Indo-European origin. It's worth mentioning that the term 'Indo-European' is a modern creation that in all likelihood is being used to describe the ancient peoples historically known as the Aryans. It seems evident that Wotan/Odin and Cúchulainn were real people, and were either the same person or were different people from a distinct group, who traveled, taking the knowledge of the spiritual sun throughout the world.

Painting called
'Odin, the Wanderer'
by Georg von Rosen.

"At some definitely remote epoch, Votan came from the far East. He was sent by God to divide out and assign to the different races of men the earth on which they dwell, and to give to each its own language. The land whence he came was vaguely called *ualum uotan*, the land of Votan. His message was especially to the Tzendals. Previous to his arrival they were ignorant, barbarous, and without fixed habitations. He collected them into villages, taught them how to cultivate the maize and cotton, and invented the hieroglyphic signs, which they learned to carve on the walls of their temples. It is even said that he wrote his own history in them. Votan brought with him, according to one statement, or, according to another, was followed from his native land by, certain attendants or subordinates, called in the myth *tzequil*, petticoated, from the long and flowing robes they wore. These aided him in the work of civilization." [13]

~ DANIEL G. BRINTON, AMERICAN HERO-MYTHS

The knowledge Viracocha taught is recorded as being to do with the sun and in building megalithic sites. In Ireland, Cúchulainn was said to be a descendent of the sun, just as Virachoca and Votan were in South America.

"We learn from various narratives that the 'preaching', 'teaching', and 'instructions' of Viracocha were of a religious as well as of a practical nature. He was anxious that the Indians should consider him the representative of the sun, a divine being in spite of his human appearance, which only differed from theirs in a lighter skin and a beard, and in his attire, consisting of a long robe secured with a girdle, and the habit of carrying a staff and a book-like object in his hands. It is interesting to note from various accounts how anxious this legendary preacher was to teach the tribes that he and his followers were god-men, connected with the sun, and that they should be worshipped and obeyed accordingly as creators, lords and protectors, instead of the idols of the former age of darkness. We are told how they taught the natives agriculture and showed them which were edible plants; how they introduced irrigation of waste land; how they built stone statues either in memory of their own ancestry who survived the flood [at Pukara], or thus to 'create ancestors for the already existing tribes [at Tiahuanaco]; how they instructed their subordinates in megalithic work and other stone sculpturing..." [14]

~ THOR HEYERDAHL, AMERICAN INDIANS IN THE PACIFIC

"Cieza de Leon, writing of the period 'before the rule of the Incas in these realms, and even before they were known', says the period of barbarism ended with the appearance of the personification of the sun on the Island of Titicaca: And immediately after this event, they tell that from the south [of Cuzco] there came and stayed a white man of tall stature, who, in his appearance and person, showed great authority and veneration... In many places they tell how he gave rules to men how they should live, and that he spoke lovingly to them with much kindness, admonishing them that they should be good with each other and not do any harm or injury, but that instead they should love each other and show charity. In most places they generally call him Ticciviracocha... In many parts, temples were built to him, in which they placed stone statues in his likeness..." [15]

~ THOR HEYERDAHL, THE BEARDED GODS SPEAK

"...highland legend that says that Viracocha 'was very shrewed and wise and said he was a child of the sun'. All the highland traditions agree that his first place of residence was on Titicaca Island, before he set forth with a fleet of reed boats to a site on the south shore of the lake, where he built the megalithic city of Tiahuanaco. He and his white and bearded followers were expressly referred to as Mitimas, the Inca word for colonist or settlers. They introduced cultivated crops and taught the Indians how to grow them in irrigated terraces; they showed the Indians how to build stone houses and live in organized communities with law and order; they introduced cotton clothing, sun worship, and megalithic carving; they built step-pyramids and erected monolithic statues said to represent the ancestors of each individual tribe over which they claimed dominion... After instructing the Indians of Cuzco in how to behave after his departure, he descended to the Pacific coast and gathered with his Viracocha followers near the port of Manta in Equador, from whence these sun worshippers sailed westward into the Pacific, departing from almost the exact point where the Equator crosses the South American continent." [16]

~ THOR HEYERDAHL, THE BEARDED GODS SPEAK

The physical description of Viracocha shares some remarkable similarities with depictions of ancient Druidic priests, many of whose religious rites and practices were adopted by Christianity, and were likely adopted by the Celtic Druids themselves from a more ancient source. Viracocha was also described as wearing the symbol of the red cross, and was depicted with the sun and spirals on his robe—symbols which are found at many ancient sites aligned to the sun.

"The chronicler Betanzos, who took part in the discovery of Peru, recorded:... When I asked the Indians what shape this Viracocha had when their ancestors had thus seen him, they said that according to the information they possessed, he was a tall man with a white vestment that reached to his feet, and that this vestment had a girdle;

and that he carried his hair short with a tonsure on the head in the manner of a priest; and that he walked solemnly, and that he carried in his hands a certain thing which today seems to remind them of the breviary that the priests carry in their hands.'" [17]

~ THOR HEYERDAHL, THE BEARDED GODS SPEAK

IMAGE LEFT: This illustration of a Druid priest shows him also with giant ear plugs, which Viracocha is also represented as having. Painting is 'An Arch Druid in His Judicial Habit' from *The Costume of the Original Inhabitants of the British Islands* by S. R. Meyrick and C. H. Smith, 1815.

IMAGE RIGHT: This depiction of a Druid also mirrors the legendary descriptions of Viracocha/ Votan as having fair skin, a long beard, and carrying a staff in one hand and book in the other. Illustration from *Britannia Antiqua Illustrata*, 1676.

IMAGE CENTER: Ceramic figurines from pre-Columbian northern Peru depicting Viracocha looking just like a Druid priest with long robe, beard, and large ear plugs, and also with the turban he is sometimes described as wearing. The earliest evidence for elongating ears using ear plugs was found in people who had arrived by boat to the Indus Valley in India—another place where the knowledge of the spiritual sun emerged.

THE SPREAD OF THE CIVILIZATION AND RELIGION OF THE SUN

There is much evidence that many so-called "Viracochas" or "fair skinned bearded men" remained in South America and settled there in outposts that became part of a network of sites throughout the world on well-traveled sea routes. For example, thousands of mummies with red, blonde, and light brown hair, and European-like features, have been discovered in Peru near the Nazca Lines—a site these people built before they and their civilization were wiped out by invading cultures. Frescos at the Temple of the Warriors at Chichen Itza show scenes of a fair skinned people, who had once helped establish and build the site under the guidance of Kukulcan, being killed and driven out sometime later in its history—with some depicted as scrambling to get into their ships to escape via sea.

The Chachapoyas were a pre-Incan culture that survived by living in the remote mountain ranges of Peru until relatively recently, when they were finally wiped out by the diseases brought by the Spanish invaders, after having just been conquered by the Incas. They were described as fair skinned (some so much so that the Spanish invader Pizarro, who conquered the Incan empire, noted they would not stand out amongst "white blondes"), and many of their buildings feature techniques and designs also found in the British Isles. The Chachapoyas told the Spanish conquistadors that they were the descendants of the idols, meaning they were descended from the peoples of Viracocha.

Their city at Kuelap high up in the mountains is one of the largest ancient ruins in the world and has been compared to Machu Picchu, which they are likely to have been involved in building, and closely resembles the ancient stone city in Zimbabwe built by another fair skinned people. The Chachapoyas also left behind statues of Viracocha/Quetzalcoatl that depict him as a bearded man, and these statues look just like those on Easter Island.

The presence of the "Viracochas" is also found on Easter Island, where the ancient stone statues were built in the image of Viracocha. It's worth noting that the same hand position carved onto the Easter Island statues, where the hands are arranged around the navel, has also been used on statues at the ancient site of Göbekli Tepe in Turkey dated to around 9,500 BC—indicating that this knowledge has very early origins, and was carried by peoples across the world in ancient times. The oral history of the most recent inhabitants of Easter Island say that the original builders of the statues had fled a partly submerged island, again revealing that the people who constructed these ancient sites were the survivors of a flood.

The people carrying the ancient knowledge of the sun also got as far as the island country of New Zealand, described by some as the "ends of the earth," as it is almost the farthest place they could have traveled by boat from Egypt and Eurasia. The evidence of their occupation there also reveals a lot about where these people came from. Legends of the local Maori people, whose ancestors colonized New Zealand in around 1300 AD, described the civilization of people they found when they arrived as having fair skin, red hair, and green eyes.

> "In Maori oral traditions and history, these more ancient residents that the first Maori immigrants encountered were universally described as "uru-kehu" and "kiri-puwhero", which in physical terms means people with light, reddish-pinkish skin colouration and reddish hair. Other general descriptions recorded that they had all of the hues of hair colour of European people, ranging from white-blond, golden-blond, red, auburn, the various shades of brown through to black hair. They were also described as having green, blue or all the other hues of eye colour that one would associate with European-Caucasoid peoples." [18]
>
> ~ MARTIN DOUTRÉ, ARCHEOASTRONOMER AND AUTHOR OF
> WWW.CELTICNZ.CO.NZ

Extensive research by the archeoastronomer Martin Doutré has identified standing stones that align to the solstices and equinoxes throughout New Zealand.

Many of the stone markers of these peoples contain "bullauns," which are like small cup holes carefully carved into the rock. Bullauns are characteristic of ancient sites in the British Isles, and standing stones with solar alignments are found throughout the British Isles and Europe.

> "The use of bullauns, stemming from Neolithic Age ritual cleansing and 'holy wells' traditions still practised in Continental Europe and Britain, was equally prevalent in New Zealand. The Pagan Euro-pean bullaun ritual practices were adopted by the early Christian church and bullaun bowls became the 'baptismal fonts' or holy water vessels of the church for baptism, sprinkling or christening rituals." [19]
>
> ~ MARTIN DOUTRÉ, THE ANCIENT SURVEYING STRUCTURES ON THE BOMBAY HILLS

Cave burials and mass graves that have been accidentally unearthed across New Zealand have been found to contain the remains of Caucasian skeletons.

> "Burial caves all over New Zealand contain the remains of red, brown or blond haired Indo-European skeletons." [20]
>
> ~ MARTIN DOUTRÉ, MEGALITHIC NEW ZEALAND

This prior civilization in New Zealand was mostly wiped out by Polynesian tribes who eventually took over the island. However, a very small number of these ancient inhabitants survived by hiding in remote places. Some of the last remaining people in New Zealand that trace their lineage to these inhabitants are called the Ngati-Hotu, whose descendants today still retain their light hair, fair skin, and green eyes.

A lot of other evidence of the presence of these people in New Zealand still exists, too numerous to detail here. Much of their culture was absorbed by the Polynesians (who came to be known as a distinctive group called the Maori) who had been welcomed into their society and taught their practices. The identical spiraling patterns of the famous Maori facial tattoos for example, which the Maori record as having been taught to them by these fair skinned people, were also found on the faces of ancient Indo-European mummies discovered in China. The double spiral was one of the most prominent symbols of ancient Europe as a symbol of the movements of the sun, and is found throughout the megalithic artwork of the British Isles, where it adorned sites in Ireland like Newgrange, Loughcrew, and Knowth—which are all sites aligned to the solstices and equinoxes and said to have been built by the Tuatha Dé Danaan people whom Cúchulainn belonged to.

The Indo-European peoples whose mummies were found in western China, are also very likely to have been related to those who built the numerous and sometimes huge pyramids (one is larger than the Great Pyramid of Egypt) found in central and northern China, along with the dolmens (standing stones) of North Korea. The pyramid complex, found in central China at Xi'an is located at one of the main places where civilization emerged in China and is one of its most ancient cities.

"XI'an was China's old capital city, where emperors reigned for about 3000-years. Many of these royal dignitaries, or others accorded the high honour, were buried in the pyramids of the district. Old Mongolian-Tibetan-Lama monastery records and oral traditions, however, attest to the fact that these pyramids were not built as mausoleums during the reign of the Chinese dynasties, but were considered to be old already 5000-years ago.

The pyramids seem to have been built at a remote epoch after the ice age, when several racial groups were crisscrossing this region of China, trading and settling or in transit to the Bering Strait and the Americas.

The complex of pyramids at XI'an form a typical "open air university", just like one finds at England's Avebury Henge or Stonehenge and their many outlying marker-mounds, as well as around the Octagon geometric earthworks of Newark, Ohio, USA or the Nazca lines of Peru and at Easter Island, etc., etc...

The pyramid complex at XI'an provided very sophisticated tutorials related to the size of the Earth and how to navigate around it safely.

In the opinion of this researcher, based upon artefact and other evidence coming out of old Europe and Asia, these edifices could easily be up to 8000-years old." [21]

~ MARTIN DOUTRÉ, CODES OF POSITION AMIDST THE XI'AN COMPLEX OF PYRAMIDS AND MOUNDS

Facial tattoo of a Maori chief. "Note the use of the double spirals, in miniature, on each side of the nose and larger spirals on each cheek. The cheek spirals are marked by double lines, which track the Sun's movement inward to the centre of the spiral (Solstice) where it turns and moves toward the Equinox (marked by the bridge of the nose). The Sun then continues its journey to the other Solstice position on the opposite side of the face." [22] ~ Martin Doutré. The lines found on the face and forehead represent the days between equinoxes—a similar concept, as Martin has pointed out, found in the nemes headdress worn by Egyptian pharaohs. The traditional Tiki pendant he is wearing is a symbol of the Polynesian solar god who was also known as Tici in Peru, and based on Viracocha.

"[A] well-preserved Caucasian mummy from Ürumchi, China shows a 'double spiral' design painted on the face adjacent to the nose. The unravelling spiral straightens then crosses to the nose. An identical spiral, unravelling in the same clockwise direction, is fashioned on the opposite side of the face. Archaeologists assessing these 3000-4000 year-old mummies, recognise that the people were Sun worshippers and the designs painted onto the faces of the dead were in veneration of their Deity.

The double spiral design has been used by European peoples since before megalithic times, as one of the foremost symbols of antiquity. It was prominently displayed in Megalithic Great Britain until the Iron Age, when its usage began to diminish...

Long after the Northern Europeans had their former Sun aligned religion supplanted through ruthless Christianisation, the selfsame pre-Christian beliefs, far beyond the reach of Rome, remained intact and unthreatened in New Zealand. Although enforced amnesia terminated age-old astronomical knowledge in the North, it persisted pure and undefiled at the base of the South Pacific...until the coming of the Pa or fortress Maori warrior/ cannibals.

Evidence would suggest that the "double spiral" represented the Sun sitting at a Solstice position (the innermost part of the spiral), then winding out of that position to the Equinox and continuing yet further to the other Solstice position. The distance travelled in Sun's annual journey down the horizon and back depends on the latitude where the observer resides. At Stonehenge the Solstice positions (mid summer and mid winter) are about 79 degrees apart on the horizon. In the North Island of New Zealand the two positions are about 60 degrees apart. Inasmuch as early Europeans, either in the Mediterranean Basin or in the far-flung colonies, used the Sun as the vicarious representation of their spiritual God RA, the annual movements of the Sun were of tremendous religious significance...

Maori oral traditions clearly state that the art of moko facial tattooing was taught to Maori-Polynesians by the Turehu people who occupied New Zealand for thousands of years before the arrival of the Maori...

The Maori Moko [which is the spiral Maori facial tattoo]... is a sophisticated solar calendar. Virtually every part of the design celebrates the movements of the Sun God RA, who, in pre-colonial New Zealand was known by that exact name and vocal rendition. The endless journey of RA is shown again in the design around the mouth, with the Vernal and Autumn Equinoxes occurring at the position of each nostril and the Sun's Solstice change of direction occurring each side of the chin cleft...

Many researchers can readily see the glaring similarity between Maori and pre-Celtic design, sufficient to show that both art forms stem from the same origins. These artistic expressions were used equally by the Pictish, Hebrew, Assyrian, Mayan, Mycenaean and Scythian civilisations." [23]

~ MARTIN DOUTRÉ, MEGALITHIC NEW ZEALAND

The sun god was most prolifically called Ra in ancient Egypt, which clearly connects this early civilization of people in New Zealand and their spiritual knowledge to Egypt, along with large amounts of other evidence.

However, Egypt is not the only place they have connections with. Family history, passed down by the surviving ancient fair skinned people of New Zealand, recounts how their ancestors had traveled to New Zealand by boat from India and Persia—many fleeing a conflict that may have been the historical basis of the legendary war of Kurukshetra in the ancient Hindu text the Mahabharata, fought and narrated by the Aryans (a term used to describe them in ancient Hindu texts).

Monica Matumua of the Ngati-Hotu tribe in New Zealand, whose family has preserved the story of their origins in Persia, underwent a DNA test as part of the National Geographic DNA Ancestry Project in 2005. Her results revealed a strong link to the region of Iran. Monica believes that her descendants did not find New Zealand by mistake, but mapped their way to the country and have been there for at least 74 generations (from at least as early as 3,000 BC).

> "There are 800 in our whanau. When the seven warrior waka arrived in New Zealand, my people were here. Our history says that our people first came to Aotearoa a long time back from what is now called Iran. If you go there today, the women still have moko, the black lips. Our people came here through Borneo." [24]
>
> ~ MONICA MATUMUA, NGATI-HOTU AND DESCENDENT OF THE TUREHU PEOPLE

This connects the ancient inhabitants of New Zealand with the ancient Indo-Europeans/Aryans who were the progenitors of the most ancient Hindu texts called the Vedas, and the most ancient sacred writings of Persia (now modern-day Iran) called the Zend Avesta, and of the vast Indo-European civilization that once spread throughout parts of Eurasia.

To give some idea of the scale of influence of this ancient civilization, 50 percent of all world languages have descended from the Proto-Indo-European language, including the Sanskrit language which the Vedas were written in. The evidence also reveals that not only the language of this civilization, but also their religion of the sun diffused throughout the ancient world.

Ancient peoples with a similar appearance also lived in Egypt at one time. Although they're unlikely to have built the Great Pyramids, which seem to date from an even earlier age, they are likely to have built other sites around the pyramids and elsewhere in Egypt that are now completely buried under the sand. They then carried the astronomical and mathematical knowledge that was encoded into the design of the Great Pyramids to other parts of the world, where it was used to build many ancient megalithic sites.

"It must be realised that the Egyptian pyramids of the Giza Plateau or those at Saqqara are far older than 'officially' recognised. The measurement standards found encoded onto these 'Bureau of Standards' edifices survived for further millennia within the European nations and were, over time, carried abroad to far-flung locations like New Zealand, by European explorers and settlers such as the Vikings.

The commonly known and preserved measurements of ancient Europe, despite their wide variety, are a part of a single and widely versatile integrated mathematical system, with traceable root origins and pedigrees extending back to Egypt..." [25]

~ MARTIN DOUTRÉ, VIKING NAVIGATION

The evidence for how they carried this knowledge abroad can even be found in such remote places as New Zealand. Oral tradition in New Zealand records how the ancient people who preceded the later Polynesian immigrants were known as "The Surveyors."

"...in a very stimulating conversation with a learned Maori kaumatua-historian, he recounted an oral tradition passed down within his family that spoke of his ancestors arriving in New Zealand from India in 700 AD. Upon making landfall, his ancestors encountered a well-established civilisation that they called 'The Surveyors' ... because of their preoccupation with marking the landscape for overland surveying purposes. Although I was aware of many other names or terms used to describe the earlier civilisation (such as 'The Stonebuilders') this was the first time I had heard of them being called, specifically, 'The Surveyors' in the Maori oral histories." [26]

~ MARTIN DOUTRÉ, ANCIENT NEW ZEALAND SURVEYORS AND ASTRONOMERS

Evidence for this skill in surveying the landscape is found at sacred sites throughout the British Isles, which align to one another across vast distances, as well as in many ancient sites that align to each other from across the globe. It was this knowledge they precisely encoded into monuments, megaliths, and ancient cities around the world, and which they used to navigate across the earth.

Another place that served as a remnant time capsule of this civilization of the sun until relatively recently, just as New Zealand did, was the Canary Islands, located off the northwest coast of Africa. For at least thousands of years, Indo-European people described as fair skinned and blonde haired, lived with Stone Age technology (there is no metal in the Canary Islands), in a tropical paradise, until they were invaded and finally wiped out by Spanish conquistadors in 1496. The Spanish recorded their observations of these native people whom they called the Guanches. They wrote how they practiced a solar religion, built stepped pyramids that they aligned to the solstices from which they offered prayers to the sun, and practiced mummification—all characteristics of those who formed part of this once great lost civilization of the sun.

> "An ancient network of pyramids are scattered across the earth in places like China, India, the Maldives, Mesopotamia, Bosnia, Egypt, Sardinia, Canary Islands, Antigua, Polynesia, Mexico, Peru, and others. These pyramid-building nations who also practiced mummification, were outposts established by those culture bearers who came at the dawn of history, to introduce civilization to native people all over the earth, and had direct or indirect inspiration from the same source about 5000 years ago. The Guanches outlasted nearly all of the others due to their island remoteness and homogeneous population that were never conquered until the Middle-Ages." [27]
>
> ~ GORDON KENNEDY, THE WHITE INDIANS OF NIVARIA

It's not clear however, where the Guanches came from. The Canary Islands are located beyond the Pillars of Hercules in the Atlantic Ocean, precisely where the ancient Egyptians located Atlantis. These islands may be the remnants of the lost continent of Atlantis, and the Guanches their descendants—but the histories of the Guanches neither confirm nor deny this. Their oral histories recount only that sixty of their ancestors came to the Canary Islands far back in time, and settled there, from where they knew not. Their language however, provides clues as to whom they were related to, as it contains words of Proto-Indo-European origin, as well as words that share similarities with those spoken in other places where Indo-European peoples with a religion of the sun existed—including Central and South America, ancient Egypt, and in Northern Europe and Scandinavia (where Teutonic, which is the Germanic branch of Indo-European, was spoken). For example, the Guanche word for "heaven," which is "Atuman," contains the ancient Egyptian word "Atum" which was the name of their supreme creator god. The word "Amen" was used by the Guanches as their word for the "sun"—the same word which is now used to finish Christian prayers, and is closely related to a variation of the name of the ancient Egyptian creator god "Atum" as "Amun."

> "The Guanches recognized themselves as custodians of an ancient spiritual legacy, and they were very devoted to their religion and spiritual practices. Like their European cousins, the Celts and Teutons, they looked upon the sun as the mighty emblem and instrumentality of the Godhead. Menceys were priest-kings within tribal territories

on the islands, and like in ancient Peru they built solar temples and step-pyramids and claimed their descent and divinity from the sun.

Solar religion manifests itself not simply in acknowledgement of the overt functions of the sun as provider of light and heat, but also in recognition of influences that are more wide-ranging than the elemental force itself. The sun is the great source of energy in almost all terrestrial phenomena, from the meteorological to the geographical, from the geological to the biological. Solar energy equals life." [28]
~ GORDON KENNEDY, THE WHITE INDIANS OF NIVARIA

"...the Guanches were monotheistic, but had a complex form of expressing the divine principle. Concepts like *"Life of the sky," "Sun God," "Sun spirit of the mountains," "Indweller of the universe"* and dozens of other spiritual metaphors were all part of the daily language, with religion being the central theme of their existence. " [29]
~ GORDON KENNEDY, THE WHITE INDIANS OF NIVARIA

The Guanches provide further evidence of the ancient lost civilization of the sun, as one of its various outposts that survived right to the end of the Middle Ages.

The Indo-European symbol of the swastika, as well as the double spiral, which are both symbols related to the cycles of the sun, are also almost always found like footprints wherever the people of this civilization tread in their journeys. The swastika is one of the most prolific symbols of the ancient world; its earliest representation was found in Ukraine carved into the tusk of a woolly mammoth and dated to 13,000 BC. These symbols emerge in such widespread places as the Americas, India, Asia, Russia, Europe, and China. The Indo-European mummies found in the Tarim Basin in Xinjiang province in China, with the spiral patterns on their face like those adopted by the Maori, were found buried with an artifact that has the symbol of the swastika on it.

Many of their journeys were made by boat as it may have been easier and much faster to traverse the seas than to travel over treacherous terrain sometimes inhabited by hostile people. And there is much evidence that these people already possessed a highly advanced sea-faring and navigational capability, as well as ships that could make these journeys.

The ancient spiritual knowledge of the sun influenced and formed the basis of many spiritual traditions: including the religion of Dynastic Egypt; the Vedas of India, which later birthed Hinduism, Buddhism, and Jainism; many of the so-called "pagan" religions of old Europe, such as those of the Thracians, Norse, and Minoans; the Druidism of the Celts, which later influenced the early Christians, who in turn influenced the Essenes; the spirituality of the Maya, Aztecs, Inca, and pre-Columbian peoples of North America; and probably many other spiritual wisdom traditions lost in time.

The esoteric schools that Gurdjieff encountered in remote parts of Central Asia, around one hundred years ago, may have also been established as part of the spread of this knowledge in ancient times all the way from Egypt, through Mesopotamia and Central Asia, down into India and across to western China, and then also throughout parts of Europe. He writes about one in particular, which he claims to have visited for some months, as having been established at least as early as 2,500 BC:

> "What struck us most was the word Sarmoung, which we had come across several times in the book called Merkhavat. This word is the name of a famous esoteric school which, according to tradition, was founded in Babylon as far back as 2500 B.C., and which was known to have existed somewhere in Mesopotamia up to the sixth or seventh century AD.; but about its further existence one could not obtain anywhere the least information.
>
> This school was said to have possessed great knowledge, containing the key to many secret mysteries." [30]
>
> ~ GURDJIEFF, MEETINGS WITH REMARKABLE MEN

Schools of knowledge were said to have been established in different places as part of a network, which sincere seekers of knowledge could have traveled between in ancient times when the peoples who carried the knowledge of the sun spread throughout Eurasia and different outposts around the world.

> "In India there are only 'philosophical' schools. It was divided up in that way long ago; in India there was 'philosophy,' in Egypt 'theory,' and in present-day Persia, Mesopotamia, and Turkestan— 'practice.'" [31]
>
> ~ GURDJIEFF SPEAKING TO OUSPENSKY ON ESOTERIC SCHOOLS, IN SEARCH OF THE MIRACULOUS

These esoteric schools have now closed their doors due to rampant violence and upheaval in the places they used to operate; their closure is a sign of the dark times we are now living in.

WHERE DID THIS CIVILIZATION COME FROM?

So where did these wisdom bringers come from? Complex knowledge of huge astronomical cycles like the 26,000 year precession of the equinox, and of advanced surveying and navigational techniques, doesn't emerge overnight.

The legendary Hyperboreans, who were said to have once inhabited a kind of mythical paradise, were described by the Greeks as coming from the north—the Greek descriptions place their origins possibly somewhere in the Arctic Circle or the now submerged landmass of Doggerland.

"In the regions beyond the land of the Celts there lies in the ocean an island no smaller than Sicily. This island, the account continues, is situated in the north and is inhabited by the Hyperboreans, who are called by that name because their home is beyond the point whence the north wind (Boreas) blows; and the island is both fertile and productive of every crop, and has an unusually temperate climate." [32]

~ HECATAEUS OF ABDERA WRITING IN THE 4TH CENTURY BC

Doggerland has been called "the Atlantis of the Celts" as it was a vast and fertile plain that connected Britain to mainland Europe, but which gradually submerged beneath the North Sea until a tsunami finally destroyed the remaining island of Dogger Bank around 7,000 BC almost overnight due to a sudden rise in sea level after the receding of the last glacial maximum. Many archeologists believe this would have been the heart of Europe many thousands of years ago as its most abundant hunting and gathering ground. The occurrence of red-hair centers largely around this area, as well as near the Ural Mountains in Russia where many sacred sites have been found. Viracocha was sometimes described as having a red beard, the ancient inhabitants of New Zealand were described as having red hair, and the mummies found in connection with the ancient religion of the sun often have red and blonde hair.

Others believe that the wisdom bringers came from somewhere in the Arctic. Author, astronomer, and political leader of India, Lokmanya Bâl Gangâdhar Tilak, presented the theory in his book *The Arctic Home in the Vedas* that the knowledge preserved in the Vedas must have come from a people who had once lived in the Arctic Circle. He came to this conclusion after a detailed analysis of the astronomical observations contained in the Vedas and Zend Avesta, which he said could only have been made if the observer was in the Arctic.

Then there are records of the ancient Egyptians that chronicle vast spans of time in history. The list of Egyptian pharaohs begins in 3,000 BC, but other lists detail the time preceding this in which a lineage of gods ruled Egypt for 23,200 years. This was a time called "Zep Tepi;" the exact sentence found on the walls of the temple of Edfu is "Ntr ntri hpr m sp tpy," which has been translated by British Egyptologist E. A. Reymond as "when the gods manifested as humans." This period was followed by those called "Sheshu Hor" or "divine pharaohs who came from elsewhere," who reigned for 13,400 years. This would place the beginning of the Egyptian lineage somewhere around 39,500 BC, which may have been when the Great Pyramids were actually built.

These "Sheshu Hor" or "divine pharaohs who came from elsewhere" are recorded as migrating to Egypt as their name suggests. The Greek Historian Diodorus of Sicily in his epic *Library of History* wrote:

> "The Egyptians were strangers, who, in remote times, settled on the banks of the Nile, bringing with them the civilization of their mother country, the art of writing, and a polished language. They had come from the direction of the setting sun [the West] and were the most ancient of men." [33]

The direction of west places their origin somewhere off the west coast of Africa, in the Atlantic ocean, where the island of Atlantis is said to have sunk beneath the sea many thousands of years ago.

The ancient Egyptians themselves gave an account, which was retold by Plato, of their origin in Atlantis. And incredibly, still today, there are peoples in North Africa who say they are descendants of the survivors of Atlantis.

> "The Berber people call themselves Amazigh: Berber is a name that has been given them by others and which they themselves do not use. Their often dark appearance is caused by the sun: they are ethnologically and genetically White. Ethnologically, the Tuaregs of North Africa (the so-called "Blue People of the Sahara") are Berbers who speak an ancient dialect of Berber called Tamachek. Genetically light-skin and blue-eyes prevail. With their aquiline noses, high cheekbones (often with blonde or reddish hair), they are said to resemble their alleged Atlantean ancestors—many individuals are over six feet tall. When questioned, they do not hesitate to name Atlantis as their lost homeland.
>
> Back in the early 1980s an investigative journalist, Ken Krippene, travelled to Marrakech, Morocco, to search out tribal leaders and speak to them concerning their traditional origins. They told him that Atlantis, their homeland, was lost during a cataclysm when 'the earth began to tremble violently... then slowly, as the storm still raged, Atlantis sank into the sea.' (Krippene, 1981) Escaping in small boats, they made their way to the shores of North Africa." [34]
>
> ~ R. CEDRIC LEONARD, LINGUISTIC CONNECTIONS: A PALEOLITHIC LANGUAGE

There is evidence that the survivors of Atlantis arrived firstly to the areas of North Africa, and re-established the center of their civilization in Egypt. At this time the last glacial maximum would have extended into north-western Europe, with permafrost extending as far as Bulgaria, making Europe a very inhospitable place. However, as the ice receded and the climate improved, there is evidence that these people from Egypt settled around the Mediterranean, and migrated through Europe to the British Isles where they may have centered their populations around Doggerland.

"Prior to 2000-BC especially, Egyptians were of Caucasoid-European ethnicity. This is evidenced by the physical anthropology of oldest mummies found, as well as busts or statues of the Pharaohs and their wives, coloured wall paintings and descriptions in historical accounts. Beyond about 1500 BC the population became increasingly mixed with Nubians from the South of Egypt and present day Egyptians stem from this latter era admixture. The last few Pharaohs of Egypt were Nubians. Shabaka (721 to 706 BC) consolidated the Nubian Kingdom's control over all of Egypt from Nubia down to the Delta region.

The majority of the Caucasoid-European occupants of Egypt began to exodus the increasingly arid country as early as 5000 BC, preferring the verdant climes of Europe which had shed its glaciers and was becoming increasingly more habitable over vast regions. The migrants left waymark trails out of Egypt, all along the seacoast of North Africa to the Pillars of Hercules, where they crossed the thin strip of water into Europe. They left their waymark trails up the coast of Spain and Portugal towards France and Scandinavia and these survived intact into the late 19th century. Those coming out of Egypt brought their harps, bagpipes, plinn rhythms, mathematics, measurements, astronomical knowledge, navigational knowledge and even the venerable Oak tree with them.

The same measurements that were used to build the Pyramids were also in use within Europe prior to 5000 BC. The thousands of large menhirs (obelisks) erected at Carnac and other areas of Brittany in France represent a huge library of mathematical information from Egypt. These French obelisk sites were built from as early as 5000 BC and contain the same information and using the same modus operandi (by way of distance and angle from hubstone positions to individual outer-marker components), as one finds at sites like Nazca in Peru." [35]

~ MARTIN DOUTRÉ, THE PREDYNASTIC AND MOST EARLY DYNASTIC EGYPTIANS WERE CAUCASOID-EUROPEANS

The inhabitants of ancient Egypt also recorded having a wisdom bringer called Thoth, who appears to have led the survivors of Atlantis to Egypt where he oversaw the establishment of a civilization. Like other wisdom bringers, he is credited with giving this civilization their writing and sciences.

"Scattered though they may be, an interesting picture emerges from the numerous references to Thoth in the earliest writings of the ancient Egyptians—and that picture fits the theory of an Atlantean origin for this intriguing character. Although late writings depict him as a god, the earliest texts depict him as a king (The Palermo Stone versus The Coffin Texts; Faulkner, 1974).

Thoth had just been described (Chapter LXXXV, Papyrus of Nu) as ruler of the "Western Domain"; but by the end of the New Kingdom he is called the "Lord of the West" (Seth, 1912). He is accredited with the invention of writing, mathematics, astronomy, and civilization in general (Budge, 1960). In addition to being the author of a large number of esoteric books, Thoth is also called the Scribe (Pyramid Texts; Book of the Dead, et al.); his Egyptian name, Tehuti, means "the measurer" (Budge, 1960)...

In summation, a catastrophe occurred which darkened the sun and disturbed the gods, but Thoth led them across the sea to an eastern country [Egypt]. Thoth is depicted as the "controller of the Flood," (Leyden Papyrus) and the Theban Recension includes the Island of Fire in the Flood story. (Papyrus of Ani, Chap. CLXXV) Thus it appears that Thoth was once the ruler of an Island Kingdom beyond the western horizon before the Egyptian priests turned him into a god. The question therefore is: Was the Egyptian Tehuti-Thoth originally a migrant from Atlantis, and did he once rule as a king there?" [36]

~ R. CEDRIC LEONARD, WRITINGS OF THE EGYPTIANS

Although Thoth has been referred to as a "god," this term is largely misunderstood in this context. In an out-of-body experience, some time after I was initiated into the mysteries of the pyramids, I saw Thoth present as an awakened being where he was taking accounts of my inner deeds in a book. He was likely to have been that person who arrived to Egypt as the wisdom bringer. At some time he would have done the spiritual work and awakened, and now has a role in higher dimensions, which I saw him carrying out. Those of us who have experiences like this bring back the knowledge of who the different awakened beings are and what roles they have, and these often become depicted in sacred texts and temples, that later become mythologized, etc., where awakened people become referred to as "gods" in many cases as though they had never been human. Some of the divine kings of Egypt and Hinduism could have been awakened people like this, and the ages of these divine kings may have been times when people had enough understanding to choose their leaders based on their level of spiritual wisdom—meaning they were times when a profound spirituality was much more valued and understood.

The ancient Egyptian god Osiris was said to have been a divine king of Egypt, who like Thoth, is also credited with establishing civilization there, and like other wisdom bringers such as Viracocha, was said to have traveled to the rest of the world establishing it elsewhere—taking with him the ancient religion of the sun that was brought from Atlantis and re-established in ancient Egypt.

> "Having become king, he devoted himself to improving the condition of his subjects. He weaned them from their miserable and barbarous manners, he taught them how to till the earth and how to sow and reap crops, he formulated a code of laws for them, and made them to worship the gods and perform service to them. He then left Egypt and travelled over the rest of the world teaching the various nations to do what his own subjects were doing. He forced no man to carry out his instructions, but by means of gentle persuasion and an appeal to their reason, he succeeded in inducing them to practise what he preached." [37]
>
> ~ E. A. WALLIS BUDGE, OSIRIS AND THE EGYPTIAN RESURRECTION

Possible references to Atlantis are not just found in ancient Egyptian sources, but also in Hindu texts, in which they refer to a White Island where they practiced the religion of the sun.

> "Atala and Sveta Dwipa ('White Island') are not the only names for Atlantis in Sankrit lore. Another name, Saka Dwipa, is used just as often in the Puranas; and according to the Sanskrit Dictionary (1974), Saka Dwipa means 'island of fair skinned people.'... The terms 'Atala' and 'White Island' are used also by the Bhavishya Purana (4th cent. B.C.). Here it is stated that Samba, having built a temple dedicated to Surya (the Sun), made a journey to Saka Dwipa, located 'beyond the salt water' looking for the Magas (magicians), worshippers of the Sun. He is directed in his journey by Surya himself (i.e., journeys west following the Sun), riding upon Garuda (the flying vehicle of Krishna and Vishnu) he lands at last among the Magas.
>
> The Mahabharata (circa. 600 B.C.) also refers to 'Atala, the White Island', which is described as an 'island of great splendour.' It continues: 'The men that inhabit that island have complexions as white as the rays of the Moon and they are devoted to Narayana... Indeed, the denizens of White Island believe and worship only one God.' (Santi Parva, Section CCCXXXVII)" [38]
>
> ~ R. CEDRIC LEONARD, PRE-PLATONIC WRITINGS PERTINENT TO ATLANTIS

Legends recited by Gurdjieff's father, who was one of the last remaining bards/ashokhs in an ancient tradition, also refer to certain wise men and survivors of a flood.

"There was another legend I had heard from my father, again about the 'Flood before the Flood'... In this legend it was said, also in verse, that long, long ago, as far back as seventy generations before the last deluge (and a generation was counted as a hundred years), when there was dry land where now is water and water where now is dry land, there existed on earth a great civilization, the centre of which was the former island Haninn, which was also the centre of the earth itself.

The sole survivors of the earlier deluge were certain brethren of the former Imastun Brotherhood [meaning brotherhood of wise men], whose members had constituted a whole caste spread all over the earth, but whose centre had been on this island.

These Imastun brethren were learned men and, among other things, they studied astrology. Just before the deluge, they were scattered all over the earth for the purpose of observing celestial phenomena from different places. But however great the distance between them, they maintained constant communication with one another and reported everything to the centre by means of telepathy."[39]
~ GURDJIEFF, MEETINGS WITH REMARKABLE MEN

If this legend proved to be true, it could be the reason why there are observations in the Vedas that could have only been made in the Arctic. It would also explain how this civilization would have been able to gather such advanced astronomical and navigational knowledge.

There is record of another wisdom bringer associated with the divine lineage of ancient Egypt, which traces its roots to Atlantis, who brought civilization to Mesopotamia and was possibly involved in the building of the ancient megalithic site in Turkey called Göbekli Tepe that dates to around 9,500 BC. Like Thoth and Votan/Viracocha, this wisdom bringer set out by boat to establish civilization in a new land. They were from among the so-called Shebtiu, or divine pharaohs of the ancient Egyptian king lists, who are said to have sailed to another place to "continue their creative task undisturbed." Interestingly, the name has Indo-European connections, as does much of the knowledge of the spiritual sun that spread throughout the world.

"...in the name A'a we are now presented with an Indo-European form of Mesopotamia's great civiliser. This is important, for as we know from the Edfu Building Texts [texts inscribed on the temple of Edfu in Egypt], the names given to the leaders of the Shebtiu who 'sailed' away to another primordial world after completing the second period of creation at Wetjeset-Neter [an island destroyed by a catastrophe which had been inhabited by the gods of ancient Egypt] are Wa and 'Aa. This second name, which is composed of two letter As prefixed by an *aleph*, is phonetically the same as the Hurrian A'a. Both are pronounced something like ah-ah.

Since we have already identified the Shebtiu as one of the primary names of the Elder gods who departed Egypt for the Near East in around 9,500 BC, I find it beyond coincidence that one of their two leaders bears exactly the same name as the great wisdom-bringer of Hurrian tradition." [40]

~ ANDREW COLLINS, GODS OF EDEN

Incredibly, as in ancient Egyptian and Indian civilizations, there are records in the most ancient recorded Mesopotamian civilization, called Sumer, of a period before a flood in which divine kings ruled. The ancient Sumerian king list is written in cuneiform script on a tablet dated to 2,100 BC. It begins by stating that these kings began their rule "after the kingship descended from heaven," but ended when "the flood swept over."

The Mesopotamian civilization of Sumer is often referred to as "the cradle of civilization," although civilization is also evidenced as developing very early on in Egypt and the Indus Valley in India. Each of these places, where civilization suddenly seems to emerge, are associated with the ancient wisdom bringers, who appeared to have set out together on a divine task to bring civilization to the world, and their knowledge of the spiritual sun.

"The precision science, geometry, orientation, stone cutting, hole drilling and architectural planning of the Great Pyramids was the result of a legacy preserved not simply by the wise old priests of Egypt, but by a number of diverse cultures across the Near East. Their most distant ancestors were the Neolithic gods of Eden, whose own forebears had left Egypt for the fertile valleys of eastern Anatolia during the geological and climatic upheavals that had accompanied the end of the last Ice Age. It is to these unique individuals, the living descendants of a divine race with a lifestyle that would seem almost alien today, that we owe the genesis of civilisation." [41]

~ ANDREW COLLINS, GODS OF EDEN

As recorded in both ancient Egyptian and Hindu texts, the knowledge of the spiritual sun was the knowledge preserved from a previous civilization and passed down by a lineage of divine kings. These divine kings may have been many of the wisdom bringers who were forewarned of the catastrophe and who traveled to different places, re-establishing civilization based on their spiritual knowledge as part of a divine mission.

It appears they established civilizations in at least Egypt, Mesopotamia, North America, and Central and South America. Then possibly, as civilizations were established as part of a global sea-faring network, outposts grew up and continued to spread to nearby areas. The knowledge would have then continued to be diffused throughout the world as people migrated into new lands. With them they took the same symbols, megalithic building techniques, spirituality, etc. The civilization these people established went on to spread over land and ocean throughout the far reaches of the world—creating what was likely to be the largest civilization to have existed since the last global cataclysm, i.e. in approximately the last 12,000 years.

The peoples who carried this knowledge throughout much of the ancient world have links both to ancient Egypt as well as to the Aryans who were central to the texts of early Hinduism, and both the ancient Egyptian and Hindu texts record an age where "the gods manifested as humans." It seems very likely then, that the ancient religion of the sun, which has come down through the ages, is the knowledge that came from this time—and was literally based on the teachings of awakened people.

It's worth bearing in mind though, that there have been different cataclysms of varying severity that have disrupted the earth in the past, and the many legends that recollect such events may be referring to different disasters with varying impact. Some ancient histories preserved in Hinduism record ages of civilization that move in huge, approximately 24,000 year cycles. Many of these histories record times of now entirely extinct races—some who were either much, much taller (described as giants), or much shorter than modern day humans (described as dwarves), or had naturally elongated skulls. So what we are looking at could be references in some cases to a number of human ages that have come and gone.

THE CENSORING OF HISTORY

Historical records show that the outposts of those who came to foster the religion of the sun continued to survive in some of the more remote locations on earth, in some cases right up until the last two hundred years, but had met their end usually through a combination of wars, conquests, disease, religious persecution, and massacres. Many of the fair skinned peoples, who did man-age to survive, merged into the societies that European colonizers established in the last few hundred years, with only a few remembering their family history.

So why is it that we hear so little about this once huge civilization of the religion of the sun—why don't we know of its story? It appears that there is a concerted effort to destroy all record of it, with evidence in many cases being bulldozed, reburied, and disappeared, just as fast as it is being discovered.

Whatever the cause of this suppression, the effect is to rob humanity of the true understanding of its past. It's a kind of forced amnesia that com-pletely reshapes our cultural narrative—serving to cut us off from the root. We're led to believe the past was only a primitive time, so that we reject the knowledge found within it, and instead turn to embrace a one-world, uniform mono-culture of humanistic materialism. When hard evidence is destroyed and ignored, and the oral histories of those who've occupied lands for thousands of years are sidelined, history becomes an incoherent mess of confusion and supposition—like a jigsaw puzzle whose pieces no longer fit. This serves to confuse most people who look into ancient history, and lead them into a never-ending labyrinth of misinformation and conflicting so-called archeological facts.

Ultimately however, the censoring and suppression of the traces of this civilization of the sun means the re-burying of their spiritual knowledge. This is what the ancient wisdom bringers ultimately wished to give to humanity, and thus what humanity is ultimately being deprived of, which is what this book aims to restore.

"Oh, how little we know of the depths of the ages gone, how wide, how profound and deep is the knowledge we seek; a monument of stone, a stone bowl, a broken symbol, a hallowed unknown spot, a lodge of ruins, all this makes a golden page glittering with diamonds that trills the emotions with mysterious longings for truth and light in the depths unknown." [42]

~ LUCY THOMPSON, TO THE AMERICAN INDIAN; REMINISCENCES OF A YUROK WOMAN 1916

THE COSMIC KNOWLEDGE IS ETERNAL

Even though physical evidence can be decimated, the knowledge of the spiritual sun is really an inner knowledge and practice, and is taught by those who have the force known as the spiritual Son within; this force is personified by the sun, which is why people who had this divine part within were associated with it. Wisdom bringers, such as Osiris, Viracocha, Odin/Wotan, Kukulcan, Quetzalcoatl, and Jesus, have all taught this knowledge anew and have worked to establish it in the world over different ages.

Cultures, civilizations, and peoples can carry the knowledge of the spiritual sun—and they once did over vast stretches of the earth—but it is those who had the Son within that were the source of their spiritual knowledge and who ultimately came to create the conditions for all peoples to be able to learn the knowledge of the spiritual sun, and to awaken.

CHAPTER EIGHT

Ancient Sacred Sites
Aligned to the Autumn Equinox

A CAREFUL STUDY OF MATHEMATICS, ASTRONOMY, and sacred symbolism reveals that many sites encode within them very ancient, timeless, and universal messages. Intended to stand the test of time, they have delivered their messages to people searching for truth ever since. Among them include messages about our planet, the nature of reality, the interconnectedness of creation, and the purpose of life. This is why studying how and why these ancient monuments mark certain astrological events, and the symbols they used, can reveal hidden information about their greater significance and meaning.

Here are a few of the most extraordinary cases in relation to the meaning of the autumn equinox (however, any site which aligns to the autumn equinox also aligns to the spring equinox, so you can find more sites aligned to the equinox in the chapter 'Ancient Sacred Sites Aligned to the Spring Equinox').

THE GREAT PYRAMIDS ~ EGYPT

LOOKING DOWN THE DESCENDING PASSAGE OF THE GREAT PYRAMID.

At midnight on the autumn equinox in 2,170 BC, the pole star Alpha Draconis/ Thuban, the chief star of the constellation Draco, depicted as a dragon and associated with the most deadly monster of Greek mythology called Typhon, shone down the central axis of the descending passage of the Great Pyramid. This was the North Star at the time. It is calculated that at precisely the same instant in 2,170 BC, Alcyone, the star in the Pleiades group which our sun and solar system revolves around, stood exactly on the meridian of the Great Pyramid at that point in the heavens which is at a right angle to the downward inclination of the descending passage.

Alpha Draconis also aligned with the descending passage in 3,350 BC. The next alignment was much more recently in AD 2004 with the North Star Polaris, in which its light was said to shine all the way down to the subterranean pit inside the pyramid on the autumn equinox. Polaris is a star in the constellation Ursa Minor, which the Egyptians identified with the god Seth. This god was seen as the god of darkness, which the Greeks associated with their god Typhon.

The Great Pyramid itself functions as an enormous sundial. Its shadow to the north, and its reflected sunlight to the south, accurately mark the annual dates of both the solstices and the equinoxes. Two of its faces are oriented precisely due east and west, which are the exact points of the rising and setting sun, only on the spring and autumn equinoxes.

The four sides of the Great Pyramid are concave, which actually gives the pyramid eight faces instead of four. This is only perceptible from the air at dawn and sunset on the spring and autumn equinoxes.

A photo taken at the spring equinox, showing
that the Great Pyramid is eight-sided.

Professor Robert Temple believes that just before and after these dates the western vertical halves of the north and south faces would have flashed with the sunlight at dawn, when the Great Pyramid still had its white limestone outer casing. The eastern vertical halves of the same faces would have then flashed at sunset. The ceasing of the flash would prove that the equinox had arrived as the sun was briefly absolutely dead-on. This flash of light would have been visible for miles around, and is believed to have even been visible from the moon—from which the pyramid would appear to light up like a star.

CHICHEN ITZA ~ MEXICO

The seven-scaled feathered serpent at Chichen Itza descending down the nine terraces of the pyramid at the equinox.

At an ancient site called Chichen Itza, there is a pyramid known as El Castillo dedicated to Kukulcán, the feathered serpent. At the equinoxes the sun creates an undulating pattern of light on the nine terraces of the pyramid to display seven triangles of light which link up with a stone serpent head at its base. As the sun sets, the scales undulate and eventually disappear, giving the visual effect of the serpent descending the nine terraces of the pyramid.

The pyramid itself is a complex annual astronomical calendar. Its four sides each have ninety-one steps (the number of days between each of the solstices and equinoxes of the year).

The feathered serpent is an esoteric symbol found in various cultures (with the serpent symbolizing the higher feminine aspect of the person, and the feathers symbolizing the eagle and the higher male aspect). The nine terraces depict the nine layers of the underworld, which the Maya were aware of. The descent of the feathered serpent down these nine terraces enacts the symbolic descent into the underworld on the path of the spiritual sun, and the serpent with its seven scales of light, parallels the symbols of descent into the underworld with seven solar bodies in other ancient sites mentioned in this book.

Maya cultures periodically built larger temples and pyramids over the top of smaller ones. In the 1930s excavations revealed an earlier temple inside the pyramid of Kukulcán, which had been built over, revealing that this site has more ancient roots.

Oral traditions state that the site of Chichen Itza is at least as old as the legends of Kukulcán himself, who is recorded as being a real person. As explained earlier in chapter seven, he may have been the same person who was known as Cúchulainn in Ireland and who belonged to the people called the Tuatha Dé Danaan, who are connected with the religion of the sun in Ireland and the many megalithic sites aligned to the sun there.

"He [Kukulcan] instructed the people in the arts of peace, and caused various important edifices to be built at Chichen Itza. He also founded and named the city of Mayapan. It is at least interesting to note that Kukulcan is simply a translation of Quetzalcoatl. *Kukul* is the Maya term for the *Quetzal*-bird, and *kan* is a serpent. [Verrill 1929, p.101.]" [1]

~ THOR HEYERDAHL, AMERICAN INDIANS IN THE PACIFIC

Note that while Kukulcán was described as bringing a message of peace, unfortunately at some time in its history this site became known for the practice of human sacrifice and bloodletting (along with other Central American sites)—thousands of people were sacrificed at this site. Murals at the nearby Temple of Warriors even depict fair skinned people being driven out, with those who couldn't escape being taken as prisoners and later sacrificed—it was they who were probably the descendants of those who had helped establish this sacred site in the first place.

As often happens, it appears this ancient site was taken over by another culture. And in this case the original spiritual knowledge encoded into this site became overlaid and overtaken by barbarity, giving it a terrible name. It is even recorded in legend that the great teacher Quetzalcoatl (which is a variant of the name Kukulcán), was opposed to human sacrifice. Tragically, his real message was turned away from and distorted as has happened with the message of true love and compassion of so many other great spiritual teachers throughout history.

PYRAMID OF THE SUN AT TEOTIHUACÁN ~ MEXICO

THE PYRAMID OF THE SUN WHICH FACES THE EQUINOX SUNSETS.

The Pyramid of the Sun at the ancient city of Teotihuacán in Mexico faces the exact point on the horizon where the sun sets on the equinox; beneath the pyramid there is a cave with four chambers. In ancient Mexico, caves were seen as passageways to the underworld, and so this ancient site connects the time of the autumn equinox with the descent into the underworld.

This site also shares many similarities with the Great Pyramids of Egypt. The base area of the Pyramid of the Sun is almost the same as that of the Great Pyramid of Egypt—the size of the Pyramid of the Sun's base is approximately 97 percent of that of the Great Pyramid. Both have an autumn equinox alignment, and both have subterranean chambers that were used for religious purposes most likely at the time of the autumn equinox. The three pyramids at Teotihuacán, including the Pyramid of the Sun, are laid out in almost the same footprint as the three Great Pyramids of Egypt—a footprint that mirrors the three stars in the belt of the constellation of Orion. Given the similarities, it seems likely that the site of Teotihuacán was established by people who carried the same knowledge and religion of the sun that once existed in Egypt.

INTIHUATANA STONE ~ PERU

THE PYRAMID OF THE SUN WHICH FACES THE EQUINOX SUNSETS.

At the ancient city of Machu Picchu in Peru there is a stone called the Intihuatana stone (meaning "Hitching Post of the Sun"), which is a precise indicator of the date of both the spring and autumn equinoxes and other significant celestial periods. At midday on the equinoxes, the sun stands almost directly above the pillar, creating no shadow at all. It is said that the Incas held ceremonies at the stone at these times. There is also an Intihuatana alignment with the summer solstice (which is in December in the southern hemisphere), when at sunset the sun sinks behind Pumasillo (the Puma's claw), the most sacred mountain of the western Vilcabamba range. Intihuatana stones were venerated as supremely sacred objects by the Inca people, and were most probably established much earlier as part of the spread of the religion of the sun.

THE MOAI OF AHU AKIVI ~ EASTER ISLAND

On Easter Island, the most remote inhabited island in the world, there are numerous megaliths with astronomical alignments. Seven giant statues called moai at the Ahu Akivi site look out to the ocean. They face the sunset during the autumn (and spring) equinox. They also faced the helical setting of the constellation of Orion in AD 1300 (helical describes the conjunction of a star or constellation with the sun as it rises or sets). In the period 5,000 BC to 3,000 BC they would have also faced the setting of the constellation of Orion on the autumn equinox. Alignments to the constellation of Orion, as well as to the solstices and equinoxes, are found at connected ancient sites throughout the world, including the Great Pyramids of Egypt.

THE MOAI FACING THE EQUINOX SUNSET AT AHU AKIVI.

In Egyptian culture, the constellation Orion corresponded to the god Osiris, whose life events, like those of Jesus, followed the process of spiritual awakening. The descent of Orion beneath the horizon may have symbolized the descent into the underworld in the work of spiritual awakening, which is represented in myths around the world at the time of the autumn equinox.

These statues were built to resemble Viracocha, the ancient wisdom bringer who was recorded as being fair skinned and red-bearded, and arriving on the shores of South America teaching the religion of the sun. Viracocha was described as having elongated ear lobes and a beard, which is why these statues all have elongated ear lobes and beards. They were built at least thousands of years ago by a pre-Polynesian culture that also built many of the ancient sites in South and Central America, including the Nazca Lines, as part of the spread of the religion of the sun throughout the world in ancient times. The statues of Easter Island, and the ancient sites of Machu Picchu and the Nazca Lines in Peru, all align to one another, and to the Great Pyramids of Egypt, revealing their shared Indo-European connection. Like Viracocha and his followers, the earliest inhabitants of Easter Island were described as fair skinned and red-haired people who practiced ear elongation, and because of this were actually nicknamed the "Long Ears." The earliest evidence for this practice is found in the Indus Valley in northern India; Buddha is also depicted with elongated ear lobes. These fair skinned and red-haired people even got as far as New Zealand, where they built numerous sites aligned to the solstice and equinox.

According to the author Jean-Michel Schwartz, the position of the hands of the moai statues over their sacrum/sacral area point out what Chinese medicine calls the "she men" or "stone door," which they say is the ancestral center of procreational energy and vitality, and the seat of immortality.[2] This sacral area is also known in Hinduism as the place from which the kundalini, or creative sexual energy rises; it is the seat from which the path to spiritual enlightenment and immortality begins. Statues with the same hand position are found at the ancient site of Tiwanaku in Bolivia, which Viracocha was said to have been involved in building, and at the ancient site of Göbekli Tepe in Turkey, dated to around 9,500 BC.

Statues of Viracocha built by the Indo-European derived Chachapoya culture in Peru, in which Viracocha is depicted as a bearded man, and which look very similar to the statues of Easter Island.

DZIBILCHALTÚN ~
THE YUCATAN PENINSULA IN MEXICO

At the ancient site of Dzibilchaltún, there is a temple called the "Temple of the Seven Dolls" because seven small clay human figures were found buried in the ground there. The temple has openings in the form of arches at each of the four cardinal points. The rising sun on the spring and autumn equinoxes shines through the central doorway of the temple in a beautiful display of light toward a single erect stone.

The "Temple of the Seven Dolls" at Dzibilchaltún—at the equinox the sun shines through the central doorway.

The seven dolls found here parallel the seven moai on Easter Island that face the autumn equinox sunset. Perhaps they too were meant to symbolize the descent of the initiate with their seven solar bodies into the underworld at the time of the autumn equinox, as the dolls were found buried in the ground.

THE PALACE OF KNOSSOS ~ THE GREEK ISLAND OF CRETE

The ancient settlement of Knossos on the Greek island of Crete is believed to be Europe's oldest city. It was first established by Neolithic peoples around 7,000 BC. Later, sometime before 2,000 BC, the ancient Minoan culture began building their central complex there, consisting of 1,300 rooms over 6 acres.

The central palace of this city was known as the legendary home of King Minos. Greek myths recount how King Minos built a labyrinth to imprison the Minotaur—a horrific beast that was half man, half bull. Many are said to have entered this labyrinth, never to come out. Some believe that the palace at Knossos is the fabled labyrinth, whilst others believe the Labyrinthos Caves at Gortyn 20 miles from the palace were used instead. The Minotaur and Labyrinth have a special esoteric meaning, and formed a central part of the spiritual ceremonies of the Minoans that were likely conducted on the autumn equinox.

Studies done by Blomberg and Henriksson reveal that the central religious area of the palace aligns with the autumn equinox sunrise. Evidence shows that this area was built over an earlier Neolithic site, perhaps indicating that the esoteric knowledge of the Minoans has more ancient roots. At sunrise on the equinox, the light travels up the corridor of the so-called house of tablets, which contains a bowl that would have been filled with water, and a wall inscribed with the symbol of the labrys, or double-headed axe.

> "On the morning of the equinoxes the rays of the sun strike the middle of the water-filled bowl, and a reflection occurs on the western wall of the sanctuary. At the same time the shadow on the southern wall just touches the tip of the double axe inscribed there." [3]
> ~ G. HENRIKSSON AND M. BLOMBERG, THE EVIDENCE FROM KNOSSOS ON THE MINOAN CALENDAR, 2011

The symbol of the double-headed axe was also very much connected with the time of the autumn equinox, explained as follows.

> "We have found that our constellation Orion could have played an important part in connection with the Minoan new year at the autumn equinox. In the Middle Bronze Age it dominated the southeastern sky at Knossos in the evening on the autumn equinox and would have done so for a very long time. If a line is drawn connecting the eastern most star in Orion's belt (ζ Orionis) and Sirius, then the figure formed and the inclination of the handle is very like that of the double axe touched by the shadow on the southern wall of the corridor. The double axe seems to have been the most important

Minoan symbol. There are large numbers of them carved into the walls and pillars of the central palace sanctuary and they occur in other parts of the palace, in other Minoan buildings, and on objects of all kinds... The bright star Betelgeuse in Orion rose in the evening of the autumn equinox in the middle of the doorway of the corridor in the Middle Bronze Age, also over a very long period of time." [4]

~ G. HENRIKSSON AND M. BLOMBERG, THE EVIDENCE FROM KNOSSOS ON THE MINOAN CALENDAR, 2011

As well as at the palace of Knossos, the Minoans also aligned other structures to the autumn equinox.

"At the peak sanctuary on Mt. Juktas, which lies about 15 kilometres southwest of Knossos, we had discovered orientations to equinoctial sunrise and to sunrise eleven days after the autumn equinox, both marked by natural foresights (Blomberg, Henriksson and Papathanassiou 2002). At the peak sanctuary on Petsophas, which is just above the Minoan town Palaikastro on the east coast of Crete, sunset at the equinoxes was marked by a natural foresight, the conical peak of Modi, and there are walls oriented to the heliacal rising and setting, in the Middle Bronze Age, of the bright star Arcturus. Its rising occurred one synodic month before the autumn equinox (Henriksson and Blomberg 1996)." [5]

~ G. HENRIKSSON AND M. BLOMBERG, THE EVIDENCE FROM KNOSSOS ON THE MINOAN CALENDAR, 2011

The double-headed axe, called a labrys, is a symbol of the equinox, much like the infinity symbol as the figure eight, as its symmetrically curved blades, protruding from a central handle like an axis, form the same fundamental shape. The labrys always accompanied the goddess, and was used ceremonially on Crete by Minoan priestesses. A Minoan inscription at the palace of Knossos reads "Mistress of the Labyrinth" as it was the goddess who presided over this site so associated with the autumn equinox.

An ancient ceremonial Minoan labrys, symbol of the equinox.

CHAPTER NINE

Ancient Sacred Sites
Aligned to the Winter Solstice

THERE ARE ALMOST COUNTLESS ANCIENT SITES that align to the winter solstice—just a few of these are included here. They have encapsulated a profound esoteric wisdom that can still be grasped even in our modern world—outlasting books and texts, which are easily lost and destroyed. These monuments speak to us through thousands of years about the true spiritual significance of the winter solstice.

Someone who understands the symbolic language used to build these sites can see the builders knew the winter solstice was the cosmic embodiment of the process of creation and the birth of the spiritual Son. This knowledge pre-dates Christian times, which reveals that spiritual deities born at the winter solstice, such as Jesus, Horus, Krishna, Attis, Mithras, etc., symbolize something much greater than one event in history. They also symbolize a spiritual event of universal significance, in which the birth of the spiritual Son within a spiritually prepared individual is a central event.

GLASTONBURY TOR ~ ENGLAND

GLASTONBURY TOR RISING OUT OF THE MIST.

This ancient site is undated and unexcavated, and is believed by many to be the mysterious Isle of Avalon from the legend of King Arthur. It is a giant man-made seven-terraced mound, which was once surrounded by water. Today it is topped by a church tower, which was built in place of a much earlier site.

From what appears to be an ancient man-made observation mound on nearby Windmill Hill, someone can watch the winter solstice sun appear at the bottom of the terraces of Glastonbury Tor, and "roll" up the northern side of the terraces until clipping the top of the tower. In approximately 3,000 BC, only the top rim of the sun would have been visible, allowing someone to observe this incredible event without being blinded by the sun's light.

The constellation Orion rises over the Tor in the winter months, followed by the star Sirius, which rises soon after. During the period around 3,150 BC, Sirius rose in the same place as the winter solstice sun. Orion is associated with the Egyptian father god Osiris, and Sirius is associated with his wife, the Egyptian mother goddess Isis. Horus, their son, is associated with the sun, and is born at the winter solstice. Thus at Glastonbury Tor, during the winter solstice someone could witness a cosmic nativity of Father, Mother, and Son, along with the symbolism created by the Tor.

The rising sun on the winter solstice connected with the birth of the spiritual Son at the base of the terraces, is a symbol of the spiritual Son, which is born in the darkness of the earth (matter), from where it rises through the terraces to reach resurrection. This same design has been used at the next site, which is found in a very different part of the world.

CHICHEN ITZA ~ MEXICO

The pyramid of the feathered serpent (which is a symbol
of the union of the earthly and heavenly) at Chichen Itza.

At an ancient sacred site called Chichen Itza, there is a pyramid dedicated to Kukulcán, the feathered serpent.

On the winter solstice the interaction between the sun and the temple is very similar to that of Glastonbury Tor. When one stands looking at the western face of the pyramid, the sun appears to climb up the terraces until it rests momentarily directly above the pyramid on the pinnacle of the temple room that sits on top of the pyramid. Like Glastonbury, it enacts the same theme of the sun being born at the lowest level of the mound or pyramid, before rising to crown its tower and peak. Here at Chichen Itza, the spiritual Son—who is born at the base of the nine terraces, symbolizing the nine regions of the psyche, underworld, and heavens—will gradually grow and ascend through them until he resurrects.

GOSECK CIRCLE ~ GERMANY

The Goseck circle is an ancient neolithic henge in Germany, and lies on the same latitude as Stonehenge in England, and Arkaim in Russia. Each of these sites have prominent alignments to the solstices.

Goseck circle is dated to 5,000 BC and was a series of concentric circles constructed out of wooden posts and ditches. Two of the openings to the circle aligned to the sunrise and sunset on the winter solstice, funneling the rays of sunlight through wooden posts into the center of the circle.

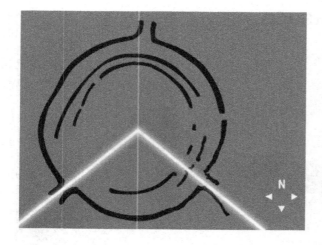

A diagram of Goseck circle from above. The two yellow lines show the alignment of the winter solstice sunrise and sunset through openings in the circle to reach its center.

NEBRA SKY DISK ~ GERMANY

The Nebra Sky Disk is a handheld device for determining the solstice and equinox, made out of bronze with a diagram of the stars, sun and moon embossed on it in gold. It is dated to 1,600 BC, and was made by pre-Celtic people. It was discovered on the hilltop of Mittelberg, which is just twenty-five kilometers away from the location of Goseck circle in Germany just mentioned.

Like the Goseck circle, it too marks the dates of the solstice, but the Nebra disk is transportable. Two arcs which run along either side of the Nebra disk mark the sun's positions at sunrise and sunset on both the winter and summer solstice from Mittelberg hill where it was discovered. Additionally, if the Nebra disk is laid flat on this hilltop and oriented north, one of these arcs points to Brocken mountain, the highest peak of the Harz mountain range. When viewed from Mittelberg hill, the sun sets on the summer solstice precisely behind Brocken mountain.

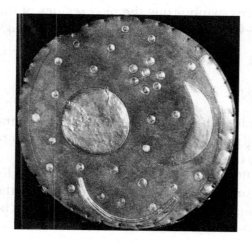

The Nebra Sky Disk. The outer gold rim on the right was also matched by one on the left, which is now missing. These marked the sunsets and sunrises of the winter and summer solstice. The moon and sun are represented in the middle, and are surrounded by stars, which are believed to represent a number of star formations, including possibly the Pleiades.

THE KARNAK TEMPLE COMPLEX ~ EGYPT

The Temple of Amun-Ra at Karnak, was known to the ancient Egyptians as the most hallowed of places, and the very center of the world dedicated to the supreme creator god Amun, where he first brought forth creation. Karnak is the largest temple complex in the world, and houses the largest room of any religious building in the world. Its main axis, which runs down the center of this colossal complex, is aligned to the winter solstice sunrise. Construction on it is said to have begun during Egypt's Middle Kingdom, dated between 2,055–1,650 BC.

The Goddess Mut has a dedicated temple as part of the Karnak complex, in probably one of the most ancient areas of it. Enclosed in her precinct is a sacred lake in the shape of a crescent, symbolizing the waters of creation and the womb. Here we have the presence of the father god Amun and mother goddess Mut at a temple complex aligned to the winter solstice sunrise, which is the time of the birth of the Son.

Pylon architecture was used at Karnak, and was used for the main entrance to the temple complex, which the rising winter solstice sun shone through. A pylon is a huge entrance wall which appears to be divided in two, with a winged solar disk rising in between over the doorway. Pylons were seen as symbols of first creation and of rebirth, which is central to the spiritual meaning of the winter solstice. Pylons depict in architecture the hieroglyph of the sun rising over the horizon between two mountains as it was said to have done on the first day.

An example of pylon architecture from the Temple of Horus; at the Temple of Karnak the winter solstice sun shines out of the doorway in a spectacular recreation of first creation.

When the sun rises on the morning of the winter solstice, it aligns to and enters the temple's most inner sanctuary dedicated to the creator god Amun. Doors from this sanctuary could be opened to allow the sun's rays to funnel along the main axis of the massive temple, out through its rear entrance (a pylon) and along a massive causeway lined with ram-headed sphinxes toward the river Nile.

The sanctuary of Amun is a small stone room, and is reminiscent of a womb that is penetrated by the creative force to give birth to the spiritual Son. Interestingly, this sanctuary aligns to the temple of Luxor nearby, which itself is laid to the proportions of a human body. Sometimes called the Temple of Man, the Luxor Temple depicts an annunciation scene in which the God Amun announces to the mother Goddess Mut that she will give birth to a divine child.

Both in the Karnak Temple Complex and Luxor Temple the golden number and the Fibonacci sequence are found. These sacred numbers are key to the growth and development of all life. In fact, the Karnak Temple Complex was built upon and expanded over hundreds of years, according to the Fibonacci sequence. The entrance to the complex is flanked by rows of giant ram-headed sphinxes that symbolized Amun, and the Fibonacci sequence can be found in the growth of a ram's horns, just as it is found in a nautilus shell. This temple complex was dedicated to life, its growth, the birth of the Son, and creation—and was specifically aligned to the winter solstice.

Ram-headed sphinx at the Karnak Temple Complex with the figure of a pharaoh between its paws. The pharaoh or divine king was often used in place of the spiritual Son.

NEWGRANGE ~ IRELAND

NEWGRANGE

Newgrange is a giant one acre mound, and grass-topped temple, said to have been built around 3,200 BC. Once a year, at the winter solstice, the rising sun enters the mound through a specially built roofbox above the main entrance and shines directly along the nineteen meter long passage, gradually widening until illuminating the inner chamber for about seventeen minutes. Today the first light enters about four minutes after sunrise, but calculations based on the precession of the earth show that five thousand years ago the first light would have entered exactly at sunrise.

The inner chamber of the mound is laid out in the shape of a cross, and beautiful neolithic artwork can be found etched into the stone both on the inside and outside of the mound. Particularly prevalent are spiral designs, including the famous tri-spiral design found inside the chamber.

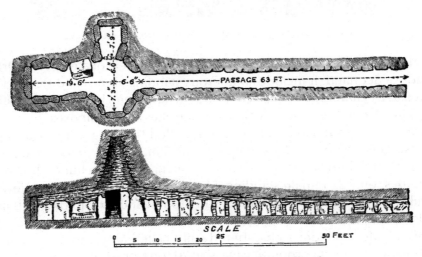

Plan and Section of Chamber in Newgrange Tumulus.

A DIAGRAM OF THE CHAMBER INSIDE NEWGRANGE SHOWING ITS CROSS SHAPE.

Here the symbol of the cross appears in connection with the winter solstice, the time of the birth of the spiritual Son, long before the birth of Jesus. The cross represents the crossing of male and female forces, which give birth to all life. The tri-spiral symbol also shows the union of the three forces of Father, Mother, and Son—positive, negative, and neutral, which give rise to creation. The single spiral is often referred to as "the spiral of life" as it shows the expansion of life.

The mound itself appears to be like a great womb of the earth. Just as the birth of Jesus, Mithras, and Viracocha was said to have taken place in a cave, so too at Newgrange the birth of the sun is enacted inside the dark chamber of the mound.

NESS OF BRODGAR ~ SCOTLAND

THE GIANT STANDING STONES OF THE RING OF BRODGAR.

The Ness of Brodgar is an ancient megalithic complex located in the Orkney Islands of Scotland. It includes numerous standing stones and stone circles, as well as a chambered cairn, all believed to have been built around 3,000 to 2,500 BC. A number of stones mark the solstices and equinoxes.

One of the stone circles at this site is called the Ring of Brodgar, which has also been referred to as a Temple of the Sun. It is 104 meters in diameter (making it the third largest stone circle in the British Isles), but of the original 60 stones, only 27 remain standing. From the circle someone can view various alignments between the solstice sun, stones, and surrounding hills in the landscape.

The site also includes a chambered cairn called Maeshowe—a canonical man-made mound incorporating massive 30 ton stone blocks—aligned to the winter solstice sunrise. Its passage and inner corbeled roof has been compared to the design of the King's Chamber of the Great Pyramid, with its huge stones placed with similar precision so that a knife blade cannot be inserted between them. Like the site of Newgrange mentioned previously, the rising sun on the winter solstice illuminates its inner chamber and lights up its back wall—again perhaps signifying the birth of the sun within the womb of the earth.

Looking out from the large inner chamber of Maeshowe
to its entrance, which aligns to the winter solstice sun.

The Ness of Brodgar obviously served as a spiritual center of some kind, and there is even evidence that it was a staging post on journeys to the Americas in ancient times. For example, similar sites incorporating woodhenges and man-made mounds (canonical and in the shape of serpents) that align to the solstices and equinoxes, are found in Scotland and elsewhere in the British Isles, and are also found in North America (see Serpent Mound and Monks Mound later in this book).

"The advanced mathematical principles, found encoded into precisely positioned, purpose-built surveying markers around Ring o' Brodgar and the greater Orkney Islands, tell us the following facts with indisputable clarity:

By about 3000 BC the cousin Caucasoid nations living around the Mediterranean and throughout Continental Europe, were making ocean traversals to the Americas in their very seaworthy, large, planked sailing ships. For this otherwise dangerous undertaking they used Britain as a main staging area and had established several expansive open-air universities for teaching mathematical principles of navigation and cyclic astronomy. In the British Isles great sprawling schools, offering intensive-comprehensive courses, were laboriously built at Avebury Henge and Durrington Walls Henge in Wiltshire, England, as elsewhere.

This European preoccupation with exploration would go a long way towards explaining why such a high percentage of the Algonquain Indian language of North America, extending to the Great Lakes region and almost across the entire continent, contains many clearly identifiable ancient Basque words (the same word used for elbow, foot, head, breast, shoulder, guts, lake, river, louse, birch bark, ocean, boat, snow (falling), snow (on ground) etc.). Moreover, it's a very ancient form of the Basque tongue, uninfluenced by Indo-Aryan admixtures that crept into the Basque language at later epochs.

Added to that is the fact that the oldest skeletons or mummified remains found across the length and breadth of the Americas are those of Europeans. Also, ancient European structures, cultural-symbolism and writing are found in profusion up and down the Eastern seaboard of the United States, with Hebrew, Phoenician, runic or ogham scripts, etc., seen as far inland as Minnesota, Oklahoma, Ohio, New Mexico, etc. Caucasoid remains are found in Nevada, extending to the Windover bog of Florida or from Mexico to Peru (the Cloud People) & Bolivia, etc. A very high percentage North American Indians carry the European "Y" chromosome and many tribes in both North and South America have oral traditions of the white tribes that their ancestors vanquished. The same measurement & angle standards employed to build ancient Mediterranean-European structures were used to build the huge geometric earthmound complexes of Ohio and Pennsylvania, as well as the temple structures of South America." [1]

~ MARTIN DOUTRÉ, RING O' BRODGAR, ORKNEY ISLANDS: GATEWAY TO THE AMERICAS

The site called "Mystery Hill," which is located in New Hampshire in the United States, also bears a striking resemblance to the ancient megalithic sites of Europe and Britain. It includes a chambered mound similar in design to Maeshowe in Scotland, and its various standing stones align to the solstice and equinox. Carbon dating places the building of the site at least as early as 2,000 BC, and inscriptions found at the site are said to represent Ogham, Phoenician, and Iberian scripts.

We have also been contacted by the owners of a site in Clay County, Kentucky in the United States, as they have discovered a natural cave on their property that aligns to the winter solstice sunrise, and which is inscribed with petroglyphs. The presence of the petroglyphs clearly indicates that the alignment of this site was recognized by ancient peoples. The use of this site potentially connects it in some way to the same peoples who built Newgrange and Maeshowe, as the same theme appears at each of these sites, in which a mound or cave receives the rays of the winter solstice sunrise to its interior.

This begs the question: how much of the spiritual knowledge of the ancient world was shared and transmitted by peoples who traveled across the globe in ancient times? Add this together with the many ancient sites around the world that lie on the same latitude, with each incorporating alignments to the solstice and equinox into their design as well as similar spiritual symbols and themes, and you have evidence for an ancient civilization of the sun that extended throughout much of the world. For example, the following sites of Easter Island, the Great Pyramids, Machu Picchu, the Nazca Lines, and Angkor Wat, all lie along the same line around the earth, and all incorporate alignments to the winter solstice.

THE FOUR-HANDED MOAI STATUE ~ EASTER ISLAND

MOAI ON EASTER ISLAND.

A lone moai statue in the center of Easter Island, at a site called Ahu Huri A Urenga, faces the rising sun on the winter solstice. Unlike any other statue on the island, it has four hands instead of the usual two. This moai is seen as one of the most important astronomical observatories on the island, as it appears that the altar together with five cupules etched on a nearby rock functioned as a "solar-ranging device" which marked the winter solstice and possibly the equinoxes.

THE GREAT PYRAMIDS ~ EGYPT

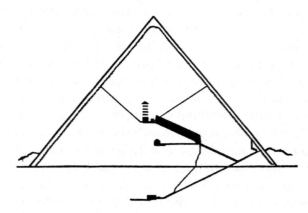

Diagram of the Great Pyramid of Egypt showing its interior passages and chambers. Both the ascending passage (leading to what is called the "King's Chamber") and the descending passage (leading down into the subterranean chamber) are at an angle of 26 degrees, 33 minutes, and 54 seconds.

As the sun set on the winter solstice, researcher Professor Robert Temple noticed that the second largest pyramid cast a shadow on the southern face of the Great Pyramid beside it at the same angles as the ascending and descending passages inside the Great Pyramid—therefore alluding to what was inside. The angle of the shadow and the passages in the Great Pyramid is 26 degrees, 33 minutes, and 54 seconds.

> "It just so happens that this odd angle of slightly more than 26 degrees is the only acute angle possible for a right triangle to be formed that is known as 'the golden triangle', because it embodies the famous Golden Mean Proportion. And it also just so happens that the Golden Mean Proportion is at the basis of the entire canon of ancient Egyptian art and architecture... And in fact, the shadow if truncated by a vertical line running up the middle of the south face of the Great Pyramid, does actually form a golden triangle, which once again is mirrored on the inside, because it is a similar golden triangle which determines the precise point of commencement of the Grand Gallery on the interior of the pyramid... And as for the vertical line running up the pyramid, that too is real, and has been shown from an aerial photograph, although it is invisible to the naked eye or by any perceptual means at ground level. There is actually a purposeful slight indentation of a few inches in the construction of the side of the pyramid, discovered in measurements made by Petrie. This 'apothegm', as geometers call such vertical lines, forms the right angle to transform the solstice shadow into a perfect golden triangle." [2]
>
> ~ PROFESSOR ROBERT TEMPLE

This golden angle was used throughout the design of the site of the Great Pyramids and in Egyptian artwork in relation to the process of spiritual resurrection. It is the spiritual Son born on the winter solstice that will later resurrect, and so perhaps the illustration of this passage was to symbolize that with the setting sun on the winter solstice, the journey toward this spiritual resurrection would now begin.

THE SUN GATE AT TIWANAKU ~ BOLIVIA

THE SUN GATE AT TIWANAKU, WITH THE CREATOR GOD VIRACOCHA FEATURED IN THE CENTER.

At the ancient sacred city of Tiwanaku (also written Tiahuanaco), the rays of the rising sun on the winter solstice pass through a stone entrance called "the Sun Gate" and hit an obelisk directly behind it. The creator god Viracocha is carved into the center of the gate and is surrounded by winged beings. On it are also believed to be the instructions for interpreting a giant wall made of eleven pillars nearby (one of which is lying on the ground) as a solar calendar. When standing at the observation stone, it is said that one could have seen the sun set over each of the pillars, depending on the time of year, including at the equinoxes and solstices—which you can see in animation here: http://www.atlantisbolivia.org/tiwanaku.htm

Although settlements around Tiwanaku have been dated back as far as 1,500 BC, the dating of the ancient ruins of the city of Tiwanaku have been debated and remain surrounded in controversy. Arthur Posnansky, a respected avocational archeologist, and the archeoastronomer Rolf Müller, have argued that Tiwanaku was constructed at approximately 15,000 BC based upon studies of its astronomical alignments.

Additionally, there are other mysteries surrounding Tiwanaku that seem to indicate the site was constructed at a much earlier date than accepted in mainstream circles. Among these are the ancient myths from throughout the Andean region that tell of its founding and use in a pre-flood time. When the Spanish arrived in South America, the Incas told them that they did not build these ancient cities, but that they moved into them. They stated that they were built by giants and by Viracocha himself. The Tiwanaku people believed that Viracocha created giants to move the massive stones, but that he grew unhappy with them and created a flood to destroy them. This myth parallels many others around the world, which also say that a great flood ended a prior race on earth. Viracocha was also said to have arrived to this site by sea and established the construction of megaliths there to commemorate those peoples wiped out by the flood, and those who would now occupy it.

Viracocha is described as a man with long beard, with fair colored skin, dressed in a long white robe, and holding a staff, which is not the appearance of an indigenous Incan, but more closely resembles depictions of Druid priests and the Norse god Odin.

These myths from the Andean region correlate to archeological evidence. The massive stone docks of Tiwanaku are ringed with ocean fossils, as it appears the city was used as a seaport, and yet today it rests miles from water, on an Andean plateau, 13,300 feet above sea level. Stephen Robins, Ph.D., has offered an explanation for this apparent paradox by discussing a worldwide event that occurred at the end of the preceding geological epoch called the Pleistocene, around twelve to thirteen thousand years ago, which suddenly made many mountain ranges around the world rise up. Studies have also found evidence for a cataclysmic flood that swept the Andean Altiplano Plateau around the same time, and the utensils, tools, and fragments of human skeletons around the Tiwanaku site are mixed in with the deepest layers of the flood alluvia—indicating possible human use of the site prior to this great flood and adding support to theories that the site of Tiwanaku was first established in 12,000 BC or before. It's possible that Viracocha knew of the site at Tiwanaku and came to re-establish civilization there after the cataclysmic flood.

MACHU PICCHU ~ PERU

At the ancient mountaintop city of Machu Picchu in Peru there is a semi-circular structure called the "Temple of the Sun" that was constructed around a large boulder. During the winter solstice, the sun shines through the central window and strikes the stone boulder within while also aligning with the tip of a nearby mountain peak.

Machu Picchu is also home to the Intihuatana stone which aligns to the equinoxes, and the city is situated on a mountain ridge above the Urubamba Valley, which also has a winter solstice alignment as described next.

The Temple of the Sun at Machu Picchu, which is the circular building that encases a large stone boulder that aligns to the winter solstice sunrise.

THE URUBAMBA SACRED VALLEY ~ THE ANDES OF PERU

In this sacred valley in the Andes facing the ancient Inca ruins of Ollantaytambo, there is a mountain sacred to the Incas called Cerro Pinkuylluna believed to have the profile of the creator god Viracocha. The formation, standing at 140 meters high, is made up of indentations that form the eyes and mouth, whilst a protruding carved rock makes his nose. Ruins built on top of the face are considered to represent a crown on his head. When the sun strikes the profile of Viracocha during the winter solstice, the mineral content of the mountain reflects and refracts the rays.

IMAGE RIGHT: Looking over the shoulder of the bearded wisdom bringer Viracocha at his face in the side of the Ollantaytambo mountain. If you look closely you can see the ruins built on top of his head, forming the crown.

In the legends of the pre-Inca and Inca people, the creator sun god Viracocha, who is depicted with a crown of the sun, is said to have risen from Lake Titicaca (or in some sources the cave of Pacaritambo) during the time of darkness to bring forth light, and is said to have made the earth, the stars, the sky, and mankind. This ties in with the spiritual meaning of the winter solstice as the time of the birth of the spiritual Son, and his bringing forth of creation, which is why at the sites of Tiwanaku and the Urubamba Sacred Valley, his image aligns to the winter solstice sunrise.

AJANTA CAVES ~ INDIA

The cave at Ajanta called number nineteen,
which aligns with the winter Solstice sunrise.

The Ajanta Caves are an extraordinary group of around thirty man-made caves cut into the side of a sheer cliff face. The cliff is naturally U-shaped and was hidden in a remote part of the jungle. The caves are believed to have been built by Buddhist monks by carving into the cliff face—what they created were elaborate shrines and temples, all cut into one single giant rock.

Work is believed to have begun on the caves in around 200 BC and ended around AD 480–650. The caves contained sculptures and artwork centered around the life of Buddha.

Two of the caves align to celestial events. Cave nineteen aligns to the winter solstice sunrise. It contains a statue of Buddha standing within a stupa, which is illuminated by the rays of the rising sun on the winter solstice.

A stupa is a symbolic monument which it is said Buddha uses to ascend and descend.

The winter solstice is a time when the force of the spiritual Son descends into a spiritually prepared person.

GREAT ZIMBABWE ~ ZIMBABWE, AFRICA

The ruins of Great Zimbabwe. The large circular structure is called the Great Enclosure, which is surrounded by various other ruins in the landscape.

In sub-Saharan Africa there lie the stone ruins of an abandoned ancient city; this region is one which could have easily been reached by boat on voyages from ancient Egypt, India, or Europe on the way to the Americas, where similar sites were established. Oral histories of the local Bantu people state that their people did not build this site, but attribute it to a fair skinned people they call the Ma-iti. Incredibly the same lozenge style patterns built into the walls of this circular fortressed city appear in another that looks just like it, built by people also described as fair skinned, at the ancient fortressed city of Kuélap in Peru. These patterns were also used by ancient peoples in their artwork in Europe.

A number of stone monoliths at the site line up with certain bright stars in the constellation Orion as they rise on the morning of the winter solstice. Perhaps this was intended to signify the birth of the spiritual Son—as the Egyptians saw the constellation of Orion as a representation of the god Osiris, whose life shares similarities with Jesus and other deities who represented the divine Son.

Great Zimbabwe is just one of many ancient sites with alignments to both Orion and to the solstices and equinoxes—all of which were built to encode the same spiritual knowledge.

NAZCA LINES ~ PERU

The giant figure known as the astronaut as seen on the side of a mountain from the air at the site known as the Nazca Lines.

In the Nazca Desert in southern Peru, hundreds of giant lines and figures were drawn into the ground by removing the layers of red desert pebbles to expose the white soil beneath. The figures are best viewed from the sky, and one figure has been called an astronaut because of how similar it looks to one. This has led some to theorize that the builders of the lines could have been in contact with extra-terrestrials.

Research by Dr. Paul Kosok and Maria Reiche has revealed that a number of the lines align to the winter and summer solstices, along with other figures that could have aligned to the constellation of Orion. The lines themselves are not able to be dated, so it is difficult to determine when they aligned to celestial movements as due to the precession of the equinoxes these alignments shift over time. However, on the winter solstice the sun used to set over one line, exactly between the sixth and first century BC.

The culture that mainstream opinion believes to be indigenous to the area, however, was only active from 100 BC to AD 1 onward, which means that an earlier people created these lines. Horrifically, the later culture that took over this site practiced human decapitation, which apparently dramatically increased from about AD 450.

The original builders were very different people however; evidence for their earlier occupation of the area is found in the tens of thousands of fair-haired European-featured mummies unearthed at the edge of the Nazca valley.

"According to our experts, the Nazca builders were very superstitious and, as recently as 550 AD, built the lines for the purpose of appeasing and stroking the egos of the "gods", in an attempt to get them to send rain during an extended drought of 40-years duration. The fact that Nazca is about the driest place on earth, where a small rain every few years causes a sensation when it happens, or that there has been no significant rainfall there since the end of the last ice-age, tends to make such a hypotheses laughable in the extreme. As it turns out, the expansive sprawl of the Andes mountain ranges just inland, offer a huge catchments area and the Nazca desert region is fed by a multitude of subterranean springs and wells, making water sources, for the most part, eternally abundant.

Before Nazca desert region could be made habitable, to sustain the sizeable population that settled there several thousand years ago, over 93-miles (150-kilometers) of mostly subterranean aqueducts had to be dug. Along with these, there were 28 filtration galleries, some of which penetrate underground over two thirds of a mile into the hard conglomerate deposits and bring out 25 litres of water per second.

The trussed mummy, with the very fine, auburn-red hair... is typical of the tens of thousands of mummies that have been found in the region. This reddish hair colour is found on only a very small percentage of the world's population (about 1-2%). The largest, present-day concentration of redheads in the world is in the United Kingdom, where 13-percent of the population has red hair and 40-percent carry the recessive red gene. The gene is strongly represented in England, Ireland, Wales, Scotland or amongst the Germanic and Scandinavian tribes, Finns, Russians, Basques and extending to the most ancient occupants of Egypt in the Eastern Mediterranean (where the early mummies have red, blond, or other European hues of hair colour) to the former population of the Canary Islands in the Atlantic (the Gaunche ... where the early mummified people found were ethnic Europeans).

Red hair was very prominent in the ancient Pacific, from Easter Island (where the giant, long faced statues had "red" top-knot stones placed on their heads) to New Zealand. In fact, the earliest cave burials of New Zealand (at the very ends of the Earth) were observed to be Caucasoid people with red hair. These most ancient New Zealanders also buried their dead in a trussed, sitting position, alongside personal possessions, in much the same manner as is found with the Nazca mummies. A huge amount of artefact, flora and cultural evidence shows a direct link between ancient New Zealand and Peru.

Well watered, fertile pockets of farmland sit adjacent or very near to the Nazca lines and ancient people, etching or using the lines, could return a reasonably short distance each evening to locations offering hospitable conditions of shelter and sustenance. In essence, the Nazca region would have been an exceptional centre for an "open-air university" if the lines were set out for the purpose of offering tutorials, of some sort, to initiate students.

Based upon the mummy evidence of the region, these tall stature, Caucasoid, dolichocephalic-cranium, long thin faced people with typical European hues of multi-coloured hair, built the Nazca aqueducts, settled the area and made the farms productive. They then undertook the huge task of etching 800 lines and other geometric shapes and glyphs into the desert to indelibly encode their ages-old sciences, brought with them to the region from the Mediterranean and Europe." [3]

~ MARTIN DOUTRÉ, NAZCA

Dr. Paul Kosok, who first discovered their astronomical link, called the Nazca Lines "the largest astronomy book in the world." The native name for the site is "Intiwatana," which means "the place to where the sun is tied," indicating its cosmological link. Just as the builders of the Great Pyramids wished to create a link between heaven and earth when they mirrored the cosmic "duat" with their ancient sites, so too did the creators of this site who carried with them the knowledge of ancient Egypt. Incredibly, the Nazca Lines lie along the same line around the earth as the Great Pyramids of Egypt and a number of other sacred sites.

MYNYDD DINAS ~ RHONDDA, WALES

According to local legend, the ancient Druids used to gather every winter solstice to watch the sunrise on the winter solstice over the mountain called Mynydd Dinas—believed to be their sacred mountain Morganwg. They believed the sun god Hu Gadarn was born as a baby boy as the winter solstice sun, and would grow as the year progressed toward the summer solstice. [4] Later the Romans celebrated the birth of Mithras and Christians the birth of Jesus at the winter solstice, and yet both had their influence upon the destruction of the Druids' traditions.

Also nearby the Dinas Mountain in Wales there is a cave that goes by a Welsh name meaning "Voice of God" where the Druids enacted the birth of their solar god Hu Gadarn (the Mabyn Taliesun) from within the cave. The Druid priest acting as Hu Gadarn was said to have given a loud musical shout to which the gathered crowds would reply "Ein Hoes," meaning "Our Life!" [5]

The mountain of Mynydd Dinas held as sacred by the Druids, who would watch the sun rise over its peak at the winter solstice.

ANGKOR WAT ~ CAMBODIA

A model of the temple of Angkor Wat, with its layout incorporating cruciform shapes. The center of the temple receives shafts of light on the winter solstice.

At the giant Hindu temple complex of Angkor Wat, shafts of light shine on the exact geometric center of the Preau Cruciforme on the winter solstice. The temple is dedicated to the Hindu god Vishnu and is laid out in a cruciform shape, a shape that is incredibly significant to the time of the winter solstice and the birth of the spiritual Son/sun, not only to the Christians, but also in the ancient sites and traditions of the Britons and Druids.

The cross is also an alchemical symbol—the union of male (vertical) and female (horizontal) forces gives spiritual birth to the divine child within. At Angkor Wat the light of the sun shines on the cross on the winter solstice, just as it does within the cruciform chamber of Newgrange in Ireland.

ARKAIM AND SURROUNDING MEGALITHIC SITES ~ RUSSIA

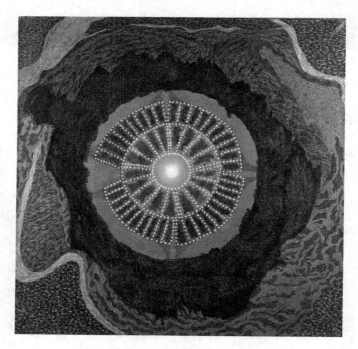

An artist's impression of the ground
plan of Arkaim, titled "Arkaim Shining."

Arkaim was an ancient city located on the Southern steppe of the Ural moun-tain region of Russia, just north of the border with Kazakhstan, and is said to have been built sometime between 2,000 to 1,700 BC, although, as with many ancient sites, further dating has suggested it may be even older. It is one of at least twenty similar settlements in the region (it's believed there are another fifty in addition to this that are still buried) that were possibly each home to approximately 1,500 people. A link has been established between the inhabitants of this site and the peoples who authored the Rig Veda—one of the oldest known sacred texts in the world—leading many to believe that it was the ancient home of the Aryans and progenitors of the Vedic religion.

It has been called "Russia's Stonehenge" as it is located at the same latitude as Stonehenge in England as well as Goseck Circle in Germany. Each of these three sites are laid out in concentric circles and have multiple astronomical alignments, providing strong evidence that they are all connected to each other in some way.

> "These sites lie on the exact latitude at which the midsummer sunrise and sunsets are at 90° to the Moon's northerly setting and southerly rising. This particular phenomena is only possible within a band of less than one degree of which Stonehenge and Goseck lies in the middle-third. The sites also sit on one of two unique latitudes in the world where the full Moon passes directly overhead on its maximum zeniths. Coincidence?" [6]
>
> ~ DEBORAH SCHERRER, STANFORD SOLAR CENTER

According to the research of Konstantin Bystrushkin, Arkaim's alignments include the sunrises and sunsets on the solstices and equinoxes.

The ancient city has also been called "Swastika City" as the layout of the structure resembles a swastika; the city itself is round and has four entrances that are laid out in the four cardinal directions. Excavations in the area have revealed numerous pottery shards covered in the symbol of the swastika, which is a symbol illustrating the movement of the sun, and the solstices and equinoxes—and is one of the oldest and most universal symbols in the ancient world.

> "The truth is that Arkaim was a troy town, so-called after the city in Asia Minor that the Greek king Agammenon destroyed during the Trojan Wars. Built on the same circular principle as Troy, as described in Homer's Iliad, but at least six hundred years older, Arkaim finds its prototype in Plato's Atlantis with its three concentric circles of canals; in legendary Electris, the Hyperborean city some said was built under the Pole Star by the sea-god Poseidon; and in Asgard, the sacred city dedicated to the Norse god Odin that is described in the Icelandic saga, the Edda. All these legendary troy towns have the same circular ground plan. They have gone down in history as neolithic Wisdom centres and the seats of ancient god-kings... Built in the unique architectural mould of nordic Asgard, the most sacred shrine of the Aesir of which the Prose Edda relates that 'men call it Troy,' **Arkaim may have been a shrine dedicated to the Aryan Sun**

religion... Troy towns like Electris — and Arkaim — were built as stellar observatories. Their function was to unite earth to the starry cosmos above according to the principle of 'as above so below' by means of a central axis symbolised by a stone pillar. Thus Diodorus Siculus of the first century BCE, quoting the historian Hecataeus, described the sanctuary of Electris as a troy town after the pattern of the spheres, 'by which he meant an astronomical design similar to that of Stonehenge and other ancient sun temples, in which the scheme of the heavenly spheres or astral shells surrounding the earth was represented diagrammatically by a series of concentric circles marked by walls, ditches or moats around a central pillar-stone.'" [7]

~ VICTORIA LEPAGE, NOV-DEC 2008 ISSUE NEW DAWN MAGAZINE

Little remains of Arkaim, as it was burnt to the ground at some time in history—and the inhabitants mysteriously disappeared, leaving almost nothing behind.

Today we can only speculate as to the meaning of the site. It has a circular design laid out in a swastika type formation, with an inner passageway that is a clockwise spiral leading to the center of the city. As the summer solstice approaches, the sun traces a tightening clockwise spiral on the earth, and so it has been said that this city was laid out in the same pattern so that people entering the city walked the way/path of the sun, with the swastika symbolizing the movement of the sun.

The city of Arkaim provides further evidence of an ancient religion of the sun. The Aryans are thought to have migrated to different parts of the world, including India and Europe, most probably taking their ancient knowledge with them, and the sacred symbols of concentric circles, the spiral, and swastika, which emerged in other ancient sites.

Arkaim is located in the Southern Ural region in Russia; in the Central and Southern Ural region there are also hundreds of megalithic and standing stone sites, most of which have been termed Dolmens and Menhirs, and some of which have been found to align to the solstices and equinoxes. The largest megalithic complex in the Ural region is located on Vera Island.

"Among the most interesting monuments of the isle are its megaliths, similar to the famous megaliths of the Western Europe and Middle East. The largest of them is about 18 meters long, and weighs about 17 tons. Most likely, it is a temple complex related to the sun calendar cult. These megaliths are at average six thousand years old. Their further study may possibly change the history of the mountain forest zone of the Urals in the end of the Stone Age." [8]

~ STANISLAV GRIGORYEV, SENIOR RESEARCH SCIENTIST OF THE CHELYABINSK RESEARCH CENTER OF THE INSTITUTE FOR HISTORY AND ARCHEOLOGY OF THE URALS DEPARTMENT OF RAS.

A megalith on Vera Island, which has portals that may
have been built to allow shafts of sunlight into it.

CHAPTER TEN

Ancient Sacred Sites Aligned to the Spring Equinox

THIS CHAPTER BRINGS TOGETHER ANCIENT SACRED SITES from around the world which align to the spring equinox. Even though they are separated by vast distances and time, they share a knowledge of the symbolic spiritual significance of the spring equinox as a time of resurrection and attainment of eternal life.

The following sacred sites from around the world reveal an incredible knowledge of the spiritual significance of the spring equinox and its relationship to the internal spirituality of humankind.

THE SPHINX AND GREAT PYRAMID OF GIZA ~ EGYPT

One of the most dominant alignments (as there are many both solar and stellar) of the Giza plateau, home to the Sphinx and the Great Pyramids, occurs at the spring equinox.

THE SPHINX, WHICH GAZES PRECISELY AT SUNRISE ON THE EQUINOX.

The Sphinx gazes due east to where the sun rises on the morning of the spring equinox. It is estimated that during the era of 10,970 to 8,810 BC (but also prior to that at approximately 36,500 BC) it also gazed directly toward the rising of its own celestial image (known today as the constellation of Leo in the form of a recumbent lion), which would have preceded the sun at dawn on the spring equinox. Due to what is called "the precession of the equinoxes," the sun rises in a different constellation on the spring equinox approximately every 2,150 years. At that time, the spring equinox sun rose in the constellation of Leo. This reveals, along with archeological evidence of weathering and esoteric evidence of what the Sphinx was originally intended to symbolize, that the Sphinx is much older than mainstream Egyptologists say—who date it to around 2,500 BC.

Furthermore, the causeway connecting the Sphinx to the second of the three Great Pyramids is slightly offset. Again, mainstream Egyptologists argue that this was a design flaw to accommodate the Sphinx into the layout of the Giza pyramids. But it was actually done for a specific esoteric reason—as everything was in the original design of the ancient Giza plateau.

Standing on the causeway facing the rising sun on the spring equinox during this era, one could have witnessed the constellation of Leo rising over the horizon just before dawn with its head appearing first before being followed by its recumbent body. Looking across at the Sphinx from the same point on the causeway, this same image is mirrored by the Sphinx itself with only its head visible above the plateau and its recumbent body set down inside a carved out enclosure.

The design of the Sphinx interwoven into the spring equinox and the constellations has an important esoteric meaning. It pinpoints the celestial parts while integrating them into an earthly design, which symbolically re-enact the process of the resurrection of Osiris as found in the ancient Pyramid Texts—the oldest surviving sacred texts of Egypt and possibly the world.

Close by, the Great Pyramid is designed in such a way that at noon on the spring equinox it casts no shadow.

The Sphinx and Great Pyramid are giant symbols, and both are part of a plan on the ground that forms a greater symbol.

The pyramids were never built as tombs for pharaohs and evidence has come to light that the Sphinx was not originally built as a man-headed lion, and possibly not even a lion at all, but as the deity Anubis in his form as recumbent African golden wolf who resurrected Osiris. Going back into the most ancient accounts, the Sphinx was a spiritual symbol of incredible significance, which was successively restored, re-carved, and vandalized over thousands of years. It symbolizes the resurrection of Osiris at the dawning of the sun on the spring equinox. This is explored further in the chapter 'Decoding the Ancient Meaning of the Sphinx and Its Origin as Anubis,' which looks at the symbolism of the spring equinox alignment with the Sphinx in more detail.

ANGKOR WAT ~ CAMBODIA

The spring equinox sun rising to crown
the pinnacle of Angkor Wat in Cambodia.

Angkor is an ancient city with a massive complex of stone temples in the jungle of Cambodia. The temple of Angkor Wat is the most famous and aligns to the rising sun of the spring equinox. The temple is said to be a representation of Mount Meru, the ancient Hindu home of the gods, and the North Pole. The five central towers symbolize the five peaks of the mountain, and the walls and moat the surrounding mountain ranges and ocean.

The axis of the temple is offset to give a three day anticipation of the coming spring equinox alignment. On the morning of the spring equinox, the sun rises up the side of the central tower (mountain peak) of the temple and crowns its pinnacle. Due to precession, the spring equinox sun gradually rises through the twelve different constellations of the zodiac over an approximately 26,000 year cycle. This constellation would have been observable before dawn over the tower of Mount Meru.

Angkor Wat is decorated with a massive stone mural that depicts the ancient Hindu story of "the churning of the milky ocean" (along with scenes from the sacred texts the Mahabharata and Ramayana) in which the asuras (demons) and devas (angels) are in a giant tug of war using a serpent wrapped around a mountain, which churns the great milky ocean as they pull back and forth. This churning produces Amrita, the nectar of immortality, eventually consumed by the devas and which allows Indra to return to his abode as the King of Heaven. The churning of the milky ocean reveals a fundamental spiritual principle found in the universe—the role of darkness and light in creation, within ourselves, and on the path of the spiritual sun.

The central segment of the mural of the churning of the milky ocean at Angkor Wat. Vishnu is the large central figure—above him is Indra, below him the turtle in the ocean, and on either side the demons and devas pulling.

This giant relief is found carved into an eastern wall, and is associated with the spring equinox, while other reliefs are associated with the other four points of the year. Like the Pyramids of Giza, Angkor Wat also features stellar alignments around 10,500 BC. Researcher Graham Hancock discovered that Angkor Wat and a number of surrounding temples (around fifteen) mirror the constellation of Draco as it would have appeared in the sky at the time of the spring equinox in the year 10,500 BC, many thousands of years before it is said to have been built. It's most likely that the site was chosen and at least part of its ground plan was built by those who had a connection to the knowledge of ancient Egypt at a far earlier time, and to the lost civilization of the sun, as Angkor Wat lies along the same line around the earth as other sites connected to this civilization. It's even located 72 symbolic degrees from the Great Pyramids—and 72 is a key number in the cycle of precession that both sites encode, as the earth cycles through one degree in its precession every 72 years.

The central tower of Angkor Wat was built to symbolize the axis of the North Pole. Due to precession, the North Pole changes the star (called the Pole star) it points to very slowly over the same approximately 26,000 year cycle of precession—tracing an almost perfect circle in the sky as it does.

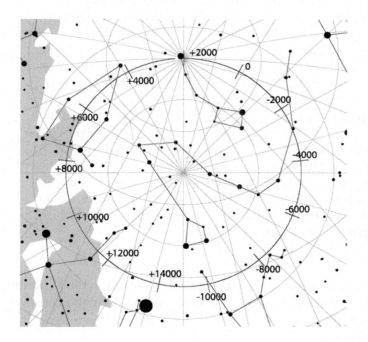

The path of the north celestial poles among the stars due to precession. Draco is the central constellation that appears to wind around the very center of the picture.

The constellation of Draco (which is depicted as a dragon or serpent) appears in the region of the circumpolar stars, where it literally wraps around the center of the circle that the North Pole traces through the sky in its processional cycle. The constellation of Draco is therefore the celestial depiction of the great serpent of the churning of the milky ocean, wrapped around the tower of Angkor Wat as the North Pole, with the stars that make its constellation mirrored in the temples on the ground.

With the combination of the constellation of Draco, which is shaped like a giant serpent, and the tower of the temple said to represent Mount Meru, all aligned at the spring equinox, Angkor Wat brings together the counterparts of the churning of the milky ocean in symphony with the earth and the sky.

In the mural depicting this scene, the number of demons on the left represents the days between the winter solstice and the spring equinox, and the number of devas on the right represents the number of days from the spring equinox to the summer solstice. Each side of either demons or devas measures 54 cubits—which together adds to 108, a number sacred in Buddhism and Hinduism.

The numbers 108 and 54, along with 72 and 36, have been incorporated into the design of Angkor Wat and surrounding temples. These numbers are part of the mathematics of the phenomena known as "the precession of the equinoxes," a cosmic cycle of the earth related to the spring equinox, which the churning of the milky ocean is also said to symbolize.

> "At the temple of Phnom Bakheng there are 108 surrounding towers. The number 108, considered sacred in both Hindu and Buddhist cosmologies, is the sum of 72 plus 36 (36 being ½ of 72). The number 72 is a primary number in the sequence of numbers linked to the earth's axial precession, which causes the apparent alteration in the position of the constellations over the period of 25,920 years, or one degree every 72 years. Another mysterious fact about the Angkor complex is its location 72 degrees of longitude east of the Pyramids of Giza. The temples of Bakong, Prah Ko and Prei Monli at Roluos, south of the main Angkor complex, are situated in relation to each other in such a way that they mirror the three stars in the Corona Borealis as they appeared at dawn on the spring equinox in 10,500 BC. It is interesting to note that the Corona Borealis would not have been visible from these temples during the 10th and 11th centuries when they were constructed." [1]
>
> ~ MARTIN GRAY, SACRED EARTH

Even the causeway of Angkor Wat incorporates cosmic symbolism and numbers encoding the cycles of time. The axial lengths along the causeway of Angkor Wat were designed to represent the great world ages of Hindu cosmology called Yugas.

TIKAL ~ GUATEMALA

Tikal is an ancient series of temples located deep in the jungle of Guatemala. Like many ancient sites in Central America, the temples here were successively built over, which means that their origins are actually much older. Here, tall pyramid style temples rise out of the canopy of the rainforest.

On the spring equinox, the sun rises up the middle of The Temple of the Grand Jaguar with its nine terraces to crown its pinnacle. In doing so, it causes the temple to cast a perfect shadow over the much smaller Temple of the Moon, which has three terraces and was decorated with a wooden lintel showing the image of a royal woman (the original stone mantle of the temple is too dilapidated to make out whether there was anything originally carved into it). This visual "absorption" of the feminine moon temple into the shadow of the Temple of the Jaguar—may have represented how someone becomes one with the Mother at the stage of resurrection.

TEMPLE OF THE GRAND JAGUAR AT TIKAL.

The Temple of the Grand Jaguar was decorated with a wooden lintel depicting a jaguar with water lilies sprouting from its head, protecting the King (again the original stone mantle is worn away).

The jaguar is an ancient Maya and Olmec symbol dating back to the earliest recorded cultures in Central and South America, with depictions that date from around 1,500 BC. The water-lily jaguar was considered a transformer, and could also be depicted amidst flames. The meaning of the water-lily jaguar remains obscure in Maya culture, however the jaguar itself has parallels in many esoteric teachings as the tiger the Hindu warrior goddess Durga rides upon, the lion-headed warrior goddess of Egypt Sekhmet, and the Buddhist lion-headed goddess Senge Dongma—each also associated with fire.

The jaguar of Central America (like the lion and tiger) is the equivalent symbol of the fierce war against darkness and evil within the initiate. Known as the god of terrestrial fire in Central America, it is symbolically related to the inner alchemical fire which transforms someone spiritually.

The jaguar was considered the night sun—the form the sun takes in its journey through the underworld. At the time of the spring equinox the sun rises from out of the underworld to defeat the darkness. The rising of the sun was very much associated with resurrection to the Maya, and again resurrection is symbolized at this site at the spring equinox as in many other ancient esoteric sites around the world. A plate illustrating the resurrection of the Maya maize god of resurrection was also found at Tikal.

The complex at Tikal includes many other solar and stellar alignments, including to the solstices and to the star cluster the Pleiades.

Like other Central American sites, Tikal descended into human sacrifice and bloodletting. Graffiti inside the temples depicts scenes of sacrificial victims. Again, this was a horrific distortion of the original spiritual teaching as has happened so many times in the past, and why spiritual knowledge is continually given anew.

CAHOKIA MOUNDS ~ UNITED STATES

THE CENTRAL COLUMN OF CAHOKIA'S "WOODHENGE."

Cahokia Mounds, located in the U.S. state of Illinois, is considered the largest and most sophisticated prehistoric civilization north of Mexico. It covered an area of 6 square miles or 16 square kilometres, contained 120 man-made earthen mounds, and at one stage became home to around 40,000 inhabitants.

This city contained a woodhenge, which was a sacred circle made of wooden posts (like the one built near Stonehenge in England). The wood used was red cedar, which was considered sacred. When standing at the center of the circle, where a large "observation post" was located, the sun on the solstices and equinox aligned with some of the posts of the circle.

The most visually spectacular of the alignments at the site was the sunrise on the equinox. One of the wood posts that aligned with the equinox also aligned with the front of Monks Mound—the largest mound in the entire complex, with a footprint larger than that of the Great Pyramid of Egypt.

On the equinox, Monks Mound is described as appearing to give birth to the rising sun. However, given that the time of the spring equinox was associated with resurrection to the Maya of Central America, perhaps the mound symbolized not the birth of the sun, but its resurrection. At the spring equinox the Maya god Hun Hunahpu resurrected from the earth and underworld symbolized as a turtle. Monks Mound, which the sun "resurrects" from, was actually built in the shape of a turtle.

> "Monks mound is prominently situated as the central feature of the Cahokia Mounds group, a group of around 120 mounds in the region. From an aerial and profile view, the mound is composed in the shape of a turtle effigy. These projections may represent the turtles hind legs on the north side, constructed to indicate movement. The front projections on the first terrace represent legs of the turtle. I suggest the possibility is that this is an effigy of a turtle burying its eggs, or possibly a turtle walking south. Several versions of this account are found throughout North America. I concur with the late Oscar Schneider, 'Monks Mound, that giant earthwork built in four stages with a projecting ramp to the south, is actually a giant turtle figure.' If it was a sacred 'National Monument' for Turtle Island, presently known as North America, which was once held in the highest regards as among the world's most sacred places. Monks Mound was used for ceremonies that relate to the 'big house' ceremony, in which the sky people sat on the north and the earth people sat on the south of the path of the sun. They contemplated the intricate workings of the cosmos, their ancestors, and their descendants." [2]
>
> ~ VINCE BARROWS

Additionally, a symbolic carving of a turtle was found at Monks Mound and is described by researcher Vince Barrows as having a trident on its left side, which depicts death and darkness, and a symbol of the sun on its right, which depicts birth. Perhaps this carving symbolizes the dual aspects of creation—of darkness and light, which rotate on the point of balance at the equinox. Incredibly, it contains the same elements of the churning of the milky ocean scene illustrated at Angkor Wat in Cambodia, where the forces of darkness and light are depicted as being on either side of a turtle. And like Monks Mound, Angkor Wat is also aligned to the spring equinox.

CAIRN T ~ IRELAND

Thousands of years ago, Ireland was inhabited by the Tuatha Dé Danann—a mysterious god-like people most closely connected with the ancient mega-lithic sites of Ireland. They were said to be preceded by the Fir Bolg, another mythical ancient people. While the ancient history of Ireland turned into legends and myth passed on verbally over thousands of years, what is known as set in stone is that Ireland was once inhabited by a highly astronomically advanced people who had knowledge of esoteric principles, which they incorporated into the design of their megalithic temples.

Cairn T is the name given to an ancient neolithic mound with an inner chamber that aligns to the equinoxes, and is believed to have been built around 3,500 BC (and was even possibly built on an older sacred site). It is the main and central mound in a group of neolithic sites at a place called Loughcrew, which originally had around forty monuments. It is thirty-five meters in diameter and was once covered in a thick mantle of quartz. The rising sun on the spring equinox enters the mound and travels into its inner chamber which is in the shape of a cross/cruciform, to alight the back stone, called the Equinox Stone, which is covered in astronomical symbols.

CAIRN T AT THE SITE OF LOUGHCREW.

You can explore Loughcrew and its beautiful art through videos and photos at this website: http://www.knowth.com/loughcrew.htm

The equinox sun, viewed from Cairn T, rises over the Hill of Slane, which is a sacred hill that is framed by the view looking back out from the chamber of Cairn T. The Hill of Slane formed part of a larger equinox alignment in ancient Ireland as described in the Millmount-Croagh Patrick alignment further on.

KNOWTH ~ IRELAND

Nearby Cairn T at Loughrew is another ancient neolithic site called Knowth, also thought to have been built around 3,500 BC. It is the largest ancient monument in Ireland and contains the largest collection of megalithic artwork in all of Europe. Some believe it could have served as an ancient repository of wisdom that was carved symbolically into its stone (much like the temples of Egypt).

It is a giant man-made mound one acre in size with two inner chambers—one aligned to the east, and the other the west. These chambers are eighteen days off aligning to the spring and autumn equinoxes, so that the sunrise enters the east chamber and is funneled along its passage near the spring equinox, while the west chamber captures the sunset near the autumn equinox. The reason for this is still unknown, and further investigation is currently trying to determine whether these passages used lunar alignments to foretell the equinoxes instead. What seems clear is that this mound is connected to the equinox in its alignments in some way.

KNOWTH

The east chamber (the direction of east is typically associated with the spring equinox) is in a cruciform shape—it is the biggest in Ireland and houses the Dagda Cauldron. The Dagda Cauldron is a large stone basin with a symbolic design carved into it, thought to be placed inside Knowth before the temple mound was built, as it is too large to have been brought into it later. It is shaped like a cauldron—an important motif in Irish mythology. The most well-known cauldron in Irish myth belonged to Dagda, a chieftain of the Tuatha Dé Danann. His cauldron was one of the four chief treasures that the Tuatha Dé Danann are said to have brought to Ireland—the others being the Stone of Destiny at Tara, the Sword of Light, and Spear of Lugh.

Cauldrons later became associated with witches, however, the cauldron was originally a spiritual symbol.

In Irish myth the cauldron was said to have had the power to regenerate life so that dead bodies could be placed into the cauldron and drawn out alive and whole again. This is symbolic of resurrection. The mound and cauldron are symbols of the womb, from which all life comes forth. The symbol of the cross in the east chamber connects this part of the mound with the spring equinox, the time of Jesus' resurrection, thousands of years before he enacted the same cosmic principle.

Another sexual symbol is present at Knowth, again revealing the knowledge of the forces of creation and life in spirituality—there is a pair of large standing stones outside its west entrance. One is tall and thin, a phallic symbol representing the masculine force, and the other is squat and round, representing the feminine.

THE MILLMOUNT-CROAGH PATRICK ALIGNMENT ~ IRELAND

The ancient man-made mound at Millmount—once a sacred astronomical observatory, now a fort with canon fire displays.

The Millmount-Croagh Patrick alignment to the spring equinox is not just to one particular site, but is created from the alignment of a number of sites in relation to each other, which were built from the east to the west coast of Ireland stretching over 135 miles.

The ancient peoples were aware of how the natural land formations aligned at certain times of the year, and incorporated them into the design of their sacred sites—again bringing the earthly and celestial together on the ground as was done in Egypt and at Angkor Wat. These types of alignments, which incorporate different sites that stretch for miles, are found around Britain.

This alignment starts at a place called Millmount (near the east coast of Ireland), which is an ancient temple mound that later became used as a fort and has been built over and left unexcavated. In Irish myth, it is identified as the burial place of Amergin mac Míled, an ancient Druid warrior and chief.

Standing at Millmount, one can watch the sun, around two days after the spring equinox (around March 23rd), set directly over the Hill of Slane, which stands 158 meters tall. The Hill of Slane was named after Sláine, the king of the Fir Bolg (a mythological race that used to inhabit Ireland), who is said to have been buried there. The Hill of Slane was also supposed to have been the location of a mythical healing well, which was used by the Tuatha Dé Danann to heal their wounds during battle. Later, it was believed to be the place where Saint Patrick lit the Easter fire on March 23rd (coinciding with the setting sun on this date). There is an artificial mound on the western end of the hilltop, and two neolithic standing stones in the burial yard of the Christian abbey that stands there today, indicating that this was once an ancient sacred site built over by the Christians, who did the same with so many other ancient sites across Britain.

The alignment continues west with the spring equinox sunset, skirting the hills of Loughcrew (home of Cairn T which aligns to the equinox sunrises) on its way, and traveling directly through Rathcroghan (or Cruachan Aí), one of the largest archeological complexes in the world, with two hundred monuments located in a ten-mile radius. These include Oweynagat (Cave of the Cats) the entrance to the Celtic Otherworld and home to the Goddess Morrigan, Daithi's Mound with its standing stone, and the main site called Rathcroghan mound—a man-made mound ninety meters wide at its base on which once stood buildings. Electric scans have now detected further enclosures beneath the ground which surround this mound. It is believed by many that queen Medb was the local earth goddess, and that becoming king meant marrying the earth, with the inauguration more than likely taking place on Rathcroghan mound itself.

The alignment ends on the west coast of Ireland at Croagh Patrick, one of Ireland's sacred mountains, intersecting the Christian church built on its summit precisely. Again, this was an ancient sacred site that was taken over by the Christians. The mountain's top is shaped like a pyramid, which can be seen from miles around. The old name for the mountain is Croghan Aigle, which might be translated as "the Eagle's Peak." The mountain is ringed by old sites, monuments, and standing stones—revealing that it was a place held sacred from ancient times.

CAIRNPAPPLE AND ARTHUR'S SEAT ALIGNMENT ~ SCOTLAND

Ancient cairn, stone circle, wooden post holes, and man-made ditch atop of Cairnpapple.

This alignment to the spring equinox is another created by natural formations that became sacred sites and observation points of the spring equinox sunrise.

Cairnpapple is an ancient megalithic complex set on top of a hill in Scotland, which is said to have been used as a sacred site for around four thousand years, starting around 3,500 BC. It includes a standing stone circle. Here, evidence was found that this site had been used by the Beaker people, who are believed to have built part of Stonehenge.

From the site of Cairnpapple, the spring equinox sun rises over Arthur's Seat, associated with King Arthur, and also Huly Hill, which is another site of an ancient cairn and standing stones, forming a sacred landscape of alignments to the sun.

CHAPTER ELEVEN

Ancient Sacred Sites Aligned to the Summer Solstice

SOME OF THE MOST FAMOUS ANCIENT MEGALITHIC SITES in the world align to the summer solstice, from numerous different cultures: Paleolithic (second period of the Stone Age which lasted until the end of the last ice age), Egyptian, Pagan, Maya, Essene, Buddhist, pre-Columbian North American, and Easter Islander. Below are some examples—there are many others that have not been included, and may be many more that have not yet been discovered.

THE GREAT PYRAMIDS ~ EGYPT

At the Great Pyramids of Egypt, when standing looking at the front of the Sphinx, the sun on the summer solstice sets precisely between the two largest of the Great Pyramids. The sun's descent between the two pyramids seems to enact the moment of creation where the sun emerged from between two mounds, but in reverse, signifying the return of the spiritual Son/sun to the source of creation.

An artist's rendition of the actual alignment of the summer solstice sun setting between the two largest Great Pyramids of Egypt, crowning the Sphinx in the foreground.

The sun also forms a halo of light around the head of the Sphinx, symbolizing the consciousness crowned by the higher Being.

THE OSIREION ~ EGYPT

The Osireion temple at Abydos in Egypt. It shares many architectural similarities with the Valley Temple beside the Sphinx. Both these sites were also connected to the deity Anubis in alignment with the sun and constellation of Leo.

There is an incredibly mysterious temple at the ancient site of Abydos in Egypt. For thousands of years Abydos was believed to be the final resting place of the Egyptian god Osiris. Then in AD 1902 the Osireion temple was unearthed, which many speculated could have been Osiris' tomb.

The Osireion shares incredible similarities with the Valley Temple, which is located next to the Sphinx. Both the Valley Temple and Osireion are made out of huge unadorned granite blocks (which also look very similar to Stonehenge), share the same construction methods, and a number of mathematical characteristics (for example, both feature the number seventeen). The Valley Temple was built at the same time as the Sphinx, and its similarities with the Osireion seem to indicate that the Osireion may too have been built by the builders of the Sphinx.

The Valley Temple located beside the Great Sphinx of Egypt. It shares remarkable similarities in building style with the Osireion, another ancient temple. Both are made out of huge unadorned granite blocks.

The Osireion is dated to 6,000–3,100 BC, although it is possibly much older. It had been unearthed at least once before when the Pharaoh Seti I uncovered it during the construction of his temple in around 1,280 BC.

Like the Great Pyramids and Sphinx, the Osireion has a summer solstice sunset alignment. On the summer solstice, the light of the setting sun shines through a nearby gap in the Libyan Hills, which intersects the Osireion temple.

The temple was constructed near a natural spring, which was used to feed a pool of water inside the temple that forms a moat around its central part. Some believe this was intended to symbolize the mound that rose from the primeval waters at the beginning of creation in ancient Egyptian texts, while others draw similarities to the sacred pagan healing well springs of the ancient Britons.

Other mysterious aspects of the site include a flower of life symbol found inscribed on some of the pillars of the temple, believed to have been left there by Greeks possibly around 300 BC. Ancient hieroglyphs of what appear to be hovercraft, and various flying machines like helicopters, can be found in the temple of Seti I next door.

THE ESSENE MONASTERY ~ QUMRAN, EGYPT

The Essene community is believed to have existed between around 200 BC to the first century AD and lived together in various places in Palestine, Syria, and Egypt.

The largest room of their stone communal building at Qumran is aligned so that the rays of the setting sun on the summer solstice illuminate the eastern wall where there are two altars.

Additionally, a limestone sundial was discovered there, designed to measure the sun throughout the year rather than the day, and which could measure the solstices and equinoxes. The historian Josephus Flavius describes how the Essenes addressed prayers to the sun.

THE RUINS OF WHAT IS BELIEVED TO HAVE BEEN THE ESSENE COMMUNITY AT QUMRAN.

However, there were many different groups in the region where the Essenes are said to have lived, which have been broadly defined as Essene, but historically had different names.

Two different historians, Philo and Epiphanius, describe groups in the area which practiced a form of sun worship. Jesus is believed to have spent time with one or some of these groups, and perhaps even gave rise to them, as the author below describes them as a remnant of the Essenes who accepted a so-called spurious form of Christianity. The author probably sees it as "spurious" because it was based on Jesus' esoteric teachings and is therefore considered unorthodox.

> "Philo relates of the Therapeutes (*Vit. Cont.* II, II. p. 485), that they 'stand with their faces and their whole body towards the East, and when they see that the sun is risen, holding out their hands to heaven they pray for a happy day and for truth and for keen vision of reason...'
>
> Epiphanius (*Haer.* xix. 2, xx. 3, pp. 40 sq., 47) speaks of a sect called the Sampsæans or 'Sun-worshippers,' as existing in his own time in Peræa on the borders of Moab and on the shores of the Dead Sea. He describes them as a remnant of the Ossenes (i.e. Essenes), who have accepted a spurious form of Christianity and are neither Jews nor Christians...
>
> In this heresy we have plainly the dregs of Essenism, which has only been corrupted from its earlier and nobler type by the admixture of a spurious Christianity. But how came the Essenes to be called Sampsæans? What was the original meaning of this outward reverence which they paid to the sun? Did they regard it merely as the symbol of Divine illumination, just as Philo frequently treats it as a type of God, the center of all light (e.g. *de. Somn.* i. 13 sq., I. p. 631 sq.), and even calls the heavenly bodies 'visible and sensible gods' (*de Mund.* Op. 7, I. p. 6)? Or did they honour the light, as the pure ethereal element in contrast to gross terrestrial matter, according to a suggestion of a recent writer (Keim I. p. 289)?... We cannot fail therefore to recognize the action of some foreign influence in this Essene practice—whether Greek or Syrian or Persian, it will be time to consider hereafter." [1]
>
> ~ J. B. LIGHTFOOT, ON SOME POINTS CONNECTED WITH THE ESSENES

This influence may have come from Jesus and the Gnostics, or from mystery schools that understood the significance of the spiritual sun.

STONEHENGE ~ ENGLAND

The giant megalithic stone circle of Stonehenge aligns most prominently to the summer solstice—with alignments at sunrise, midday, and sunset.

At sunrise on the summer solstice, the sun rose between two Heel Stones outside Stonehenge, and penetrated into its center to the altar stone.

A giant ancient avenue leading from Stonehenge to the nearby River Avon also aligns to the summer solstice sunrise. The ancient stone circle called Bluehenge lies where this avenue and the river meet.

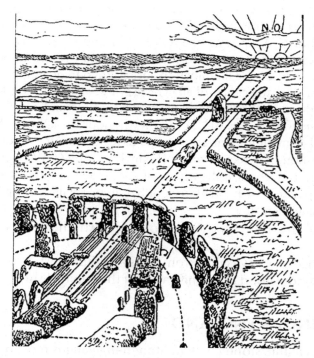

The summer solstice sunrise aligns with the avenue off the circle around Stonehenge. At sunrise the sun shines down the avenue, between the two heel stones, into the center of the stone circle.

At midday on the summer solstice, the sun shines directly overhead Stonehenge into its center.

Next to Stonehenge there is a large area called the Stonehenge Cursus which is an area of earthen ditches and banks around three kilometers long and 100-150 meters wide. Within this area are two huge pits around sixteen feet across and three feet deep that, when viewed from the Heel Stone just outside Stonehenge, align to the summer solstice sunrise and sunset.

Yet another ancient site called Durrington Walls lies two miles northeast of Stonehenge. It contains a henge called the Southern Circle consisting of six concentric circles that would have been made out of large timber posts. The circle is aligned to the winter solstice sunrise, but has a paved avenue leading to the River Avon and a post which acted as the Heel Stone aligned to the summer solstice sunset.

It is possible that Stonehenge was part of a sacred landscape in which a number of sites were used ceremoniously during various celestial occasions, but it appears they were used particularly at the summer solstice.

NABTA PLAYA ~ EGYPT

A REPLICA OF THE STONE CIRCLE AT NABTA PLAYA FROM THE ASWAN NUBIA MUSEUM.

Nabta Playa is the name of a location in the Egyptian desert where there is an ancient stone circle dated to around 4,800 BC (although its alignments would indicate it is far older) that acts as an astronomical calendar, much like Stonehenge. A number of other large stone megaliths are located around the circle and also align to the stars. Together it is claimed they have some astonishing stellar, solar, and even galactic alignments, including to the summer solstice—marking not only the positions of the stars but even the distance of these stars from Earth!

The stones align to the rising sun on the summer solstice, as well as the star Sirius (the brightest star in the night sky), Dubhe (the brightest star in Ursa Major), and stars in the belt of the constellation Orion. Interestingly, the summer solstice, Sirius, and Orion were also used in the design of the Great Pyramids and Sphinx—these and other similarities have led many to theorize that the builders of the site at Nabta Playa and the site of the Great Pyramids at Giza (around eight hundred kilometers away) are connected. Additionally, the site was built in the Tropic of Cancer, which many believe was done on purpose so that the vertical stones at the site marked the sun's zenith passage at the summer solstice (which occurs three weeks before and after it) so that they cast no shadow at all during this time.

The astrophysicist Thomas G. Brophy discovered that the stones marked the helical rising (which is the conjunction of a star or constellation with the sun as it rises or sets) of a number of stars in the constellation of Orion on the spring equinox, the star Vega on the autumn equinox (Vega was the pole star around 12,000 BC), and the rising of the galactic center on the spring equinox at around 17,700 BC. An alignment of the pole star on the autumn equinox is incorporated into the design of the descending passage of the Great Pyramid, which you can read about in the chapter on the ancient sites aligned to the autumn equinox—and so it is interesting to see that this combination of alignments was also part of this site.

Most incredibly of all however, Brophy discovered that the distance between the megaliths that marked these helical risings matched the distance of the stars they marked from Earth on a scale of roughly 1 meter to 0.8 light years—within the margin of error found in calculating astronomical distances today.

TALLAGHT HILL OF THE FAIR GODS ~ MOUNT SESKIN, IRELAND

On Mount Seskin, the tallest of the Tallaght Hills (outside of the town of Tallaght) there are a number of ancient stone ruins including standing stones and passage cairns. The summer solstice sun rises in the distance, right beside the Lambay Volcano and reflects off a pool of water on the hill called Lin Oir, meaning golden pond.

See pictures here: http://www.druidschool.com/site/1030100/page/882207

EXTERNSTEINE ~ GERMANY

The Externsteine rocks are a chain of naturally occurring sandstone spires dating from about seventy million years ago. They were a sacred place of pilgrimage in prehistoric, Celtic, and early Saxon times and a site of pagan ritual until the eighth century AD, when Charles the Great cut down the sacred Irmensul tree, the German tree of life. At the top of the tallest spire is a mysterious prehistoric temple; no one knows for certain who built it. It is centered around a round hole above an altar carved into a small stone shrine. This hole looks out at the surrounding landscape and aligns to the moon at its northern extreme and the sun at sunrise on the summer solstice.

The temple atop of Externsteine near Horn-Bad Meinberg, Germany.
The hole in the shrine aligns to the summer solstice sunrise.

AJANTA CAVES ~ INDIA

The Ajanta Caves are an extraordinary group of around thirty man-made caves cut into the side of a sheer cliff face. The cliff is naturally U-shaped and was hidden in a remote part of the jungle. The caves are believed to have been built by Buddhist monks by carving into the cliff face—what they created were elaborate shrines and temples, all cut into one single giant rock.

Work is believed to have begun on the caves in around 200 BC and ended around AD 480–650. The caves contain sculptures and artwork centered around the life of Buddha.

Two of the caves align to celestial events.

Cave twenty-six aligns to the summer solstice sunrise. It contains a statue of Buddha seated within a stupa, which is illuminated by the rays of the rising sun on the summer solstice.

The cave at Ajanta called number twenty-six, which aligns to the summer solstice sunrise. As the sun rises, a beam of light penetrates this cave and illuminates the stupa and the statue of Buddha within.

A stupa is a symbolic monument which is said Buddha uses to ascend and descend.

The summer solstice is a time of ascent. In the cave aligned to the summer solstice Buddha is seated with his feet on a pedestal. Perhaps this was symbolic of him no longer being on the earth—similarly, ancient Egyptian gods were sometimes portrayed upon pedestals to show their heavenly status.

The creator god Amun being worshiped, seated with his feet raised above the level of the ground similar to the statue of Buddha at Ajanta.

SERPENT MOUND ~ OHIO, UNITED STATES

The serpent mound is a giant earthwork in the shape of a serpent made by an ancient people who once lived in North America. The head of the serpent faces the summer solstice sunset.

The serpent mound in Ohio, whose head
aligns with the summer solstice sunset.

The mound is around 1,370 feet (420 meters) long. The serpent holds an oval in its mouth, has seven undulating coils along its body, and the tip of its tail is coiled three times. Its coils point to the winter solstice and equinox sunrises. It is believed there was an altar inside the oval at the head, in which ceremonies could have been conducted while watching the summer solstice sunset.

Interestingly, there exists another very similar site in a very different part of the world—Scotland. At a place called Loch Nell there is an ancient serpent mound, around three hundred feet long, and which used to have a circle of stones which contained an altar at its head. It too faced west, although not to the summer solstice sunset, but so that looking back east across its body it had a special view of three mountain peaks. Someone who viewed the site in the mid-nineteenth century before much of it was damaged and dismantled wrote:

> "The mound was built in such a manner that the worshipper standing at the altar would naturally look eastward, directly along the whole length of the Great Reptile, and across the dark lake, to the triple peaks of Ben Cruachan. This position must have been carefully selected, as from no other point are the three peaks visible." [2]

A drawing published in 1883 of the Loch Nell serpent mound in Scotland. The altar in the stone circle at the head of the serpent is in the foreground, and the three mountain peaks in the background. The design of this particular serpent mound shares a number of similarities with the one in Ohio.

There are other serpent mounds in Scotland and Ireland. At least one dated to around 2,000 BC used fire burnt stones, which were also apparently used in the building of the serpent mound in Ohio. The oval at the heads of these serpents may have represented the sun, thus forming the same symbol of a serpent with a sun disk on its head found throughout Egypt.

Could Ohio's serpent mound be part of a lineage of people and knowledge that ran from Egypt, through ancient Britain and Europe, and is now barely traceable in North America?

CHACO CANYON ~ NEW MEXICO, UNITED STATES

The giant kiva in Chaco Canyon whose window let in the light of the summer solstice sunrise. Kivas were sacred circular temples that had thatched ceilings.

The ancient city of Chaco Canyon was one of the sites established by the Anasazi/Hopi under the guidance of their wisdom bringer Maasaw, who directed them to build their sites and cities in alignment with the constellations and the solstices and equinoxes.

"The Hopi migrations were the divine instructions of Maasaw, but according to author Gary A. David, they are far more interesting than what most have assumed so far. In *The Orion Zone*, David argues that '[the constellation] Orion provided the template by which the Anasazi determined their villages' locations during a migration period lasting centuries. Spiritually mandated by a god the Hopi call Masau'u, this 'terrestrial Orion' closely mirrors its celestial counterparts, with prehistoric 'cities' corresponding to all the major stars in the constellation. By its specific orientation the sidereal pattern projected on the Arizona high desert also encodes various sunrise and sunset points of both summer and winter solstices.'

David has shown that the three Hopi Mesas can overlap the three stars of Orion's Belt, with other key Ancestral Puebloan sites corresponding to other stars of this constellation — and neighbouring stars: Chaco Canyon coincides with Sirius. Orion itself is made up (amongst others) from the Betatakin Ruin in Tsegi Canyon and Keet Seel Ruin as representing the double star Rigel, the left foot or knee of Orion; Homol'ovi Ruins State Park is Betelgeuse, while Wupatki is Bellatrix and Canyon de Chelly Saiph. Even the Sipapu in the Grand Canyon is mapped, and corresponds with Pi 3 Ori.

Orion's Belt is therefore sacred to the Hopi, the 'Centre of the World', but it was also very important to the Mayans, who actually saw it as the point where the creation of the Fourth World occurred. Specifically, the Mayan creation myth sees Orion's Belt as a huge Cosmic Turtle, whose back was cracked open by a lightning stone. From this crack, the Maize Gods grew and it is therefore a place of emergence too. That Orion's Belt features so prominently in the layout of the Hopi homeland therefore suggests that they had strong links with the Mayans, as plenty of evidence near the mesas — e.g. Wupatki — has demonstrated.

David believes that the stone tablets given by Maasaw to guide the Hopi in their journeys must have contained this 'grand scheme.' Their purificational migrations are therefore literally 'as above, so below': in accordance with the movements of the stars, the deities." [3]

~ PHILIP COPPENS, THE WANDERERS OF THE FOURTH WORLD

Located near the ruins of the ancient city of Chaco Canyon is the famous Sun Dagger. Found high up on the top of what is called the Fajada Butte, a giant volcanic outcrop, is a stone carving in a spiral. Stone slabs especially arranged around it direct the sunlight so that on the summer solstice, a dagger of sunlight pierces the center of the spiral. Daggers of sunlight over different parts of the spiral also mark the winter solstice and the equinoxes.

Down below, the Casa Rinconada, which is one of the five great kivas (temple buildings) of the Chaco Canyon city, aligns to the summer solstice sunrise. As the sun rises, a beam of light shines through a lone window and moves across the room until it illuminates one of the five niches on the western wall.

AHU TONGARIKI ~ EASTER ISLAND

The Ahu Tongariki is the largest ahu (or stone platform) on Easter Island. On it stand fifteen moai (giant stone statues). These fifteen statues face the summer solstice sunset, watching it disappear over the ocean. One of the fifteen statues is the heaviest ever erected on the island, weighing eighty-six tons.

These fifteen moai statues, which includes the heaviest on
Easter Island ever erected, stand facing the summer solstice sunset.

THE TEMPLE OF THE DESCENDING GOD AT TULUM
~ YUCATÁN, MEXICO

The Temple of the Descending God at the site of Tulum. According
to some accounts, it aligns to the rising sun on the summer solstice.

The ancient Maya city of Tulum is dedicated to the Maya "descending god"
and consists of a number of sacred and ceremonial buildings. The ruins of
this ancient city stand on a bluff overlooking the ocean. The original name of
this site was "Zama" which means "City of Dawn" because it faces the sunrise.

The information about the alignments of this site are inconsistent, but a number of accounts state that the sun at sunrise on the summer solstice shines through a tiny opening on the back wall of the Temple of the Descending God to create the effect of a beam of light shining from out of the doorway of the temple.

This temple was built over an even older structure that was filled in to make the foundation of the temple, and artifacts have been found dated to the first century AD although many of the buildings were erected around AD 1200.

The descending god is portrayed throughout the site descending from heaven, with his legs in the air and his head crowned. He is believed by some to be a representation of the Maya god Kukulcán and Aztec god Quezalcoatl, the feathered serpent, and is associated with the planet Venus, the "Morning Star," just as Jesus was.

> "I Jesus have sent mine angel to testify unto you these things in the churches. I am the root and the offspring of David, and the bright and morning star." [4]
>
> ~ JESUS IN REVELATION 22:16

The descending god carved above the doorway
of The Temple of the Descending God.

Throughout the site there are frescoes that depict scenes of feathered serpents, the act of creation, and are particularly focused on death and rebirth.

> "There is an architectural expression of rebirth at Tulum. The eastern- most structure at Tulum, Structure 45, is a round-based structure.

Round structures are associated with Kukulcan. One of Kukulcan's most important manifestations is Venus as Morning Star. According to the widespread pan-Mesoamerican myth, Kukulcan was reborn in the east in the form of Venus as Morning Star after descent and death in the west and a long passage in the Underworld." [5]

~ ARTHUR G. MILLER, WEST AND EAST IN MAYA THOUGHT: DEATH AND REBIRTH AT PALENQUE AND TULUM

The story of Jesus' death, descent to hell, and resurrection are well known, and bear a striking similarity with these sacred Maya teachings.

THE PYRAMID OF THE MAGICIAN AT UXMAL ~ YUCATÁN, MEXICO

The Pyramid of the Magician at the Maya city of Uxmal in Mexico.
Its western staircase faces the summer solstice sunset.

Uxmal is a Maya city that is said to date between AD 600 to 1000. The city's tallest structure is called The Pyramid of the Magician—so-called because local legends say that it was built by a magical race of dwarves who moved the stones in place by using the power of sound by whistling. The pyramid's western staircase faces the setting sun on the summer solstice.

This first pyramid temple was successively built upon four times, meaning that the pyramid is now made of five layered temples in total. This was a common Maya building practice, thought to capture and amplify the power of the underlying structure.

Unfortunately human sacrifice and ritual bloodletting was practiced here, as it was in other Maya cities. However, it's very likely the original culture did not practice these rites, but were taken over by those who did as happened at many other Maya sites.

THE LOST WORLD PYRAMID AT TIKAL ~ GUATEMALA

The Lost World Pyramid at Tikal. It started as a small platform before 700 BC that faced three structures aligned to the solstices and equinoxes.

At the ancient Maya city called Tikal, located in the dense jungles of Guatemala, there is evidence for the practice of cosmological knowledge. The oldest part of Tikal is called the Lost World and consists of thirty-eight structures. They are believed to have been set aside entirely for the observance of the cosmos.

The main structure of the Lost World is a great pyramid, which was built in five successive layers over hundreds of years, just like the Pyramid of the Magician at Uxmal. It began as a platform and is believed to be the most ancient of any structure at Tikal. The platform faced east, looking over three other structures that aligned with the winter solstice, equinoxes, and summer solstice sunrise.

A similar grouping of structures, in which a pyramid is used as a viewing platform to see the sunrise on the winter solstice, equinoxes, and summer solstice over three temples, was also found in Guatemala at Uaxactun. The ancient Mayan name for this site was Siaan K'aan, which means "Born in Heaven."

WURDI YOUANG STONE ARRANGEMENT ~ VICTORIA, AUSTRALIA

At Mount Rothwell in Australia, there is a stone ovoid-shaped arrangement around fifty meters in diameter. It aligns to the solstice and equinox sunsets, including the summer solstice sunset. It is unable to be dated, and could have been built anywhere between 25,000 years ago right up to AD 1835.

To see images of the site, visit: http://aboriginalastronomy.blogspot.com. au/2011/03/wurdi-youang-aboriginal-stone.html

LASCAUX CAVE PAINTINGS ~ FRANCE

Lascaux cave. Prehistoric Sites and Decorated Caves of the Vézère Valley (France).

Lascaux is a cave complex located in France, decorated with a vast number of cave paintings and engravings—with over 1,500 engravings and 600 drawings—estimated to be around 17,300 years old.

Most of the paintings are of large animals and geometric shapes, but recent research suggests that there is much more to these paintings than it first seems. Dr. Michael Rappenglueck of the University of Munich argues that some of the dots made within the animal scenes depict the constellation of Taurus, the Pleiades, and the star grouping known as the "Summer Triangle." French researcher Chantal Jègues-Wolkiewiez has also proposed that the paintings in the Great Hall area of the caves represent an extensive star map of the main constellations as they appeared in the Paleolithic.

As further evidence of the people who painted these caves having an interest in the cosmos, the entrance to the caves aligns with the summer solstice sunset—at this time of year, the sun's light enters the cave and illuminates it for almost one hour each day, for a few days surrounding the solstice. Chantal Jègues-Wolkiewiez also calculated that the light of the full-moon would enter the cave directly on the morning of the winter solstice, and that other painted caves in the area align to the setting sun on the winter solstice.

No one knows what the purpose of these caves or paintings were, but it's been suggested that they were possibly ceremonial and sacred places as most of the paintings are located at a distance from the entrance, and many of the chambers are hard to get to. If this was their purpose, Lascaux would be one of the most ancient known sites in the world where spiritual rites took place on the solstice.

PART III

Ceremonies and Rituals for Celebrating the Solstices and Equinoxes

CHAPTER TWELVE

A Guide to Celebrating the Solstices and Equinoxes

ANCIENT PEOPLE OF NEARLY EVERY RACE and culture have celebrated the solstices and equinoxes as evident in hundreds if not thousands of ancient sites, myths, and texts, and the most famous spiritual figures of the world such as Jesus, Osiris, Hu Gadarn, Mithras, Dionysus, Hun Hunahpu, Quetzalcoatl, etc., experienced major events in their life stories at these times. While some of these traditions were simple and based on an appreciation of the natural world, many celebrated the profound and universal spiritual significance of these special times of year.

Many ancient people knew that the natural world and its cycles contain the principles of creation, and that these principles are spiritual in their nature. That is why some of the world's most famous and universal religious symbols can actually be found in the natural world, such as the yin and yang, the swastika, cross, spiral, etc., and why the study of science and mathematics ultimately comes upon a fabric of life that is intelligent in its design.

The maxim of wisdom, "as above, so below," indicates how cosmic and natural phenomena are intimately connected to the human being and journey of consciousness. We are undeniably part of the universe, and so too therefore is the process of spiritual awakening. The sun (and stars) is the source of light and life in our universe, just as the spirit is the source of light and life within us. Spiritual figures and texts placed so much emphasis on the journey of the sun, as the path of the sun is symbolic of the path of consciousness/spirit in its journey to awakening, and the solstices and equinoxes are this journey's major stages.

WHY CELEBRATE THE SOLSTICES AND EQUINOXES?

THE PYTHAGOREANS (AN ANCIENT ESOTERIC SCHOOL IN GREECE) CELEBRATING THE RISING SUN.

Some ancient peoples and mystics throughout history were in touch with a different way of gaining knowledge than most are familiar with. This way of learning is timeless, and is gained through individual practice, experience, and observation of the natural world, rather than just reading.

Today, although we as a human race have become distant from and even hostile toward our environment, the principles of creation remain eternal. They are there within and all around us for anyone who opens their eyes enough to see.

These principles have, throughout history, been extremely relevant to every human being, no matter what race, sex, religion, or nationality, and are in fact what unites us.

Although the solstices and equinoxes are celestial events, they are also very personal ones. They communicate not only cosmic principles, but inner ones too, as the inner and outer world are connected.

Each individual can have their own reasons for celebrating the solstices and equinoxes, but these celebrations give everyone participating an opportunity to experience spiritual principles directly. The spirit in life teaches—through these celebrations an individual can learn something personal about their own journey of consciousness, and a group celebrating can learn and perceive something together. Some people who celebrated the ceremony for the summer solstice given here for the first time found afterward that they had all felt something powerfully spiritual and significant from it, and that they had been so moved by it that they would never be the same again.

CELEBRATING ACCORDING TO YOUR CIRCUMSTANCES

Your circumstances will really determine how you'll be able to celebrate, but there is still lots of flexibility and room for creativity. It can be celebrated all the way from a detailed ritual to simply being present for the sunrise/sunset.

IN A GROUP AT A DEDICATED LOCATION

The ideal way to celebrate any solstice and equinox is out in the open air, where the sun is clearly visible, with a large group of people who are open to the spiritual side of the event. Chanting mantras becomes especially moving with lots of voices, and the energy of a focused gathering of people can be really uplifting. It would be great if every city had a place where people could go and celebrate together in a large group.

The ceremonies I've created in this book are really tailored for a group who has their own dedicated sacred space where they can feel comfortable and relaxed in practicing the spirituality of their choice.

If you're unable to do it outside due to a lack of privacy or difficult weather conditions, a gathering of people could always practice in a room that lets the light of the sun in at the moment of sunrise or sunset on the solstice or equinox. There are many examples of ancient peoples celebrating in this way. For example, the Pueblo peoples of North America created kivas (which were their temples) that were entirely enclosed except for a window that let in a shaft of light on the winter solstice.

While it's not within everyone's budget to build a room like this, there are some fairly simple ways of doing it. A cheap do-it-yourself tepee or cabin could be put on a site and its door aligned to the solstice or equinox. Then, only the door need be opened, or perhaps a cabin window could be aligned instead.

WINTER SOLSTICE CEREMONY IN CALIFORNIA.

IN A GROUP AT A PUBLIC LOCATION

If you only have venues open to you where people who are not involved in the celebration may be staring or even insulting, then you will probably want to simplify the ceremony to the point where you feel comfortable, and may omit special clothing and ceremonial items—perhaps just chanting mantras together and doing readings.

Another idea could be to find ancient or sacred sites in your area and watch the sunrise or sunset together there. For example, there are ancient standing stones, mounds, mountains, springs, etc., across Europe that are hardly visited. North and Central America are also full of sacred sites and places. It's important though, whenever visiting ancient sites, to take care not to damage or alter the site in any way. Make sure not to climb on or walk over things that are fragile and liable to break or move, nor to remove anything from the site as a souvenir, or to show someone, etc., as each stone and plant may form a unique part of the site's character and history. Some of these sites may still be considered sacred by peoples today, so it's important to be respectful and to treat the site as if you wanted it to remain intact and protected as far into the future as possible.

WITH A SMALL NUMBER OF PEOPLE

Some of the ceremonies I've created require a certain number of participants to fulfill the different ceremonial roles. If you find that you don't have enough people to fulfill all the roles, just cut the ceremony back until you can fulfill the most crucial ones; or, you could simplify the ceremony so that although not every action is performed, the main essence of the ceremony remains.

ON YOUR OWN

If you're celebrating on your own, you could find a nice private spot in your garden or patio to watch the sunrise or sunset. You could even create a very simple outdoor sacred space with stones and candles. Alternatively, you could also celebrate indoors in a room that catches the sunlight and make a simple sacred space there by incorporating the colors related to the ceremony, using candles, aromas, and even music.

For the event, you could try constructing your own simple ceremony, or chant mantras, or sit in quietness, prayer, or reflection. You could even just sit in awareness and watch the rising sun.

However, there is no substitute for attending an actual ceremony with other people, which is why pilgrimages to sacred sites were so important to ancient people at these times of year.

WORK OUT A CALENDAR AND PREPARE IN ADVANCE

The solar year can be mapped out in advance. There are many websites that give the upcoming dates for the solstices and equinoxes, which occur more or less on the same days every year, giving plenty of time to prepare the celebrations for each.

One thing to be aware of is that the solar calendar in the Northern Hemisphere is opposite to the one in the Southern Hemisphere. So when it's the winter solstice in the Northern Hemisphere in a place like the United States, it is actually the summer solstice in the Southern Hemisphere in a place like Australia. Likewise, the autumn equinox in the north is the spring equinox in the south.

So although the world celebrates Christmas at the time of the winter solstice (around December 21) in the Northern Hemisphere, those in the Southern Hemisphere who wish to celebrate Christmas according to its true meaning should celebrate it at the time of their actual winter solstice, which would instead be around June 21 (the solstice) and the three days following. The same applies to Easter, which is a celebration of the spring equinox.

The precise time of the solstice or equinox is usually given in Universal Time (UT), which you'll need to convert into your local time. Once you do that, you will probably end up with a time that is not exactly sunrise or sunset. To work out when to celebrate the solstice or equinox, simply find the sunrise or sunset closest to the local time you have. So for example, if the time given is 3am in your local time zone and you are celebrating the winter solstice sunrise, then celebrate it the morning of that day a few hours later. If you're celebrating the autumn equinox sunset, then celebrate it at sunset the day before.

Make sure you have your sacred space and things for the ceremony prepared well in advance so you are not rushed beforehand. Take some time leading up the ceremony to practice any mantras you'll be doing, and rehearse your ceremony until you feel confident remembering it. This will help it go smoothly on the day, so that you aren't distracted by trying to remember things and can relax into the perception of the moment.

CREATING A SACRED SPACE

Having a sacred space is very important. As humans wishing to connect with the divine, we've always created them as temples, churches, sacred circles, etc. A dedicated space like this helps us to move from an ordinary state of mind, full of the thoughts of the day, etc., to one of inner quietness, awareness of the moment, reverence for divinity, and receptivity to spiritual feelings and learning.

A sacred space can be anything from a huge temple to a room in your house that is dedicated to practice and prayer. Whatever the resources, the principle is the same—it becomes an energetically focused place for connecting with the spiritual.

GATEWAYS AND PROCESSIONS AS A TRANSITION TO A SPIRITUAL PLACE

Entering a sacred place always has its requirements, as the sacredness and energy of the space must be preserved. The most powerful sacred places are where this energy has been built up and maintained by the people who used it, which they did through consciousness.

The gate to the Ki Monastery in the Himalayas, signifying the entrance into a sacred place.

A sacred place is always entered by some sort of gate, entrance, or doorway that one has to pass through. This can serve as a reminder of the transition needed before entering the sacred space, into awareness of the present moment, reverence for the divine, respect for the principles of spirituality, etc. In ancient times and still at many religious sites today, before passing through, a person had to repeat a special phrase, bow, or say a small prayer. Some even ritually cleansed in water and put on white garments as a symbol of purifying oneself inwardly before presenting themselves before the spiritual. This kind of practice was important, for example, to the Buddhist monks in the high places of Tibet.

A gateway to an area which has a sacred space could be a timber arch, two standing stones, or something even simpler, and decorated with special plants and symbols as was done in ancient times. A doorway into a room that is used for spiritual purposes serves in the same way. So if you're looking to create a sacred space of any kind, you might want to have a dedicated entrance.

You could also incorporate a sense of journey to your sacred space, so that even before you reach the entrance, you begin to attune yourself to the event. Pilgrimages and processions have long been a part of sacred ceremonies; there is evidence that they formed a major part of summer solstice celebrations at Stonehenge in ancient times.

To do this, all the participants could gather at a meeting point some distance from the sacred site where you're going to conduct your ceremony, and then walk together in a procession chanting a mantra, or in awareness of the present moment in silence, or with someone playing an uplifting tune on an instrument like a wooden flute, bell, singing bowl, or harp, etc. If it is safe and practical to do so, each person could carry a lit candle to the sacred site in a procession symbolizing the spiritual light we carry within; this would look especially beautiful before dawn.

CHOOSING YOUR SITE DESIGN

For celebrating the solstices and equinoxes, it's best to create a space that aligns to the moment of either sunrise or sunset of the particular solar event you are celebrating, and gives all the participants a clear view of it. As ancient people did, you could either create one site that has multiple solar alignments, such as the Lost World Pyramid at the ancient city of Tikal in Guatemala, or as they did in the ancient British Isles, create different sites for different alignments, such as Newgrange and Knowth in Ireland.

You can get a lot of ideas of how to create a sacred site from the ancient sites of the world, which are written about in this book (and there are also many others not included). While creating most of these is far beyond most people's resources, it is possible to take the concepts and designs they were based on and replicate them in simple ways.

A GUIDE TO CREATING YOUR OWN STANDING STONE/WOOD CIRCLE

One of the simplest site designs that has been used for thousands of years to celebrate the solstice and equinox is a sacred standing stone and/or wood circle. These types of circles are still made by communities today, and can be put together using wooden posts and stones that can be moved into place without machinery.

A MODERN SACRED CIRCLE IN LITHUANIA.

The circle can be made of wood, stone, or a combination of the two, like the modern example you see in the picture above in Lithuania. It can even be made of or include plants and trees, like the sacred groves of the Druids, which there are no traces of left today.

CEREMONIAL CLOTHING

There's something about wearing special clothing for special occasions. Monks/nuns, priests/priestesses, and yogis/yoginis have worn them for thousands of years, and even today non-religious people still wear traditional garments for weddings.

Different colors have different vibrations and affect the way we feel. They also represent and symbolize different spiritual principles. White for example, has always been used as a color of spirituality, while black has been used to evoke dark forces, which is why we don't use black in any of our ceremonies, unless dark forces are being represented. White is by default the best color for any ceremony, including those of the sun. The ancient Druids believed it was the color of the sun, and they were right. The sun's light contains all the colors of the

The sun when photographed in space is seen as white.

visible spectrum, appearing to our eyes as white, which is why when the sun's light is refracted, we see it split into all its colors, creating a rainbow. The sun photographed from space is white, but we mostly see it as a golden yellow (and sometimes orange, or red) from Earth, as the blue end of the light spectrum is scattered by Earth's atmosphere. The sun is actually sending out most of its photons (packets of light) in the green portion of the light spectrum—the same color as the leaves and grass, which are being nourished by its light through photosynthesis.

The standard dress used for the ceremonies in this book is white with a yellow or gold trim or sash. The white symbolizes the sun generally. The yellow or gold is the color of the spiritual Son, as the golden, yellow light of the spectrum that reaches our eyes on Earth has a symbolic significance. It represents the light of the spiritual Son as being the mediator between heaven and earth, as it is the color of the sun that we can see from Earth. It is also related to the element of helium, which was discovered as a yellow spectral line in the sun. The element was named after the Greek sun god Helios, and is the second lightest and most abundant element in the universe—having been formed during the first acts of creation in the universe at the Big Bang. It then went on to form stars along with hydrogen. As life is multidimensional, these elements and processes have higher, spiritual origins and properties, and why aspects like their color are used in the ceremonies.

Depending on your circumstances, the clothing for the ceremonies can range from being whole custom made garments to colored headbands or scarves worn with normal clothing, or even normal clothing in the desired color (e.g. a yellow t-shirt or red jacket).

ROMUVAN CEREMONY IN LITHUANIA.

Either way, the kind I would recommend are garments made of natural fabrics that are elegant and based on traditional designs, as natural fibers have certain properties that synthetic fibers don't. A good example are those worn by the Romuvan community in Lithuania who are reviving the ancient celebrations of their people, which include the solstices and equinoxes.

If you live somewhere that has an existing tradition or culture, you could wear the traditional costumes of your people or country for the ceremonies, but in the colors specified in the ceremonies if that's possible. The same applies if you feel a connection to a particular culture; you could adopt the traditional costumes and symbols of that culture in the ceremonies. So for example, if

A ROMUVAN CEREMONY IN LITHUANIA.

in the ceremony it says that a woman playing a role wears the color blue, your culture may have ceremonial dresses that women wear, which can be made out of the color blue and used in the ceremony. Or for example, in a couple of the ceremonies it says that a person wears the symbol of the sun, so you could use the icon that symbolizes the sun in your culture.

RESOURCES PAGE

A webpage of resources has been put together to accompany this book. There you'll find videos of the ceremonies being performed, more detailed suggestions for mantras and chanting for the ceremonies with pronunciations and recordings, as well as other helpful material such as guides to creating your own sacred circles.

If you are planning to do a ceremony based on one in this book, I'd recommend taking a look at the resources page before you do, as any updates or further materials for the ceremonies will be posted there. We'll be continuing to add resources as we find them.

You can find the page at the URL:
www.belsebuub.com/path-of-the-spiritual-sun-resources
or just look for The Path of the Spiritual Sun Resources on my website.

WORKING OUT THE CEREMONIES AND ACTIVITIES

I've put together detailed instructions for ceremonies for each of the four points in the year. They are based on an understanding of their deeper meaning and incorporate ancient symbols and rituals from all around the world that were used in actual ancient ceremonies at the solstices and equinoxes.

Depending on your circumstances, you may do the entire ritual to the letter, or may simplify it to suit what you are able and feel comfortable doing. It could be as simple as chanting mantras at sunrise on your own or with a few friends.

MAKING YOUR OWN CEREMONY

To make your own ceremony, you could look at the contents of the ceremonies in the following chapters, and use the elements you like. If you're part of a group of people, you could decide amongst yourselves what you want to incorporate.

There are many places in the world where remnants of solstice and equinox celebrations still survive. If you are in one of those places, you could try analyzing your existing traditions to see if you can find meanings in each of the elements they comprise of, such as any symbols or actions performed. Over time many traditions can become distant from the original meaning, but with a grasp of the universal principles involved, you could reconstruct a ceremony based upon your tradition, but one that is closer to its original meaning and purpose.

SUGGESTED READINGS

Sacred texts are read aloud as part of all the ceremonies. I've included a number of suggestions. You could choose to read some or all of them, or could use other readings that are relevant. There are many references in ancient texts and traditions to the themes found in the ceremonies, such as descent into the underworld, creation, resurrection, ascension, and the return to source.

If for example you are celebrating the winter solstice, which is to do with creation, you could find other readings that describe this event that you would like to read either instead of or in addition to those suggested. You might also find readings you'd like to use from your own culture and tradition on the themes relevant to the ceremony.

If you're looking for extra readings, I have a page on my website where I list sacred texts I recommend as being of the spiritual sun. It is always being added to as more texts are found, so you could have a look through that list to find readings for the ceremonies if you like.

CHANTS USED IN THE CEREMONIES

Sound is used in all the ceremonies through spiritual chant. I've suggested some simple chants and mantras which anyone can do, as many people are not familiar or experienced with spiritual chanting. The idea is that anyone can pick up this book and do the ceremonies in it without needing to look through other resources, like how to pronounce mantras. This is why I have decided to keep the main suggestions in the ceremonies very simple.

However, a chant doesn't have to be complex to be effective. What is most important is the tone and harmony it's sung with, even if it's just a vowel that is being chanted. The ancient Egyptians for example, were well known in ancient times for their sacred chants, which were a series of vowels sung like hymns. Similar chants appear in the texts of the early Christian Gnostics, and the same principle used in Gregorian chanting.

Ideally, a chorus of voices would sing in a harmony of sound to evoke the mood of the event and its meaning, which could even incorporate musical instruments. If you're inexperienced with music, the simplest way to chant harmoniously is to have everyone chant at the same musical note. It can take some practice to get this right and find a note that everyone in the group is comfortable singing, so it's worth rehearsing ahead of the ceremony.

For those who would like to explore more complex mantras and chants and incorporate them as part of the ceremonies, I do have a resources page on my website, as mentioned before, where you can find a list of suggestions. As part of the resources there are audio recordings and explanations of mantras, which will be developed into the future.

Throughout the ceremonies you will see references, such as "chant Autumn Equinox Chant 1" or "chant Winter Solstice Chant 2." This is for those who would like to use a more complex chant, and who have access to the resources page on my website. To find the chant, you can look it up in the resources section; it is listed there with its words, how to pronounce it, and its meaning if it has one, etc. Having them numbered like this also gives me the flexibility to update and change any chants as they are developed.

For those who aren't able to access the resources page, the main chant used in all the ceremonies is the Vedic mantra Om. It's probably the most well-known mantra in the world. Here is some information about it for those who'll be using it as part of their ceremonies.

OM (ALSO KNOWN AS AUM)

~ from the Upanishads

In the ancient texts of the Upanishads, the syllable Om (written out as Aum) represents Brahman, the Absolute source of all creation, as well as the whole of creation. It is said to be the greatest of all mantras; it is also a mantra of the spiritual sun.

The following excerpts from the Maitrāyanīya Upanishad describe Om as the syllable of Brahman, which is light—and which is the sun. This spiritual sun is said to reside both within us and within the sun as our higher Being (our Soul). Brahman, like the mantra Om, which is composed of three letters, is said to be a trinity of masculine, feminine, and neuter (just like the trinity of Father, Mother, and Son), which everything in creation is woven upon. The text also refers to the path of the sun as being the path to emancipation.

> "This (Soul) verily bears a twofold form, Prāna [life force/cosmic energy] and yonder Sun... Yonder sun is the external soul, Prāna is the internal; hence it is said that from the external soul's motion is inferred the motion of the internal soul. But whosoever is wise, void of sin, the master of his senses, clear-minded, firmly abiding in Him, having his eyes withdrawn (from all external objects) he indeed says that from the internal soul's motion is inferred the motion of the external soul. Now that golden being within the sun who beholds this earth from his golden sphere, is the same who abiding within, in the lotus of the heart, devours food.

> Now that which dwelling within the lotus of the heart devours food, the same, dwelling as the solar fire in the sky, being called Time, and invisible, devours all beings as its food. (The Vālakhilyas asked) What is its lotus and of what composed? (Prajāpati answered), Its lotus is the same as the ether; the four quarters and the four intermediate points are its petals. These two, Prāna and the Sun, revolve near to each other; —let him worship them both, by the syllable Om, by the mystical words, and by the Gāyatrī.

> There are two forms of the supreme Brahman, the material and the immaterial; the material is unreal, the immaterial is real, is Brahman. That which is Brahman is light; that which is light is the Sun. This Sun was identical with Om; it divided itself into three parts, for Om consists of three *mātrās*. 'By these are woven the warp and woof of all things, and this am I,' thus He speaks...

> It hath been also elsewhere said: —the sound-endowed form of this (Prāna-Āditya Soul) is Om; masculine, feminine, and neuter, —this is the gender-endowed form...

> As the lamp consists of the union of the wick, the vessel, and the oil, so from the union of the individual body and the world exist the Individual Soul and the pure Sun.

> Therefore let him devoutly honour the aforesaid (round of ceremonial rites) by repeating the word Om (at their commencement.) Unbounded is its might, and located in three sites, —in the fire, the Sun, and in Prāna...

> The syllable Om is verily the essential nature of that ether which abides in the cavity of the heart. By this syllable, Om, that (splendor)

germinates, it shoots upward, it expands, it becomes continuously the vehicle of the worship of Brahman...

The king named after the wind, having made his obeisance to him and duly offered his homage, went, with his aim attained, to the northern path. There is here no going by any by-way. This is the path to Brahman. Bursting open the door of the sun, he departed by the upward path. On this point the sages declare;

Endless are the rays of that soul which abides like a lamp in the heart, —white and black, brown and blue, tawny and reddish. One of these rises upward which pierces the orb of the sun; by this, having passed beyond the world of Brahman, they attain to the supreme abode...

Therefore yonder adorable Sun is the cause of creation, of heaven, and of emancipation..." [1]

~ THE MAITRĀYANĪYA UPANISHAD, TRANSLATED BY E. B. COWELL

The mantra OM is pronounced as in the word "home" and the sound elongated as in "ooooommmmm." It is sometimes written as AUM as the "au" sound is a subtle intonation that naturally arises when OM is pronounced. Each letter of the mantra is said to have its own significance.

"In Hindu mythology, the letter A also represents the process of creation, when it is said that all existence issued forth from Brahma's golden nucleus; the letter U refers to Vishnu, the god who is said to preserve this world by balancing Brahma on a lotus above himself; the M symbolizes the final part of the cycle of existence, when it is said that Vishnu falls asleep and Brahma has to breathe in so that all existing things have to disintegrate and are reduced to their essence to him... Finally, the silence at the end of the mantra symbolizes the period between death and rebirth. One must not forget that this silence is an important part of the mantra." [2]

~ AUM, NEW WORLD ENCYCLOPEDIA

Interestingly, the Egyptian supreme creator deity is called Atum, containing the same letters as this sacred mantra.

THE DAY AND DAYS SURROUNDING THE EVENT

In ancient times, celebrations for the solstices and equinoxes not only consisted of a special ceremony at sunrise or sunset, but carried on throughout the days and nights surrounding them. Depending on the meaning of the occasion, the days surrounding the event can be filled with lots of spiritual practice, singing spiritual songs, pilgrimages to sacred sites, processions by candlelight, readings of sacred texts, spiritual dancing, mantras, music, bonfires, times of prayer, reflection, meditation, etc.

It's especially nice to gather around a fire and sing spiritual songs and mantras. Fire itself is living and divine, and very much connected to the sun and its own fire, as well as to the fire of the spirit within. This is why fire has always held a special place in religious rites and places throughout the world.

With that in mind, the ceremonies in this book could form just one part of a much larger and longer celebration. To work out how you'd like to do it, you could look at the meaning of these times of year provided in this book, and put together a program of activities surrounding the ceremony that reflect this spiritual meaning.

BACKGROUND INFORMATION ON THE MEANING BEHIND THE CEREMONIES

It helps to understand the meaning of the event you're celebrating, at least on some level. You could be surprised, however, to find that you feel an understanding during the celebration itself that touches you in a direct way beyond words and thought, and which may even be difficult to explain to somebody else.

In this book I've put together detailed descriptions of the meanings of the solstices and equinoxes based on universal spiritual principles and ancient texts and sites from all over the world, and even if some things "go over your head" at the moment, it's worth reflecting on them and the ancient texts they quote before your event.

THE VALUE OF EXPERIENCE

The aim of this book is not only to re-kindle an interest in the cosmic nature of spirituality, but also the experience of it. My hope is that people all over the world start celebrating the solstices and equinoxes again as major events in their towns and cities, with celebrations based on cosmic principles that everyone can enjoy—connecting again with the spirit in nature through bonfires and spiritual music. Creating your own ceremony at home or with friends can connect you to the ancients and make you feel part of the spiritual, cosmic order of the universe.

The more involved ceremonies, outlined in the following chapters, are best practiced at dedicated locations, and could become part of an annual calendar of spiritual events that people take part in and even travel to four times a year.

One of the great things about the solstice and equinox is that a tradition of their celebration exists in many cultures, so it is possible for people to celebrate it according to the culture they feel most affinity with, whilst at the same time, connecting with its universal meaning. If enough people took up the universal principles of spirituality contained in these celebrations, they could help to give birth to a sense of spiritual harmony while at the same time celebrating the richness of cultural diversity throughout the world.

PEOPLE CELEBRATING THE SUMMER SOLSTICE CALLED IVAN KUPALA, IN RUSSIA.

Autumn Equinox

A Ceremony to Celebrate the Autumn Equinox

THE TIMING OF THE CEREMONY

This ceremony begins just before the sun starts to set on the day of the autumn equinox.

ITEMS NEEDED

- A sword.

- A labrys (the ancient Greek/Minaon symbol of the double-headed axe).

- The symbol of infinity as the figure eight on the end of a pole that can stand upright in the ground.

- A handful of seed (corn, rice, or wheat).

- A candle in a non-flammable container which can be carried and held safely. A tealight candle placed in a purpose-made candle holder would be an example of this.

- One or a number of handheld drums.

- A headdress of the Mother goddess based on any of the goddesses related to the autumn equinox, e.g. Inanna, Durga, Kali, Sekhmet, Senge Dongma, or Hecate.

- Seven symbols of a serpent that can be worn (as headpieces, necklaces, etc.).

- A headdress of a bull.

The symbol for infinity (like the number 8 turned on its side), which is also a symbol of the equinox.

THE SETUP OF THE SACRED CIRCLE

The ceremony takes place in a sacred circle from where you can see the setting sun, with a place for a fire in the middle. The fire is not lit until the ceremony is underway, as lighting it is part of the ceremony. Make sure to have everything needed to light the fire ready by the fire before the ceremony begins.

Before the ceremony, dig a hole inside the circle close to the bonfire, just big enough to bury a handful of seeds in. The symbol of infinity on a pole should be stood up in the ground near the fire, facing toward the participants.

The inside of the circle represents the underworld, so there should be a passage created using wood or stones into the circle to represent the passage into the underworld. If possible, the passage should align with the sunset on the equinox and be built on the eastern side of the circle, so that when people enter the circle, they walk toward the direction of west.

The nine regions of the underworld also need to be symbolized in some way. Ideally, if you have a big enough outdoor space, you could create a large sacred circle and mark out eight concentric circles inside it, making the center where the fire is the ninth. You could do this by pegging a string of natural fibers into the ground or by using sand sprinkled in circles. Just make sure that however you do it, you leave a walkway from the edge of the sacred circle, through the concentric circles, to the area where the fire is, so that people can walk to the bonfire without tripping on anything. If you are constricted with space, you can symbolize the nine layers by stacking nine smooth stones upon each other on the ground by the fire.

If you can only celebrate indoors, create a workaround to suit your circumstances. Likewise, if you don't have enough people for the ceremony, modify it as you consider best.

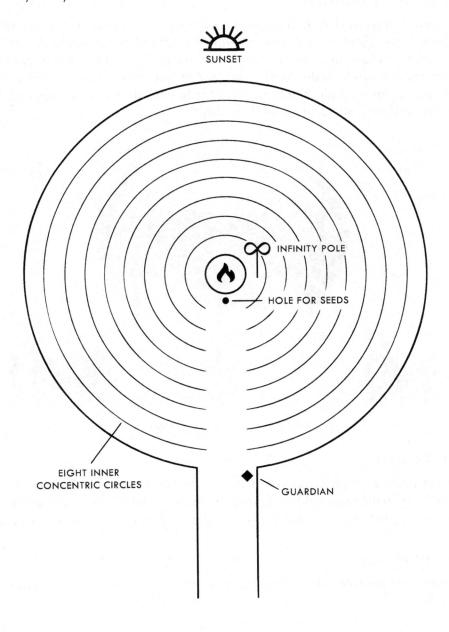

THE PARTICIPANTS

THE GUARDIAN

A man acts as the guardian of the underworld and of the ceremony. He stands at the entrance to the circle (where the passageway meets the circle) and carries a sword. He dresses the same as the General Participants.

THE MOTHER GODDESS

A woman plays the role of the Mother goddess. She is dressed in red, making sure her chest and legs are fully covered. As part of her costume she wears a headdress belonging to any of the goddesses related to the autumn equinox. These goddesses include Inanna, Durga, Kali, Sekhmet, Senge Dongma, and Hecate. So for example, she could wear the lion headdress of Sekhmet, or the crown of Durga. She also carries the labrys.

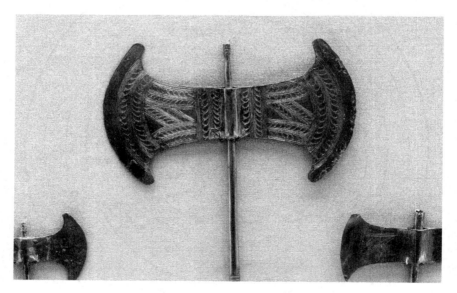

AN ANCIENT CEREMONIAL MINOAN LABRYS.

THE INITIATE

A male participant plays the role of the initiate. He carries an unlit candle in his right hand that can be held safely once it is lit, and a handful of seeds in his left hand (as wheat, rice, or corn). He dresses the same as the General Participants.

THE MINOTAUR

A man plays the role of the Minotaur. They dress in red, and wear a headdress of a bull.

An ancient Minoan rhyton which would have been
used in ceremonies, housed in a museum in Crete.

SEVEN SOLAR BODIES

Seven people (they can be men and women) dress in yellow to symbolize the
seven solar bodies. Each of the seven wears a symbol of a serpent. If there
aren't enough people, then just one person could represent the solar bodies
by wearing seven serpent symbols.

GENERAL PARTICIPANTS

All the remaining participants dress in white with gold or yellow trims or sashes.

DRUMMERS

At least one of the General Participants should carry a handheld drum which
they will play in the ceremony.

AN ORATOR

Another General Participant will read from sacred texts in the ceremony.

INSTRUCTIONS FOR THE CEREMONY

STEP 1. Everyone takes their positions for the ceremony. The fire in the center of the circle should be unlit as lighting it is part of the ceremony, but everything should be ready beside it so that it can be lit. The symbol of infinity should be by the fire, as well as the pre dug hole. The Initiate and the Mother stand at the beginning of the passageway into the circle, facing the setting sun, with the Mother on the left of the Initiate. The Guardian stands at the entrance to the circle with his sword held upright at his chest with both hands, so that the blade is in front of his face. The Minotaur stands inside the circle at a distance from the fire, facing the Mother and the Initiate. The Solar Bodies stand in a row outside the circle, facing the sunset. The General Participants also stand outside the circle facing the sunset, positioned so that everyone can see the ceremony taking place inside the circle.

STEP 2. The General Participants begin chanting Autumn Equinox Chant 1 or the mantra Om for a short time.

STEP 3. The Mother and the Initiate walk side-by-side down the passageway to the beginning of the circle. The Guardian holds his sword horizontally across the entrance so they cannot enter.

STEP 4. The Guardian says aloud, *"The mysteries are revealed to those who keep silence."* At that moment all the participants who are chanting stop. The silence represents the silence that must be kept when going through esoteric mysteries.

STEP 5. The Mother says to the Initiate, *"Lux in Tenebris Lucem"* and then its translation into the local language, *"The light shines in darkness."* And then, *"Go into the darkness and bring back light."*

STEP 6. The Guardian lifts his sword and allows the Mother and the Initiate to enter the circle.

STEP 7. The Drummers begin to drum slowly and rhythmically. The Minotaur walks over to the Mother and the Initiate and sways with the drum beat as they do.

STEP 8. The Mother and the Initiate walk slowly into the circle to stand by the central fire. The Minotaur walks alongside the Mother and Initiate to the center of the circle.

STEP 9. Once the Mother and the Initiate reach the central fire, the drumming stops. They face the fire in the direction of the setting sun. The Minotaur faces the setting sun but stands at a distance away from the Mother and the Initiate.

STEP 10. The Initiate bends down and places the seeds they were holding into the hole in the ground by the bonfire. The Mother then covers them over with earth using her hand, so they are buried.

STEP 11. While waiting for the sun to begin to set, the General Participants chant Autumn Equinox Chant 2 or the mantra Om.

STEP 12. The Mother lights the fire in the center of the circle as the sun begins to set, which is when the first visible part of the sun begins to set. If the view of the horizon is obscured by terrestrial objects such as mountains or trees, light the fire when you see the sun begin to set behind the terrestrial object, even though the sun may not have yet set below the actual horizon.

STEP 13. The Mother then lights the candle of the Initiate.

STEP 14. The Orator lifts their hand to signal that the General Participants should stop chanting, and they become silent.

STEP 15. The Mother pronounces the Egyptian words, *"Hbs m pht"* (pronounced khebs m pekht), and then its translation into the local language, *"Attain the star."* Both the Mother and the Initiate remain standing together, facing the setting sun.

STEP 16. The Orator begins reading some relevant excerpts from sacred texts (there are suggestions that can be used at the end of this chapter).

STEP 17. Once the reading is finished, the General Participants chant Autumn Equinox Chant 3 or the mantra Om.

STEP 18. Once the sun has fully set and the readings have finished, the Mother and the Initiate then turn and walk together out of the circle, and out the passageway to join the General Participants chanting the mantra for a few minutes. The Initiate still holds their lit candle as they do.

STEP 19. The Orator then signals for the chanting to end and everyone becomes silent.

STEP 20. The Mother and the Initiate begin walking away from the ceremonial area together. The Solar Bodies follow them, then the General Participants, and then the Guardian who leaves the passageway, and finally the Minotaur leaves the circle and follows behind everyone else. Once everyone has left the ceremonial area, the ceremony has ended.

After the ceremony you could gather around a fire, sing songs, chant mantras, or do further readings. Any activities should conclude before midnight.

THE MEANING OF THE CEREMONY

Every stage on the path begins with a descent into inner darkness and one's own inner abyss, as to ascend spiritually, we must first descend.

The ceremony symbolizes the descent into our own inner underworld to extract the light of knowledge and consciousness from our psychological inner darkness. This descent is depicted at ancient sites aligned to the autumn equinox, such as the Great Pyramid of Egypt, the Pyramid of the Sun in Mexico, the pyramid of the feathered serpent at Chichen Itza in Mexico, and legendary Minoan labyrinth of Knossos in Crete.

The seven people dressed in yellow represent the seven solar bodies and the kundalini risen in each in preparation for the birth of the spiritual Son at the winter solstice. These find their representation in the seven moai on Easter Island that face the setting sun on the equinox, as well as the descent of the seven scaled serpent at Chichen Itza.

The guardian of the circle represents the guardians of the gates of the underworld.

The Mother is the Mother of our higher Being who helps us on the path of the spiritual sun. The red color she wears represents our sexual energies converted into lust, which all our egos feed from, which is why in the ceremony the ego wears the same red color as the Mother. The red is the color of the womb, of the earth, and the infra-red light of the underworld. Incredibly, it's the energies of our spiritual Mother that are used to create our egos. These egos are needed for us to be able to acquire the knowledge of both darkness and of light; it's in overcoming the darkness of the egos that we gain knowledge and consciousness, which is light. The energies of the Mother in their lower aspect are ultimately behind the egos, sexual desire, and the underworld, which is why she is referred to as "Maya" by the Hindus, meaning "illusion." However, because her energies create "Maya," she also has the power to free us from it, as symbolized by the many warrior goddesses around the world. The Mother carries a weapon because she destroys our egos. Thus she provides the means for our own salvation by providing the world of darkness, matter, and the egos, which we go into as our place of learning, and then by liberating us from it through her ability to transform our inner energies and disintegrate our egos. The fire she lights is the sexual fire. It represents the "cremation ground" Kali is said to inhabit, where the egos are destroyed in the inner fire activated in the practice of alchemy.

The circle is divided into nine regions because there are nine regions of the underworld, and the initiate descends through them to reach the center which is the ninth sphere—the location of the central fire both within the earth and within our sexual energies. These nine regions were depicted by the Maya as the nine terraces the feathered serpent descends at Chichen Itza, and by the Minoans as a dark cavernous labyrinth.

A stone engraving of a labyrinth found in North Cornwall in England. This depiction is used to create the layered sacred circle in the ceremony, representing the regions of the underworld.

The symbolic underworld of the Minoans was said to be inhabited by the Minotaur, which was a mythological beast that was half man and half bull; this is symbolic of the person turned into an animalistic beast by the egos. The bull or buffalo is often used as a symbol of the ego. The Hindus also used it in this way, as the Hindu Mother goddess Durga wages her symbolic war against the buffalo demon. Our egos inhabit our psychological underworld, which is why the labyrinth is the symbolic abode of the Minotaur.

The initiate enters the circle with their candle unlit, because they descend in darkness; the Mother lights their candle in the ceremony because she is the one who releases our consciousness from the egos. The lighting of the candle is symbolic of the initiate gaining knowledge from the depths of the underworld and coming back out with it.

The seeds symbolize the latent potential of our inner seeds contained in the sexual energies, which need to be placed in the earth (through the practice of alchemy) where they can germinate and give rise to the birth of the spiritual within.

SUGGESTED READINGS

The following reading describes the experience of consciousness in the underworld. It is taken from the text called Pistis Sophia, which is an account Jesus gives to the disciples of the journey of consciousness from chaos, through many perils, until finally ascending to the Treasury of Light, the divine source. In these readings, Pistis Sophia, speaking symbolically as the consciousness, is describing how it feels to be trapped in psychological darkness. The chaos is the underworld, and the self-willed, whom she refers to as her foes, are the egos.

PISTIS SOPHIA

~ translated by G. R. S. Mead
From the first repentance of Sophia

O Light of lights, in whom I have had faith from the beginning, hearken now then, O Light, unto my repentance. Save me, O Light, for evil thoughts have entered into me.

I gazed, O Light, into the lower parts and saw there a light thinking: I will go to that region, in order that I may take that light. And I went and found myself in the darkness which is in the chaos below, and I could no more speed thence and go to my region, for I was sore pressed by all the emanations of Self-willed...

And I cried for help, but my voice hath not reached out of the darkness. And I looked unto the height, that the Light, in which I had had faith, might help me...

Suffer me no more to lack, O Lord, for I have had faith in thy light from the beginning; O Lord, O Light of the powers, suffer me no more to lack my light.

For because of thy inducement and for the sake of thy light am I fallen into this oppression, and shame hath covered me.

And because of the illusion of thy light, I am become a stranger to my brethren, the invisibles, and to the great emanations of Barbēlō.

This hath befallen me, O Light, because I have been zealous for thy abode; and the wrath of Self-willed is come upon me...

And I was in that region, mourning and seeking after the light which I had seen in the height...

But I looked up unto the height towards thee and had faith in thee. Now, therefore, O Light of lights, I am sore pressed in the darkness of chaos.

If now thou wilt come to save me,—great is thy mercy,—then hear me in truth and save me.

Save me out of the matter of this darkness, that I may not be submerged therein, that I may be saved from the emanations of god Self-willed which press me sore, and from their evil doings.

Let not this darkness submerge me... and let not this chaos shroud my power.

Hear me, O Light, for thy grace is precious, and look down upon me according to the great mercy of thy Light.

Turn not thy face from me, for I am exceedingly tormented.

Haste thee, hearken unto me and save my power...

My power looked forth from the midst of the chaos and from the midst of the darkness, and I waited for my pair, that he should come and fight for me, and he came not, and I looked that he should come and lend me power, and I found him not.

And when I sought the light, they gave me darkness; and when I sought my power, they gave me matter...

They have taken my light from me, and my power hath begun to cease in me and I am destitute of my light.

Now, therefore, O Light, which is in thee and is with me, I sing praises to thy name, O Light, in glory.

May my song of praise please thee, O Light, as an excellent mystery, which leadeth to the gates of the Light, which they who shall repent will utter, and the light of which will purify them.

Now, therefore, let all matters rejoice; seek ye all the Light, that the power of the stars which is in you, may live.

For the Light hath heard the matters, nor will it leave any without having purified them.

Let the souls and the matters praise the Lord of all æons, and let the matters and all that is in them praise him.

For God shall save their soul from all matters, and a city shall be prepared in the Light, and all the souls who are saved, will dwell in that city and will inherit it.

And the soul of them who shall receive mysteries will abide in that region, and they who have received mysteries in its name will abide therein. [1]

These excerpts dedicated to the goddess Durga are taken from the text Devi Mahatmyam, used in the celebration of the spiritual Mother in India around the autumn equinox. The text describes the battles of the Mother goddess against demons. The battlefield is said to be our consciousness and the demons symbolic of the egos.

DEVI MAHATMYAM

~ translated by Swami Jagadiswarananda

Salutation be to You, Devi Durga

Mother, I bow to Thee again and again, destroyer of worldly sufferings, embodiment of bliss, dispenser of wisdom and devotion.

You are the nectar of immortality, oh eternal and imperishable One
The supreme Mother of the devas
By you this universe is born,
By you this universe is created,
By you it is protected oh Devi
And you always consume it at the end.

Oh you who are of the form of the whole world, at the time of creation
You are the form of the creative force, at the time of the sustentation
You are the form of the protective power,
And at the time of dissolution of the world, You are the form of the destructive power
Armed with sword, spear, club, discus, conch, bow, arrows, slings and mace
You are terrible
And at the same time pleasing,
You are more pleasing than all the pleasing things and exceedingly beautiful
You are indeed the Supreme Ishvari, beyond high and low.

You are the resort of all! This entire world is composed of an infinitesimal portion of Yourself! You are verily the Supreme Primordial Prakriti untransformed.

O Devi, You are Bhagavati, the Supreme Vidya, which is the cause of liberation and great inconceivable penances. You, the Supreme Knowledge, are cultivated by sages desiring liberation, whose senses are well restrained, who are devoted to Reality, and have shed all the blemishes.

You are the sustenance whereby life is maintained.
You are the Supreme Destroyer of the pain of all the worlds.

You are Durga, the boat that takes men across the difficult ocean of worldly existence, devoid of attachment.

When called to mind in a difficult pass, You remove fear for every person.

When called to mind by those in happiness, You bestow a mind still further pious.

Which Goddess but You, O Dispeller of poverty, pain and fear, has an ever sympathetic heart for helping everyone?

Don't You reduce to ashes all asuras by mere sight? But You direct Your weapons against them so that even the unfriendly ones, purified by the missiles, may attain the higher worlds. Such is Your most kindly intention towards them.

If the eyes of the asuras had not been put out by the terrible flashes of the mass of light issuing from Your sword or by the copious lustre of Your spearpoint it is because they saw Your face resembling the moon, giving out cool rays.

What is Your prowess to be compared to? Where can one find this beauty of Yours most charming, yet striking fear in enemies? Compassion in heart and relentlessness in battle are seen, O Devi, O Bestower of boons, only in You in all the three worlds.

Oh Devi, protect us with Your spear. O Ambika, protect us with Your sword, protect us by the sound of Your gong and by the twang of Your bow-string. O Candika, guard us in the east, in the west, in the north and in the south by the brandishing of Your spear, O Ishwari.

You are the sole substratum of the world, because You subsist in the form of the earth. By You, who exist in the shape of water, all this universe is gratified, O Devi of inviolable valour.

O Devi, You are that power of Lord Vishnu, and have endless valour. You are the primeval maya, which is the source of the entire universe; by You all this universe has been thrown into an illusion, O Devi. If You become gracious, You become the cause of final emancipation in this world.

May Your bell that fills the world with its ringing, and destroys the prowess of the daityas, guard us, O Devi, as a mother protects her children, from all evils.

Oh Queen of all, You who exist in the form of all and possess every might Save us from error, Oh Devi

Salutation be to You, Devi Durga
Mother, I bow to Thee again and again, destroyer of worldly sufferings, embodiment of bliss, dispenser of wisdom and devotion. [2]

Winter Solstice

CHAPTER FOURTEEN

A Ceremony to Celebrate the Winter Solstice

THE TIMING OF THE CEREMONY

The ceremony takes place on the morning of the winter solstice, starting just before sunrise.

ITEMS NEEDED

- ☸ A pine tree or branch of a pine tree standing upright.

- ☸ A symbol of the sun on a long pole/staff so it stands around 2.2 meters high. It can be any symbol of the sun or an object that looks like the sun (such as a monstrance), and should be a gold color.

- ☸ The headdress of the Egyptian goddess Hathor.

- ☸ A headdress of an eagle.

- ☸ Candles in non-flammable containers which can be carried and held safely. Tealight candles placed in purpose-made candle holders would be an example of this.

A picture of a Christian monstrance, which looks like the sun and can be used as a symbol of it in the ceremony.

THE SETUP OF THE SACRED CIRCLE

A fire is built at the center of a sacred circle. It is not lit until the ceremony is underway, as lighting it is part of the ceremony, so whatever is needed to light the fire should be ready beside the fire before the ceremony begins.

A cross with four arms of equal length is drawn (using sand, or any other material to create a visible line), so that its arms intersect the central fire of the circle, but extend a distance beyond the circle, into what I'll call the outer-expanse.

The axis of the cross should align with the rising sun on the winter solstice, as well as the entrance to the circle.

At the end of each of the four arms, arcs should be drawn that reach the halfway point between the next arm and point clockwise, to form a swastika symbol.

Along each arm of the cross, from where they extend beyond the outside of the circle to where they finish, eight equidistant marks should be made. In the ceremony, a woman playing the role of the Mother goddess will use these markers to walk clockwise in an ever-tightening spiral nine times until she reaches the entrance of the circle, where she will then enter it.

A pine tree is placed at the end of the swastika arm on the opposite side of the circle to the sunrise and just to the right (when facing the sunrise). The monstrance is placed lying down on cloth near the central fire, and is covered with a white cloth to hide it.

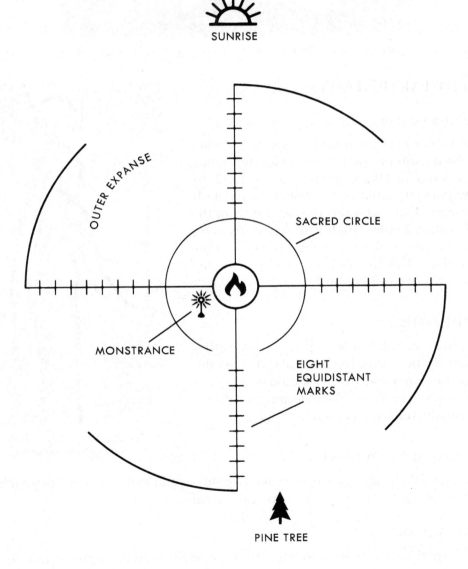

THIS WINTER SOLSTICE CEREMONY BEING PERFORMED IN SCOTLAND.

THE PARTICIPANTS

THE MOTHER

A woman plays the role of the spiritual Mother. She dresses in a pinkish red color (the subtle pink red the Hindu goddess Lakshmi and the Virgin Mary usually wear, rather than a gaudy, bright pink) and wears the headdress of the Egyptian goddess Hathor, which has two cow horns (not real horns) with a sun disk in the middle. This headdress can also have the symbol of a serpent on it.

THE FATHER

A man plays the role of the spiritual Father. Ideally the man and woman playing the roles of the Father and Mother should be a couple. The man wears the color blue and a headdress with the representation of an eagle.

The Egyptian goddess Hathor showing her headdress.

GENERAL PARTICIPANTS

General Participants wear white with a gold or yellow trim or sash. They each hold an unlit candle which can be carried safely.

AN ORATOR

One of the General Participants reads from sacred texts during the ceremony.

INSTRUCTIONS FOR THE CEREMONY

STEP 1. Everyone takes their positions for the ceremony. The Father and Mother stand together at some distance from the sacred circle. The Father stands on the right side of the Mother. The General Participants in the ceremony sit or stand behind the Mother and Father, and face the direction of the rising sun in a semi-circle, holding their unlit candles. The participants remain seated where they are throughout the duration of the ceremony or can stand if it is not practical to sit.

STEP 2. The Father and Mother walk together side-by-side to the pine tree. The Father stays at the pine tree. Both stand facing the direction of the rising sun.

STEP 3. The Father begins chanting Winter Solstice Chant 1 or the mantra Om and the attendees join in the chant, each at their own pace so there is a continuous sound.

STEP 4. The Mother leaves the Father's side and begins walking around the circle in the outer-expanse (with the circle to her right) nine times in a clock-wise direction, using the markers on the arms of the cross as a guide, in an ever-tightening spiral until she reaches the circle.

STEP 5. When the Mother reaches the circle she goes inside it and stands slightly to the left, facing the direction of the rising sun.

STEP 6. The Father and General Participants begin chanting Winter Solstice Chant 2 or continue chanting the mantra Om while waiting for the sun to rise.

STEP 7. Just as the sun begins to rise, the Mother lights the fire in the center of the circle.

STEP 8. The Orator stands up, or steps forward, and lifts their hand to signal that the chanting should stop. The General Participants stop chanting and become silent. The Orator then says:

> "The Lord of Love is the sun that dispels our darkness. He is the supreme Lord, who through his grace moves us to seek him in our own hearts. He is the light that shines forever. Let us adore the Lord of Life!" [1]

STEP 9. The Mother takes the monstrance out of the cloth and stands it up. She stands holding it facing the rising sun and the fire.

STEP 10. The Orator then says:

"Hear, O children of immortal bliss! You are born to be united with the Lord. Follow the path of the illumined ones and be united with the Lord of Life." [2]

STEP 11. The General Participants light their candles using a lighter of some kind, as they should not light them from the fire in the center of the circle.

STEP 12. The Orator says, "Lord, Lead me from ignorance to truth."

> The General Participants repeat together,
> "Lord, Lead me from ignorance to truth."

> The Orator then says, "Lead me from darkness to light."

> The General Participants repeat this line.

> The Orator says, "Lead me from death to immortality."

> The General Participants repeat this line.

> The Orator says, "Let There Be Peace, Peace, Peace."

> The General Participants repeat this line.

STEP 13. The Orator begins chanting Winter Solstice Chant 3 or the mantra Om and the General Participants join in, continuing until the sun is fully risen.

STEP 14. The Orator stops chanting and raises their hand to signal that the chanting should stop. All the participants become silent, and the Orator reads some relevant sacred texts.

STEP 15. The Orator signals to the General Participants to stand if they have been seated, and the General Participants stand.

STEP 16. The Mother leaves the circle by walking along the arm of the swastika that has the pine tree at the end of it to the edge of the outer-expanse, carrying the monstrance high, and meets the Father at the pine tree.

STEP 17. The General Participants turn to watch the Father and Mother if they need to from where they are standing.

STEP 18. The Father and Mother walk together away from the ceremonial area, with the Mother still carrying the monstrance.

STEP 19. The General Participants follow the Father and Mother in single file and the ceremony ends.

Afterward everyone can sit inside the circle, get warm around the fire, and chant mantras, sing spiritual songs, do extra readings, or relax if they wish.

In the evening an optional informal gathering around the bonfire can be held at sunset, with music and mantras, to finish before midnight.

DOING THE CEREMONY IN A COLD CLIMATE

For those who live in a cold climate and who are doing this ceremony outdoors, here are a few suggestions to make sure everyone keeps as warm as they can. One idea is to create a large enough bonfire within the sacred circle that will keep everyone warm enough even at a bit of distance.

The participants, instead of remaining seated outside the ceremonial area, should follow the Mother in single file as she walks in a spiral around the circle. They should not go inside the circle however, but stand or be seated in a semi-circle around the fire just outside of the circle, facing the rising sun. Once the ceremony has ended, they can then follow the Mother and Father once they walk away from the ceremonial area in single file, along the same way that the Mother left the circle.

It's important that everyone has proper clothing for cold temperatures, like thermals, gloves, boots, warm hats, etc., which can always be worn underneath any ceremonial clothing. It's also a good idea to have hot soup, teas/coffees, waiting inside a heated room after the ceremony ends to revive everyone from the cold.

If the weather is too poor to hold a ceremony outdoors, you could always improvise one indoors instead. The bonfire can be substituted by a candle or a candlestick of seven.

THE BIRTH OF THE MIDNIGHT SUN AT CHRISTMAS EVE

The birth of the spiritual Son has been widely celebrated three days following the winter solstice, which generally falls on the 25th of December (in the northern hemisphere). More specifically, Jesus is said to have been born at midnight the night before on what is known as Christmas Eve, which is traditionally celebrated with a Midnight Mass. This birth symbolizes the birth of the spiritual Son within a person. It is the celebration of the midnight sun, which is when the sun is born into the time of greatest darkness (our greatest psychological darkness), before it begins to "grow."

Holding your own midnight Christmas can be something very special and magical. You can work out when to celebrate it by finding out what day the sun will start to ascend after standing still for three days from the winter solstice. A midnight Christmas would be held the night before that day.

Traditionally, Midnight Mass is celebrated with lighting candles, singing traditional songs, and reading from sacred texts. It can be especially magical to celebrate just by candlelight (turning the electric lights off). In some parts of the world, a large white pillar candle is lit to symbolize the spiritual Son as the light of the world. You could celebrate by lighting your own handheld candle and any other candles in the room, from a main white pillar candle, to symbolize light coming into each person and the world. The monstrance from the ceremony or any monstrance can also be used for this celebration to symbolize the spiritual Son.

Then by candlelight you could sing spiritual songs, as well as mantras, and read relevant sacred texts.

It's also very nice to set up your own nativity scene with a knowledge of its meaning, lit by candlelight.

CHRISTMAS DAY

Traditionally, Christmas day, which is the day following Christmas Eve, when the sun begins to ascend after standing still for three days, is celebrated with lots of joy and merriment. You could celebrate the sun this day with lots of spiritual music, song, and meals shared together with friends and family, as this symbolizes the happiness, hope, spiritual gifts, and abundance that the spiritual Son brings by his birth within us. Ultimately, the spiritual Son is a gift from our higher Mother and Father on a personal level, and from the divine source of creation on a universal level.

THE MEANING OF THE CEREMONY

This ceremony is very similar to ones which were practiced in ancient times. It was created using a knowledge of esoteric principles. A little later, I discovered that there is an account by ancient Greeks of an ancient Egyptian winter solstice ceremony that closely resembles this one.

It symbolizes the central processes contained in the birth of the spiritual Son, which is symbolized by the rising sun of the winter solstice.

The ceremony enacts how at the dawn of existence, the feminine aspect of the creator (the chaos, the seedbed of life) is in the continuous movement of creation, initiated by the masculine aspect, and from the womb of the Mother the neutral force, the spiritual Son is born.

The cross created in the sacred circle forms a swastika, which symbolizes the forces of creation in continuous movement. The cross represents the alchemical forces of creation in the union of male and female.

The pine tree represents the Father (eternal, thus evergreen), as does the man who plays the role of the Father. He instigates creation, and impregnates the womb of the Mother, yet his remaining out of the circle altogether represents how he remains hidden. He chants Om, as it is said to be the primordial sound that was present at the creation of the universe.

The woman represents the great Mother of creation, the chaos, the darkness of the uncreated absolute source. The monstrance represents the child born from her womb—the spiritual Son. The cow's horns of her headdress symbolize her as the nourisher and also because the shape made by the head and horns of a cow looks like a womb. The sun disk between the horns represents her divinity and the sun child who is born from her womb.

The rising sun (in the sky) represents the Son that is born from the union of male and female, as does the monstrance the Mother carries.

The spiral of nine circles that the Mother walks represent the nine regions of creation, as there are nine heavens and nine hells. They also symbolize the nine months of gestation before birth, which correlate to these nine regions which the Son gestates within.

The entrance stone to the ancient megalithic temple of Newgrange, which aligns to the winter solstice sunrise. It is covered in the symbol of the spiral, which is significant to the time of the winter solstice and used in this ceremony.

The sacred circle represents the womb, the earth, the world, and the stables in which the Son is born—at the center of which is the divine Treasury, represented by the fire.

The Mother moves in darkness, representing the primeval chaos at the beginning of the creation of the universe, the seabed of life, which is fertilized with the word and from which life springs.

The sacred circle is similar in design to the ancient city of Arkaim in Russia, which was aligned to the solstices and equinoxes, and which was laid out around a main spiral pathway within a swastika type formation. The way the Mother walks in a clockwise spiral has been called "walking the way of the sun," as the sun traces this path on the earth leading up to the summer solstice.

The participants chanting the mantras represent the divine androgynous beings who are created from the divine source. Each being is a Monad who later divides into the different parts of someone's higher Being, and as part of that process, sends down a spark of itself called consciousness, which comes into the world of matter to learn and awaken.

The words the Orator reads out in steps 8, 10, and 12 are taken from sacred texts. Steps 8 and 10 are from the Shvetashatvara Upanishad, and step 12 is from the Vedas.

SUGGESTED READINGS

There are many readings that could be used at this ceremony, as it represents such a widely important part of spirituality. Here are some suggestions:

THE GOSPEL ACCORDING TO JOHN

In the beginning was the Word, and the Word was with God, and the Word was God. The same was in the beginning with God. All things were made by him; and without him was not any thing made that was made. In him was life; and the life was the light of men. And the light shineth in darkness; and the darkness comprehended it not.

There was a man sent from God, whose name was John. The same came for a witness, to bear witness of the Light, that all men through him might believe. He was not that Light, but was sent to bear witness of that Light.

That was the true Light, which lighteth every man that cometh into the world. He was in the world, and the world was made by him, and the world knew him not. He came unto his own, and his own received him not. But as many as received him, to them gave he power to become the sons of God, even to them that believe on his name: Which were born, not of blood, nor of the will of the flesh, nor of the will of man, but of God. [3]

JESUS IN THE APOCRYPHON OF JOHN FROM THE NAG HAMMADI LIBRARY

~ translated by Frederik Wisse

I, therefore, the perfect Pronoia of the all, changed myself into my seed, for I existed first, going on every road. For I am the richness of the light; I am the remembrance of the pleroma.

And I went into the realm of darkness and I endured till I entered the middle of the prison. And the foundations of chaos shook. And I hid myself from them because of their wickedness, and they did not recognize me.

Again I returned for the second time, and I went about. I came forth from those who belong to the light, which is I, the remembrance of the Pronoia. I entered into the midst of darkness and the inside of Hades, since I was seeking (to accomplish) my task. And the foundations of chaos shook, that they might fall down upon those who are in chaos and might destroy them. And again I ran up to my root of light, lest they be destroyed before the time.

Still for a third time I went—I am the light which exists in the light, I am the remembrance of the Pronoia—that I might enter into the midst of darkness and the inside of Hades. And I filled my face with the light of the completion of their aeon. And I entered into the midst of their prison, which is the prison of the body. And I said, "He who hears, let him get up from the deep sleep." And he wept and shed tears. Bitter tears he wiped from himself and he said, "Who is it that calls my name, and from where has this hope come to me, while I am in the chains of the prison?" And I said, "I am the Pronoia of the pure light; I am the thinking of the virginal Spirit, who raised you up to the honored place. Arise and remember that it is you who hearkened, and follow your root, which is I, the merciful one, and guard yourself against the angels of poverty and the demons of chaos and all those who ensnare you, and beware of the deep sleep and the enclosure of the inside of Hades."

And I raised him up, and sealed him in the light of the water with five seals, in order that death might not have power over him from this time on. [4]

THE GOSPEL ACCORDING TO MATTHEW

Jesus said:

Blessed are the poor in spirit,
for theirs is the kingdom of heaven.

Blessed are those who mourn,
for they will be comforted.

Blessed are the meek,
for they will inherit the earth.

Blessed are those who hunger and thirst for righteousness,
for they will be filled.

Blessed are the merciful,
for they will be shown mercy.

Blessed are the pure in heart,
for they will see God.

Blessed are the peacemakers,
for they will be called children of God.

Blessed are those who are persecuted because of righteousness,
for theirs is the kingdom of heaven.

Blessed are you when people insult you, persecute you and falsely say all kinds of evil against you because of me. Rejoice and be glad, because great is your reward in heaven... [5]

THE LORD'S PRAYER

Our Father, which art in heaven,
Hallowed be thy Name.
Thy Kingdom come.
Thy will be done on earth,
As it is in heaven.
Give us this day our daily bread.
And forgive us our trespasses,
As we forgive those who trespass against us,
And lead us not into temptation,
But deliver us from evil.

THE ESSENE GOSPEL OF PEACE
~ translated by Edmond Bordeaux Szekely

"I am sent to you by the Father, that I may make the light of life to shine before you. The light lightens itself and the darkness, but the darkness knows only itself, and knows not the light... When you can gaze on the brightness of the noonday sun with unflinching eyes, you can then look upon the blinding light of your Heavenly Father, which is a thousand times brighter than the brightness of a thousand suns. But how should you look upon the blinding light of your Heavenly Father, when you cannot even bear the shining of the blazing sun? Believe me, the sun is as the flame of a candle beside the sun of truth of the Heavenly Father. Have but faith, therefore, and hope, and love. I tell you truly, you shall not want your reward. If you believe in my words, you believe in him who sent me, who is the lord of all, and with whom all things are possible. For what is impossible with men, all these things are possible with God. If you believe in the angels of the Earthly Mother and do her laws, your faith shall sustain you and you shall never see disease. Have hope also in the love of your Heavenly Father, for he who trusts in him shall never be deceived, nor shall he ever see death." [6]

The following reading from the ancient text The Wisdom of Jesus Christ describes the creation of the Monad from the source of creation, which is the eternal Being of each person, and its division into its different parts, including the Father, Mother, and Son. The Monads coming out of the source is symbolized in the winter solstice ceremony when the participants light their candles. In the text below, they are called "self-begotten ones" and "The Generation over Whom There Is No Kingdom." The "drop from the light" is a reference to the spiritual part of us that has come into the world, called consciousness.

THE WISDOM OF JESUS CHRIST
~ translated by Douglas M. Parrott

The Savior said: "He Who Is is ineffable. No principle knew him, no authority, no subjection, nor any creature from the foundation of the world until now, except he alone, and anyone to whom he wants to make revelation through him who is from First Light. From now on, I am the Great Savior. For he is immortal and eternal. Now he is eternal, having no birth; for everyone who has birth will perish. He is unbegotten, having no beginning; for everyone who has a beginning has an end. Since no one rules over him, he has no name; for whoever has a name is the creation of another. He is unnameable. He has no human form; for whoever has human form is the creation of another.

And he has a semblance of his own - not like what you have seen and received, but a strange semblance that surpasses all things and is better than the universe. It looks to every side and sees itself from itself. Since it is infinite, he is ever incomprehensible. He is imperishable and has no likeness to anything. He is unchanging good. He is faultless. He is eternal. He is blessed. While he is not known, he ever knows himself. He is immeasurable. He is untraceable. He is perfect, having no defect. He is imperishability blessed. He is called 'Father of the Universe'...

Because of his mercy and his love, he wished to bring forth fruit by himself, that he might not enjoy his goodness alone, but that other spirits of the Unwavering Generation might bring forth body and fruit, glory and honor, in imperishableness and his infinite grace, that his treasure might be revealed by Self-begotten God, the father of every imperishableness and those that came to be afterward...

Seeing himself within himself in a mirror, he appeared resembling himself, but his likeness appeared as Divine Self-Father... He is indeed of equal age with the Light that is before him, but he is not equal to him in power.

And afterward was revealed a whole multitude of confronting, self-begotten ones, equal in age and power, being in glory and without number, whose race is called 'The Generation over Whom There Is No Kingdom' from the one in whom you yourselves have appeared from these men...

I want you to know that First Man is called 'Begetter, Self-perfected Mind'. He reflected with Great Sophia, his consort, and revealed his first-begotten, androgynous son. His male name is designated 'First Begetter, Son of God', his female name, 'First Begettress Sophia, Mother of the Universe'. Some call her 'Love'. Now First-begotten is called 'Christ'...

All who come into the world, like a drop from the Light, are sent by him to the world of Almighty, that they might be guarded by him. And the bond of his forgetfulness bound him by the will of Sophia, that the matter might be revealed through it to the whole world in poverty, concerning the Almighty's arrogance and blindness and the ignorance that he was named. But I came from the places above by the will of the great Light, I who escaped from that bond; I have cut off the work of the robbers; I have awakened that drop that was sent from Sophia, that it might bear much fruit through me, and be perfected and not again be defective, but be joined through me, the Great Savior, that his glory might be revealed, so that Sophia might also be justified in regard to that defect, that her sons might not again become defective but might attain honor and glory and go up to their Father, and know the words of the masculine Light. And you were sent by the Son, who was sent that you might receive Light..."[7]

Spring Equinox

Spring Equinox

CHAPTER FIFTEEN

A Ceremony to Celebrate the Spring Equinox

THE TIMING OF THE CEREMONY

The ceremony begins just before sunrise on the day of the spring equinox.

ITEMS NEEDED

⚙ A human sized cross made of wood, which is light enough for a man to carry on his own.

⚙ An open coffin without a lid and with straight sides so it is rectangular in shape like the sarcophagus in the Great Pyramid of Egypt. It can be handmade out of wood or any other materials available, and should be large enough for the person playing the role of Initiate to lie down comfortably in. Ideally the sides of the coffin should be high enough so that when someone lies down in it, they can't be seen by the General Participants in the ceremony. If you're unable to make a coffin like this, you could simply use a board or platform of some kind that can be placed on the ground, which someone can lie on. It's a good idea to have a mat and small pillow placed inside the coffin or on the board, so that the person lying down is comfortable.

☸ A copper cauldron (or bowl) filled with water. If you can't find one made of copper, then any other material can be used except iron. The cauldron is symbolic of the womb, and the water symbolizes the sexual waters of creation. On the outside of the cauldron make nine equidistant markings, signifying nine layers of the underworld, and the ninth sphere. The top marking is at the level of the water, indicating the descent and re-ascent the Initiate must make before resurrection.

☸ An altar or table that the cauldron can be placed on.

☸ A white cloth that is placed next to the cauldron on the altar, which will be dipped in the water inside the cauldron.

☸ A torch which can be lit and stand upright in the ground.

☸ An Anubis face mask which has small, white feathered wings fanning out from the top of it.

☸ A necklace with a serpent pendant. The serpent should be upright, so that its head is higher than its tail. This could be handmade using any materials you have, such as cardboard, string, and gold foil. A small brass statue of a serpent could also be tied to a necklace, etc.

☸ A crown with a raised serpent on it, like those found on the foreheads of the gods and pharaohs of ancient Egypt. They are called a "uraeus."

IMAGE RIGHT: Photograph showing a woman wearing a uraeus headpiece, which is worn by the woman playing the role of the Mother in this ceremony.

THE SETUP OF THE SACRED CIRCLE

There should be a sacred circle, or other sacred space, with a place for a fire in the middle. The sacred circle will act as the tomb in the ceremony, much like the King's Chamber of the Great Pyramid. The fire is unlit as lighting it takes place as part of the ceremony. The passageway to the circle should align to the sunrise on the spring equinox.

Inside the circle, place the coffin to the left of the fire, orientated north south, so that the person who lies in the coffin has their head at the southern end and feet at the northern end.

Place the copper cauldron or equivalent bowl inside the circle, near the coffin, on the altar or table. Place the white cloth and pendant next to the cauldron on the table.

A lit torch of fire should also be placed inside the circle where Anubis will stand just before the ceremony begins, so that it does not catch anything else alight and can be used to light the fire easily at the appropriate moment in the ceremony.

A post-hole needs to be dug just outside the entrance to the sacred circle, on the left side, so that the wooden cross can be stood upright in it so that it doesn't fall over.

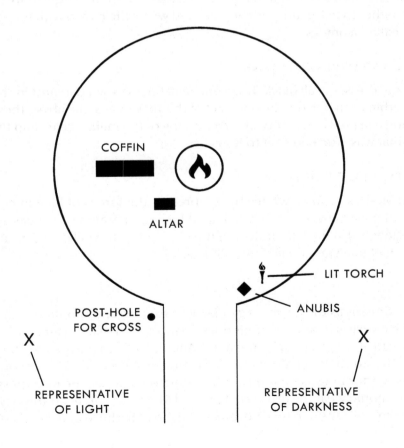

THE PARTICIPANTS

THE INITIATE

A man plays the role of the Initiate, and dresses in white with the symbol of the sun in gold or yellow on his back. Any symbol of the sun can be used. He also wears a white cape over his shoulders, which covers over the symbol of the sun on his back. He wears this cape from the beginning of the ceremony, but takes it off to reveal the sun symbol on his back at a specific stage of the ceremony. The cape should be able to easily be untied or unbuttoned at the front so it can be removed without having to lift it over one's head.

THE BETRAYER

A person plays the role of the betrayer and dresses as all the General Participants do.

THE MOTHER

A woman plays the role of the spiritual Mother. She wears a pinkish red color (the subtle pink red the Hindu goddess Lakshmi and the Virgin Mary usually wear, rather than a gaudy, bright pink) and wears the crown with the serpent on it, called a uraeus.

REPRESENTATIVE OF DARKNESS

A person dresses in all black. They represent the forces of darkness in creation and within each person, the dark half of the year, chaos, the abyss, the asuras (demons) in the Hindu story of the churning of the milky ocean, and the bad thief that was crucified next to Jesus.

REPRESENTATIVE OF LIGHT

A person dresses in all white. They represent the forces of light in creation and within each person, the light half of the year, harmony, the heavens, the devas (angels) in the Hindu story of the churning of the milky ocean, and the good thief that was crucified next to Jesus.

ANUBIS

A man dresses as the ancient Egyptian god Anubis, and should be tall if possible. He wears a mask as Anubis does, that covers his face. Murals in ancient Egypt actually depict people dressed as Anubis and wearing a mask—the artists made sure to show the ties of the mask to indicate that these were ordinary people performing a ceremony. In addition to the mask, the man dressed as Anubis should wear the feathers of the god Mercury in his headdress (symbolizing rising)—they stand up vertically at the top of his head and fan out slightly.

GENERAL PARTICIPANTS

All the other participants dress in white with a yellow or gold trim, or sash.

AN ORATOR

Someone from the General Participants reads the excerpts from sacred texts in the ceremony. They can carry pieces of paper with the readings on them, so they don't have to memorize the words.

INSTRUCTIONS FOR THE CEREMONY

STEP 1. The ceremony begins before sunrise. The coffin, cauldron on the altar with pendant and white cloth, the unlit fire in the center, and lit torch should be ready inside the circle.

STEP 2. Everyone takes their places for the ceremony. The Initiate stands some distance away from the circle (about forty meters away if you have enough room) facing the direction of the rising sun. The General Participants stand together near the Initiate, facing the Initiate and the direction of the rising sun. The Betrayer and Orator stand amidst the General Participants. The Initiate stands a short distance away from the General Participants on their own, and the Mother stands near the Initiate but not near the General Participants. Next to the Initiate, lying on the ground, is the wooden cross. Anubis stands at the entrance of the sacred circle, just inside the circle on the right side when facing the direction of the rising sun (which is the opposite side to where the cross is placed in the post-hole). The Representative of Darkness stands on the south side of the entrance to the sacred circle, a short distance from it, and faces north. The Representative of Light stands on the north side of the entrance to the sacred circle, a short distance from it, and faces south.

STEP 3. The ceremony begins when the Initiate says, "Father, let your will be done and not mine."

STEP 4. The General Participants then begin singing Spring Equinox Chant 1 or a somber O tone, which they continue with until step 15.

STEP 5. The Betrayer emerges from the General Participants and walks up behind the back of the Initiate and holds them by one arm.

STEP 6. The Betrayer turns the Initiate around to face the General Participants and says, "I hand the Son, who gave me his trust, over to the evil of the world."

STEP 7. The Orator, who is amongst the General Participants calls out "See the Son whom the world condemns!"

STEP 8. The Betrayer lets go of the Initiate.

STEP 9. The Initiate picks up the cross that is lying on the ground beside them and puts it over their right shoulder.

STEP 10. The Betrayer then merges back into the crowd of General Participants.

STEP 11. The Initiate walks to the sacred circle, carrying the wooden cross over their right shoulder. The Mother walks beside the Initiate on their left side.

STEP 12. The General Participants, Betrayer and Orator follow the Initiate in a crowd, and gather outside the sacred circle to watch the rest of the ceremony, facing the direction of the rising sun.

STEP 13. The Initiate and Mother walk down the passageway to the sacred circle. Once the Initiate reaches the entrance to the circle, he stops and places the cross he has been carrying in the post-hole so that it stands upright.

STEP 14. The Representative of Darkness and the Representative of Light both walk over to the Initiate at the same time. The Representative of Darkness holds the left arm of the Initiate out straight, and the Representative of Light, the right arm of the Initiate out straight, so that the Initiate's arms are out-stretched in the shape of a cross. They stay like this for a short time.

STEP 15. The Orator signals the General Participants should stop chanting, and they become silent. The Orator says,

"For truly, no one can reach the Heavenly Father unless they return through the womb of the Earthly Mother.[1] The Son of Man will be three days and three nights in the heart of the earth.[2] Whoever has ears to hear about the infinities, let him hear! I have addressed those who are awake. Everything that came from the perishable will perish, since it came from the perishable. But whatever came from imperishableness does not perish but becomes imperishable." [3]

STEP 16. The Representative of Darkness and Representative of Light both let go of the arms of the Initiate at the same time. The Initiate lets their arms lower completely, closes their eyes, and bows their head. The two Representatives turn to face the rising sun, and remain standing where they are throughout the remainder of the ceremony.

STEP 17. The Orator says, "Enter the secret ways of Ro-Setawe, The gate of the gods... The secret way to which only Anubis has access in order to conceal the body of Osiris." [4]

STEP 18. Anubis, who is standing at the entrance to the circle, holds the Initiate's right arm and walks them over to the coffin. The Mother follows behind them.

STEP 19. The Initiate climbs into the coffin and lies down in it. He opens his eyes to get to the coffin and closes them again once he lays down.

STEP 20. The General Participants begin quietly chanting Spring Equinox Chant 2 or the mantra Om continuously at their own pace so that there is a constant sound, and continue with it until step 24.

STEP 21. Anubis and the Mother stand over the coffin looking in at the Initiate. Anubis raises his hands over the Initiate just as is shown in the ancient Egyptian temple relief, depicting this same scene, in the image below. After a short time (once his arms feel tired), Anubis lowers his arms, and both he and the Mother look up to face the rising sun.

STEP 22. Just as the rising sun starts to become visible (where you can start to see the first part of the sun over the horizon or any terrestrial objects like trees), Anubis walks over and picks up the lit torch, and uses it to light the fire. Depending on the torch used, he can either throw it into the fire (if it is too damaged or not reusable) or continue holding it throughout the rest of the ceremony. He then stands facing the sun.

STEP 23. As the fire is being lit, the Initiate opens his eyes, stands up, and gets out of the coffin. They take off their cape, and let it fall to the ground, to reveal the symbol of the sun on their back. The Initiate then walks over to stand before the fire, facing the rising sun.

STEP 24. As the Initiate stands up and walks over to the fire, as in the step above, the Orator signals the General Participants should stop chanting, and they become silent. The Orator says,

"He comes indeed, weary of the Nine, an Imperishable spirit, he that bore more than you, he that suffered more than you, he that is more weary than you, he that became greater than you, he who will be happier than you, he who roars louder than you. You have no more time there! [5]

Atum, this your son is here, whom you have preserved alive. He lives! He lives! Osiris lives! He is not dead, Osiris is not dead! He is not gone down, Osiris is not gone down! He has not been judged, Osiris has not been judged! He judges, Osiris judges!" [6]

STEP 25. The Mother walks over to the cauldron and dips the cloth in the water, and then walks over to the Initiate. She wipes the cloth on both cheeks of his face, as if gently cleaning them.

STEP 26. The Orator says,

"Your Mother the Celestial Serpent has cleansed you. Bathe in the Jackal Lake, be cleansed in the Lake of the Netherworld, be purified. You travel the Winding Waterway because you are pure, the son of a pure one. I say to the door-keeper of the firmament, 'Let him come, for he is pure.' Run your course, row over your waterway like the sun god Ra on the banks of the sky. Raise yourself, go in your spirit-state." [7]

STEP 27. The Mother walks back over to the altar, puts down the cloth and picks up the serpent pendant, walks over to the Initiate and puts it on him. The Mother and the Initiate then both turn and face the rising sun, standing next to one another.

STEP 28. The Orator says,

"Anubis, the counter of hearts, deducts Osiris from the gods who belong to the earth, and assigns him to the gods who are in heaven. [8]

The earth speaks: The doors of the earth-god are opened for you, the doors of Geb are thrown open for you, you come forth at the voice of Anubis, he makes a spirit of you. [9]

How pleasant is your condition! You become a spirit, among your brothers the gods. How changed, how changed is your state! [10]

You are not like the dead, who are dead, you are living, you are alive, together with them, the spirits, the imperishable stars." [11]

STEP 29. The Initiate then takes a piece of paper from somewhere concealed on them, like a pocket, and reads aloud the excerpts from the Odes of Solomon found in the suggested reading section of this chapter.

STEP 30. The General Participants chant Spring Equinox Chant 3 or the mantra Om until step 33.

STEP 31. After some time of chanting, the Initiate turns and walks out of the circle on their own, and continues walking completely away from the ceremonial area alone.

STEP 32. The Mother and Anubis both walk out of the circle, and begin walking away from the ceremonial area. They are followed by the Representatives of Light and Darkness.

STEP 33. The General Participants stop chanting, and follow the Mother, Anubis, and Representatives away from the ceremonial area. The ceremony has then finished.

After the end of the ceremony you could gather in the sacred circle and chant any mantras, as well as read any sacred texts that are relevant to the occasion.

THE MEANING OF THE CEREMONY

This ceremony is based upon how an ancient one may have looked. I've used research, my own experience of having gone through the actual initiation it symbolizes while out of my body, and the oldest known evidence for the celebration of the event.

The journey to enlightenment is told in the heavens if you know how to read its signs. Central to that journey is death and resurrection; these are primary events in the return of consciousness to its origin. Sunrise on the spring equinox signifies the resurrection, following the darkness of winter that preceded it. From this time onward until the summer solstice, the sun increases in its strength and time in the sky.

The spring equinox symbolizes the Initiate's triumph over darkness and absorption into the eternal Mother. Before resurrection, the Initiate dies symbolically and spends three days in a tomb (symbolic of the womb, the underworld, and chaos of creation). In this ceremony, the sacred circle and the coffin represent the womb of the Mother.

The Mother accompanies the Initiate throughout the ceremony, as spiritually she always accompanies us. Our body is of the earth, which is of the Mother, and so she accompanies the Initiate through everything, right until the very end. It is she, along with Anubis, who resurrects the Initiate, which was described in the life of Osiris who was resurrected by the goddess Isis and Anubis. The serpent is symbolic of the Mother, which is why she wears it in this ceremony. The Mother puts the serpent pendant on the Initiate to signify how he has become one with the Mother. The water she cleanses the Initiate in represent the waters of the underworld, which are the sexual energies. She works with the Initiate to purify their energies in the practice of alchemy, and these energies restore and heal the Initiate.

The Betrayer plays an important role in the process of inner death, as they bring out the egos of the Initiate and form the circumstances that test them. They are someone in the Initiate's life, which is why they emerge from within the crowd of General Participants in the ceremony.

The Initiate taking up the cross themselves and carrying it represents the suffering they voluntarily put themselves through as an act of self-sacrifice, in order to continue with their work to help humanity, despite the unjust attacks and persecution they suffer as a result of their own betrayal.

The Representatives of both Light and Darkness represent the struggle the Initiate goes through between these forces, both externally in their life, and also within themselves—represented in the Hindu story of the churning of the milky ocean. They go into darkness as they go into the coffin, which is symbolic of their "death" to the world—in that they are totally shunned and persecuted by it. It also represents the womb of creation and the underworld, where they must go through hellish psychological states and achieve an inner death of those egos. The sun rising symbolizes the Initiate rising up slowly from the underworld to resurrect, and the triumph of the light within them.

The cape the Initiate wears, in the beginning of the ceremony, conceals the sun on their back, symbolizing how they have the Son within and yet appear as a normal person just like everyone else. Removing the cape in the ceremony after they rise out of the coffin, reveals the sun on their back, and symbolizes the resurrection of the Son within.

The figure of Anubis is present as he presides over the process from inner death to resurrection.

In an initiation of the inner death that occurs before resurrection—which I went through out of the body—I lay in a tomb in an open granite coffin with straight sides. It was dark inside the tomb, but I looked to my side and Anubis was standing at the doorway, silhouetted by the light behind him, and with the wings of Mercury on his head. Years later, looking through ancient sites and texts, I found references to Anubis (and his equivalent in other cultures) depicted in the exact event I went through. So many of the symbols I'm discovering now I also discovered while going through the initiation. Some of the hieroglyphs of ancient Egypt that depict resurrection are not speaking of a process of actual death, nor are they representing just cosmic events, but they describe the hidden initiations of the inner worlds.

Anubis attending the initiate who lies
symbolically dead, to resurrect them.

The role of Anubis in this ceremony is also the symbolic role the Sphinx has in the design of the Great Pyramids where a similar ceremony to this one is described as being performed in the Pyramid Texts. The symbolic meaning of the Sphinx is described in chapter five "Decoding the Ancient Meaning of the Sphinx and Its Origin as Anubis."

The Initiate walking away from the sacred circle on their own at the end of the ceremony signifies how someone who has gone through this stage leaves behind a circle of life and society they were formerly bound to, and eventually even the entire circle of humanity, as they instead become part of a circle of solar Beings.

The spring equinox can be celebrated in many ways—not just with a ceremony like the one I describe, but simply by being present at the rising sun, without any ceremony, or by chanting a mantra or by simply improvising something, perhaps by selecting some of the themes in this ceremony. It's especially difficult to be in a suitable place to see the sunrise in a city, so it can be celebrated at home or wherever you think best. The more complex ceremony is better suited to a retreat or outdoor situation where all the facilities are already in place for it.

This can be done as a stand-alone ceremony, but it is really part of a three day event, which begins with the symbolic death on the first day. The second day is the time spent in the tomb, and on the third day is resurrection. Three days of ceremonies could even be held to celebrate the event.

SUGGESTED READINGS USED IN THE CEREMONY

THE ODES OF SOLOMON

~ Translated by James H. Charlesworth

ODE 28

As the wings of doves over their nestlings,
And the mouths of their nestlings toward their mouths,
So also are the wings of the Spirit over my heart.
My heart continually refreshes itself and leaps for joy,
Like the babe who leaps for joy in his mother's womb.
I trusted, consequently I was at rest,
Because trustful is He in whom I trusted.
He has greatly blessed me;
And my head is with Him.
And the dagger shall not divide me from Him,
Nor the sword.
Because I am ready before destruction comes;
And I have been placed in His incorruptible arms.
And immortal life embraced me,
And kissed me.
And from that life is the Spirit that is within me.
And it cannot die because She is life.
Those who saw Me were amazed,
Because I was persecuted.
And they thought that I had been swallowed up,
Because I appeared to them as one of the lost.
But My defamation
Became My salvation.
And I became their abomination,
Because there was no jealousy in Me.
Because I continually did good to every man,
I was hated.
And they surrounded me like mad dogs,
Those who in stupidity attack their masters,
Because their mind is depraved,
And their sense is perverted.
But I was carrying water in My right hand.
And their bitterness I endured by My sweetness.

And I did not perish, because I was not their brother,
Nor was My birth like theirs.
And they sought My death but were unsuccessful,
Because I was older than their memory;
And in vain did they cast lots against Me.
And those who were after Me
Sought in vain to destroy the memorial of Him who was before them.
Because the mind of the Most High cannot be prepossessed;
And His heart is superior to all wisdom. [12]

ODE 31

And they condemned Me when I stood up,
Me who had not been condemned.
Then they divided My spoil,
Though nothing was owed them.
But I endured and held My peace and was silent,
That I might not be disturbed by them.
But I stood undisturbed like a solid rock,
Which is continuously pounded by columns of waves and endures.
And I bore their bitterness because of humility. [13]

ODE 5

Even if everything should be shaken,
I shall stand firm.
And though all things visible should perish,
I shall not be extinguished;
Because the Lord is with me,
And I with Him. [14]

EXTRA SUGGESTED READINGS

THE PRAYER OF ST FRANCIS OF ASSISI

Lord, make me an instrument of Your peace.
Where there is hatred, let me sow love;
where there is injury, pardon;
where there is doubt, faith;
where there is despair, hope;

where there is darkness, light;

where there is sadness, joy.

O, Divine Master, grant that I may not so much seek
to be consoled as to console;

to be understood as to understand;

to be loved as to love.

For it is in giving that we receive;

it is in pardoning that we are pardoned;

it is in dying that we are born again to eternal life.

THE ESSENE GOSPEL OF PEACE
~ translated by Edmond Bordeaux Szekely

I tell you in very truth, Man is the Son of the Earthly Mother, and from her did the Son of Man receive his whole body, even as the body of the newborn babe is born of the womb of his mother. I tell you truly, you are one with the Earthly Mother; she is in you, and you in her. Of her were you born, in her do you live, and to her shall you return again. Keep, therefore, her laws, for none can live long, neither be happy, but he who honors his Earthly Mother and does her laws. For your breath is her breath; your blood her blood; your bone her bone; your flesh her flesh; your bowels her bowels; your eyes and your ears are her eyes and her ears.

I tell you truly, should you fail to keep but one only of all these laws, should you harm but one only of all your body's members, you shall be utterly lost in your grievous sickness, and there shall be weeping and gnashing of teeth. I tell you, unless you follow the laws of your Mother, you can in no wise escape death.

And he who clings to the laws of his Mother, to him shall his Mother cling also. She shall heal all his plagues, and he shall never become sick. She gives him long life, and protects him from all afflictions; from fire, from water, from the bite of venomous serpents.

For your Mother bore you, keeps life within you. She has given you her body, and none but she heals you. Happy is he who loves his Mother and lies quietly in her bosom. For your Mother loves you, even when you turn away from her. And how much more shall she love you, if you turn to her again? I tell you truly, very great is her love, greater than the greatest of mountains, deeper than the deepest seas. And those who love their Mother, she never deserts them. As the hen protects her chickens, as the lioness her cubs, as the mother her newborn babe, so does the Earthly Mother protect the Son of Man from all danger and from all evils. [15]

Summer Solstice

A Ceremony to Celebrate the Summer Solstice

THE TIMING OF THE CEREMONY

The first ceremony begins before sunrise on the morning of the summer solstice. The second ceremony begins before sunset on the afternoon of the summer solstice.

SUNRISE CEREMONY

ITEMS NEEDED FOR THE SUNRISE CEREMONY

- ✿ A bowl of water. The water should be clear and clean, and ideally the bowl would be transparent, and made out of glass for example. This bowl of water should never be placed on the ground.

- ✿ An altar covered in a white cloth.

- ✿ A golden crown, which is placed on the altar.

- ✿ A pole/staff with the three ring symbol of the Absolute attached to the top of it and painted gold, so that it stands about 2.2 meters high.

- ✿ A ladder, ideally that is made of wood or looks ceremonial. It doesn't have to be a real ladder, but can be something handmade that looks like one.

- ✿ A pine tree or pine branch which can be stood up.

- ✿ Candles in non-flammable containers which can be carried and held safely. Tealight candles placed in purpose-made candle holders would be an example of this.

- ✿ The marigold flower called Calendula (however, any flower can be used which looks like the sun).

- ✿ Optional: wreaths of flowers to be worn by women.

- ✿ Optional: wreaths of leaves to be worn by men. Pick a tree which is deciduous (which means it drops its leaves in autumn and winter, and has leaves which come into their full growth at summer) if possible and if it is not too difficult.

THE SETUP OF THE SACRED CIRCLE FOR THE SUNRISE CEREMONY

To celebrate the summer solstice, it's best to create a space that aligns with the sunrise precisely on the morning of the summer solstice.

Create a passageway to walk to the circle, which aligns with the sunrise on the summer solstice and the center of the circle (like at Stonehenge).

Next to the passageway on the right side when walking into the circle, a ladder should be placed on the ground lying down. Place it so that it runs parallel to the passageway but does not block the passage in any way.

Create a place for a fire inside the circle in the middle. The fire is unlit as lighting it is part of the ceremony. Everything needed to light it should be ready beside it.

Place the altar near it but not so it is in danger of catching fire. Place the bowl of water on the altar, and next to it the gold crown.

The staff with the symbol of the Absolute is placed standing upright in the ground next to the altar.

The pine tree or branch is also placed inside the circle near the staff standing upright in some way, whether it is in a stand of some kind, dug into the ground, or in a plant pot if it is potted.

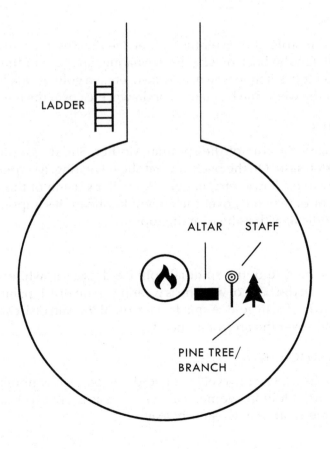

The summer solstice sunrise aligns with the avenue leading into the circle of Stonehenge. At sunrise the sun shines down the avenue into the center of the stone circle.

THE PARTICIPANTS FOR THE SUNRISE CEREMONY

THE FATHER

A man plays the role of the spiritual Father. He dresses in white and wears a golden sash. On the back of what he is wearing, an eagle or the wings of an eagle are painted, stitched, sewn, or drawn, etc., in gold. A smaller version of this eagle or the wings can be painted or drawn, etc., over the area of his heart.

THE MOTHER

A woman plays the role of the spiritual Mother. She dresses in white and wears a golden sash. On the back of what she is wearing, a serpent is painted, stitched, sewn, or drawn, etc., in gold. A smaller version of this serpent can be painted or drawn, etc., over the area of her heart. It's important that the serpent is vertical, with its head at the top.

THE SON

A man plays the role of the spiritual Son. He dresses in white and wears a golden sash. On the back of what he is wearing, a sun disk is painted, stitched, sewn, or drawn, etc., in gold. A smaller version of this sun disk can be painted or drawn, etc., over the area of his heart.

GENERAL PARTICIPANTS

Everyone wears white with a yellow or gold trim or sash, symbolizing the sun. For an optional addition, women can wear wreaths of flowers around their heads, and men can wear wreaths of leaves.

Each participant wears the marigold flower called Calendula (however, any flower can be used which looks like the sun). This can either form part of their wreath, or be pinned onto the front of their clothing, or incorporated into what they are wearing in some other way.

AN ORATOR

One of the General Participants takes the role of Orator, and will read from sacred texts during the ceremony.

INSTRUCTIONS FOR THE SUNRISE CEREMONY

STEP 1. Everyone takes their places for the ceremony before sunrise. The fire in the center of the circle should be unlit, as lighting it takes place in the ceremony. Everything needed to light it should be ready beside it. The Father stands inside the center of the circle facing the fire and the direction of the rising sun, next to the altar and the staff with the symbol of the Absolute as well as the pine tree. The General Participants line up outside the sacred circle each carrying a lit candle. The Mother and Son stand together with the Mother standing on the left side of the Son. The Mother and Son stand apart from the General Participants, and further away than them from the circle.

STEP 2. The Orator announces the start of the ceremony and then the General Participants go through the passageway in single file chanting Summer Solstice Sunrise Chant 1 or the mantra Om.

STEP 3. The General Participants take a seat inside the circle, in a semi-circle, facing the fire and the sunrise, leaving the passageway clear. They put their candles beside them if they like.

STEP 4. The Mother and Son walk together up the passageway into the sacred circle, with the Mother on the left of the Son. Both walk up to and stand next to the Father. They stand so that the Mother stands to the left of the Son, and the Father to the right of the Son, with the Son in the middle, and all of them facing the direction of the rising sun, with the fire in front of them. The General Participants should be behind them.

STEP 5. Just as the sun begins to rise (when you can see it first appear over the horizon or any terrestrial objects like trees), the Mother lights the fire in the center of the circle.

STEP 6. The Orator stands and signals that the chanting should stop. All the General Participants become quiet. The Orator says,

"Blessed is the Child of Light
Who is pure in heart,
For they shall see God...
Let thy love be as the sun
Which shines on all the creatures of the earth...
And this love shall flow as a fountain...
And as it is spent,
So shall it be replenished.
For love is eternal.
Love is stronger
Than the currents of deep waters.
Love is stronger than death." [1]

STEP 7. The Father then takes the crown from the altar and holds it up. The Mother turns to the Son. The Son turns to the Father and bows his head.

STEP 8. The Father says to the Son:

"Peace I bring to thy body, Guided by the Angel of Power;
Peace I bring to thy heart, Guided by the Angel of Love;
Peace I bring to thy mind, Guided by the Angel of Wisdom.
Through the Angels of Power, Love and Wisdom,
Thou shalt travel the Seven Paths of the Infinite Garden,
And thy body, thy heart and thy mind shall join in Oneness
In the Sacred Flight to the Heavenly Sea of Peace." [2]

STEP 9. The Father places the crown upon the Son's head, and says:

"He who overcomes—I will make him a pillar in the Temple of God and he will not go outside again." [3]

STEP 10. The Son says to the Father,

"You have crowned me with light in your compassion and you have saved me...
There is a river, which floweth to the Eternal Sea.
Beside the river stands the holy Tree of Life.
There doth my Father dwell, and my home is in him.
The Heavenly Father and I are One."

STEP 11. The General Participants raise their candles.

STEP 12. After a short time, the Orator raises their hand and the General Participants lower their candles again.

STEP 13. The Orator says:

> "Even from everlasting to everlasting,
> Hath there been love
> Between the Heavenly Father
> And his children.
> And how shall this love be severed?
> From the beginning
> Until the ending of time
> Doth the holy flame of love
> Encircle the heads
> Of the Heavenly Father
> And the Children of Light:
> How then shall this love be extinguished?...
>
> For the Heavenly Father is love: And he that dwelleth in love dwelleth in the Heavenly Father, and the Heavenly Father in him. Let him that love him be as the sun." [4]

STEP 14. With her right hand, the Mother takes the left hand of the Son and holds it. The Son then takes the left hand of the Father with his right hand, and holds it. The three stand facing the rising sun.

STEP 15. The Orator says,

> "FOR YOUR HEAVENLY FATHER IS LOVE.
> FOR YOUR EARTHLY MOTHER IS LOVE.
> FOR THE SON OF MAN IS LOVE.
>
> It is by love, that the Heavenly Father and the Earthly Mother and the Son of Man become one. For the spirit of the Son of Man was created from the spirit of the Heavenly Father, and his body from the body of the Earthly Mother...
>
> Behold, the Tree of Life... mystery of mysteries, growing everlasting branches for eternal planting, to sink their roots into the stream of life from an eternal source.
>
> See... the branches of the Tree of Life reaching toward the kingdom of the Heavenly Father. And see the roots of the Tree of Life

descending into the bosom of the Earthly Mother. And the Son of Man is raised to an eternal height and walks in the wonders of the plain; for only the Son of Man carries in his body the roots of the Tree of Life; the same roots that suckle from the bosom of the Earthly Mother; and only the Son of Man carries in his spirit the branches of the Tree of Life; the same branches that reach to the sky, even so to the kingdom of the Heavenly Father." [5]

STEP 16. The Orator sits down.

STEP 17. The Father takes the staff with the symbol of the Absolute out of the ground.

STEP 18. The Father, Mother, and Son release their hands.

STEP 19. The Father hands the staff to the Son.

STEP 20. The Son holds the symbol of the Absolute up high for about thirty seconds.

STEP 21. The General Participants begin singing Summer Solstice Sunrise Chant 2 or the mantra Om in a high tone in celebration for some time. If possible, the idea is to emulate a heavenly choir. The Son lowers the staff so it is supported on the ground (so their arms don't get tired).

STEP 22. At this point, the Orator can stand, signal that the General Participants should stop chanting, and then read some excerpts from sacred texts if wished; otherwise the Orator remains seated and the chant continues.

STEP 23. The Mother, Son, and Father walk side-by-side, together out of the circle with the Son holding the symbol of the Absolute up high, toward the rising sun.

STEP 24. The General Participants stand and follow behind. The ceremony has then ended.

People can then gather again around the fire to do more readings, to chant mantras, sings songs, etc., if they wish.

* Excerpts in this ceremony are from The Essene Gospel of Peace, translated by Edmond Bordeaux Szekely, except for the reading at step 9, which is from the book of Revelation, chapter 3:12, and the first line of step 10, which is based on The Odes of Solomon.

MEANING OF THE SUNRISE CEREMONY

This ceremony celebrates the stage of ascension in the spiritual work, which is a return to the Father of one's Being.

The spring equinox symbolizes the Son's return to the Mother to become a serpent of light; the summer solstice symbolizes the return to the Father to become a feathered serpent.

The Mother and Son begin by standing together to symbolize how they have already become one at the spring equinox. They walk together to the Father to symbolize ascension.

This ceremony celebrates the Son becoming the feathered serpent, where the three primary forces of creation—Father, Mother, and Son—become one. This is represented in the ceremony by the Father, Mother, and Son joining hands, and by the Father handing the Son the three ring symbol of the Absolute, which is a symbol of the three unified forces.

The symbol of the Absolute can also be represented as a crown; the placement of the crown on the Son's head symbolizes the unity of the source and the person becoming one with their unified Being.

The pine tree represents the Father because it is evergreen and therefore represents the eternal.

The Calendula flower is used because of its significance to the summer solstice. The Druids believed this flower had special properties at the time of the summer solstice. It has also been used in sacred rituals by the Romans, Aztecs, and Hindus. The head of the flower follows the direction of the sun, and opens its petals at sunrise, and closes them at sunset. It also bears a resemblance to the sun and has been called "summer's bride." As the summer solstice symbolizes the union of masculine and feminine parts of someone's higher Being, of heaven and earth, this flower is relevant in that it symbolizes the joining of these forces, as the flower sprouts from the earth and yet contains the energy of the sun.

> "The Golden Flower is the light. What colour is the light? One uses the Golden Flower as a symbol. It is the true energy of the transcendent great One." [6]
>
> ~ THE SECRET OF THE GOLDEN FLOWER, TRANSLATED BY RICHARD WILHELM

SUGGESTED READINGS FOR THE SUNRISE CEREMONY

THE ODES OF SOLOMON

~ translated by James H. Charlesworth

The following are some suggested excerpts from this text to choose from. I recommend choosing the last two paragraphs and any one or two others to read.

> Like a wreathed-crown on my head is the Lord,
> And never shall I be without Him.
> The wreathed-crown of truth is plaited for me,
> Causing Your branches to blossom within me,
> For it is not like a parched crown
> That fails to blossom.
> But You have lived upon my head,
> And You have blossomed upon me.
> Your fruits are full, even complete;
> They are full of Your salvation.

> I am putting on the love of the Lord.
> And His members are with Him,
> And I am dependent on them; and He loves me.
> For I should not have known how to love the Lord,
> If He had not loved me continuously.
> Who is able to distinguish love?
> Surely, it is only the one who is loved.
> I love the Beloved and I myself love Him;
> And where His rest is, there am I also.
> And I shall be no rejected stranger,
> Because no jealousy is with the Lord Most High and Merciful.
> I have been united to Him, because the lover has found the Beloved;
> Because I love Him that is the Son, I shall become a son.
> Indeed he who is joined to Him who is immortal,
> Truly, he shall become immortal.
> And he who delights in the Life
> Will become living.
> This is the Spirit of the Lord, which is not false,
> Which teaches the sons of men to know His ways.
> Be wise, and understanding, and vigilant.

Open your ears,
Then I shall speak to you.
Give me yourself,
So that I may also give you Myself;
The word of the Lord and His desires,
The holy thought which He has thought concerning His Messiah.
For in the will of the Lord is your life,
And His purpose is eternal life,
And your perfection is incorruptible.
Be enriched in God the Father;
And receive the purpose of the Most High.
Be strong and saved by His grace.
For I announce peace to you, His holy ones,
So that none of those who hear will fall in the war.
And also that those who have known Him may not perish,
And so that those who receive Him may not be ashamed.
An everlasting wreathed-crown is Truth;
Blessed are they who set it on their head.
It is a precious stone,
For the wars were on account of the wreathed-crown.
But Righteousness has taken it;
And She has given it to you.
Put on the wreathed-crown in the true covenant of the Lord,
And all those who have conquered will be inscribed in His book.
For their book is the justification which is for you,
And She sees you before Her and wills that you will be saved.

From the beginning until the end
I received His knowledge.
And I was established upon the rock of truth,
Where He set me.
And speaking waters touched my lips
From the spring of the Lord generously.
And so I drank and became intoxicated,
From the living water that does not die.
And my intoxication was not with ignorance;
But I abandoned vanity;
And turned toward the Most High, my God,
And was enriched by His favors.
And I abandoned the folly cast upon the earth,
And stripped it off and cast it from me.

And the Lord renewed me with His garment,
And possessed me by His light.
And from above He gave me immortal rest;
And I became like the land which blossoms and rejoices in its fruits.
And the Lord is like the sun
Upon the face of the land.
My eyes were enlightened,
And my face received the dew;
And my breath was refreshed
By the pleasant fragrance of the Lord.
And He took me to His Paradise,
Wherein is the wealth of the Lord's pleasure.
I contemplated blooming and fruit-bearing trees,
And self-grown was their wreathed-crown.
Their branches were flourishing
And their fruits were shining;
Their roots were from an immortal land.
And a river of gladness was irrigating them,
And the region around them in the land of eternal life.
Then I adored the Lord,
Because of His magnificence.

As the sun is the joy to them who seek its daybreak,
So my joy is the Lord;
Because He is my sun,
And His rays have restored me.
And His light has dismissed all darkness from my face.
Eyes I have possessed in Him;
And I have seen His holy day.
Ears I have acquired;
And I have heard His truth.
The thought of knowledge I have acquired;
And I have lived fully through Him.
I abandoned the way of error;
And I went towards Him and received salvation from Him generously.
And according to His generosity He gave to me;
And according to His majestic beauty He made me.
I put on incorruption through His name;
And I stripped off corruption by His grace.
Death has been destroyed before my face;
And Sheol has been vanquished by my word.

Since eternal life has arisen in the Lord's land,
And become known to His faithful ones,
And been given without limit to all that trust in Him.

The Lord's gentle shower overshadowed me with serenity,
And it caused a cloud of peace to remain over my head,
That it might guard me at all times.
And it became salvation for me.
Everyone was disturbed and afraid,
And there flowed from them smoke and judgement.
But I was tranquil in the Lord's legion;
More than a shade was He to me, and more than foundation.
And I was carried like a babe by its mother;
And He gave me milk, the dew of the Lord.
And I grew strong in His favor.
And I rested in His perfection.
And I extended my hands in the ascent of my soul.
And I directed myself near the Most High.
And I was saved near Him.

I rested on the Spirit of the Lord.
And She raised me up to heaven.
And She caused me to stand on my feet in the Lord's high place,
Before His perfection and His glory,
Where I continued praising Him by the composition of His odes.
The Spirit brought Me forth before the Lord's face.
And because I was the Son of Man,
I was named the Light, the Son of God,
Because I was the most praised among the praised,
And the greatest among the great ones.
For according to the greatness of the Most High, so She made Me;
And according to His newness He renewed Me.
And He anointed Me with His perfection;
And I became one of those who are near Him.
And My mouth was opened like a cloud of dew,
And My heart gushed forth like a gusher of righteousness.
And My approach was in peace,
And I was established in the spirit of providence. [7]

THE ESSENE GOSPEL OF PEACE

~ translated by Edmond Bordeaux Szekely

At last, shall the Son of Man seek peace with the kingdom of his Heavenly Father; for truly, the Son of Man is only born of his father by seed and of his mother by the body, that he may find his true inheritance and know at last that he is the Son of the King.

The Heavenly Father is the One Law, who fashioned the stars, the sun, the light and the darkness, and the Holy Law within our souls. Everywhere is he, and there is nowhere he is not. All in our understanding, and all we know not, all is governed by the Law. The falling of leaves, the flow of rivers, the music of insects at night, all these are ruled by the Law.

In our Heavenly Father's realm there are many mansions, and many are the hidden things you cannot know of yet. I tell you truly, the kingdom of our Heavenly Father is vast, so vast that no man can know its limits, for there are none. Yet the whole of his kingdom may be found in the smallest drop of dew on a wild flower, or in the scent of newly-cut grass in the fields under the summer sun. Truly, there are no words to describe the kingdom of the Heavenly Father.

Glorious, indeed, is the inheritance of the Son of Man, for to him only is it given to enter the Stream of Life which leads him to the kingdom of his Heavenly Father. But first he must seek and find peace with his body, with his thoughts, with his feelings, with the Sons of Men, with holy knowledge, and with the kingdom of the Earthly Mother. For I tell you truly, this is the vessel which will carry the Son of Man on the Stream of Life to his Heavenly Father. He must have peace that is sevenfold before he can know the one peace which surpasses understanding, even that of his Heavenly Father.

The Heavenly Father planted the holy Tree of Life,
Which standeth forever in the midst of the Eternal Sea
High in its branches sings a bird,
And only those who have journeyed there,
And have heard the mysterious song of the bird,
Only those shall see the Heavenly Father.
They shall ask of him his name,
And he shall answer, I am that I am,
Being ever the same as the Eternal I am.
O thou Heavenly Father!...
Whither shall I go from thy spirit?

Or whither shall I flee from thy presence?
If I ascend up into heaven, thou art there;
If I make my bed in hell, behold, thou art there.
If I take the wings of the morning,
And dwell in the uttermost parts of the sea,
Even there shall thy hand lead me,
And thy right hand shall hold me.
If I say, "Surely the darkness shall cover me,"
Even the night shall be light about me;
Yea, the darkness hideth not from thee
But the night shineth as the day:
The darkness and the light are both alike to thee,
For thou hast possessed my reins. [8]

EXTRA SUGGESTED READING FOR THE SUNRISE CEREMONY

Although it's too long to reproduce here, another suggested reading relevant to this time of year is the Hymn of the Pearl, which is a poem that appears in the ancient text the Acts of Thomas. There are many translations of it that are freely available on the internet.

SUNSET CEREMONY

ITEMS NEEDED FOR THE SUNSET CEREMONY

- ☸ A bowl of water on an altar covered in a white cloth (this bowl of water should never be placed on the ground).

- ☸ A white robe with the symbol of a feathered serpent either painted, drawn, or sewn onto it.

- ☸ A high chair which is covered completely in white cloth. The cloth on the back of the chair is painted with the three ring symbol of the Absolute in gold.

- ☸ Candles in non-flammable containers which can be carried and held safely. Tealight candles placed in purpose-made candle holders would be an example of this.

- ☸ The marigold flower called Calendula (however, any flower can be used which looks like the sun).

- ☸ Optional: wreaths of flowers to be worn by women.

- ☸ Optional: wreaths of leaves to be worn by men.

- ☸ Optional: Tibetan singing bowl or bowls, or other equivalent kind of instrument.

THE SETUP OF THE SACRED CIRCLE FOR THE SUNSET CEREMONY

The sacred circle for the sunset ceremony should have an entrance that aligns to sunset on the summer solstice, but on the opposite side of the circle from the sunset, so that participants enter the circle facing the setting sun.

As in the sunrise ceremony, a fire should be in the middle; however, this time the fire is already lit before the ceremony begins.

An altar is placed nearby covered in white cloth (but not so that it is in danger of catching fire), with the same bowl of water on it.

If instruments are used, they are also placed in the circle ready.

In the distance, around eighty to fifty meters away if possible, the chair with the symbol of the Absolute on it is placed so that aligns with the sunset when looking toward it from inside the circle. It is positioned so that someone sitting on it faces the sunset, and the symbol of the Absolute on the back of it faces the sacred circle.

SUNSET

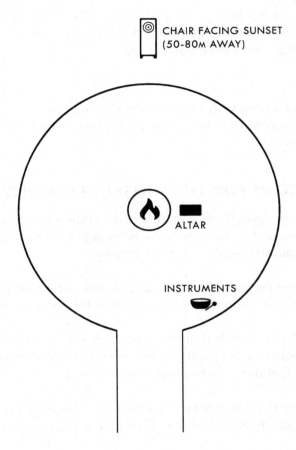

CHAIR FACING SUNSET
(50-80M AWAY)

ALTAR

INSTRUMENTS

THE PARTICIPANTS FOR THE SUNSET CEREMONY

GENERAL PARTICIPANTS

The participants for the sunset ceremony wear the same clothing and optional wreaths as they did for the sunrise ceremony.

Each participant carries a candle that can be held safely and the Calendula flower (or other flower representing the sun).

FEATHERED SERPENT

A man wears a white robe with a symbol of the feathered serpent on the back of it. The symbol should incorporate a serpent, wings, and a sun disk. The serpent should be ascending, rather than descending.

MUSICIANS

As an option, a man and woman from the General Participants (preferably a couple) can each play Tibetan singing bowls or equivalent instruments at some point during the ceremony. They represent the united masculine and feminine parts of the being, the forces of yang and yin. These instruments could be placed inside the sacred circle before the ceremony begins, in a place where they can easily be picked up.

AN ORATOR

Someone from amongst the General Participants reads from sacred texts during the ceremony. They should be a different person than those who play the instruments.

INSTRUCTIONS FOR THE SUNSET CEREMONY

STEP 1. Someone lights the fire in the center of the sacred circle some time before it begins, and makes sure there is enough wood in the fire to keep it going throughout the duration of the ceremony.

STEP 2. Everyone gathers at the sacred circle just before sunset. The General Participants line up in the order they plan to enter the circle in.

STEP 3. The Orator signals that the ceremony will begin, and the General Participants begin chanting Summer Solstice Sunset Ceremony Chant 1 or the mantra Om so that they create a continuous sound.

STEP 4. The Feathered Serpent walks into the circle on their own, and stands near the altar, facing the setting sun. They do not carry anything with them.

STEP 5. The General Participants walk in single file into the circle. As they enter, one by one, they place their candles before the altar.

STEP 6. As each one does, they then take their place standing in a semi-circle facing the sunset with the fire at the center of the circle in front of them.

STEP 7. As an optional step, once everyone is in position, the Musicians begin playing their instruments—however best to create a harmonious sound with the chant.

STEP 8. As the sun begins to set below the horizon, or behind terrestrial objects like trees, the Feathered Serpent slowly begins to walk out of the circle in the direction of the setting sun, toward the chair which has been prepared and placed in the distance. They do not walk out the passageway, but through the edge of the circle in the most direct way from the fire to the chair.

STEP 9. The Feathered Serpent continues walking slowly all the way to the chair, and then sits down on the chair. They sit so that, as much as possible, they can't be seen by the General Participants, while still remaining comfortable. They remain seated this way for the rest of the ceremony.

STEP 10. The Orator then makes a signal for the mantra and instruments to stop, and reads aloud from some texts relevant to the occasion (we suggest the excerpts from the Upanishads and Vedas included at the end of this chapter).

STEP 11. After the readings, the Orator then signals for the General Participants to start singing a chant again. The General Participants sing Summer Solstice Sunset Ceremony Chant 2 or the mantra Om (without instruments).

STEP 12. As the chant continues, one by one, from right (when facing the sun) to left, each person steps forward and places their flower in the bowl of water.

STEP 13. Everyone continues singing the mantra until a short time after the sun sets, gradually becoming quieter until there is silence.

STEP 14. One by one, each person leaves the circle. Once the last person has left the circle, the ceremony has ended.

Following this there can be a more relaxed celebration. You could sing songs or chant mantras around the fire, improvising as you feel, making sure to leave before midnight.

THE MEANING OF THE SUNSET CEREMONY

This ceremony celebrates the return to the source of creation. This was symbolized at sunset on the summer solstice at the Great Pyramids of Egypt.

The symbol of the feathered serpent represents the divine androgynous Being—in which the parts of someone's higher Being called Father, Mother, and Son, have become one. The feathers represent the Father, the serpent the Mother, and the sun disk the Son. We can only return to the source of creation as we left, which is as one.

This return to the unknowable, unmanifest source of creation is represented by the setting of the summer solstice sun. It is symbolized in the ceremony by the feathered serpent walking toward the sun, and disappearing behind the symbol of the Absolute, the source of creation, painted on the back of the chair.

The feathered serpent leaving the circle represents the fully awakened person leaving the circle of matter, and of humanity. They carry nothing with them because they now contain everything within themselves.

The fire is already lit because the Being is already ascended and whole.

The candles the General Participants place before the fire represent the small part of the Being we each have within, which is of the same substance as the bigger fire, and of the fire of the sun.

The flowers each person places within the bowl of water, represent the return to source. The flower symbolizes the earth (as the flower grows from the earth), united with the heavens and the sun (as the flower itself looks like the sun). It represents the unified Being and placing it in water represents it returning to the source of creation.

SUGGESTED READINGS FOR THE SUNSET CEREMONY

THE NARAYANA SUKTAM FROM THE YAJUR VEDA

~ translated by Swami Krishnananda

This universe is the Eternal Being (Narayana), the imperishable, the supreme, the goal, the omnipresent and omniscient, the resplendent, the source of delight for the whole universe.

This universe is the Supreme Being alone; hence, it subsists on That, the Eternal which transcends it in every way—the Omnipresent Absolute which destroys all sins.

The protector of the universe, the Lord of all souls, the perpetual, the auspicious, the indestructible, the Goal of all creation, the Supreme object worthy of being known, the Soul of all beings, the Refuge unfailing.

The Lord Narayana is the Supreme Absolute; Narayana is the Supreme Reality; Narayana is the Supreme Light; Narayana is the Supreme Self; Narayana is the Supreme Meditator; Narayana is the Supreme Meditation.

Whatever all this universe is, seen or heard of—pervading all this, from inside and outside alike, stands supreme the Eternal Divine Being.

He is the Limitless, Imperishable, Omniscient, residing in the ocean of the heart, the Cause of the happiness of the universe, the Supreme End of all striving, manifesting Himself in the ether of the heart which is comparable to an inverted bud of the lotus flower.

There in the heart effulges the Great Abode of the universe, as if adorned with garlands of flames.

Surrounded on all sides by nerve-currents, the lotus-bud of the heart is suspended in an inverted position. In it is a subtle space, and therein is to be found the Substratum of all things.

In that space within the heart resides the great flame of fire, undecaying, all-knowing, with tongues spread out in all directions, with faces turned everywhere, consuming food presented before it, and assimilating it unto itself.

His rays, spreading all round, sideways as well as above and below, warm up the whole body from head to foot. In the centre of That Flame abides the Tongue of Fire as the topmost among all subtle things.

Brilliant like a streak of lightning set in the midst of the blue rain-bearing clouds, slender like the awn of a paddy grain, yellow like gold in colour, in subtlety comparable to the minute atom, this Tongue of Fire glows splendid.

In the middle of that Flame, the Supreme Self dwells. This Self is Brahma (the Creator), Siva (the Destroyer), Hari (the Protector), Indra (the Ruler), the Imperishable, the Absolute, the Autonomous Being.

We bow again and again to the Omni-formed Being, the Truth, the Law, the Supreme Absolute, the Purusha of blue-decked yellow hue, the Centralised-force Power, the All-seeing One.

We commune ourselves with Narayana, and meditate on Vaasudeva; May that Vishnu direct us to the Great Goal. [9]

THE ISHA UPANISHAD

~ translated by Eknath Easwaran

The Lord is enshrined in the hearts of all.
The Lord is the supreme Reality.
Rejoice in him through renunciation.
Covet nothing. All belongs to the Lord.
Thus working may you live a hundred years.
Thus alone will you work in real freedom.
Those who deny the Self are born again
Blind to the Self, enveloped in darkness,
Utterly devoid of love for the Lord.
The Self is one. Ever still, the Self is
Swifter than thought, swifter than the senses.
Though motionless, he outruns all pursuit.
Without the Self, never could life exist.

The Self seems to move, but is ever still.
He seems far away, but is ever near.
He is within all, and he transcends all.
Those who see all creatures in themselves
And themselves in all creatures know no fear.
Those who see all creatures in themselves
And themselves in all creatures know no grief.
How can the multiplicity of life
Delude the one who sees its unity?
The Self is everywhere. Bright is the Self,
Indivisible, untouched by sin, wise,
Immanent and transcendent. He it is
Who holds the cosmos together.
In dark night live those for whom
The world without alone is real; in night
Darker still, for whom the world within
Alone is real. The first leads to a life
Of action, the second to a life of meditation.
But those who combine action with meditation
Cross the sea of death through action
And enter into immortality
Through the practice of meditation.
So have we heard from the wise.
In dark night live those for whom the Lord
Is transcendent only; in night darker still,
For whom he is immanent only.
But those for whom he is transcendent
And immanent cross the sea of death
With the immanent and enter into
Immortality with the transcendent.
So have we heard from the wise.
The face of truth is hidden by your orb
Of gold, O sun. May you remove your orb
So that I, who adore the true, may see
The Glory of truth. O nourishing sun,
Solitary traveller, controller,
Source of life for all creatures, spread you light
And subdue your dazzling splendour
So that I may see your blessed Self.
Even that very Self am I!
May my life merge in the Immortal

When my body is reduced to ashes.
O mind, meditate on the eternal Brahman.
Remember the deeds of the past.
Remember, O mind, remember.
O god of fire, lead us by the good path
To eternal joy. You know all our deeds.
Deliver us from evil, we who bow
And pray again and again. [10]

SHVESTASHVATARA UPANISHAD

~ translated by Eknath Easwaran

What is the cause of the cosmos? Is it Brahman?
From where do we come? By what live?
Where shall we find peace at last?
What power governs the duality
Of pleasure and pain by which we are driven?
Time, nature, necessity, accident,
Elements, energy, intelligence—
None of these can be the First Cause.
They are effects, whose only purpose is
To help the self rise above pleasure and pain.
In the depths of meditation, sages
Saw within themselves the Lord of Love,
Who dwells in the heart of every creature.
Deep in the hearts of all he dwells, hidden
Behind the gunas of law, energy,
And inertia. He is One. He it is
Who rules over time, space, and causality.
The world is the wheel of God, turning round
And round with all living creatures upon its rim.
The world is the river of God,
Flowing from him and flowing back to him.

On this ever-revolving wheel of life
The individual self goes round and round
Through life after life, believing itself
To be a separate creature, until
It sees its identity with the Lord of Love
And attains immortality in the indivisible whole.
He is the eternal reality, sing

The scriptures, and the ground of existence.
Those who perceive him in every creature
Merge in him and are released from the wheel
Of birth and death.
The Lord of Love holds in his hand the world,
Composed of the changing and the changeless,
The manifest and the unmanifest.
The separate self, not yet aware of the Lord,
Goes after pleasure, only to become
Bound more and more. When it sees the Lord,
There comes an end to its bondage.
Conscious spirit and unconscious matter
Both have existed since the dawn of time,
With maya appearing to connect them,
Misrepresenting joy as outside us.
When all these three are seen as one, the Self
Reveals his universal form and serves
As an instrument of the divine will. [11]

MAITRI UPANISHAD

~ translated by E. B. Cowell

The Spirit supreme is immeasurable, inapprehensible, beyond conception, never-born, beyond reasoning, beyond thought. His vastness is the
vastness of space.

At the end of the worlds, all things sleep: He alone is awake in Eternity.
Then from his infinite space new worlds arise and awake, a universe
which is a vastness of thought. In the consciousness of Brahman the
universe is, and unto him it returns. [12]

KRISHNA IN THE BHAGAVAD GITA

~ translated by Shri Purohit Swami

The worlds, within the whole realm of creation, come and go; but, O
Arjuna, whoso Comes to Me, for him there is no rebirth.

Those who understand the cosmic day and cosmic night know that
one day of creation is a thousand cycles, and that the night is of
equal length.

At the dawning of that day all objects in manifestation stream forth from the Unmanifest, and when evening falls they are dissolved into It again.

The same multitude of beings, which have lived on earth so often, all are dissolved as the night of the universe approaches, to issue forth anew when morning breaks. Thus is it ordained.

In truth, therefore, there is the Eternal Unmanifest, which is beyond and above the Unmanifest Spirit of Creation, which is never destroyed when all these beings perish.

The wise say that the Unmanifest and Indestructible is the highest goal of all; when once That is reached, there is no return. That is My Blessed Home.

O Arjuna! That Highest God, in Whom all beings abide, and Who pervades the entire universe, is reached only by wholehearted devotion.

Now I will tell thee, O Arjuna, of the times at which, if the mystics go forth, they do not return, and at which they go forth only to return.

If knowing the Supreme Spirit the sage goes forth with fire and light, in the daytime, in the fortnight of the waxing moon and in the six months before the Northern summer solstice, he will attain the Supreme.

But if he departs in gloom, at night, during the fortnight of the waning moon and in the six months before the Southern solstice, then he reaches but lunar light and he will be born again.

These bright and dark paths out of the world have always existed. Whoso takes the former, returns not; he who chooses the latter, returns. [13]

SUMMER SOLSTICE MIDDAY

The time of summer solstice corresponds to midday in the daily cycle of the sun. The midday sun on the summer solstice is when the light is at its absolute maximum. In many parts of the world, the strength of the sun is so great at this time that it is too difficult to do anything outside. For those in a milder climate, you could do an optional reflection, reading, or practice at midday, making sure however that you are protected from the sun by being properly shaded.

CHAPTER SEVENTEEN

Conclusion

I HOPE THIS BOOK PROVIDES A CATALYST that contributes to the re-kindling of the celebration of the path of the spiritual sun and the spiritual knowledge contained within it. This knowledge is helpful to anyone wishing to participate in the process of enlightenment that ancient people once read in creation.

In the great cycle of the sun and the earth are reflected the principles that are the very keys to enlightenment. The west and the autumn equinox, which the Maya associated with the color black, is symbolic of inner death. The south and winter solstice, associated with the color yellow, is symbolic of inner birth and creation. The east and spring equinox, associated with red, is symbolic of self-sacrifice. And the north and summer solstice, associated with the color white, is symbolic of completion in the process of inner transformation, as the color of the sun and its light beyond the atmosphere of the earth.

"The red wild bees are in the east. A large red blossom is their cup. The red Plumeria is their flower.

The white wild bees are in the north. The white pachca is their flower. A large white blossom is their cup.

The black wild bees are in the west. The black laurel flower is their flower. A large black blossom is their cup.

The yellow wild bees are in the south. A large yellow blossom is their cup ...is their flower." [1]

~ THE BOOK OF CHILAM BALAM OF CHUMAYEL, TRANSLATED BY RALPH L. ROYS

The three principles of inner death, birth, and self-sacrifice signify the basis of the practice that leads someone along the path to enlightenment, the path of the spiritual sun, to reach its completion, to the principle of ascension—thereby returning to their Being and the divine source, symbolized as the region of the stars and sun in the north.

This kind of esoteric knowledge today may be largely derided as fantasy by some, but it wasn't in the past—it was greatly valued. Humanity's rich heritage of spiritual, mythological, and religious texts, art, and archeology are a testimony to the central role esoteric knowledge played in the lives of those for whom the solstices and equinoxes and the spiritual principles reflected in them held significant meaning.

Although the key components of this ancient knowledge can be known, this is a different humanity and a different world today. It is a time when the material dominates the spiritual, where humanity has lost the understanding of its universal, cosmic principles, and where the majority of people think a lot, but don't perceive spiritual truths.

Until now, the ancient knowledge of the spiritual sun has been all but lost to humanity. Yet I hope this book will contribute to its lasting re-emergence; moreover, that the wisdom of the sun will once again serve as a guiding light for all those seeking the return to their higher Being.

I hope that in time, people in many cities and towns throughout the world will come together to celebrate the solstices and equinoxes, and that sites will be created where four times a year people go to celebrate this ancient and wondrous festival, keeping alive the awareness of the spiritual sun and the incredible knowledge it conveys.

··· References ···

Note: Translations from the Pyramid Texts have been modified to replace references to "Unas" (the name of the pharaoh whose tomb the texts were written upon, and who was believed to be going through events Osiris goes through), with the name "Osiris" for readability.

PREFACE

1. *Gurdjieff's Search for Esoteric Knowledge*, Learning Institute for Growth, Healing and Transformation, p. 5. Available from: <http://gurdjiefffourthway.org/pdf/search.pdf>.

CHAPTER ONE

1. Lionel Giles (Trans.), L. Cranmer-Byng and Dr. S. A. Kapadia (Eds.), *The Sayings of Lao-Tzŭ*, E. P. Dutton and Company, Inc., New York, 1905, p. 21.
2. Manly P. Hall, The Secret Teachings of All Ages, H.S. Crocker Company, San Francisco, 1928, p. 85.
3. G. R. S. Mead (Trans.), *Pistis Sophia*, J. M. Watkins, London, 1921, pp. 155-156.
4. Manly P. Hall, op. cit., p. 51.
5. Brian Browne Walker (Trans.), *Hua Hu Ching: The Unknown Teachings of Lao Tzu*, HarperCollins, San Francisco, 1995, p. 43.
6. Manly P. Hall, op. cit., p. 39.
7. Lionel Giles (Trans.), op. cit., p. 19.
8. Manly P. Hall, op. cit., p. 40.
9. Ibid., p. 51.
10. E. A. Wallis Budge (Trans.), *The Book of the Dead: The Papyrus of Ani*, British Museum, 1895, p. liii.

11. Swami Swarupananda (Trans.), *Srimad-Bhagavad-Gita*, Advaita Ashrama, Mayavati, Almora, 1909, p. 330.

12. Thomas O. Lambdin (Trans.), "The Gospel of Thomas" in James M. Robinson (Ed.), *The Nag Hammadi Library in English*, HarperCollins, San Francisco, 1990, p. 135. Copyright © 1978, 1988 by E. J. Brill, Leiden, The Netherlands. Used by permission.

13. Scripture taken from the Holy Bible, NEW INTERNATIONAL VERSION®, NIV® Copyright © 1973, 1978, 1984, 2011 by Biblica, Inc.® Used by permission. All rights reserved worldwide.

14. Wesley W. Isenberg (Trans.), "The Gospel of Philip" in James M. Robinson (Ed.), *The Nag Hammadi Library in English*, op. cit., p. 144.

15. F. Max Müller (Trans.), *Vedic Hymns: Part 1, Hymns to the Maruts, Rudra, Vâyu, and Vâta*, Oxford University Press, Clarendon, 1891, p. 1.

16. Malcolm L. Peel and Jan Zandee (Trans.), "The Teachings of Silvanus" in James M. Robinson (Ed.), *The Nag Hammadi Library in English*, op. cit., p. 387.

17. Shri Purohit Swami (Trans.), *The Bhagavad Gita*.

18. Ralph T. H. Griffith (Trans.), *The Hymns of the Rigveda*, 1896.

19. American Institute of Vedic Studies, *The Sacred Fire and Agni*, 2012. Available from: <https://vedanet.com/2012/06/13/the-sacred-fire-and-agni/>.

20. Ralph T. H. Griffith (Trans.), op. cit.

21. American Institute of Vedic Studies, op. cit.

22. L. H. Mills (Trans.), *The Zend Avesta, Part III, Sacred Books of the East, Vol. 31*, Oxford University Press, 1887, pp. 255, 346.

23. Manly P. Hall, op. cit., p. 39.

24. Loc. cit.

25. Thomas O. Lambdin (Trans.), op. cit., p. 135.

26. E. A. Wallis Budge (Trans.), op. cit., p. 317.

27. Shri Purohit Swami (Trans.), op. cit.

28. Loc. cit.

29. Swami Krishnananda (Trans.), "Narayana Sukta" in *Daily Invocations*, The Divine Life Society, Rishikesh, pp. 67-70.

30. From The Upanishads, translated by Eknath Easwaran, founder of the Blue Mountain Center of Meditation, copyright 1987, 2007; reprinted by permission of Nilgiri Press, P. O. Box 256, Tomales, Ca 94971, www.easwaran.org. p. 188.

31. Shri Purohit Swami (Trans.), op. cit.

32. Eknath Easwaran (Trans.), op. cit., pp. 226-227.

33. John P. Lundy, *Monumental Christianity*, J W Bouton, New York, 1876, p. 165.

34. Martin Brennan, *The Stars and the Stones: Ancient Art and Astronomy in Ireland*, Thames & Hudson Ltd, 1986.

35. Charles Ross, "Biography." Available from: <http://charlesrossstudio.com/biography/>.

36. Thomas Smith (Trans.), Alexander Roberts, James Donaldson, and A. Cleveland Coxe (Eds.), *Ante-Nicene Fathers*, Vol. 8, Christian Literature Publishing Co., Buffalo, NY, 1886.

37. Ibid.

38. Ibid.

39. Allen J. Christenson (Trans.), *Popol Vuh: The Sacred Book of the Maya*, O Books, Winchester, UK, 2003, p. 220.

40. Ibid., pp. 238, 250.
41. M. R. James (Trans.), *The Apocryphal New Testament*, Clarendon Press, Oxford, 1924.
42. Thomas Smith (Trans.), op. cit.
43. Thor Heyerdahl, "The Bearded Gods Speak" in Geoffrey Ashe, *The Quest for America*, Praeger, New York, 1971.
44. Edmond Bordeaux Szekely (Trans.), *The Essene Gospel of Peace: Book One*, International Biogenic Society, USA, 1981, p. 13.

CHAPTER TWO

1. Stephen Emmel (Trans.), "The Dialogue of the Savior" in James M. Robinson (Ed.), *The Nag Hammadi Library in English*, op. cit., p. 250.
2. Scripture quotation taken from the New American Standard Bible® (NASB). Copyright © 1960, 1962, 1963, 1968, 1971, 1972, 1973, 1975, 1977, 1995 by The Lockman Foundation. Used by permission. www.Lockman.org
3. *Holy Bible*, NEW INTERNATIONAL VERSION®, NIV®, op. cit.
4. Hippolytus of Rome, *Refutation of All Heresies*, 5.8.39.
5. Eknath Easwaran (Trans.), op. cit., p. 227.
6. *Holy Bible*, NEW INTERNATIONAL VERSION®, NIV®, op. cit.
7. Karen Bassie, "Maya Creator Gods," Mesoweb, 2002, p. 8. Available from: <www.mesoweb.com/features/bassie/CreatorGods/CreatorGods.pdf>. Cites: Bassie-Sweet, Karen, 1999 Maya Corn Deities and the Male/Female Principal in Maya Mythology, paper presented at the Tercera Mesa Redonda de Palenque. Bassie-Sweet, Karen, 2001 Corn Deities and the Complementary Male/Female Principle, (September 2000 revision of a paper presented at the Tercera Mesa Redonda de Palenque.) Mesoweb.com <http://www.mesoweb.com/features/bassie/corn/index.html>. Edmonson, Munro, 1971 The Book of Counsel: the Popol Vuh of the Quiché Maya of Guatemala, New Orleans: Middle American Research Institute. Thompson, J. Eric S, 1970 Maya History and Religion. Norman: University of Oklahoma Press. Allen J. Christenson, personal communication 2001.
8. R. H. Charles (Trans.), *The Book of Enoch*, Society for Promoting Christian Knowledge, London, 1917, p. 44.
9. Ralph L. Roys (Trans.), *The Book of Chilam Balam of Chumayel*, Carnegie Institution, Washington D.C., 1933, p. 65.
10. Allen Mandelbaum (Trans.), *The Divine Comedy of Dante Alighieri: Inferno*, University of California Press, Berkeley and Los Angeles, 1980.
11. M. R. James (Trans.), "The Acts of Thomas," *The Apocryphal New Testament*, op. cit.
12. Samuel A. B. Mercer (Trans.), *The Pyramid Texts*, Longmans, Green & Co., New York, 1952, p. 302.
13. Douglas Wile (Trans.), *True Transmission of the Golden Elixir*.
14. Payam Nabaraz, "Mithras and Mithraism," *White Dragon*, 1999. Available from: <http://whitedragon.org.uk/articles/mithras.htm>.
15. M. R. James (Trans.), "The Acts of Thomas," op. cit.
16. Ibid.
17. Edmond Bordeaux Szekely (Trans.), *The Essene Gospel of Peace: Book Four*, International Biogenic Society, USA, 1981, p. 16.

18. John D. Turner (Trans.), "The Book of Thomas the Contender" in James M. Robinson (Ed.), *The Nag Hammadi Library in English*, op. cit., p. 206.
19. Donald A. Mackenzie, *Teutonic Myth and Legend*, Gresham Publications, London, 1912, pp. 14, 18.
20. E. A. Wallis Budge (Trans.), *The Book of the Dead: Papyrus of Ani*.
21. Douglas M. Parrott and R. McL. Wilson (Trans.), "The Acts of Peter and the Twelve Apostles" in James M. Robinson (Ed.), *The Nag Hammadi Library in English*, op. cit., p. 291.
22. Shri Purohit Swami (Trans.), op. cit.
23. Ralph L. Roys (Trans.), op. cit., p. 104.
24. E. A. Wallis Budge (Trans.), *The Book of the Dead: Papyrus of Ani*.
25. Douglas Wile (Trans.), op. cit.
26. Kisari Mohan Ganguli (Trans.), *The Mahabharata*, c. 1883-1896.
27. Devadatta Kali (Trans.), *In Praise of the Goddess: The Devimahatmya and Its Meaning*, Nicolas-Hays, Berwick, 2003, pp. 65, 66-67.
28. Daniel A. Lord, "Mount Carmel Novena," *The Queen's Work*, Sodality of Our Lady, St. Louis, 1947.
29. Devadatta Kali (Trans.), op. cit.

CHAPTER THREE

1. *The Kolbrin*, e-book copyright 2014, The Culdian Trust, originally published 1994 by The Hope Trust, New Zealand.
2. Thomas O. Lambdin (Trans.), op. cit., p. 126.
3. Manly P. Hall (Trans.), op. cit., p. 40.
4. Garcilaso de la Vega, *The Royal Commentaries of the Incas*.
5. *Holy Bible*, NEW INTERNATIONAL VERSION®, NIV®, op. cit.
6. G. R. S. Mead (Trans.), *Echoes from the Gnosis, Vol. X: The Hymn of the Robe of Glory*, 1908, pp. 14, 15-16.
7. *Holy Bible*, NEW INTERNATIONAL VERSION®, NIV®, op. cit.
8. Manly P. Hall, op. cit., p. 29.
9. Douglas Wile.
10. Brian Browne Walker (Trans.), op. cit., p. 47.
11. Swami Prabhavananda and Frederick Manchester (Trans.), *The Upanishads: Breath from the Eternal*, Signet Classic, New York, 2002, p. 35.
12. Allen J. Christenson (Trans.), op. cit., pp. 65-66.
13. Edmond Bordeaux Szekely (Trans.), *The Essene Gospel of Peace: Book One*, op. cit., p. 19, and *The Essene Gospel of Peace: Book Four*, op. cit., p. 14.
14. F. Max Müller (Trans.), *The Upanishads, Part II*, Sacred Books of the East, Vol. XV, Oxford, Clarendon Press, 1884, pp. 85-86.
15. James Legge (Trans.), *The Yî King*, Sacred Books of the East Vol. 16, The Sacred Books of China, vol. 2, Oxford, Clarendon Press, 1882, pp. 358, 395, 435.
16. A. E. Waite (Trans.), *The Alchemical Writings of Edward Kelly*, James Elliott and Co., London, 1893, p. 35.
17. Sigismund Bacstrom (Trans.), *The Emerald Tablet of Hermes*, in Manly P. Hall, op. cit., p. 158.
18. Swami Prabhavananda and Frederick Manchester (Trans.), op. cit., p. 74.
19. Norbert Guterman (Trans.), Jolande Jacobi (Ed.), *Paracelsus: Selected Writings*, Princeton University Press, New Jersey, 1995, p. 21.

20. Edmond Bordeaux Szekely (Trans.), *The Essene Gospel of Peace: Book Four*, op. cit., p. 13.
21. Douglas Wile (Trans.), op. cit.
22. Wesley W. Isenberg (Trans.), op. cit., pp. 148, 150, 151, 158.
23. Brian Browne Walker (Trans.), op. cit., p. 84.
24. Richard Wilhelm (Trans.), *The Secret of the Golden Flower*, translated from German to English by Cary F. Baynes, Harcourt Brace & Company, San Diego, 1962, p. 31.
25. King James Version, op. cit.
26. Richard Wilhelm (Trans.), op. cit., p. 71.
27. Edmond Bordeaux Szekely (Trans.), *The Essene Gospel of Peace: Book Three*, International Biogenic Society, USA, 1981, p. 93
28. Shri Purohit Swami (Trans.), op. cit.
29. James Donaldson (Trans.), Alexander Roberts, James Donaldson, and A. Cleveland Coxe (Eds.), *Ante-Nicene Fathers*, Vol. 8, op. cit.
30. G. R. S. Mead (Trans.), *Pistis Sophia*, op. cit., pp. 148, 149-150.
31. Thomas Smith (Trans.), op. cit.
32. Eknath Easwaran (Trans.), op. cit., pp. 76-77.
33. Shri Purohit Swami (Trans.), op. cit.
34. Swami Tapasyananda (Trans.), *Shrimad Bhagavad Gita*, Sri Ramakrishna Math, Mylapore, 2003, p. 239.
35. Douglas M. Parrott and R. McL. Wilson (Trans.), op. cit., p. 290.
36. Morien O. Morgan, *The Royal Winged Son of Stonehenge and Avebury*, Glarmorgan Free Press, Cardiff, 1900.
37. Ibid.
38. Manly P. Hall, op. cit., p. 173.
39. Lionel Giles (Trans.), op. cit, p. 22.
40. Douglas M. Parrott (Trans.), "Eugnostos the Blessed and The Sophia of Jesus Christ" in James M. Robinson (Ed.), *The Nag Hammadi Library in English*, op. cit., pp. 229-230.
41. Frederik Wisse (Trans.), "The Apocryphon of John" in James M. Robinson (Ed.), *The Nag Hammadi Library in English*, op. cit., p. 122.
42. Ralph L. Roys (Trans.), op. cit., p. 105.
43. E. B. Cowell (Trans.), *The Maitri or Maitrāyanīya Upanishad*, Asiatic Society of Bengal, Calcutta, 1870.
44. Allen J. Christenson (Trans.), op. cit.

CHAPTER FOUR

1. Eleanor Mannikka, *Angkor Wat: Time, Space, and Kingship*, University of Hawaii Press, 2000.
2. G. R. S. Mead (Trans.), *Pistis Sophia*, op. cit., p. 262.
3. *Holy Bible*, NEW INTERNATIONAL VERSION®, NIV®, op. cit.
4. Ibid.
5. Ibid.
6. Ibid.
7. Ibid.
8. Carolyne Larrington (Trans.), *The Poetic Edda*, Oxford University Press, 1999, p. 34.

9. Shri Purohit Swami (Trans.), op. cit.
10. Devi Chand (Trans.), *The Yajur Veda*, All India Dayanand Salvation Mission, Hoshiarpur, 1959, p. 23.
11. Eknath Easwaran (Trans.), op. cit., p. 76.
12. Rodolphe Kasser, Marvin Meyer, and Gregor Wurst (Trans.), in collaboration with François Gaudard, *The Gospel of Judas*, National Geographic Society, Washington D. C., 2006, p. 43.
13. *Holy Bible*, NEW INTERNATIONAL VERSION®, NIV®, op. cit.
14. Eknath Easwaran (Trans.), op. cit., p. 91.
15. Terence DuQuesne, *Jackal at the Shaman's Gate*, 1991. Quoted in Robert Temple with Olivia Temple, *The Sphinx Mystery*, Inner Traditions, 2009.
16. Samuel A. B. Mercer (Trans.), op. cit., p. 239.
17. Ralph T. H. Griffith (Trans.), op. cit.
18. J. Zandee, *Death as an Enemy: According to Ancient Egyptian Conceptions*, translated from Dutch to English by Mrs W. F. Klasens, E. J. Brill, Leiden, 1960, p. 58.
19. Richard Wilhelm (Trans.), op. cit., p. 23.
20. Ralph T. H. Griffith (Trans.), op. cit.
21. *Holy Bible*, NEW INTERNATIONAL VERSION®, NIV®, op. cit.
22. Douglas M. Parrott (Trans.), op. cit., p. 226.
23. Edmond Bordeaux Szekely (Trans.), *The Essene Gospel of Peace: Book Four*, op. cit., pp. 37-38.
24. Edmond Bordeaux Szekely (Trans.), *The Essene Gospel of Peace: Book One*, op. cit., p. 18.
25. Samuel A. B. Mercer (Trans.), op. cit., p. 289.

CHAPTER FIVE

1. Robert Temple with Olivia Temple, *The Sphinx Mystery*, Inner Traditions, 2009.
2. Based on translations by Faulkner, Piankoff and Speleer. Available from: <http://www.pyramidtextsonline.com/translation.html>.
3. Terence DuQuesne, op. cit.
4. Robert Temple with Olivia Temple, op. cit.
5. R. O. Faulkner (Trans.), *The Ancient Egyptian Pyramid Texts*, Clarendon Press, Oxford, 1998, p. 291.
6. Robert Temple with Olivia Temple, op. cit.
7. Ibid.
8. Terence DuQuesne, *The Jackal Divinities of Egypt*, Darengo Publications, London, 2005. Quoted in Robert Temple with Olivia Temple, op. cit., p. 299.
9. R. O. Faulkner (Trans.) in Robert Temple with Olivia Temple, op. cit., p. 184.
10. R. O. Faulkner (Trans.) in Robert Temple with Olivia Temple, op. cit., pp. 185-186.
11. Based on translations by Faulkner, Piankoff and Speleer. Available from: <http://www.pyramidtextsonline.com/translation.html>.
12. R. T. Rundle Clark (Trans.), *Myth and Symbol in Ancient Egypt*, Thames & Hudson, London, 1959, pp. 130-40.
13. Samuel A. B. Mercer (Trans.), op. cit., p. 58.

14. Based on translations by Faulkner, Piankoff and Speleer. Available from: <http://www.pyramidtextsonline.com/translation.html>.
15. R. O. Faulkner (Trans.), *The Ancient Egyptian Pyramid Texts*, op. cit.
16. Samuel A. B. Mercer (Trans.), op. cit., p. 239.
17. Robert Temple with Olivia Temple, op. cit., p. 222.
18. Based on translations by Faulkner, Piankoff and Speleer. Available from: <http://www.pyramidtextsonline.com/translation.html>.
19. Ibid.
20. Ibid.
21. R. O. Faulkner (Trans.), *The Ancient Egyptian Pyramid Texts*, op. cit.
22. Vincent Bridges, *Abydos, the Osireion and Egyptian Sacred Science*, 2000. Available from: <http://vincentbridges.com/post/145759129272/abydos-the-osireion-and-egyptian-sacred-science>.
23. Samuel A. B. Mercer (Trans.), op. cit.
24. Robert Temple, "Lost Technology of the Ancients: The Crystal Sun," *New Dawn Magazine*, No. 65, 2001. Available from: <http://www.newdawnmagazine.com.au/Article/The_Crystal_Sun.html>.
25. Robert Temple with Olivia Temple, op. cit.
26. Alexandre Piankoff (Trans.), *The Wandering of the Soul*, Princeton University Press, 1974.

CHAPTER SIX

1. Edmond Bordeaux Szekely (Trans.), *The Essene Gospel of Peace: Book One*, op. cit., p. 19.
2. *Holy Bible*, NEW INTERNATIONAL VERSION®, NIV®, op. cit.
3. Frederik Wisse (Trans.), op. cit., p. 105.
4. Douglas Wile (Trans.), op. cit.
5. Allen Mandelbaum (Trans.), *The Divine Comedy of Dante Alighieri: Paradisio*.
6. *Holy Bible*, NEW INTERNATIONAL VERSION®, NIV®, op. cit.
7. G. R. S. Mead (Trans.), *Pistis Sophia*, op. cit., pp. 12-13.
8. Ibid., pp. 5-6.
9. Ibid., p. 190.
10. Stephen Patterson and Marvin Meyer (Trans.), "Gospel of Thomas" in Robert J. Miller (Ed.), *The Complete Gospels: Annotated Scholars Version*, Polebridge Press, 1994.
11. Wesley W. Isenberg (Trans.), op. cit., p. 160.
12. Stephen Patterson and Marvin Meyer (Trans.), op. cit.
13. G. R. S. Mead (Trans.), *Pistis Sophia*, op. cit., pp. 191, 192.
14. Douglas Wile (Trans.), op. cit.
15. Eknath Easwaran (Trans.), op. cit., pp. 143-144.
16. G. R. S. Mead (Trans.), *Pistis Sophia*, op. cit., p. 1.
17. Donald A. Mackenzie, op. cit., p. 146.
18. *Poetic Edda*, Völuspá, stanza 2.
19. Edmond Bordeaux Szekely (Trans.), *The Essene Gospel of Peace: Book Two*, International Biogenic Society, USA, 1981.
20. Edmond Bordeaux Szekely (Trans.), *The Essene Gospel of Peace: Book Four*, op. cit., p. 11.

21. G. R. S. Mead (Trans.), *Pistis Sophia*, op. cit., p. 313.
22. Thomas O. Lambdin (Trans.), op. cit., p. 129.
23. Manly P. Hall, op. cit., p. 39.
24. Douglas M. Parrott (Trans.), op. cit., p. 228.
25. G. R. S. Mead (Trans.), *Pistis Sophia*, op. cit., pp. 99, 100.
26. Lady Gregory, *A Book of Saints and Wonders*, 1906.
27. Gordon Kennedy, *The White Indians of Nivaria*, Nivaria Press, Mecca, California, 2010, p. 46.
28. William C. Robinson, Jr. (Trans.), "The Exegesis on the Soul" in James M. Robinson (Ed.), *The Nag Hammadi Library in English*, op. cit., p. 192.
29. Douglas M. Parrott (Trans.), op. cit., pp. 234-235.
30. William C. Robinson, Jr. (Trans.), op. cit., pp. 195, 196.
31. Samuel A. B. Mercer (Trans.), op. cit., p. 59.
32. Ralph L. Roys (Trans.), op. cit., p. 131.
33. James H. Charlesworth (Trans.), *The Earliest Christian Hymnbook: The Odes of Solomon*, Wipf and Stock, Eugene, 2009, pp. 32-33. Used by permission of Wipf and Stock Publishers. www.wipfandstock.com
34. Morien O. Morgan, op. cit.
35. Wesley W. Isenberg (Trans.), op. cit., p. 142.
36. G. R. S. Mead (Trans.), *Pistis Sophia*, op. cit., p. 117.
37. James H. Charlesworth (Trans.), op. cit., p. 1.
38. G. R. S. Mead (Trans.), *Pistis Sophia*, op. cit., pp. 3, 4.
39. Samuel A. B. Mercer (Trans.), op. cit., pp. 59-60.
40. G. R. S. Mead (Trans.), *Pistis Sophia*, op. cit., p. 118.
41. Samuel A. B. Mercer (Trans.), op. cit., pp. 186-187.
42. Ibid., p. 240.
43. Based on translations by Faulkner, Piankoff and Speleer. Available from: <http://www.pyramidtextsonline.com/translation.html>.
44. Rodolphe Kasser, Marvin Meyer, and Gregor Wurst (Trans.), op. cit.
45. Manly P. Hall, op. cit., p. 40.

CHAPTER SEVEN

1. Lucy Thompson, *To the American Indian*, Self-Published, Eureka, California, 1916, p. 65.
2. Martin Doutré, personal communication.
3. Thor Heyerdahl, op. cit.
4. Manly P. Hall, op. cit., pp. 21-22.
5. Shri Purohit Swami (Trans.), op. cit.
6. David Frawley, *The Vedic Literature of Ancient India and Its Many Secrets*, 2008. Available from: <https://grahamhancock.com/frawleyd1/>.
7. Thomas Paine, "Origin of Free-Masonry" in Moncure Daniels Conway (Ed.), *Writings of Thomas Paine*, G.P. Putnam's Sons, 1896.
8. Martin Doutré, *The Chinese Pyramids at Xi'an, Shaanxl*, 2000. Available from: <http://www.celticnz.co.nz/ChinesePyramids/Chinese%20Pyramids%20l.htm>.
9. Lucy Thompson, op. cit., pp. 64-65, 66.
10. Philip Coppens, *The Wanderers of the Fourth World*. Available from: <http://www.philipcoppens.com/hopi.html>.

11. Thor Heyerdahl, *American Indians in the Pacific*, Allen & Unwin, London, 1952, pp. 230, 257-258. Cites: William H. Prescott, *History of the Conquest of Peru*, Harper and Brothers, New York, 1847.

12. Ibid., pp. 278-279. Cites: Daniel G. Brinton, *American Hero-Myths*, H. C. Watts & Co., Philadelphia, 1882. A. Hyatt Verrill, *Thirty Years in the Jungle*, John Lane, London, 1929.

13. Daniel G. Brinton, *American Hero-Myths*, H. C. Watts & Co., Philadelphia, 1882.

14. Thor Heyerdahl, *American Indians in the Pacific*, op. cit., pp. 251-252.

15. Thor Heyerdahl, *The Bearded Gods Speak*, op. cit.

16. Ibid.

17. Ibid.

18. Martin Doutré, personal communication.

19. Martin Doutré, *The Ancient Surveying Structures on the Bombay Hills*, 2000. Available from: <http://www.celticnz.co.nz/AucklandAlignment1.htm>.

20. Martin Doutré, *Megalithic New Zealand*, 2000. Available from: <http://www.celticnz.co.nz/mnz_pt1.html>.

21. Martin Doutré, *Codes of Position Amidst the Xi'an Complex of Pyramids and Mounds*, 2009. Available from: <http://www.celticnz.co.nz/ChinesePyramids/Chinese%20Pyramids%203.htm>.

22. Martin Doutré, *Megalithic New Zealand*, op. cit.

23. Ibid.

24. Monica Matumua in Raynor Capper, "Listen to the People. Talking with an Extinct Race. Part 1," *eLocal*, Adbonanza NZ Ltd, Pukekohe, 2011. Available from: <http://www.elocal.co.nz/view_Article~id~266~title~Listen_to_the_People._Talking_with_an_Extinct_Race._Part_1.html>.

25. Martin Doutré, *Viking Navigational Techniques*, 2000. Available from: <http://www.celticnz.co.nz/VikingNavigation.htm>.

26. Martin Doutré, *Ancient New Zealand Surveyors & Astronomers*, 2000. Available from: <http://www.celticnz.co.nz/SurveyorsNZ/Ancient%20New%20Zealand%20Surveyors.htm>.

27. Gordon Kennedy, op. cit., p. 82.

28. Ibid., p. 45.

29. Loc. cit.

30. G. I. Gurdjieff, *Meetings with Remarkable Men*.

31. P. D. Ouspensky, *In Search of the Miraculous: Fragments of an Unknown Teaching*, Harcourt, Brace, New York, 1949.

32. Diodorus Siculus, *Bibliotheca historica*.

33. Ibid.

34. R. Cedric Leonard, *Linguistic Connections: A Paleolithic Language*, 2011. Available from: <http://www.atlantisquest.com/Linguistics.html>.

35. Martin Doutré, *The Predynastic and Most Early Dynastic Egyptians Were Caucasoid-Europeans*, 2007. Available from: <http://www.celticnz.co.nz/Nazca/Ancient%20Caucasoid%20Egyptians.htm>.

36. R. Cedric Leonard, *Writings of the Egyptians: Egyptian Vignettes of the story of Atlantis*, 2012. Available from: <http://www.atlantisquest.com/Hiero.html>. Cites: Raymond O. Faulkner, (Trans.) *Ancient Egyptian Coffin Texts*, Oxford, 1974. K. Sethe, *Zur altagyptischen Sage vom Sonnenauge, das in der Fremde war, Untersuchungen zur Geschichte und Altertumskunde Aegyptens*,

1912. E. A. Wallis Budge, (Trans.) *The Book of the Dead*, University Books, New York, 1960.

37. E. A. Wallis Budge, *Osiris and the Egyptian Resurrection, Vol. 1*, Philip Lee Warner, London, 1912, p. 2.

38. R. Cedric Leonard, *Ancient Writings: Pre-Platonic Writings Pertinent to Atlantis*, 2011. Available from: <http://www.atlantisquest.com/Writings.html>. Cites: Arthur A. MacDonnell, *A Practical Sanskrit Dictionary*, Oxford University Press, London, 1974.

39. G. I. Gurdjieff, op. cit.

40. Andrew Collins, *Gods of Eden*, Bear & Company, Rochester, Vermont, 2002, pp. 295-296.

41. Ibid., p. 299.

42. Lucy Thompson, op. cit., p. 65.

CHAPTER EIGHT

1. Thor Heyerdahl, *American Indians in the Pacific*, op. cit., pp. 278, 279. Cites: A. Hyatt Verrill, *Thirty Years in the Jungle*, John Lane, London, 1929.

2. Jean-Michel Schwartz, *The Mysteries of Easter Island*, Avon, New York, 1975, p. 193.

3. G. Henriksson and M. Blomberg, "The Evidence From Knossos on the Minoan Calendar," *Mediterranean Archaeology and Archaeometry*, Vol. 11, No. 1, University of the Aegean, Rhodes, 2011, p. 63. Available from: <www.rhodes.aegean.gr/maa_journal/7_Blomberg.pdf>.

4. Ibid., p. 65.

5. Ibid., p. 64. Cites: Blomberg, M., Henriksson, G and Papathanassiou, M. (2002) The calendaric relationship between the Minoan peak sanctuary on Juktas and the palace at Knossos. In Proceedings of the Conference "Astronomy of ancient Civilizations" of the European society for Astronomy in Culture (SEAC) and National Astronomical Meeting (JENAM), Moscow, May 23-27, 2000, T. M. Potyomkina and V. N. Obridko (eds.), Moscow, 81-92. Henriksson, G. and Blomberg, M. (1996) Evidence for Minoan astronomical observations from the peak sanctuaries on Petsophas and Traostalos. Opuscula Atheniensia vol. 21, 99-114.

CHAPTER NINE

1. Martin Doutré, *Ring O' Brodgar, Orkney Islands: Gateway To The Americas*, 2000. Available from: <http://www.celticnz.co.nz/Brodgar/Brodgar%201.htm>.

2. Robert Temple, *Lost Technology of the Ancients: The Crystal Sun*, op. cit.

3. Martin Doutré, *The Nazca Lines of Peru*, 2000. Available from: <http://www.celticnz.co.nz/Nazca/Nazca1.htm>.

4. Morien O. Morgan, op. cit.

5. Ibid.

6. Deborah Scherrer, *Ancient Observatories – Timeless Knowledge*, Stanford University, 2015, pp. 4-5.

7. Victoria LePage, "Arkaim: Russia's Ancient City & the Arctic Origin of Civilisation," *New Dawn Magazine*, No. 111, 2008.

8. Stanislav Grigoryev, "Urals intends to develop pilgrimage to the "Russian Stonehenge"," *Interfax*, 2008. Available from: <http://www.interfax-religion.com/?act=news&div=4653>.

CHAPTER TEN

1. Martin Gray, *Sacred Earth*, Sterling, New York, 2011, p. 168.
2. Vince Barrows, *A History of Monks Mound*, 2007. Available from: <http://www.bibliotecapleyades.net/arqueologia/monks_mound02.htm>.

CHAPTER ELEVEN

1. J. B. Lightfoot, "Saint Paul's Epistles to the Colossians and Philemon," *On Some Points Connected With The Essenes*, MacMillan and Co., London, 1875.
2. Constance Gordon-Cumming, *In the Hebrides*, Chatto and Windus, London, 1883.
3. Philip Coppens, op. cit. Cites: Gary A. David, *The Orion Zone*, Adventures Unlimited Press, Kempton.
4. King James Version, op. cit.
5. Arthur G. Miller, *West and East in Maya Thought: Death and Rebirth at Palenque and Tulum*, Yale University, 1974, p. 47. Available from: <www.mesoweb.com/pari/publications/RT02/Miller1974-OCR.pdf>.

CHAPTER TWELVE

1. E. B. Cowell (Trans.), op. cit.
2. "AUM." New World Encyclopedia, 4 Dec 2015, 20:21 UTC. 3 Jul 2016, 05:12 <http://www.newworldencyclopedia.org/p/index.php?title=AUM&oldid=992429>.

CHAPTER THIRTEEN

1. G. R. S. Mead (Trans.), *Pistis Sophia*, op. cit., pp. 37-38, 39-40, 41.
2. Swami Jagadiswarananda (Trans.), *Devi Mahatmyam*.

CHAPTER FOURTEEN

1. Eknath Easwaran (Trans.), op. cit., pp. 165, 166, 167.
2. Ibid., p. 15.
3. King James Version, op. cit.
4. Frederik Wisse (Trans.), op. cit., p. 122.
5. *Holy Bible*, NEW INTERNATIONAL VERSION®, NIV®, op. cit.
6. Edmond Bordeaux Szekely (Trans.), *The Essene Gospel of Peace: Book One*, op. cit., p. 21.
7. Douglas M. Parrott (Trans.), op. cit., pp. 224-225, 225-226, 227, 231, 234-235.

CHAPTER FIFTEEN

1. Based on Edmond Bordeaux Szekely (Trans.), *The Essene Gospel of Peace: Book One*, op. cit., p. 18.

2. *Holy Bible*, NEW INTERNATIONAL VERSION®, NIV®, op. cit.
3. Douglas M. Parrott (Trans.), op. cit., p. 226.
4. Terence DuQuesne, *The Book of the One in the Netherworld*, op. cit.
5. Based on translations by Faulkner, Piankoff and Speleer. Available from: <http://www.pyramidtextsonline.com/translation.html>.
6. Ibid.
7. Based on various excerpts from The Pyramid Texts.
8. Samuel A. B. Mercer (Trans.), op. cit., p. 239.
9. R. O. Faulkner (Trans.), *The Ancient Egyptian Pyramid Texts*, op. cit.
10. Based on translations by Faulkner, Piankoff and Speleer. Available from: <http://www.pyramidtextsonline.com/translation.html>.
11. Samuel A. B. Mercer (Trans.), op. cit., p. 289.
12. James H. Charlesworth (Trans.), op. cit., pp. 83-85.
13. Ibid., pp. 92, 94.
14. Ibid., p. 10.
15. Edmond Bordeaux Szekely (Trans.), *The Essene Gospel of Peace: Book One*, op. cit., pp. 10-11.

CHAPTER SIXTEEN

1. Edmond Bordeaux Szekely (Trans.), *The Essene Gospel of Peace: Book Two*, op. cit.
2. Ibid.
3. Revelation 3:12.
4. Edmond Bordeaux Szekely (Trans.), *The Essene Gospel of Peace: Book Two*, op. cit.
5. Edmond Bordeaux Szekely (Trans.), *The Essene Gospel of Peace: Book One*, op. cit., p. 19, and *The Essene Gospel of Peace: Book Four*, op. cit., p. 11.
6. Richard Wilhelm (Trans.), *The Secret of the Golden Flower*, translated from German to English by Cary F. Baynes, Routledge and Kegan Paul Ltd, 1965.
7. James H. Charlesworth (Trans.), op. cit., pp. 1, 3-4, 25-26, 31-33, 43-44, 102, 105-106.
8. Edmond Bordeaux Szekely (Trans.), *The Essene Gospel of Peace: Book Four*, op. cit., pp. 38-39, and *The Essene Gospel of Peace: Book Three*, op. cit., pp. 69, 70.
9. Swami Krishnananda (Trans.), op. cit., pp. 66-70.
10. Eknath Easwaran (Trans.), op. cit., pp. 57-59.
11. Ibid., pp. 159-161.
12. E. B. Cowell (Trans.), op. cit.
13. Shri Purohit Swami (Trans.), op. cit.

CHAPTER SEVENTEEN

1. Ralph L. Roys (Trans.), op. cit., p. 65.

··· Image Credits ···

All Creative Commons works in this book are derivatives which have been processed with cropping, rotation, and/or other image adjustments.

Image credits are listed by page number.

MISC
5, 241, 349. Illustration of an Aztec sun calendar by Antonio de Leon y Gama, 1792. Public domain.
49, 85, 127, 205, 369, 385, 403, 421. 'Yin Yang motifs' © Mystical Life Publications.

CHAPTER HEADING SYMBOLS
Symbol images re-created by Mystical Life Publications.

1, 7, 243, 351, 449. Sun cross symbol found in the Aukstaitija region of Lithuania.

51, 277, 371. Double spiral symbol—which shows the sun moving from winter solstice, through equinox, to summer solstice and back again—found engraved at the ancient megalithic site of Newgrange in Ireland and the site of the Sun Dagger in Chaco Canyon in the United States, and in facial tattoos in the Tarim Basin of China and in New Zealand.

87, 289, 387. The oldest depiction of a swastika in the world, found carved into the tusk of a mammoth in Ukraine, and dated to 13,000 BC.

129, 171, 315, 405. North American pre-Columbian symbol of the sun and of happiness.

207, 329, 423. A sun symbol of the Guanches of Tenerife Island in the Canary Islands.

CHAPTER ONE

8. 'Summer Solstice 2005 Sunrise over Stonehenge 01' by Andrew Dunn, <https://commons.wikimedia.org/wiki/File:Summer_Solstice_2005_Sunrise_over_Stonehenge_01.jpg>. Creative Commons BY-SA 2.0.

9. *Top* 'Equinoxes-solstice-EN' by Divad. Public domain.

9. *Bottom* 'Emblem 21' by Michael Maier from Atalanta Fugiens, 1617. Public domain.

11. 'Anch and Sunwheel' from a Book of the Dead, circa 1300 BC. Public domain.

14. 'Christ Pantocrator' by Viktor M. Vasnetsov, circa 1885-1896. Public domain.

23. 'Taperet stele E52 mp3h9201' by Rama, <https://commons.wikimedia.org/wiki/File:Taperet_stele_E52_mp3h9201.jpg>. Creative Commons BY-SA 2.0 FR.

28. Photograph of the pyramid of Khafre and the Sphinx by Than217. Public domain.

31. *Top Right* 'Yin and Yang' by Klem. Public domain.

31. *Bottom* Image created for book based on web article by Allen Tsai, <http://www.chinesefortunecalendar.com/YinYang.htm>.

32. *Top Left* 'Samarra bowl' by Dbachmann, <https://commons.wikimedia.org/wiki/File:Samarra_bowl.jpg>. Creative Commons BY-SA 4.0.

32. *Top Right* 'Chromesun 4 uktenas design' by Herb Roe, <https://en.wikipedia.org/wiki/File:Chromesun_4_uktenas_design.jpg>. Creative Commons BY-SA 3.0.

32. *Bottom* Image created for book based on illustration by Sergey Smelyakov in his article "Crucifying The Earth On the Galactic Cross," <http://www.soulsofdistortion.nl/Galactic Alignment.html>.

33. *Bottom* 'Analemma Earth' by PAR. Public domain.

34. © Mystical Life Publications.

35. *Top* 'Newgrange Entrance Stone' by Nomadtales, <https://commons.wikimedia.org/wiki/File:Newgrange_Entrance_Stone.jpg>. Creative Commons BY-SA 3.0.

35. *Bottom* Spiraling rotation of the planets from 'Solar System 2.0 – the helical model' © DjSadhu. Source: <https://youtu.be/mvgaxQGPg7I>. Used by permission.

36. *Top* 'Golden-triangles-pentagram' by Krishnavedala. Public domain.

36. *Bottom* 'Venus pentagramm' by Cwitte, <https://commons.wikimedia.org/wiki/File:Venus_pentagramm.svg>. Creative Commons BY-SA 3.0.

37. 18th century album leaf painting of the Churning of the Milky Ocean, artist unknown. Public domain.

38. Image created for book based on information in *Episode 01, The Horizon Project: Bracing for Tomorrow*, Remote Viewing Products, 2006.

39. Photograph of hieroglyphs from a temple in Abydos, Egypt, by Olek95. Public domain.

46. © Mystical Life Publications.

47. Photograph © Lucy Pringle, 2001, <http://www.lucypringle.co.uk/photos/2001/uk2001ar.shtml#pic2 >. Used by permission.

CHAPTER TWO

52. Libra sign, used under license from Shutterstock.com.

54. Statue of Horus and Seth placing the crown of Upper Egypt on the head of Ramesses III, early 12th century BC, original photograph by A. Parrot. Public domain.

57. 'The Wicker Man burns - geograph.org.uk – 50168' by Simon Brooke, <https://commons.wikimedia.org/wiki/File:The_Wicker_Man_burns_-_geograph.org.uk_-_50168.jpg>. Creative Commons BY-SA 2.0.
59. Photograph by Bibi Saint-Pol of Demeter and Metanira, detail of the belly of an Apulian red-figure hydria, circa 340 BC. Public domain.
61. 'Descendant-grande-pyramide' © Jon Bodsworth, <https://commons.wikimedia.org/wiki/File:Descendant-grande-pyramide.jpg>. Used by permission.
64. © Mystical Life Publications.
67. Illustration of the Celestial spheres, circa 1377, artist unknown. Public domain.
68. *Top* 'Golden Mask of Psusennes I' by Brett Weinstein, <https://commons.wikimedia.org/wiki/File:Golden_Mask_of_Psusennes_I.jpg>. Creative Commons BY-SA 2.5.
68. *Bottom Left* 'Crowned Naga-Protected Buddha' circa 1150-1190, Walters Art Museum. Public domain.
68. *Bottom Right* Egyptian god Sokar-Osiris, from the Papyrus of Ani, circa 1300 BC, artist unknown. Public domain.
70. 'La Divina Commedia di Dante' by Domenico di Michelino, 1465. Public domain.
75. Kali poster by unknown artist, circa 1940s. Public domain.
76. *Left* '20041229-Coatlicue (Museo Nacional de Antropología) MQ-3' by Luidger, <https://en.wikipedia.org/wiki/File:20041229-Coatlicue_%28Museo_Nacional_de_Antropolog%C3%ADa%29_MQ-3.jpg>. Creative Commons BY-SA 3.0.
76. *Right* 'Sekhmet (British Museum)' by Stormnight, <https://commons.wikimedia.org/wiki/File:Sekhmet_%28British_Museum%29.jpg>. Creative Commons BY-SA 4.0.
77. Photograph of Sumerian cylinder seal by Daderot. Public domain.
78. *Left* 'Kali Kangra Painting' by unknown artist, circa 19th century. Public domain.
78. *Right* Hecate detail of a statuette by Richard Cosway, circa 1814. Public domain.
79. 'Our Lady of Succor' by Giovanni da Monte Rubiano, circa 1506. Public domain.
82. *Top* Minotaur in labyrinth illustration from Gemmae Antiche by P. A. Maffei, 1709. Public domain.
82. *Bottom* 'Theseus and the Minotaur' illustration from The story of Greeks by H. A. Guerber, 1896. Public domain.

CHAPTER THREE

88. *Top* 'Newgrange' by Shira, <https://commons.wikimedia.org/wiki/File:Newgrange.JPG>. Creative Commons BY-SA 3.0.
88. *Bottom* 'Christ the Judge' by Fra Angelico, 1447. Public domain.
90. Statue of Isis and Horus, Berlin Museum, from the 4th edition (1885-90) of Meyers Konversationslexikon. Public domain.
92. Drawing of a hieroglyph from the temple at Luxor by Samuel Sharpe, circa 1879. Public domain.
98. 17th century Tibetan thanka of Guhyasamaja Akshobhyavajra, author unknown. Public domain.
102. Illustration from the Donum Dei, 17th century, artist unknown. Public domain.

106. Depiction of Viracocha, artist unknown. Public domain.
107. 'St George and the Dragon' by Paolo Uccello, circa 1458-1460. Public domain.
112. 'Church of the Saviour on the Blood IMG 7407' by Deror avi, <https:// commons.wikimedia.org/wiki/File:Church_of_the_Saviour_on_the_Blood_ IMG_7407.JPG>. Creative Commons BY-SA 3.0.
113. Photograph by Marie-Lan Nguyen of statue of Mithras born from the rock, Baths of Diocletian, Epigraphical Museum. Public domain.
114. 'Das Christuskind' by Melchior Paul von Deschwanden, by 1881. Public domain.
115. 'Torre de Glastonbury' by Josep Renalias, <https://commons.wikimedia.org/ wiki/File:Torre_de_Glastonbury.JPG>. Creative Commons BY-SA 3.0.
117. 'Pyramids at Gizah' by Ricardo Liberato, <https://commons.wikimedia.org/ wiki/File:Pyramids_at_Gizah.jpg>. Creative Commons BY-SA 2.0.
118. 'Ahu-Akivi-1' by Ian Sewell, <https://commons.wikimedia.org/wiki/ File:Ahu-Akivi-1.JPG>. Creative Commons BY-SA 3.0.
120. 'The Adoration of the Shepherds' by Gerard van Honthorst, 1622. Public domain.
122. 'The Angelic Announcement' to the Shepherds by Taddeo Gaddi, circa 1327-1330. Public domain.
123. 'The Visit of the Wise-Men' by Heinrich Hofmann, circa 1900. Public domain.

CHAPTER FOUR
130. Drawing by Linda Schele © David Schele, used by permission on behalf of LACMA.
131. 18th century album leaf painting of the Churning of the Milky Ocean, artist unknown. Public domain.
132. 'Awatoceanofmilk01 - color corrected' by Markalexander100, <https:// commons.wikimedia.org/wiki/File:Awatoceanofmilk01_-_color_corrected. JPG>. Creative Commons BY-SA 3.0.
135. 'TIB lhasa sera lebensrad' by Bgabel at wikivoyage shared, <https://commons. wikimedia.org/wiki/File:TIB-lhasa-sera-lebensrad.jpg>. Creative Commons BY-SA 3.0.
137. 'Samudr manthan' by elishams, <https://commons.wikimedia.org/wiki/ File:Samudr_manthan.jpg>. Creative Commons BY 2.5.
139. Xolotl illustration from the Codex Fejervary-Mayer, artist unknown, circa 15th century. Public domain.
140. 'The Jews Took Up Rocks to Stone Jesus' by James Tissot, circa 1886-1896. Public domain.
142. 'The Last Supper' by Carl Heinrich Bloch, circa late 19th century. Public domain.
144. 'No. 31 Scenes from the Life of Christ: 15. The Arrest of Christ (Kiss of Judas)' by Giotto, circa 1304-1306. Public domain.
145. 'Joan of Arc is interrogated by The Cardinal of Winchester in her prison' by Paul Delaroche, 1824. Public domain.
146. 'Christ in front of Pilate' by Mihály Munkácsy, 1881. Public domain.
147. Kali, draped with a necklace of skulls, stands on Shiva, color lithograph lettered, inscribed and numbered 27, circa 1895, artist unknown. Public domain.

149. 'Crocifissione' by Bramantino, circa 1465-1530. Public domain.
151. 'Odin's Self-sacrifice' illustration by W.G. Collingwood, 1908, from The Elder or Poetic Edda, commonly known as Sæmund's Edda, edited and translated by Olive Bray. Public domain.
155. *Top* Anubis attending the mummy of the deceased, from a wall painting in the tomb of Sennedjem, artist unknown. Public domain.
155. *Bottom* Anubis weighing the heart of a man against a feather, from a section of plate 3 from the Papyrus of Ani, artist unknown. Public domain.
156. 'Italy Vatican' by gnuckx, <https://www.flickr.com/photos/34409164@N06/3492615876>. Creative Commons BY 2.0.
157. © Mystical Life Publications.
159. Quetzalcoatl in the Codex Telleriano-Remensis, circa 16th century, artist unknown. Public domain.
160. Depiction of the Egyptian goddess Nut, artist unknown. Public domain.
161. 'Silver cauldron' by Rosemania, <https://commons.wikimedia.org/wiki/File:Silver_cauldron.jpg>. Creative Commons BY 2.0.
162. 'Knowth entrance to second passage 2010' by Bkwillwm, <https://commons.wikimedia.org/wiki/File:Knowth_entrance_to_second_passage_2010.JPG>. Creative Commons BY-SA 3.0.
163. Painting showing Arthurian knight Sir Galahad discovering the Holy Grail, 1895, by Edwin Austin Abbey. Public domain.
165. 'Govinda' from Deccan School, Bikaner, circa 1820, bequest of Mr J. Kitto 1986. Public domain.
166. 'Christ in Limbo' by Follower of Hieronymus Bosch, circa 1575. Public domain.
168. 'Anubis, Isis, Nephthys in the Theban Tomb 335 (Nakhtamun), from the reign of Ramesses II' by ShillukinUSA, <https://commons.wikimedia.org/wiki/File:ThebanTomb335.png>. Creative Commons BY-SA 3.0.
170. 'Philae 13' by Olaf Tausch, <https://commons.wikimedia.org/wiki/File:Philae_13.jpg>. Creative Commons BY 3.0.

CHAPTER FIVE

172. *Top* © Mystical Life Publications.
172. *Bottom* Photograph of the Sphinx partially excavated by Maison Bonfils, late 18th century. Public domain.
174. *Top* Diagram of Khafre's valley area with the temples and the Sphinx, based on Lehner's and Verner's works, by Horemweb. Public domain.
174. *Bottom* 'Great Sphinx of Giza 2' by Marek Kocjan, <https://commons.wikimedia.org/wiki/File:Great_Sphinx_of_Giza_2.jpg>. Creative Commons BY-SA 3.0.
175. Anubis attending the mummy of the deceased, from a wall painting in the tomb of Sennedjem. Public domain.
176. Judgement of the dead in the presence of Osiris, from the Book of the Dead of Hunefer. Public domain.
177. Photograph of Tutankhamun jackal © Jon Bodsworth, <https://commons.wikimedia.org/wiki/File:Tutanhkamun_jackal.jpg>. Used by permission.
180. Photograph of a complete set of Canopic jars from Egypt, circa 900-800 BC, Walters Art Museum. Public domain.

181. 'kist uit de 27- 31e dynastie' (box from the 27- 31st dynasty) by Andre, <https://www.flickr.com/photos/9987501@N08/3643941456>. Creative Commons BY-SA 2.0.

183. Diagram of an atom by Wykis, edited from original. Public domain.

184. Illustration from the Book of the Dead of Khensumose, artist unknown. Public domain.

186. Photograph of Pyramid Texts from pyramid of Teti I in Saqqara, taken by Chipdawes. Public domain.

188. 'Leo constellation map' by Torsten Bronger, <https://commons.wikimedia.org/wiki/File:Leo_constellation_map.png>. Creative Commons BY-SA 3.0.

189. 'Golden wolf small', by Prof. Lee R. Berger, <https://en.wikipedia.org/wiki/File:Golden_wolf_small.jpg>. Creative Commons BY-SA 3.0.

190. *Top* 'Osireion at Abydos' by RsAzevedo, <https://commons.wikimedia.org/wiki/File:Osireion_at_Abydos.jpg>. Creative Commons BY-SA 3.0.

190. *Bottom* 'Giza Plateau - Great Sphinx - inside temple' by Daniel Mayer, <https://commons.wikimedia.org/wiki/File:Giza_Plateau_-_Great_Sphinx_-_inside_temple.JPG>. Creative Commons BY-SA 4.0.

193. 'Orion – pyramids' by Davkal, <https://commons.wikimedia.org/wiki/File:Orion_-_pyramids.jpg>. Creative Commons BY-SA 3.0.

194. 'The Great Pyramid, showing passages and mummy chambers. (1902) – TIMEA' by unknown artist, <https://commons.wikimedia.org/wiki/File:The_Great_Pyramid,_showing_passages_and_mummy_chambers._%281902%29_-_TIMEA.jpg>. Licensed from Travelers in the Middle East Archive (TIMEA). Creative Commons BY-SA 2.5.

196. 'Karnak temple 9456' by Hedwig Storch, <https://commons.wikimedia.org/wiki/File:Karnak_temple_9456.JPG>. Creative Commons BY-SA 3.0.

197. 'Giza. Pyramid of Khafre and Sphinx' photograph from Cornell University Library, circa 1865-1889. Public domain.

199. 'Egypt.LuxorTemple.03' by Hajor, <https://commons.wikimedia.org/wiki/File:Egypt.LuxorTemple.03.jpg>. Creative Commons BY-SA 3.0.

200. 'Egypt.Saqqara.Panorama.01' by Hajor, <https://commons.wikimedia.org/wiki/File:Egypt.Saqqara.Panorama.01.jpg>. Creative Commons BY-SA 3.0.

203. 'Sun Over Pyramid' by A. Parrot (derivative work of photograph by Nina Aldin Thune), <https://commons.wikimedia.org/wiki/File:Sun_Over_Pyramid.jpg>. Creative Commons BY-SA 3.0.

CHAPTER SIX

208. 'Stonehenge (sun)' by simonwakefield, <https://commons.wikimedia.org/wiki/File:Stonehenge_%28sun%29.jpg>. Creative Commons BY 2.0.

209. 'Lord Garuda' by Raja Ravi Varma, 18th century oil on canvas. Public domain.

210. *Left* Illustration of a 1st century AD marble relief in the Estense Museum in Modena, Italy, by Arthur Bernard Cook, 1914, from Zeus: a study in ancient religion. Public domain.

210. *Right* 'Messico, aztechi, serpente piumato quetzalcoatl, pietra periodo postclassico recente' by Sailko, <https://commons.wikimedia.org/wiki/File:Messico,_aztechi,_serpente_piumato_quetzalcoatl,_pietra_periodo_postclassico_recente,_1400-1510_ca._02.JPG>. Creative Commons BY 3.0.

211. 'Egypt.KV34.07' by Hajor, <https://commons.wikimedia.org/wiki/File:Egypt.KV34.07.jpg>. Creative Commons BY-SA 3.0.
213. 'Rosa Celeste: Dante and Beatrice gaze upon the highest Heaven, The Empyrean,' by Gustave Doré, 19th century, from The Divine Comedy by Dante, Illustrated, Complete (edited by Henry Francis, 1892). Public domain.
214. This work has been recreated based on the research by Roger Penrose and Vahe Gurzadyan, 2010. Background is a public domain image from NASA / WMAP Science Team.
215. 'The Ascension' by Benjamin West, 1801. Public domain.
220. *Top* © Mystical Life Publications.
220. *Bottom* Illustration from the Book of the Dead of Khensumose, artist unknown. Public domain.
221. *Left* 'Maibaum Ostfriesland967' by Matthias Süßen, <https://commons.wikimedia.org/wiki/File:Maibaum_Ostfriesland967.jpg>. Creative Commons BY 3.0.
221. *Right* © Mystical Life Publications.
223. *Top* Osiris djed illustration from Osiris and the Egyptian resurrection by Sir E. A. Wallis Budge, 1911. Public domain.
223. *Bottom* Illustration of the Norse Tree of Life as described in the Icelandic Prose Edda, from Northern Antiquities, published 1859. Public domain.
226. 'Palazzo Braschi - Vestale 1020774' by Lalupa, <https://commons.wikimedia.org/wiki/File:Palazzo_Braschi_-_Vestale_1020774.JPG>. Creative Commons BY-SA 3.0.
229. 'Invocation' by Frederic Leighton, 19th century oil on canvas. Public domain.
231. 18th century engraving based on a bas-relief found at Autun, France, depicting two druids, by Bernard de Montfaucon. Public domain.
233. 'Midsummer Crown' by Bengt Nyman, <https://commons.wikimedia.org/wiki/File:Midsummer_Crown.jpg>. Creative Commons BY 2.0.
235. Photograph of the gods Seth and Horus adoring Ramesses II in the small temple at Abu Simbel, Egypt, by Chipdawes. Public domain.
237. 'The Virgin of the Apocalypse' by Miguel Cabrera, 1760. Public domain.

CHAPTER SEVEN

244. Photograph of Lucy Thompson, 1916. Public domain.
253. 'Odin, the Wanderer' by Georg von Rosen, 1886. Public domain.
256. *Top Left* 'An Arch Druid in His Judicial Habit' from *The Costume of the Original Inhabitants of the British Islands* by S. R. Meyrick and C. H. Smith, 1815. Public domain.
256. *Top Right* Druid illustration from *Britannia Antiqua Illustrata* by Aylett Sammes, 1676. Public domain.
256. *Bottom* 'MocheBeardedMen' by Pattych at en.wikipedia, <https://en.wikipedia.org/wiki/File:MocheBeardedMen.jpg>. Creative Commons BY-SA 3.0.
260. 1910 illustration of Maori chief Hongi Hika by Major-General G. Robley, after the portrait painted in England in 1820, from The New Zealand Electronic Text Collection, <http://www.nzetc.org/etexts/SmiMaor/SmiMaorP001a.jpg>. Creative Commons BY-SA 3.0 NZ.

CHAPTER EIGHT

278. 'Descendant-grande-pyramide' © Jon Bodsworth, <https://commons. wikimedia.org/wiki/File:Descendant-grande-pyramide.jpg>. Used by permission.

279. *Top* Photograph of Giza pyramid used under license from SOTK2011/Alamy stock photo.

279. *Bottom* Photograph of Chichen Itza at the spring equinox by ATSZ56. Public domain.

281. 'Teonate' by Nateirma~commonswiki, <https://commons.wikimedia.org/ wiki/File:Teonate.JPG>. Creative Commons BY-SA 3.0.

282. 'Intihuatana Solar Clock' by Jordan Klein, <https://commons.wikimedia.org/ wiki/File:Intihuatana_Solar_Clock.jpg>. Creative Commons BY 2.0.

283. 'Ahu-Akivi-1' by Ian Sewell, <https://commons.wikimedia.org/wiki/ File:Ahu-Akivi-1.JPG>. Creative Commons BY-SA 3.0.

284. 'Karajia1' by Papiermond at the German language Wikipedia, <https:// en.wikipedia.org/wiki/File:Karajia1.jpg>. Creative Commons BY-SA 3.0.

285. Photograph of the Temple of the Seven Dolls in Yucatan, Mexico, by -Luyten-. Public domain.

286. 'Knossos - North Portico 02' by Bernard Gagnon, <https://en.wikipedia.org/ wiki/File:Knossos_-_North_Portico_02.jpg>. Creative Commons BY-SA 3.0.

287. 'AMI - Goldene Doppelaxt' by Wolfgang Sauber, <https://en.wikipedia.org/ wiki/File:AMI_-_Goldene_Doppelaxt.jpg>. Creative Commons BY-SA 3.0.

CHAPTER NINE

290. 'Street and Glastonbury Tor' by Edwin Graham, <https://commons.wikimedia. org/wiki/File:Street_and_Glastonbury_Tor.jpg>. Creative Commons BY-SA 2.0.

291. 'Chichen Itza CB' by Comvaser, <https://commons.wikimedia.org/wiki/ File:Chichen_Itza_CB.jpg>. Creative Commons BY-SA 4.0.

292. *Top* Diagram of Goseck circle by Rainer Zenz. Public domain.

292. *Bottom* '1600 Himmelsscheibe von Nebra sky disk anagoria' by Anagoria, <https://commons.wikimedia.org/wiki/File:1600_Himmelsscheibe_von_ Nebra_sky_disk_anagoria.jpg>. Creative Commons BY 3.0.

293. 'S F-E-CAMERON EGYPT 2006 FEB 00289' by Steve F-E-Cameron, <https:// commons.wikimedia.org/wiki/File:S_F-E-CAMERON_EGYPT_2006_ FEB_00289.JPG>. Creative Commons BY-SA 3.0.

294. 'Karnak temple 9456' by Hedwig Storch, <https://commons.wikimedia.org/ wiki/File:Karnak_temple_9456.JPG>. Creative Commons BY-SA 3.0.

295. *Top* 'Newgrange' by Shira, <https://commons.wikimedia.org/wiki/ File:Newgrange.JPG>. Creative Commons BY-SA 3.0.

295. *Bottom* Sketch of a cross section of the Newgrange passage grave by William Frederick Wakeman, circa 1900. Public domain.

296. Photograph of Ring of Brodgar, used under license from Shutterstock.com.

297. 'Maes Howe entrance passage' by Rob Burke, <https://commons.wikimedia. org/wiki/File:Maes_Howe_entrance_passage_-_geograph.org.uk_-_33791. jpg>. Creative Commons BY-SA 2.0.

299. Photograph of Easter Island moai statues, used under license from Shutterstock.com.

300. 'The Great Pyramid, showing passages and mummy chambers. (1902) – TIMEA' by unknown artist, <https://commons.wikimedia. org/wiki/File:The_Great_Pyramid,_showing_passages_and_mummy_ chambers._%281902%29_-_TIMEA.jpg>. Licensed from Travelers in the Middle East Archive (TIMEA). Creative Commons BY-SA 2.5.
301. Photograph of the Gateway of the Sun, Tiwanaku, Bolivia, by Mhwater. Public domain.
303. *Top* Photograph of the Temple of the Sun at Machu Picchu, Peru, by Fabricio Guzmán. Public domain.
303. *Bottom* 'Ollantaytambo, Tunupa monument' by D. Gordon E. Robertson, <https://commons.wikimedia.org/wiki/File:Ollantaytambo,_Tunupa_ monument.jpg>. Creative Commons BY-SA 3.0.
304. 'Another Stupa of Ajanta' by Ekta Abhishek Bansal, <https://commons. wikimedia.org/wiki/File:Another_Stupa_of_Ajanta.JPG>. Creative Commons BY-SA 3.0.
305. Photograph of the Great Enclosure from the Great Zimbabwe ruins by Jan Derk. Public domain.
306. 'Nasca Astronaut 2007 08' by Raymond Ostertag, <https://commons. wikimedia.org/wiki/File:Nasca_Astronaut_2007_08.JPG>. Creative Commons BY-SA 3.0.
309. *Top* 'Mynydd Dinas under snow - geograph.org.uk – 1151816' by ceridwen, <https://commons.wikimedia.org/wiki/File:Mynydd_Dinas_under_ snow_-_geograph.org.uk_-_1151816.jpg>. Creative Commons BY-SA 2.0.
309. *Bottom* 'Angkor-wat-central' by Heron, <https://en.wikipedia.org/wiki/ File:Angkor-wat-central.jpg>. Creative Commons BY-SA 3.0.
310. 'Arkaim Shining' painting by Lola Lonli, 2001, <https://commons.wikimedia. org/wiki/File:Arkaim_Shining.jpg>. Creative Commons BY-SA 3.0.
313. 'Vera Island, megalyth 2' by S.Grigoriev, <https://commons.wikimedia.org/ wiki/File:OV-M2.jpg>. Creative Commons BY-SA 3.0.

CHAPTER TEN

316. 'Egypt.Giza.Sphinx.01' by Hajor, <https://commons.wikimedia.org/wiki/ File:Egypt.Giza.Sphinx.01.jpg>. Creative Commons BY-SA 3.0.
317. 'Equinox at Angkor 21st March 2012' by Kim Heng, <https://commons. wikimedia.org/wiki/File:Equinox_at_Angkor_21st_March_2012.JPG>. Creative Commons BY-SA 3.0.
318. 'Awatoceanofmilk01 - color corrected' by Markalexander100, <https:// commons.wikimedia.org/wiki/File:Awatoceanofmilk01_-_color_corrected. JPG>. Creative Commons BY-SA 3.0.
319. 'Precession N' by Tau'olunga, <https://en.wikipedia.org/wiki/ File:Precession_N.gif>. Creative Commons BY-SA 2.5.
321. 'Tikal Temple1 2006 08 11' by Raymond Ostertag, <https://commons. wikimedia.org/wiki/File:Tikal_Temple1_2006_08_11.JPG>. Creative Commons BY-SA 2.5.
322. 'The central column of Cahokia's 'Woodhenge'' by QuartierLatin1968, <https://commons.wikimedia.org/wiki/File:Woodhenge_Cahokia_3998. jpg>. Creative Commons BY-SA 3.0.

324. 'Cairn T Loughcrew' by William Whyte, <https://commons.wikimedia.org/wiki/File:Cairn_T_Loughcrew.jpg>. Creative Commons BY-SA 2.0.

325. Photograph of the archaeological site at Knowth, Ireland, by Sitoman. Public domain.

326. 'Cannon fire at Millmount, Drogheda - geograph.org.uk – 1079077' by Kieran Campbell, <https://commons.wikimedia.org/wiki/File:Cannon_fire_at_Millmount,_Drogheda_-_geograph.org.uk_-_1079077.jpg>. Creative Commons BY-SA 2.0.

328. 'Summit of Cairnpapple - geograph.org.uk – 1062278' by James Allen, <https://commons.wikimedia.org/wiki/File:Summit_of_Cairnpapple_-_geograph.org.uk_-_1062278.jpg>. Creative Commons BY-SA 2.0.

CHAPTER ELEVEN

330. *Top* © Mystical Life Publications.

330. *Bottom* 'Osireion at Abydos' by Markh, <https://commons.wikimedia.org/wiki/File:Osireion_at_Abydos.jpg>. Creative Commons BY-SA 3.0.

331. 'Giza Plateau - Great Sphinx - inside temple' by Daniel Mayer, <https://commons.wikimedia.org/wiki/File:Giza_Plateau_-_Great_Sphinx_-_inside_temple.JPG>. Creative Commons BY-SA 4.0.

332. 'Qumran national park' by Bukvoed, 2008, <https://commons.wikimedia.org/wiki/File:Kumran-1-84.jpg>. Creative Commons BY 3.0.

334. *Top* Photograph of Stonehenge, used under license from GailJohnson/Bigstock.com.

334. *Bottom* 'Stonehenge on midsummer, 1700 BC' from Nordisk familjebok (1918), vol.27, p.115. Public domain.

335. 'Calendar aswan' by Raymbetz, <https://commons.wikimedia.org/wiki/File:Calendar_aswan.JPG>. Creative Commons BY-SA 3.0.

337. '2007-06-06-Externsteine-33' by R. Engelhardt, <https://commons.wikimedia.org/wiki/File:2007-06-06-Externsteine-33.jpg>. Creative Commons BY-SA 3.0.

338. *Top* 'Ajanta Cave' by dola.das85, <https://commons.wikimedia.org/wiki/File:Ajanta_Cave.jpg>. Creative Commons BY-SA 3.0.

338. *Bottom* Photo of Hathor chapel at the temple of Thutmosis III in Deir el-Bahari, Eqypt, by Henry Edouard Naville, 1907. Public domain.

339. 'View from Above' by Timothy A. Price and Nichole I. Stump, <https://upload.wikimedia.org/wikipedia/commons/archive/e/eb/20060424222021!Serpent_Mound.jpg>. Creative Commons BY-SA 3.0.

340. Illustration of Loch Nell serpent mound from In the Hebrides by Constance Gordon-Cumming, 1883. Public domain.

341. 'Casa Rinconada' by HJPD, <https://commons.wikimedia.org/wiki/File:Casa_Rinconada.jpg>. Creative Commons BY 3.0.

343. *Top* 'Easter Island Ahu (2006)' by Honey Hooper, <https://commons.wikimedia.org/wiki/File:Easter_Island_Ahu_%282006%29.jpg>. Creative Commons BY 2.5.

343. *Bottom* Photograph of the Temple of the Descending God, Tulum, by Evadb. Public domain.

344. 'Descending God (Tulum)' by El Comandante, <https://commons.wikimedia. org/wiki/File:Descending_God_%28Tulum%29.JPG>. Creative Commons BY-SA 3.0.
345. '0073 Uxmal' by tato grasso, <https://commons.wikimedia.org/wiki/ File:0073_Uxmal.JPG>. CC BY-SA 2.5.
346. 'Guatemala-1520' by Dennis Jarvis, <https://commons.wikimedia.org/wiki/ File:Flickr_-_archer10_%28Dennis%29_-_Guatemala-1520.jpg>. Creative Commons BY-SA 2.0.
347. Photograph of Lascaux cave by Francesco Bandarin, © UNESCO, <http:// whc.unesco.org/en/list/85/gallery/>. Creative Commons BY-SA 3.0 IGO.

CHAPTER TWELVE

352. 'Pythagoreans Anthem to the Rising Sun' by Fyodor Bronnikov, 1869. Public domain.
355. © Mystical Life Publications.
356. © Mystical Life Publications.
357. *Top* © Mystical Life Publications.
357. *Bottom* Photograph of the gate to the Ki Monastery in the Himalayas, used under license from Shutterstock.com.
359. *Top* 'Stebykla 01' by GiW, <https://commons.wikimedia.org/wiki/ File:Stebykla_01.jpg>. Creative Commons BY-SA 3.0.
359. *Bottom* 'Sun white' by Geoff Elston, <https://commons.wikimedia.org/wiki/ File:Sun_white.jpg>. Creative Commons BY 4.0.
360. 'Romuvan ceremony (10)' by Mantas Masalskis, <https://commons. wikimedia.org/wiki/File:Romuvan_ceremony_%2810%29.PNG>. Creative Commons BY 2.0.
361. 'Romuvan ceremony (6)' by Mantas Masalskis, <https://commons.wikimedia. org/wiki/File:Romuvan_ceremony_%286%29.PNG>. Creative Commons BY 2.0.
367. 'Ivan Kupala Day' by Vladimir Lobachev, <https://commons.wikimedia.org/ wiki/File:Ivan_Kupala_Day_in_2011_08.JPG>. Creative Commons BY-SA 3.0.

CHAPTER THIRTEEN

373. © Mystical Life Publications.
374. 'AMI - Goldene Doppelaxt' by Wolfgang Sauber, <https://en.wikipedia.org/ wiki/File:AMI_-_Goldene_Doppelaxt.jpg>. Creative Commons BY-SA 3.0.
375. Photograph of a Minoan rhyton, circa 1550-1500 BC, used under license from Shutterstock.com.
379. Scan from a transparency by Simon Garbutt of labyrinth patterns cut into the cliff face at Rocky Valley, Tintagel, England, unknown date. Public domain.

CHAPTER FOURTEEN

388. Monstrance illustration, used under license from Shutterstock.com.
389. © Mystical Life Publications.
390. *Bottom* 'Dendera relief' by Bernard Gagnon, <https://commons.wikimedia. org/wiki/File:Dendera_relief.jpg>. Creative Commons BY-SA 3.0.

396. 'Newgrange Entrance Stone' by Nomadtales, <https://commons.wikimedia.org/wiki/File:Newgrange_Entrance_Stone.jpg>. Creative Commons BY-SA 3.0.

CHAPTER FIFTEEN

406. Photograph of a woman wearing a uraeus headpiece, used under license from Shutterstock.com.
407. © Mystical Life Publications.
411. Photograph of Dendera Hathor Temple Complex by Csorfoly Daniel, 2007. Public Domain.
414. 'The Resurrection' by Lucas Cranach the Younger, 1558. Public domain.
416. Illustration of Anubis attending the initiate from Loring, W.W. A Confederate Soldier in Egypt, Dodd, Mead & Company: New York, 1884, in the Travelers in the Middle East Archive (TIMEA), <https://commons.wikimedia.org/wiki/File:Priest_Preparing_Mummy_for_Burial._and_Resurrection_of_the_Body._%281884%29_-_TIMEA.jpg>. Creative Commons BY-SA 2.5.

CHAPTER SIXTEEN

424. © Mystical Life Publications.
425. © Mystical Life Publications.
426. Diagram of Stonehenge by Joseph Lertola, 2007. Public domain.
439. © Mystical Life Publications.

CHAPTER SEVENTEEN

450. © Mystical Life Publications.

MysticalLifePublications.org

For more works by Belsebuub,
visit his official website

BELSEBUUB.COM

CPSIA information can be obtained
at www.ICGtesting.com
Printed in the USA
LVOW04s0533060817
544004LV00014B/387/P

9 780992 411312